Praise for *Network Security Through Data Analysis, Second Edition*

Attackers generally know our technology better than we do, yet a defender's first reflex is usually to add more complexity, which just makes the understanding gap even wider—we won't win many battles that way. Observation is the cornerstone of knowledge, so we must instrument and characterize our infrastructure if we hope to detect anomalies and predict attacks. This book shows how and explains why to observe that which we defend, and ought to be required reading for all SecOps teams.

—*Dr. Paul Vixie, CEO of Farsight Security*

Michael Collins provides a comprehensive blueprint for where to look, what to look for, and how to process a diverse array of data to help defend your organization and detect/deter attackers. It is a "must have" for any data-driven cybersecurity program.

—*Bob Rudis, Chief Data Scientist, Rapid7*

Combining practical experience, scientific discipline, and a solid understanding of both the technical and policy implications of security, this book is essential reading for all network operators and analysts. Anyone who needs to influence and support decision making, both for security operations and at a policy level, should read this.

—*Yurie Ito, Founder and Executive Director,*
CyberGreen Institute

Michael Collins brings together years of operational expertise and research experience to help network administrators and security analysts extract actionable signals amidst the noise in network logs. Collins does a great job of combining the theory of data analysis and the practice of applying it in security contexts using real-world scenarios and code.

—*Vyas Sekar, Associate Professor,*
Carnegie Mellon University/CyLab

Network Security Through Data Analysis

From Data to Action

Michael Collins

Beijing · Boston · Farnham · Sebastopol · Tokyo

Network Security Through Data Analysis

by Michael Collins

Copyright © 2017 Michael Collins. All rights reserved.

Published by O'Reilly Media, Inc., 1005 Gravenstein Highway North, Sebastopol, CA 9547.

O'Reilly books may be purchased for educational, business, or sales promotional use. Online editions are also available for most titles (*http://oreilly.com/safari*). For more information, contact our corporate/institutional sales department: 800-998-9938 or *corporate@oreilly.com*.

Editors: Courtney Allen and Virginia Wilson	**Indexer:** WordCo Indexing Services, Inc.
Production Editor: Nicholas Adams	**Interior Designer:** David Futato
Copyeditor: Rachel Head	**Cover Designer:** Karen Montgomery
Proofreader: Kim Cofer	**Illustrator:** Rebecca Demarest

February 2014:   First Edition
September 2017:   Second Edition

Revision History for the Second Edition

2017-09-08:   First Release

See *http://oreilly.com/catalog/errata.csp?isbn=9781491962848* for release details.

978-1-491-96284-8

[LSI]

Table of Contents

Preface

This book is about networks: monitoring them, studying them, and using the results of those studies to improve them. "Improve" in this context hopefully means to make more secure, but I don't believe we have the vocabulary or knowledge to say that confidently—at least not yet. In order to implement security, we must know what decisions we can make to do so, which ones are most effective to apply, and the impact that those decisions will have on our users. Underpinning these decisions is a need for *situational awareness*.

Situational awareness, a term largely used in military circles, is exactly what it says on the tin: an understanding of the environment you're operating in. For our purposes, situational awareness encompasses understanding the components that make up your network and how those components are used. This awareness is often *radically* different from how the network is configured and how the network was originally designed.

To understand the importance of situational awareness in information security, I want you to think about your home, and I want you to count the number of web servers in your house. Did you include your wireless router? Your cable modem? Your printer? Did you consider the web interface to CUPS? How about your television set?

To many IT managers, several of the devices just listed won't have registered as "web servers." However, most modern embedded devices have dropped specialized control protocols in favor of a web interface—to an outside observer, they're just web servers, with known web server vulnerabilities. Attackers will often hit embedded systems without realizing what they are—the SCADA system is a Windows server with a couple of funny additional directories, and the MRI machine is a perfectly serviceable spambot.

This was all an issue when I wrote the first edition of the book; at the time, we discussed the risks of unpatched smart televisions and vulnerabilities in teleconferencing systems. Since that time, the Internet of Things (IoT) has become even more of a thing, with millions of remotely accessible embedded devices using simple (and insecure) web interfaces.

This book is about collecting data and looking at networks in order to understand how the network is used. The focus is on analysis, which is the process of taking security data and using it to make actionable decisions. I emphasize the word *actionable* here because effectively, security decisions are restrictions on behavior. Security policy involves telling people what they shouldn't do (or, more onerously, telling people what they *must* do). Don't use a public file sharing service to hold company data, don't use *123456* as the password, and don't copy the entire project server and sell it to the competition. When we make security decisions, we interfere with how people work, and we'd better have good, solid reasons for doing so.

All security systems ultimately depend on users recognizing and accepting the tradeoffs—inconvenience in exchange for safety—but there are limits to both. Security rests on people: it rests on the individual users of a system obeying the rules, and it rests on analysts and monitors identifying when rules are broken. Security is only marginally a technical problem—information security involves endlessly creative people figuring out new ways to abuse technology, and against this constantly changing threat profile, you need cooperation from both your defenders and your users. Bad security policy will result in users increasingly evading detection in order to get their jobs done or just to blow off steam, and that adds additional work for your defenders.

The emphasis on actionability and the goal of achieving security is what differentiates this book from a more general text on data science. The section on analysis proper covers statistical and data analysis techniques borrowed from multiple other disciplines, but the overall focus is on understanding the structure of a network and the decisions that can be made to protect it. To that end, I have abridged the theory as much as possible, and have also focused on mechanisms for identifying abusive behavior. Security analysis has the unique problem that the targets of observation are not only aware they're being watched, but are actively interested in stopping it if at all possible.

The MRI and the General's Laptop

Several years ago, I talked with an analyst who focused primarily on a university hospital. He informed me that the most commonly occupied machine on his network was the MRI. In retrospect, this is easy to understand.

"Think about it," he told me. "It's medical hardware, which means it's certified to use a specific version of Windows. So every week, somebody hits it with an exploit, roots it, and installs a bot on it. Spam usually starts around Wednesday." When I asked why he didn't just block the machine from the internet, he shrugged and told me the doctors

---

wanted their scans. He was the first analyst I'd encountered with this problem, but he wasn't the last.

We see this problem a lot in any organization with strong hierarchical figures: doctors, senior partners, generals. You can build as many protections as you want, but if the general wants to borrow the laptop over the weekend and let his granddaughter play Neopets, you've got an infected laptop to fix on Monday.

I am a firm believer that the most effective way to defend networks is to secure and defend *only* what you need to secure and defend. I believe this is the case because information security will always require people to be involved in monitoring and investigation—the attacks change too frequently, and when we automate defenses, attackers figure out how to use them against us.[1]

I am convinced that security should be inconvenient, well defined, and constrained. Security should be an artificial behavior extended to assets that must be protected. It should be an artificial behavior because the final line of defense in any secure system is the *people* in the system—and people who are fully engaged in security will be mistrustful, paranoid, and looking for suspicious behavior. This is not a happy way to live, so in order to make life bearable, we have to limit security to what must be protected. By trying to watch everything, you lose the edge that helps you protect what's really important.

Because security is inconvenient, effective security analysts must be able to *convince* people that they need to change their normal operations, jump through hoops, and otherwise constrain their mission in order to prevent an abstract future attack from happening. To that end, the analysts must be able to identify the decision, produce information to back it up, and demonstrate the risk to their audience.

The process of data analysis, as described in this book, is focused on developing security knowledge in order to make effective security decisions. These decisions can be forensic: reconstructing events after the fact in order to determine why an attack happened, how it succeeded, or what damage was done. These decisions can also be proactive: developing rate limiters, intrusion detection systems (IDSs), or policies that can limit the impact of an attacker on a network.

Audience

The target audience for this book is network administrators and operational security analysts, the personnel who work on NOC floors or who face an IDS console on a

---

[1] Consider automatically locking out accounts after *x* number of failed password attempts, and combine it with logins based on email addresses. Consider how many accounts an attacker can lock out that way.

regular basis. Information security analysis is a young discipline, and there really is no well-defined body of knowledge I can point to and say, "Know this." This book is intended to provide a snapshot of analytic techniques that I or other people have thrown at the wall over the past 10 years and seen stick. My expectation is that you have some familiarity with TCP/IP tools such as `netstat`, `tcpdump`, and `wireshark`.

In addition, I expect that you have some familiarity with scripting languages. In this book, I use Python as my go-to language for combining tools. The Python code is illustrative and might be understandable without a Python background, but it is assumed that you possess the skills to create filters or other tools in the language of your choice.

In the course of writing this book, I have incorporated techniques from a number of different disciplines. Where possible, I've included references back to original sources so that you can look through that material and find other approaches. Many of these techniques involve mathematical or statistical reasoning that I have intentionally kept at a functional level rather than going through the derivations of the approach. A basic understanding of statistics will, however, be helpful.

Contents of This Book

This book is divided into three sections: Data, Tools, and Analytics. The Data section discusses the process of collecting and organizing data. The Tools section discusses a number of different tools to support analytical processes. The Analytics section discusses different analytic scenarios and techniques. Here's a bit more detail on what you'll find in each.

Part I discusses the collection, storage, and organization of data. Data storage and logistics are critical problems in security analysis; it's easy to collect data, but hard to search through it and find actual phenomena. Data has a footprint, and it's possible to collect so much data that you can never meaningfully search through it. This section is divided into the following chapters:

Chapter 1

This chapter discusses the general process of collecting data. It provides a framework for exploring how different sensors collect and report information and how they interact with each other, and how the process of data collection affects the data collected and the inferences made.

Chapter 2

This chapter expands on the discussion in the previous chapter by focusing on sensor placement in networks. This includes points about how packets are transferred around a network and the impact on collecting these packets, and how various types of common network hardware affect data collection.

Chapter 3

This chapter focuses on the data collected by network sensors including `tcpdump` and NetFlow. This data provides a comprehensive view of network activity, but is often hard to interpret because of difficulties in reconstructing network traffic.

Chapter 4

This chapter focuses on the process of data collection in the service domain—the location of service log data, expected formats, and unique challenges in processing and managing service data.

Chapter 5

This chapter focuses on the data collected by service sensors and provides examples of logfile formats for major services, particularly HTTP.

Chapter 6

This chapter discusses host-based data such as memory and disk information. Given the operating system–specific requirements of host data, this is a high-level overview.

Chapter 7

This chapter discusses data in the active domain, covering topics such as scanning hosts and creating web crawlers and other tools to probe a network's assets to find more information.

Part II discusses a number of different tools to use for analysis, visualization, and reporting. The tools described in this section are referenced extensively in the third section of the book when discussing how to conduct different analytics. There are three chapters on tools:

Chapter 8

This chapter is a high-level discussion of how to collect and analyze security data, and the type of infrastructure that should be put in place between sensor and SIM.

Chapter 9

The System for Internet-Level Knowledge (SiLK) is a flow analysis toolkit developed by Carnegie Mellon's CERT Division. This chapter discusses SiLK and how to use the tools to analyze NetFlow, IPFIX, and similar data.

Chapter 10

One of the more common and frustrating tasks in analysis is figuring out where an IP address comes from. This chapter focuses on tools and investigation methods that can be used to identify the ownership and provenance of addresses, names, and other tags from network traffic.

Part III introduces analysis proper, covering how to apply the tools discussed throughout the rest of the book to address various security tasks. The majority of this section is composed of chapters on various constructs (graphs, distance metrics) and security problems (DDoS, fumbling):

Chapter 11

Exploratory data analysis (EDA) is the process of examining data in order to identify structure or unusual phenomena. Both attacks and networks are moving targets, so EDA is a necessary skill for any analyst. This chapter provides a grounding in the basic visualization and mathematical techniques used to explore data.

Chapter 12

Log data, payload data—all of it is likely to include some forms of text. This chapter focuses on the encoding and analysis of semistructured text data.

Chapter 13

This chapter looks at mistakes in communications and how those mistakes can be used to identify phenomena such as scanning.

Chapter 14

This chapter discusses analyses that can be done by examining traffic volume and traffic behavior over time. This includes attacks such as DDoS and database raids, as well as the impact of the workday on traffic volumes and mechanisms to filter traffic volumes to produce more effective analyses.

Chapter 15

This chapter discusses the conversion of network traffic into graph data and the use of graphs to identify significant structures in networks. Graph attributes such as centrality can be used to identify significant hosts or aberrant behavior.

Chapter 16

This chapter discusses the unique problems involving insider threat data analysis. For network security personnel, insider threat investigations often require collecting and comparing data from a diverse and usually poorly maintained set of data sources. Understanding what to find and what's relevant is critical to handling this trying process.

Chapter 17

Threat intelligence supports analysis by providing complementary and contextual information to alert data. However, there is a plethora of threat intelligence available, of varying quality. This chapter discusses how to acquire threat intelligence, vet it, and incorporate it into operational analysis.

Chapter 19

This chapter discusses a step-by-step process for inventorying a network and identifying significant hosts within that network. Network mapping and inventory are critical steps in information security and should be done on a regular basis.

Chapter 20

Operational security is stressful and time-consuming; this chapter discusses how analysis teams can interact with operational teams to develop useful defenses and analysis techniques.

Changes Between Editions

The second edition of this book takes cues from the feedback I've received from the first edition and the changes that have occurred in security since the time I wrote it. For readers of the first edition, I expect you'll find about a third of the material is new. These are the most significant changes:

- I have removed R from the examples, and am now using Python (and the Anaconda stack) exclusively. Since the previous edition, Python has acquired significant and mature data analysis tools. This also saves space on language tutorials which can be spent on analytics discussions.

- The discussions of host and active domain data have been expanded, with a specific focus on the information that a network security analyst needs. Much of the previous IDS material has been moved into those chapters.

- I have added new chapters on several topics, including text analysis, insider threat, and interacting with operational communities.

Most of the new material is based around the idea of an analysis team that interacts with and supports the operations team. Ideally, the analysis team has some degree of separation from operational workflow in order to focus on longer-term and larger issues such as tools support, data management, and optimization.

Tools of the Trade

So, given Python, R, and Excel, what should you learn? If you expect to focus purely on statistical and numerical analysis, or you work heavily with statisticians, learn R first. If you expect to integrate tightly with external data sources, use techniques that aren't available in CRAN, or expect to do something like direct packet manipulation or server integration, learn Python (ideally iPython and Pandas) first. Then learn Excel, *whether you want to or not*. Once you've learned Excel, take a nice vacation and then learn whatever tool is left of these three.

All of these data analysis environments provide common tools: some equivalent of a data frame, visualization, and statistical functionality. Of the three, the Pandas stack (that is, Python, NumPy, SciPy, Matplotlib, and supplements) provides the greatest variety of tools, and if you're looking for something outside of the statistical domain, Python is going to have it. R, in comparison, is a tightly integrated statistical package where you will always find the latest statistical analysis and machine learning tools. The Pandas stack involves combining multiple toolsets developed in parallel, resulting in both redundancy and valuable tools located all over the place. R, on the other hand, inherits from this parallel development community (via S and SAS) and sits in the developer equivalent of the Uncanny Valley.

So why Excel? Because operational analysts live and die off of Excel spreadsheets. Excel integration (even if it's just creating a button to download a CSV of your results) will make your work relevant to the operational floor. Maybe you do all your work in Python, but at the end, if you want analysts to use it, give them something they can plunk into a spreadsheet.

Conventions Used in This Book

The following typographical conventions are used in this book:

Italic

Indicates new terms, URLs, email addresses, filenames, and file extensions.

`Constant width`

Used for program listings, as well as within paragraphs to refer to program elements such as variable or function names, databases, data types, environment variables, statements, and keywords. Also used for commands and command-line utilities, switches, and options.

`Constant width bold`

Shows commands or other text that should be typed literally by the user.

`Constant width italic`

Shows text that should be replaced with user-supplied values or by values determined by context.

Using Code Examples

Supplemental material (code examples, exercises, etc.) is available for download at *https://github.com/mpcollins/nsda_examples*.

This book is here to help you get your job done. In general, if example code is offered with this book, you may use it in your programs and documentation. You do not need to contact us for permission unless you're reproducing a significant portion of the code. For example, writing a program that uses several chunks of code from this book does not require permission. Selling or distributing a CD-ROM of examples from O'Reilly books does require permission. Answering a question by citing this book and quoting example code does not require permission. Incorporating a significant amount of example code from this book into your product's documentation does require permission.

We appreciate, but do not require, attribution. An attribution usually includes the title, author, publisher, and ISBN. For example: "*Network Security Through Data Analysis* by Michael Collins (O'Reilly). Copyright 2017 Michael Collins, 978-1-491-96284-8."

If you feel your use of code examples falls outside fair use or the permission given above, feel free to contact us at *permissions@oreilly.com*.

O'Reilly Safari

Safari (formerly Safari Books Online) is a membership-based training and reference platform for enterprise, government, educators, and individuals.

Members have access to thousands of books, training videos, Learning Paths, interactive tutorials, and curated playlists from over 250 publishers, including O'Reilly Media, Harvard Business Review, Prentice Hall Professional, Addison-Wesley Professional, Microsoft Press, Sams, Que, Peachpit Press, Adobe, Focal Press, Cisco Press, John Wiley & Sons, Syngress, Morgan Kaufmann, IBM Redbooks, Packt, Adobe Press, FT Press, Apress, Manning, New Riders, McGraw-Hill, Jones & Bartlett, and Course Technology, among others.

For more information, please visit *http://oreilly.com/safari*.

How to Contact Us

Please address comments and questions concerning this book to the publisher:

O'Reilly Media, Inc.
1005 Gravenstein Highway North
Sebastopol, CA 95472
800-998-9938 (in the United States or Canada)
707-829-0515 (international or local)
707-829-0104 (fax)

We have a web page for this book, where we list errata, examples, and any additional information. You can access this page at *http://bit.ly/nstda2e*.

To comment or ask technical questions about this book, send email to *bookquestions@oreilly.com*.

For more information about our books, courses, conferences, and news, see our website at *http://www.oreilly.com*.

Find us on Facebook: *http://facebook.com/oreilly*

Follow us on Twitter: *http://twitter.com/oreillymedia*

Watch us on YouTube: *http://www.youtube.com/oreillymedia*

Acknowledgments

I need to thank my editors, Courtney Allen, Virginia Wilson, and Maureen Spencer, for their incredible support and feedback, without which I would still be rewriting commentary on regression over and over again. I also want to thank my assistant editors, Allyson MacDonald and Maria Gulick, for riding herd and making me get the thing finished. I also need to thank my technical reviewers: Markus DeShon, André DiMino, and Eugene Libster. Their comments helped me to rip out more fluff and focus on the important issues.

This book is an attempt to distill down a lot of experience on ops floors and in research labs, and I owe a debt to many people on both sides of the world. In no particular order, this includes Jeff Janies, Jeff Wiley, Brian Satira, Tom Longstaff, Jay Kadane, Mike Reiter, John McHugh, Carrie Gates, Tim Shimeall, Markus DeShon, Jim Downey, Will Franklin, Sandy Parris, Sean McAllister, Greg Virgin, Vyas Sekar, Scott Coull, and Mike Witt.

Finally, I want to thank my mother, Catherine Collins.

## PART I

Data

This section discusses the collection and storage of data for use in analysis and response. Effective security analysis requires collecting data from widely disparate sources, each of which provides part of a picture about a particular event taking place on a network.

To understand the need for hybrid data sources, consider that most modern bots are general-purpose software systems. A single bot may use multiple techniques to infiltrate and attack other hosts on a network. These attacks may include buffer overflows, spreading across network shares, and simple password cracking. A bot attacking an SSH server with a password attempt may be logged by that host's SSH logfile, providing concrete evidence of an attack but no information on anything else the bot did. Network traffic might not be able to reconstruct the sessions, but it can tell you about other actions by the attacker—including, say, a successful long session with a host that never reported such a session taking place, no siree.

The core challenge in data-driven analysis is to collect sufficient data to reconstruct rare events without collecting so much data as to make queries impractical. Data collection is surprisingly easy, but making sense of what's been collected is much harder. In security, this problem is complicated by the rare *actual* security threats.

Attacks are common, threats are rare. The majority of network traffic is innocuous and highly repetitive: mass emails, everyone watching the same YouTube video, file accesses. Interspersed among this traffic are attacks, but the majority of the attacks will be automated and unsubtle: scanning, spamming, and the like. Within those attacks will be a minority, a tiny subset representing actual threats.

That security is driven by rare, small threats means that almost all security analysis is I/O bound: to find phenomena, you have to search data, and the more data you collect, the more you have to search. To put some concrete numbers on this, consider an OC-3: a single OC-3 can generate 5 terabytes of raw data per day. By comparison, an eSATA interface can read about 0.3 gigabytes per second, requiring several hours to perform *one* search across that data, assuming that you're reading and writing data across different disks. The need to collect data from multiple sources introduces redundancy, which costs additional disk space and increases query times. It is completely possible to instrument oneself blind.

A well-designed storage and query system enables analysts to conduct arbitrary queries on data and expect a response within a reasonable time frame. A poorly designed one takes longer to execute the query than it took to collect the data. Developing a good design requires understanding how different sensors collect data; how they complement, duplicate, and interfere with each other; and how to effectively store this data to empower analysis. This section is focused on these problems.

This section is divided into seven chapters. Chapter 1 is an introduction to the general process of sensing and data collection, and introduces vocabulary to describe how different sensors interact with each other. Chapter 2 discusses the collection of network data—its value, points of collection, and the impact of vantage on network data collection. Chapter 3 discusses sensors and outputs. Chapter 4 focuses on service data collection and vantage. Chapter 5 focuses on the content of service data—logfile data, its format, and converting it into useful forms. Chapter 6 is concerned with host-based data, such as memory or filesystem state, and how that affects network data analysis. Chapter 7 discusses *active domain* data, scanning and probing to find out what a host is actually doing.

## CHAPTER 1

Organizing Data: Vantage, Domain, Action, and Validity

Security analysis is the process of applying data to make security decisions. Security decisions are disruptive and restrictive—disruptive because you're fixing something, restrictive because you're constraining behavior. Effective security analysis requires making the right decision *and convincing a skeptical audience* that this is the right decision. The foundations of these decisions are quality data and quality reasoning; in this chapter, I address both.

Security monitoring on a modern network requires working with multiple sensors that generate different kinds of data and are created by many different people for many different purposes. A sensor can be anything from a network tap to a firewall log; it is something that collects information about your network and can be used to make judgment calls about your network's security.

I want to pull out and emphasize a very important point here: quality source data is *integral* to good security analysis. Furthermore, the effort spent acquiring a consistent source of quality data will pay off further down the analysis pipeline—you can use simpler (and faster) algorithms to identify phenomena, you'll have an easier time verifying results, and you'll spend less time cross-correlating and double-checking information.

So, now that you're raring to go get some quality data, the question obviously pops up: what *is* quality data? The answer is that security data collection is a trade-off between expressiveness and speed—packet capture (pcap) data collected from a span port can tell you if someone is scanning your network, but it's going to also produce terabytes of unreadable traffic from the HTTPS server you're watching. Logs from the HTTPS server will tell you about file accesses, but nothing about the FTP interactions going on as well. The questions you ask will also be situational—how you decide to deal with an advanced persistent threat (APT) is a function of how much risk you face, and how much risk you face will change over time.

That said, there are some basic goals we can establish about security data. We would like the data to express as much information with as small a footprint as possible—so data should be in a compact format, and if different sensors report the same event, we would like those descriptions to not be redundant. We want the data to be as accurate as possible as to the time of observation, so information that is transient (such as the relationships between IP addresses and domain names) should be recorded at the time of collection. We also would like the data to be expressive; that is, we would like to reduce the amount of time and effort an analyst needs to spend cross-referencing information. Finally, we would like any inferences or decisions in the data to be accountable; for example, if an alert is raised because of a rule, we want to know the rule's history and provenance.

While we can't optimize for all of these criteria, we can use them as guidance for balancing these requirements. Effective monitoring will require juggling multiple sensors of different types, which treat data differently. To aid with this, I classify sensors along three attributes:

Vantage

> The placement of sensors within a network. Sensors with different vantages will see different parts of the same event.

Domain

> The information the sensor provides, whether that's at the host, a service on the host, or the network. Sensors with the same vantage but different domains provide complementary data about the same event. For some events, you might only get information from one domain. For example, host monitoring is the only way to find out if a host has been physically accessed.

Action

> How the sensor decides to report information. It may just record the data, provide events, or manipulate the traffic that produces the data. Sensors with different actions can potentially interfere with each other.

This categorization serves two purposes. First, it provides a way to break down and classify sensors by how they deal with data. Domain is a broad characterization of where and how the data is collected. Vantage informs us of how the sensor placement affects collection. Action details how the sensor actually fiddles with data. Together, these attributes provide a way to define the challenges data collection poses to the *validity* of an analyst's conclusions.

Validity is an idea from experimental design, and refers to the strength of an argument. A valid argument is one where the conclusion follows logically from the premise; weak arguments can be challenged on multiple axes, and experimental design

---

focuses on identifying those challenges. The reason security people should care about it goes back to my point in the introduction: security analysis is about convincing an unwilling audience to reasonably evaluate a security decision and choose whether or not to make it. Understanding the validity and challenges to it produces better results and more realistic analyses.

Domain

We will now examine domain, vantage, and action in more detail. A sensor's *domain* refers to the type of data that the sensor generates and reports. Because sensors include antivirus (AV) and similar systems, where the line of reasoning leading to a message may be opaque, the analyst needs to be aware that these tools import their own biases.

Table 1-1 breaks down the four major domain classes used in this book. This table divides domains by the event model and the sensor uses, with further description following.

Table 1-1. The four domain classes

Domain	Data sources	Timing	Identity
Network	PCAP, NetFlow	Real-time, packet-based	IP, MAC
Service	Logs	Real-time, event-based	IP, Service-based IDs
Host	System state, signature alerts	Asynchronous	IP, MAC, UUID
Active	Scanning	User-driven	IP, Service-based IDs

Sensors operating in the *network domain* derive all of their data from some form of packet capture. This may be straight pcap, packet headers, or constructs such as Net-Flow. Network data gives the broadest view of a network, but it also has the smallest amount of useful data relative to the volume of data collected. Network domain data must be interpreted, it must be readable,[1] and it must be meaningful; network traffic contains a lot of garbage.

Sensors in the *service domain* derive their data from services. Examples of services include server applications like `nginx` or `apache` (HTTP daemons), as well as internal processes like `syslog` and the processes that are moderated by it. Service data provides you with information on what actually happened, but this is done by interpreting data and providing an event model that may be only tangentially related to reality. In addition, to collect service data, you need to *know the service exists*, which can be

---

1 And note that more and more network data is encrypted.

surprisingly difficult to find out, given the tendency for hardware manufacturers to shop web servers into every open port.

Sensors in the *host domain* collect information on the host's state. For our purposes, these types of tools fit into two categories: systems that provide information on system state such as disk space, and host-based intrusion detection systems such as file integrity monitoring or antivirus systems. These sensors will provide information on the impact of actions on the host, but are also prone to timing issues—many of the state-based systems provide alerts at fixed intervals, and the intrusion-based systems often use huge signature libraries that get updated sporadically.

Finally, the *active domain* consists of sensing controlled by the analyst. This includes scanning for vulnerabilities, mapping tools such as `traceroute`, or even something as simple as opening a connection to a new web server to find out what the heck it does. Active data also includes beaconing and other information that is sent out to ensure that we know something is happening.

Vantage

A sensor's *vantage* describes the packets that sensor will be able to observe. Vantage is determined by an interaction between the sensor's placement and the routing infrastructure of a network. In order to understand the phenomena that impact vantage, look at Figure 1-1. This figure describes a number of unique potential sensors differentiated by capital letters. In order, they are:

A

> Monitors the interface that connects the router to the internet.

B

> Monitors the interface that connects the router to the switch.

C

> Monitors the interface that connects the router to the host with IP address 128.2.1.1.

D

> Monitors host 128.1.1.1.

E

> Monitors a spanning port operated by the switch. A spanning port records all traffic that passes the switch (see "Network Layers and Vantage" on page 22 for more information on spanning ports).

F

> Monitors the interface between the switch and the hub.

G

Collects HTTP log data on host 128.1.1.2.

H

Sniffs all TCP traffic on the hub.

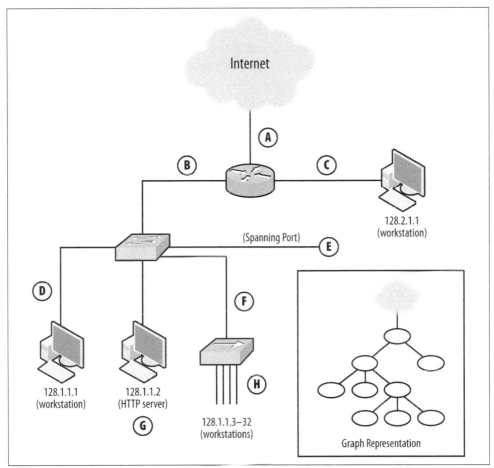

Figure 1-1. Vantage points of a simple network and a graph representation

Each of these sensors has a different vantage, and will see different traffic based on that vantage. You can approximate the vantage of a network by converting it into a simple node-and-link graph (as seen in the corner of Figure 1-1) and then tracing the links crossed between nodes. A link will be able to record any traffic that crosses that link en route to a destination. For example, in Figure 1-1:

- The sensor at position A sees only traffic that moves between the network and the internet—it will not, for example, see traffic between 128.1.1.1 and 128.2.1.1.

- The sensor at B sees any traffic that originates from or ends up at one of the addresses "beneath it," as long as the other address is 128.2.1.1 or the internet.

- The sensor at C sees only traffic that originates from or ends at 128.2.1.1.

- The sensor at D, like the sensor at C, only sees traffic that originates or ends at 128.1.1.1.

- The sensor at E sees any traffic that moves between the switches' ports: traffic from 128.1.1.1 to anything else, traffic from 128.1.1.2 to anything else, and any traffic from 128.1.1.3 to 128.1.1.32 that communicates with anything *outside* that hub.

- The sensor at F sees a subset of what the sensor at E sees, seeing only traffic from 128.1.1.3 to 128.1.1.32 that communicates with anything *outside* that hub.

- G is a special case because it is an HTTP log; it sees only HTTP/S traffic (port 80 and 443) where 128.1.1.2 is the server.

- Finally, H sees any traffic where one of the addresses between 128.1.1.3 and 128.1.1.32 is an origin or a destination, as well as traffic between those hosts.

Note that no single sensor provides complete coverage of this network. Furthermore, instrumentation will require dealing with redundant traffic. For instance, if I instrument H and E, I will see any traffic from 128.1.1.3 to 128.1.1.1 twice. Choosing the right vantage points requires striking a balance between complete coverage of traffic and not drowning in redundant data.

Choosing Vantage

When instrumenting a network, determining vantage is a three-step process: acquiring a network map, determining the potential vantage points, and then determining the optimal coverage.

The first step involves acquiring a map of the network and how it's connected, together as well as a list of potential instrumentation points. Figure 1-1 is a simplified version of such a map.

The second step, determining the vantage of each point, involves identifying every potentially instrumentable location on the network and then determining what that location can see. This value can be expressed as a range of IP address/port combinations. Table 1-2 provides an example of such an inventory for Figure 1-1. A graph can be used to make a first guess at what vantage points will see, but a truly accurate model requires more in-depth information about the routing and networking hardware. For example, when dealing with routers it is possible to find points where the vantage is asymmetric (note that the traffic in Table 1-2 is all symmetric). Refer to "The Basics of Network Layering" on page 19 for more information.

Table 1-2. A worksheet showing the vantage of Figure 1-1

Vantage point	Source IP range	Destination IP range
A	internet	128.1, 2.1.1–32
	128.1, 2.1.1–32	internet
B	128.1.1.1–32	128.2.1.1, internet
	128.2.1.1, internet	128.1.1.1–32
C	128.2.1.1	128.1.1.1–32, internet
	128.1.1.1–32, internet	128.2.1.1
D	128.1.1.1	128.1.1.2-32, 128.2.1.1, internet
	128.1.1.2–32, 128.2.1.1, internet	128.1.1.1
E	128.1.1.1	128.1.1.2–32, 128.2.1.1, internet
	128.1.1.2	128.1.1.1, 128.1.1.3–32, 128.2.1.1, internet
	128.1.1.3–32	128.1.1.1-2, 128.2.1.1, internet
F	128.1.1.3–32	128.1.1.1-2, 128.2.1.1, internet
	128.1.1.1–32, 128.2.1.1, Internet	128.1.1.3–32
G	128.1, 2.1.1–32, internet	128.1.1.2:tcp/80
	128.1.1.2:tcp/80	128.1, 2.1.1–32
H	128.1.1.3-32	128.1.1.1–32, 128.2.1.1, internet
	128.1.1.1-32, 128.2.1.1, internet	128.1.1.3–32

The final step is to pick the optimal vantage points shown by the worksheet. The goal is to choose a set of points that provide monitoring with minimal redundancy. For example, sensor E provides a superset of the data provided by sensor F, meaning that there is no reason to include both. Choosing vantage points almost always involves dealing with *some* redundancy, which can sometimes be limited by using filtering rules. For example, in order to instrument traffic between the hosts 128.1.1.3–32, point H *must* be instrumented, and that traffic will pop up again and again at points E, F, B, and A. If the sensors at those points are configured to not report traffic from 128.1.1.3–32, the redundancy problem is moot.

Actions: What a Sensor Does with Data

A sensor's *action* describes how the sensor interacts with the data it collects. Depending on the domain, there are a number of discrete actions a sensor may take, each of which has different impacts on the validity of the output:

Report
> A report sensor simply provides information on all phenomena that the sensor observes. Report sensors are simple and important for baselining. They are also useful for developing signatures and alerts for phenomena that control sensors

haven't yet been configured to recognize. Report sensors include NetFlow collectors, tcpdump, and server logs.

Event

An event sensor differs from a report sensor in that it consumes multiple data sources to produce an *event* that summarizes some subset of that data. For example, a host-based intrusion detection system (IDS) might examine a memory image, find a malware signature in memory, and send an event indicating that its host was compromised by malware. At their most extreme, event sensors are black boxes that produce events in response to internal processes developed by experts. Event sensors include IDS and antivirus (AV) sensors.

Control

A control sensor, like an event sensor, consumes multiple data sources and makes a judgment about that data before reacting. Unlike an event sensor, a control sensor modifies or blocks traffic when it sends an event. Control sensors include intrusion prevention systems (IPSs), firewalls, antispam systems, and some antivirus systems.

A sensor's action not only affects how the sensor reports data, but also how it interacts with the data it's observing. Control sensors can modify or block traffic. Figure 1-2 shows how sensors with these three different types of action interact with data. The figure shows the work of three sensors: R, a report sensor; E, an event sensor; and C, a control sensor. The event and control sensors are signature matching systems that react to the string ATTACK. Each sensor is placed between the internet and a single target.

R, the reporter, simply reports the traffic it observes. In this case, it reports both normal and attack traffic without affecting the traffic and effectively summarizes the data observed. E, the event sensor, does nothing in the presence of normal traffic but raises an event when attack traffic is observed. E does not stop the traffic; it just sends an event. C, the controller, sends an event when it sees attack traffic and does nothing to normal traffic. In addition, however, C *blocks* the aberrant traffic from reaching the target. If another sensor is further down the route from C, it will never see the traffic that C blocks.

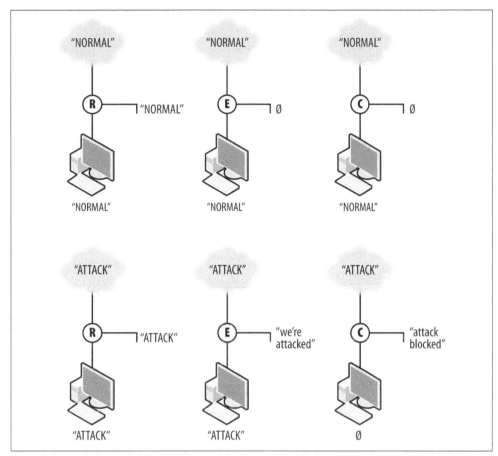

Figure 1-2. Three different sensor actions

Validity and Action

Validity, as I'm going to discuss it, is a concept used in experimental design. The validity of an argument refers to the strength of that argument, of how reasonably the premise of an argument leads to the conclusion. Valid arguments have a strong link, weakly valid arguments are easily challenged.

For security analysts, validity is a good jumping-off point for identifying the challenges your analysis will face (and you *will* be challenged). Are you sure the sensor's working? Is this a real threat? Why do we have to patch this mission-critical system? Security in most enterprises is a cost center, and you have to be able to justify the expenses you're about to impose. If you can't answer challenges internally, you won't be able to externally.

This section is a brief overview of validity. I will return to this topic throughout the book, identifying specific challenges within context. Initially, I want to establish a working vocabulary, starting with the four major categories used in research. I will introduce these briefly here, then explore them further in the subsections that follow. The four types of validity we will consider are:

Internal
> The *internal validity* of an argument refers to cause and effect. If we describe an experiment as an "If I do A, then B happens" statement, then internal validity is concerned with whether or not A is related to B, and whether or not there are other things that might affect the relationship that I haven't addressed.

External
> The *external validity* of an argument refers to the generalizability of an experiment's results to the outside world as a whole. An experiment has strong external validity if the data and the treatment reflect the outside world.

Statistical
> The *statistical validity* of an argument refers to the use of proper statistical methodology and technique in interpreting the gathered data.

Construct
> A *construct* is a formal system used to describe a behavior, something that can be tested or challenged. For example, if I want to establish that someone is transferring files across a network, I might use the volume of data transferred as a construct. Construct validity is concerned with whether the constructs are meaningful—if they are accurate, if they can be reproduced, if they can be challenged.

In experimental construction, validity is not proven, but challenged. It's incumbent on the researcher to demonstrate that validity has been addressed. This is true whether the researcher is a scientist conducting an experiment, or a security analyst explaining a block decision. Figuring out the challenges to validity is a problem of expertise—validity is a living problem, and different fields have identified different threats to validity since the development of the concept.

For example, sociologists have expanded on the category of external validity to further subdivide it into *population* and *ecological* validity. Population validity refers to the generalizability of a sampled population to the world as a whole, and ecological validity refers to the generalizability of the testing environment to reality. As security personnel, we must consider similar challenges to the validity of our data, imposed by the perversity of attackers.

Internal Validity

The *internal validity* of an argument refers to the cause/effect relationship in an experiment. An experiment has strong internal validity if it is reasonable to believe that the effect was caused by the experimenter's hypothesized cause. In the case of internal validity, the security analyst should particularly consider the following issues:

Timing

Timing, in this case, refers to the process of data collection and how it relates to the observed phenomenon. Correlating security and event data requires a clear understanding of how and when the data is collected. This is particularly problematic when comparing data such as NetFlow (where the timing of a flow is impacted by cache management issues for the flow collector), or sampled data such as system state. Addressing these issues of timing begins with record-keeping—not only understanding how the data is collected, but ensuring that timing information is *coordinated and consistent* across the entire system.

Instrumentation

Proper analysis requires validating that the data collection systems are collecting useful data (which is to say, data that can be meaningfully correlated with other data), and that they're collecting data at all. Regularly testing and auditing your collection systems is necessary to differentiate actual attacks from glitches in data collection.

Selection

Problems of selection refer to the impact that choosing the target of a test can have on the entire test. For security analysts, this involves questions of the mission of a system (is it for research? marketing?), the placement of the system on the network (before a DMZ, outward facing, inward facing?), and questions of mobility (desktop? laptop? embedded?).

History

Problems of history refer to events that affect an analysis while that analysis is taking place. For example, if an analyst is studying the impact of spam filtering when, at the same time, a major spam provider is taken down, then she has to consider whether her results are due to the filter or a global effect.

Maturation

Maturation refers to the long-term effects a test has on the test subject. In particular, when dealing with long-running analyses, the analyst has to consider the impact that dynamic allocation has on identity—if you are analyzing data on a DHCP network, you can expect IP addresses to change their relationship to assets when leases expire. Round robin DNS allocation or content distribution networks (CDNs) will result in different relationships between individual HTTP requests.

External Validity

External validity is concerned with the ability to draw general conclusions from the results of an analysis. If a result has strong external validity, then the result is generalizable to broader classes than the sample group. For security analysis, external validity is particularly problematic because we lack a good understanding of general network behavior—a problem that has been ongoing for decades.

The basic mechanism for addressing external validity is to ensure that the data selected is representative of the target population as a whole, and that the treatments are consistent across the set (e.g., if you're running a study on students, you have to account for income, background, education, etc., and deliver the same test). However, until the science of network traffic advances to develop quality models for describing normal network behavior,[2] determining whether models represent a realistic sample is infeasible. The best mechanism for accommodating this right now is to rely on additional corpora. There's a long tradition in computer science of collecting datasets for analyses; while they're not necessarily representative, they're better than nothing.

> **Information Security Datasets: A Brief Primer**
>
> Information security research is on a perpetual hunt for quality datasets. One of the most important early research papers on intrusion detection, the 1999 Lincoln Labs study (see "Further Reading" on page 16), is heavily focused on the problem of data generation and resulted in a dataset that has been used by researchers for years. The United States Department of Homeland Security supports a program called IMPACT (*https://www.impactcybertrust.org/*) that serves as a data catalog and marketplace for security data.[3]

---

2 Hint, hint.

3 IMPACT is the latest of a number of security science projects run by the DHS Science and Technology Directorate, including DETER (a testbed for security research) and PREDICT (the predecessor to IMPACT).

A number of research organizations also generate and share data. Notable sources include CAIDA (*http://www.caida.org*), UCSD's Center for Applied Internet Data Analysis. CAIDA generates and collects a number of different network-mapping data sources. The US Marine Corps maintains a number of datasets from the annual Cyber Defense Exercise (*http://www.usma.edu/crc/sitepages/datasets.aspx*), and CERT maintains a SiLK repository (*https://tools.netsa.cert.org/silk/referencedata.html*) from a past exercise. VizSec, the security visualization conference, also maintains pointers to a number of interesting datasets (*http://vizsec.org/data/*). The best single site for all of these sets is currently maintained by Mike Sconzo; his Security Repo site (*http://www.secrepo.com/*) manages links to datasets and pointers to multiple repositories for host, service, and network data.

These corpora are great for training and exploratory data analysis, but there are a number of caveats I have to mention. First, simply by virtue of being collected and published, they are out of date—be aware of when a dataset was published, because the sensor(s), network, and internet may have substantially changed. Also, be aware that information such as sensor placement is almost never available, which impacts the data observed.

All of this is predicated on the assumption that you need a general result. If the results can be constrained only to one network (e.g., the one you're watching), then external validity is much less problematic.

Construct Validity

When you conduct an analysis, you develop some formal structure to describe what you're looking for. That formal structure might be a survey ("Tell me on a scale of 1–10 how messed up your system is"), or it might be a measurement (bytes/second going to *http://www.evilland.com*). This formal structure, the *construct*, is how you evaluate your analysis.

Clear and well-defined constructs are critical for communicating the meaning of your results. While this might seem simple, it's amazing how quickly construct disagreements can turn into significant scientific or business decisions. For example, consider the question of "how big is a botnet?" A network security person might decide that a botnet consists of everything that communicates with a particular command and control (C&C) server. A forensics person may argue that a botnet is characterized by the same malware hash present on different machines. A law enforcement person would say it's all run by the same crime syndicate.

Statistical Validity

Statistical conclusion validity is about using statistical tools *correctly*. This will be covered in depth in Chapter 11.

Attacker and Attack Issues

Finally, we have to consider the unique impact of security experimentation. Security experimentation and analysis has a distinct headache in that the subject of our analysis hates us and wants us to fail. To that end, we should consider challenges to the validity of the system that come from the attacker. These include issues of currency, resources and timing, and the detection system:

Currency

When evaluating a defensive system, you should be aware of whether the defense is a reasonable defense against current or foreseeable attacker strategies. There are an enormous number of vulnerabilities in the Common Vulnerability Enumeration (CVE; see Chapter 7), but the majority of exploits in the wild draw from a very small pool of those vulnerabilities. By maintaining a solid awareness of the current threat environment (see Chapter 17), you can focus on the more germane strategies.

Resources and timing

Questions of resources and timing are focused on whether or not a detection system or test can be evaded if the attacker slows down, speeds up, or otherwise splits the attack among multiple hosts. For example, if your defensive system assumes that the attacker communicates with one outside address, what happens if the attacker rotates among a pool of addresses? If your defense assumes that the attacker transfers a file quickly, what happens if the attacker takes his time—hours, or maybe days?

Detection

Finally, questions about the detection system involve asking how an attacker can attack or manipulate your detection system itself. For example, if you are using a training set to calibrate a detector, have you accounted for attacks within the training set? If your system is relying on some kind of trust (IP address, passwords, credential files), what are the implications of that trust being compromised? Can the attacker launch a DDoS attack or otherwise overload your detection system, and what are the implications if he does?

Further Reading

1. Two generally excellent resources for computer security experimentation are the proceedings of the USENIX CSET (Computer Security Experimentation and Test) and LASER (Learning from Authoritative Security Experiment Results) workshops. Pointers to the CSET Workshop proceedings are at *https://www.usenix.org/conferences/byname/135*, while LASER proceedings are accessible at *http://www.laser-workshop.org/workshops/*.

2. R. Lippmann et al., "Evaluating Intrusion Detection Systems: The 1998 DARPA Off-Line Intrusion Detection Evaluation," *Proceedings of the 2000 DARPA Information Survivability Conference and Exposition*, Hilton Head, SC, 2000.

3. J. McHugh, "Testing Intrusion Detection Systems: A Critique of the 1998 and 1999 DARPA Intrusion Detection System Evaluations as Performed by Lincoln Laboratory," *ACM Transactions on Information and System Security* 3:4 (2000): 262–294.

4. S. Axelsson, "The Base-Rate Fallacy and the Difficulty of Intrusion Detection," *ACM Transactions on Information and System Security* 3:3 (2000): 186–205.

5. R. Fisher, "Mathematics of a Lady Tasting Tea," in *The World of Mathematics*, vol. 3, ed. J. Newman (New York, NY: Simon & Schuster, 1956).

6. W. Shadish, T. Cook, and D. Campbell, *Experimental and Quasi-Experimental Designs for Generalized Causal Inference* (Boston, MA: Cengage Learning, 2002).

7. R. Heuer, Jr., *Psychology of Intelligence Analysis* (Military Bookshop, 2010), available at *http://bit.ly/1lY0nCR*.

## CHAPTER 2

Vantage: Understanding Sensor Placement in Networks

This chapter is concerned with the practical problem of vantage when collecting data on a network. At the conclusion of this chapter, you should have the necessary skills to break an accurate network diagram into discrete domains for vantage analysis, and to identify potential trouble spots.

As with any network, there are challenges involving proprietary hardware and software that must be addressed on a case-by-case basis. I have aimed, wherever possible, to work out general cases, but in particular when dealing with load balancing hardware, expect that things will change rapidly in the field.

The remainder of this chapter is broken down as follows. The first section is a walk-through of TCP/IP layering to understand how the various layers relate to the problem of vantage. The next section covers *network vantage*: how packets move through a network and how to take advantage of that when instrumenting the network. Following this section is a discussion of the data formats used by TCP/IP, including the various addresses. The final section discusses mechanisms that will impact network vantage.

The Basics of Network Layering

Computer networks are designed in *layers*. A layer is an abstraction of a set of network functionality intended to hide the mechanics and finer implementation details. Ideally, each layer is a discrete entity; the implementation at one layer can be swapped out with another implementation and not impact the higher layers. For example, the Internet Protocol (IP) resides on layer 3 in the OSI model; an IP implementation can run identically on different layer 2 protocols such as Ethernet or FDDI.

There are a number of different layering models. The most common ones in use are the OSI seven-layer model and TCP/IP's four-layer model. Figure 2-1 shows these two models, representative protocols, and their relationship to sensor domains as defined in Chapter 1. As Figure 2-1 shows, the OSI model and TCP/IP model have a rough correspondence. OSI uses the following seven layers:

1. The *physical* layer is composed of the mechanical components used to connect the network together—the wires, cables, radio waves, and other mechanisms used to transfer data from one location to the next.

2. The *data link* layer is concerned with managing information that is transferred across the physical layer. Data link protocols, such as Ethernet, ensure that asynchronous communications are relayed correctly. In the IP model, the data link and physical layers are grouped together as the *link layer* (layer 1).

3. The *network* layer is concerned with the routing of traffic from one data link to another. In the IP model, the network layer directly corresponds to layer 2, the internet layer.

4. The *transport* layer is concerned with managing information that is transferred across the network layer. It has similar concerns to the data link layer, such as flow control and reliable data transmission, albeit at a different scale. In the IP model, the transport layer is layer 3.

5. The *session* layer is concerned with the establishment and maintenance of a session, and is focused on issues such as authentication. The most common example of a session layer protocol today is SSL, the encryption and authentication layer used by HTTP, SMTP, and many other services to secure communications.

6. The *presentation* layer encodes information for display at the application layer. A common example of a presentation layer is MIME, the message encoding protocol used in email.

7. The *application* layer is the service, such as HTTP, DNS, or SSH. OSI layers 5 through 7 correspond roughly to the application layer (layer 4) of the IP model.

The layering model is just that, a model rather than a specification, and models are necessarily imperfect. The TCP/IP model, for example, eschews the finer details of the OSI model, and there are a number of cases where protocols in the OSI model might exist in multiple layers. Network interface controllers (NICs) dwell on layers 1 and 2 in this model. The layers do impact each other, in particular through how data is transported (and is observable), and by introducing performance constraints into higher levels.

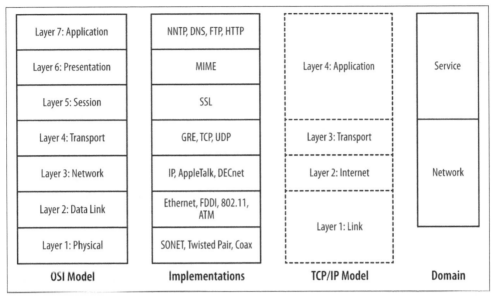

Figure 2-1. Layering models

The most common place where we encounter the impact of layering on network traffic is the *maximum transmission unit* (MTU). The MTU is an upper limit on the size of a data frame, and impacts the maximum size of a packet that can be sent over that medium. The MTU for Ethernet is 1,500 bytes, and this constraint means that IP packets will almost never exceed that size.

The layering model also provides us with a clear difference between the network and service-based sensor domains. As Figure 2-1 shows, network sensors are focused on layers 2 through 4 in the OSI model, while service sensors are focused on layers 5 and above.

Layering and the Role of Network Sensors

It's logical to ask why network sensors can't monitor everything; after all, we're talking about attacks that happen *over a network*. In addition, network sensors can't be tampered with or deleted like host logs, and they will see things like scans or failed connection attempts that host logs won't.

Network sensors provide extensive coverage, but recovering exactly what happened from that coverage becomes more complex as you move higher up the OSI model. At layer 5 and above, issues of protocol and packet interpretation become increasingly prominent. Session encryption becomes an option at layer 5, and encrypted sessions will be unreadable. At layer 6 and layer 7, you need to know the intricacies of the actual protocol that's being used in order to extract meaningful information.

Protocol reconstruction from packet data is complex and ambiguous; TCP/IP is designed on end-to-end principles, meaning that the server and client are the only parties required to be able to construct a session from packets. Tools such as Wireshark or NetWitness can reconstruct the contents of a session, but these are approximations of what actually happened.

Network, host, and service sensors are best used to complement each other. Network sensors provide information that the other sensors won't record, while the host and service sensors record the actual events.

Recall from Chapter 1 that a sensor's vantage refers to the traffic that a particular sensor observes. In the case of computer networks, the vantage refers to the packets that a sensor observes either by virtue of transmitting the packets itself (via a switch or a router) or by eavesdropping (within a collision domain). Since correctly modeling vantage is necessary to efficiently instrument networks, we need to dive a bit into the mechanics of how networks operate.

Network Layers and Vantage

Network vantage is best described by considering how traffic travels at three different layers of the OSI model. These layers are across a shared bus or collision domain (layer 1), over network switches (layer 2), or using routing hardware (layer 3). Each layer provides different forms of vantage and mechanisms for implementing the same.

The most basic form of networking is across a *collision domain*. A collision domain is a shared resource used by one or more networking interfaces to transmit data. Examples of collision domains include a network hub or the channel used by a wireless router. A collision domain is called such because the individual elements can potentially send data at the same time, resulting in a collision; layer 2 protocols include mechanisms to compensate for or prevent collisions.

The net result is that layer 2 datagrams are broadcast across a common source, as seen in Figure 2-2. Network interfaces on the same collision domain all see the same datagrams; they *elect* to only interpret datagrams that are addressed to them. Network capture tools like tcpdump can be placed in promiscuous mode and will then record all the datagrams observed within the collision domain.

Figure 2-2 shows the vantage across collision domains. As seen in this figure, the initial frame (A to B) is broadcast across the hub, which operates as a shared bus. Every host connected to the hub can receive and react to the frames, but only B should do so. C, a compliant host, ignores and drops the frame. D, a host operating in promiscuous mode, records the frame. The vantage of a hub is consequently all the addresses connected to that hub.

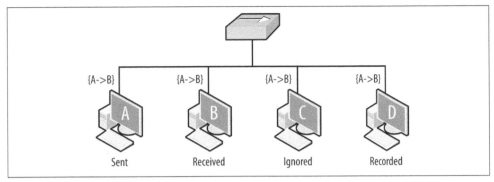

Figure 2-2. Vantage across collision domains

Shared collision domains are inefficient, especially with asynchronous protocols such as Ethernet. Consequently, layer 2 hardware such as Ethernet switches are commonly used to ensure that each host connected to the network has its own dedicated Ethernet port. This is shown in Figure 2-3.

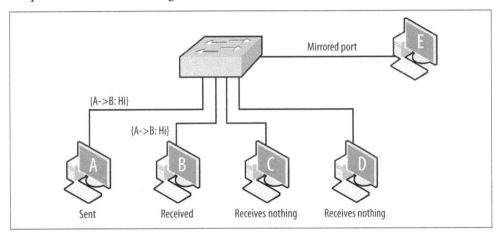

Figure 2-3. Vantage across a switch

A capture tool operating in promiscuous mode will copy every frame that is received at the interface, but the layer 2 switch ensures that the only frames an interface receives are the ones explicitly addressed to it. Consequently, as seen in Figure 2-3, the A to B frame is received by B, while C and D receive nothing.

There is a hardware-based solution to this problem. Most switches implement some form of *port mirroring*. Port mirroring configurations copy the frames sent between different ports to common mirrored ports in addition to their original destination. Using mirroring, you can configure the switch to send a copy of every frame received by the switch to a common interface. Port mirroring can be an expensive operation, however, and most switches limit the amount of interfaces or VLANs monitored.

Switch vantage is a function of the port and the configuration of the switch. By default, the vantage of any individual port will be exclusively traffic originating from or going to the interface connected to the port. A mirrored port will have the vantage of the ports it is configured to mirror.

Layer 3, when routing becomes a concern, is when vantage becomes messy. Routing is a semiautonomous process that administrators can configure, but is designed to provide some degree of localized automation in order to provide reliability. In addition, routing has performance and reliability features, such as the TTL (described shortly), which can also impact monitoring.

Layer 3 vantage at its simplest operates like layer 2 vantage. Like switches, routers send traffic across specific ports. Routers can be configured with mirroring-like functionality, although the exact terminology differs based on the router manufacturer. The primary difference is that while layer 2 is concerned with individual Ethernet addresses, at layer 3 the interfaces are generally concerned with blocks of IP addresses because the router interfaces are usually connected via switches or hubs to dozens of hosts.

Layer 3 vantage becomes more complex when dealing with multihomed interfaces, such as the example shown in Figure 2-4. Up until this point, all vantages discussed in this book have been symmetric—if instrumenting a point enables you to see traffic from A to B, it also enables you to see traffic from B to A. A multihomed host like a router has multiple interfaces that traffic can enter or exit.

Figure 2-4 shows an example of multiple interfaces and their potential impact on vantage at layer 3. In this example, A and B are communicating with each other: A sends the packet {A→B} to B, B sends the packet {B→A} to A. C and D are monitoring at the routers: the top router is configured so that the shortest path from A to B is through it. The bottom router is configured so that shortest path from B to A is through it. The net effect of this configuration is that the vantages at C and D are asymmetric. C will see traffic from A to B, and D will see traffic from B to A, but neither of them will see both sides of the interaction. While this example is contrived, this kind of configuration can appear due to business relationships and network instabilities. It's especially problematic when dealing with networks that have multiple interfaces to the internet.

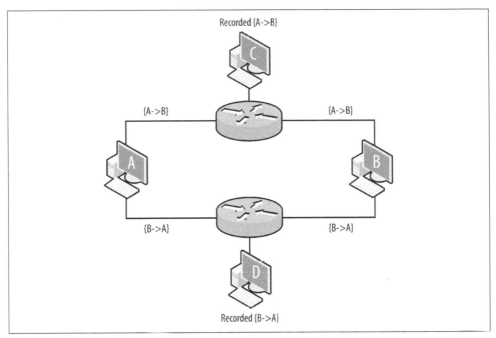

Figure 2-4. Vantage when dealing with multiple interfaces

IP packets have a built-in expiration function: a field called the *time-to-live* (TTL) value. The TTL is decremented every time a packet crosses a router (not a layer 2 facility like a switch), until the TTL reaches 0 and the packet is dropped. In most cases, the TTL should not be a problem—most modern stacks set the TTL to at least 64, which is considerably longer than the number of hops required to cross the entire internet. However, the TTL is manually modifiable and there exist attacks that can use the TTL for evasion purposes. Table 2-1 lists default TTLs by operating system.[1]

Table 2-1. Default TTLs by operating system

Operating system	TTL value
Linux (2.4, 2.6)	64
FreeBSD 2.1	64
macOS	64
Windows XP	128
Windows 7, Vista	128
Windows 10	128
Solaris	255

---

1 A more comprehensive list of TTLs is maintained by Subin Siby at *http://subinsb.com/default-device-ttl-values*.

Figure 2-5 shows how the TTL operates. Assume that hosts C and D are operating on monitoring ports and the packet is going from A to B. Furthermore, the TTL of the packet is set to 2 initially. The first router receives the packet and passes it to the second router. The second router drops the packet; otherwise, it would decrement the TTL to 0. TTL does not directly impact vantage, but instead introduces an erratic type of blind spot—packets can be seen by one sensor, but not by another several routers later as the TTL decrements.

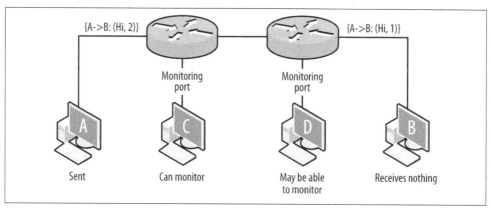

Figure 2-5. Hopping and router vantage

The net result of this is that the packet is observed by C, never received by B, and *possibly* (depending on the router configuration) observed at D.

Physical Taps

Instead of configuring the networking hardware to report data on a dedicated interface, you can monitor the cables themselves. This is done using network taps, which are objects that physically connect to the cables and duplicate traffic for monitoring purposes. Network taps have the advantage of moving the process of collecting and copying data off the network hardware, but only have the vantage of the cables to which they connect.

Network Layers and Addressing

To access anything on a network, you need an address. Most hosts end up with multiple addresses at multiple layers, which are then moderated through different lookup protocols. For example, the host *www.mysite.com* may have the IP address 196.168.1.1 and the Ethernet address 0F:2A:32:AA:2B:14. These addresses are used to resolve the identity of a host at different abstraction layers of the network. For the analyst, the most common addresses encountered will be IPv4, IPv6, and MAC addresses.

In this section, I will discuss addressing in a LAN and instrumentation context. Additional information on addressing and lookup, primarily in the global context, is in Chapter 10.

MAC Addresses

A *media access control* (MAC) address is what the majority of layer 2 protocols, including Ethernet, FDDI, Token Ring, 802.11, Bluetooth, and ATM, use to identify a host. MAC addresses are sometimes called "hardware addresses," as they are usually assigned as fixed values by hardware manufacturers.

MAC format and access

The most common MAC address format is MAC-48, a 48-bit integer. The canonical format for a MAC-48 is six zero-added two-digit hexadecimal octets separated by dashes (e.g., 01-23-45-67-89-AB), although colons and dropped padding are commonly seen (e.g., 1:23:45:67:89:AB).

MAC addresses are divided into two parts: the *organizationally unique identifier* (OUI), a 24-bit numeric ID assigned to the hardware manufacturer by the IEEE, followed by the NIC-specific element, assigned by the hardware manufacturer. The IEEE manages the registry of OUIs on its website (*http://standards-oui.ieee.org/ oui.txt*), and there are a number of sites that will return a manufacturer ID if you pass them a MAC or full address.

Routing, Spoofing, and MAC Address Uniqueness

MAC address collisions are managed through the basic unscalability of local networks. By the time you get up to a few hundred hosts, addresses should be managed by routing, and as layer 2 addresses, MAC addresses *don't route*. When a frame is transferred across a router, the addressing information is replaced with the addressing information of the router's interface.

It is hilariously easy to spoof MAC addresses. Most network configuration tools will provide you with some option for manually setting the MAC address, and as long as it's well formed, you should be able to set it to anything you like without a problem.

The routing escape hatch also deals with the risk of MAC collisions. Since manufacturers are normally assigned 16 million or so addresses to play with, the odds of running into an address overlap *should* be low.

IPv4-to-MAC lookup is managed using the Address Resolution Protocol (ARP).

IPv4 Format and Addresses

An IPv4 address is a 32-bit integer value assigned to every routable host, with exceptions made for reserved dynamic address spaces (see Chapter 10 for more information on these addresses). IPv4 addresses are most commonly represented in dotted quad format: four integers between 0 and 255 separated by periods (e.g., 128.1.11.3).

Historically, addresses were grouped into four *classes*: A, B, C, and D. A class A address (0.0.0.0–127.255.255.255) had the high order (leftmost) bit set to zero, the next 7 assigned to an entity, and the remaining 24 bits under the owner's control. This gave the owner 2^{24} addresses to work with. A class B address (128.0.0.0–191.255.255.255) assigned 16 bits to the owner, and class C (192.0.0.0–223.255.255.255) assigned 8 bits. This approach led rapidly to address exhaustion, and in 1993, *Classless Inter-Domain Routing* (CIDR) was developed to replace the naive class system.

Under the CIDR scheme, users are assigned a *netblock* via an address and a netmask. The netmask indicates which bits in the address the user can manipulate, and by convention, those bits are set to zero. For example, a user who owns the addresses 192.28.3.0–192.28.3.255 will be given the block 192.28.3.0/24. The suffix /24 here indicates that the high 24 bits are fixed, while the last 8 are open. /24s will contain 256 addresses, /27s 32, /16s 65,536, and so on.

A number of important IPv4 address blocks are reserved for special use. The IANA IPv4 Address Register (*http://www.iana.org/assignments/ipv4-address-space/ipv4-address-space.xhtml*) contains a list of the most important /8s and their ownership. More important for administration and management purposes are the addresses listed in RFC 1918.[2] The RFC 1918 local addresses define a set of IP addresses for local use, meaning that they can be used for internal networks (such as DHCP or NATed networks) that are *not* routed to the broader internet.[3]

IPv6 Format and Addresses

An IPv6 address is a 128-bit integer, solving the IPv4 address exhaustion problem by increasing the space by a factor of about 4 billion. By default, these addresses are described as a set of 16-bit hexadecimal *groups* separated by colons (e.g., 00AA:2134:0000:0000:A13F:2099:0ABE:FAAF). Given their length, IPv6 addresses use a number of conventions to shorten the representation. In particular:

---

2 *https://tools.ietf.org/html/rfc1918*, updated by RFC 6761 at *https://tools.ietf.org/html/rfc6761*.

3 You will, of course, see them routed through the broader internet because nobody will follow BCP38 until the mutant cockroaches rule the Earth. You can learn about BCP38 at *http://www.bcp38.info/*. Go learn about BCP38, then go implement BCP38.

- Initial zeros are trimmed (e.g., AA:2134:0:0:A13F:2099:ABE:FAAF).

- A sequence of zero-value groups can be replaced by empty colons (e.g., AA:2134:::A13F:2099:ABE:FAAF).

- Multiple colons are reduced to a single pair (e.g., AA:2134::A13F:2099:ABE:FAAF).

As with IPv4, IPv6 blocks are grouped using CIDR notation. The IPv6 CIDR prefixes can be up to the full length of an IPv6 address (i.e., up to /128).

All of these relationships are dynamic, and multiple addresses at one layer can be associated with one address at another layer. As discussed earlier, a single DNS name can be associated with multiple IP addresses through the agency of the DNS service. Similarly, a single MAC address can support multiple IP addresses through the agency of the ARP protocol. This type of dynamism can be used constructively (like for tunneling) and destructively (like for spoofing).

Validity Challenges from Middlebox Network Data

Security analysts evaluating a network's suitability for traffic analysis must consider not just whether they can *see* an address, but if they can *trust* it. Network engineers rely on a variety of tools and techniques to manage traffic, and the tools chosen can also affect vantage in a number of different ways.

We can categorize the general problems these tools introduce by how they impact analytics. In this section, I will discuss these effects and then relate them, in general and kind of loosely, to different common networking tools. Challenges to the validity of network data include threats to identity, causality, aggregation, consistency, and encryption. Table 2-2 shows how these are associated with the technologies we'll discuss in the following subsections.

Table 2-2. Vantage risks from networking support technologies

	Identity	Causality	Aggregation	Consistency	Encryption
NAT	X		X	X	
DHCP	X			X	
Load balancer		X		X	
Proxy	X	X	X	X	
VPN	X		X	X	X

These technologies will impact vantage, and consequently analysis, in a number of ways. Before we dig into the technologies themselves, let's take a look at the different ways analytic results can be challenged by them:

Identity

In some situations, the identity of individuals is not discernible because the information used to identify them has been remapped across boundaries—for example, a network address translator (NAT) changing address X to address Y. Identity problems are a significant challenge to internal validity, as it is difficult to determine whether or not the same individual is using the same address. Addressing identity problems generally requires collecting logs from the appliance implementing the identity mapping.

Causality

Information after the middlebox boundary does not necessarily follow the sequence before the middlebox boundary. This is particularly a problem with caching or load balancing, where multiple redundant requests before the middlebox may be converted into a single request managed by the middlebox. This affects internal validity across the middlebox, as it is difficult to associate activity between the events before and after the boundary. The best solution in most cases is to attempt to collect data before the boundary.

Aggregation

The same identity may be used for multiple individuals simultaneously. Aggregation problems are a particular problem for construct validity, as they affect volume and traffic measurements (for example, one user may account for most of the traffic).

Consistency

The same identity can change over the duration of the investigation. For example, we may see address A do something malicious on Monday, but on Tuesday it's innocent due to DHCP reallocation. This is a long-term problem for internal validity.

Encryption

When traffic is contained within an encrypted envelope, deep packet inspection and other tools that rely on payload examination will not work.

DHCP

On DHCP (RFC 2131) networks—which are, these days, most networks—IP addresses are assigned dynamically from a pool of open addresses. Users *lease* an address for some interval, returning it to the pool after use.

DHCP networks shuffle IP addresses, breaking the relationship between an IP address and an individual user. The degree to which addresses are shuffled within a DHCP network is a function of a number of qualitative factors, which can result in anything from an effectively static network to one with short-term lifespans. For example, in an enterprise network with long leases and desktops, the same host may keep the same address for weeks. Conversely, in a coffee shop with heavily used WiFi, the same address may be used by a dozen machines in the course of a day.

While a DHCP network may operate as a de facto statically allocated network, there are situations where everything gets shuffled en masse. Power outages, in particular, can result in the entire network getting reshuffled.

When analyzing a network's vantage, the analyst should identify DHCP networks, their size, and lease time. I find it useful to keep track of a rough characterization of the network—whether devices are mobile or desktops, whether the network is public or private, and what authentication or trust mechanisms are used to access the network. Admins should configure the DHCP server to log all leases, with the expectation that an analyst may need to query the logs to find out what asset was using what host at a particular time.

Sysadmins and security admins should also ask what assets are being allocated via DHCP. For critical assets or monitored users (high-value laptops, for example), it may be preferable to statically allocate an address to enable that asset's traffic to be monitored via NetFlow or other network-level monitoring tools. Alternatively, critical mobile assets should be more heavily instrumented with host-based monitoring.

NAT

NATing (network address translation) converts an IP address behind a NAT into an external IP address/port combination outside the NAT. This results in a single IP address serving the interests of multiple addresses simultaneously. There are a number of different NATing techniques, which vary based on the number of addresses assigned to the NAT, among other things. In this case, we are going to focus on Port Address Translation (PAT), which is the most common form and the one that causes the most significant problems.

NATed systems both shuffle addresses (meaning that there is no realistic relationship between an IP address and a user) and multiplex them (meaning that the same *address:port* combination will rapidly serve multiple hosts). The latter badly affects any metrics or analyses depending on individual hosts, while the former confuses user identity. For this reason, the most effective solution for NATing is instrumentation *behind the NAT*.

Figure 2-6 shows this multiplexing in action. In this figure, you can see flow data as recorded from two vantage points: before and after translation. As the figure shows, traffic before the NAT has its own distinct IP addresses, while traffic *after* the NAT has been remapped to the NAT's address with different port assignments.

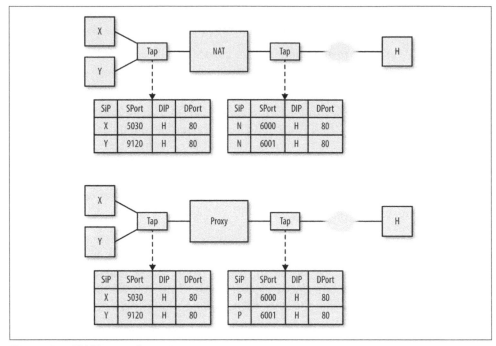

Figure 2-6. NATing and proxies

Note that correlating NATing activity across both sides of the NAT requires the NAT itself to log that translation; this is discussed in more depth in Chapter 3.

The Pain Trinity

A common and unpleasant network configuration involves multiple isolated networks with addresses allocated via DHCP, using RFC 1918 addresses, sitting behind NATs. As noted, generally when working with NATs, you're going to need instrumentation behind the NAT in order to figure out what's going on. The problem with this fragmentation is that you're going to end up with multiply redundant IP addresses.

This is basically a provenance problem, and it can be addressed in a number of different ways. When collecting the data behind the NAT, ensure it's properly labeled so you always know what subnetwork you're dealing with.

An alternative approach, and one that saves a lot of pain in the long run, is to assign a distinct set of IP addresses to each NATed subnetwork. That is, network A may use 10.0.0.0/24, network B may use 10.0.1.0/24, and so on. This way, even if the data is globally collected and stored, you can still identify the distinct segments simply by the IP addresses.

Proxies

As with NATing, there are a number of different technologies (such as load balancing and reverse proxying) that fall under the proxy banner. Proxies operate at a higher layer than NATs—they are service-specific and, depending on the service in question, may incorporate load balancing and caching functions that will further challenge the validity of data collected across the proxy boundary.

Figure 2-6 shows how proxies remap traffic; as the figure shows, in a network with a proxy server, hosts using the proxy will *always* communicate with the proxy address first. This results in all communications with a particular service getting broken into two flows: client to proxy, proxy to server. This, in turn, exacerbates the differentiation problems introduced by NATing—if you are visiting common servers with common ports, they cannot be differentiated outside of the proxy, and you cannot relate them to traffic inside the proxy except through timing.

Without logs *from* the proxy, correlating traffic across proxy boundaries has extremely dubious validity. As with NATing, individual IP addresses and events are not differentiable. At the same time, internal instrumentation is not valuable because all the traffic goes to the same address. Finally, timing across proxies is always messy —web proxies, in particular, usually incorporate some form of caching to improve performance, and consequently the same page, fetched multiple times before the proxy, may be fetched only once after the proxy.

Load balancing

Load balancing techniques split traffic to a heavily used target between multiple servers and provide a common address to those servers. Load balancing can take place at multiple layers—techniques exist to remap DNS, IP, and MAC addresses as needed.

Load balancing primarily challenges identity and consistency, as the same address will, often very quickly, point to multiple different targets.

VPNs

In a virtual private network (VPN), some process wraps traffic in one protocol within the envelope of another protocol. Examples of these include classic VPN protocols such as Generic Routing Encapsulation (GRE), ad-hoc VPN tools such as Secure Shell (SSH), and transition protocols like Teredo or 6to4.

VPNs introduce two significant challenges. First, the encryption of the data in transit obviates deep packet inspection and any technique that requires examining or interpreting the payload. The other challenge is the identity problem—outside of the VPN, the observer sees a single, long-lived flow between client and VPN. At the VPN endpoint, the client will engage in multiple interactions with clients within the network, which are returned to the VPN access point and delivered to the client. The end result is a maze of IP address relationships across the VPN barrier.

Further Reading

1. R. Bejtlich, *The Practice of Network Security Monitoring: Understanding Incident Detection and Response* (San Francisco, CA: No Starch Press, 2003).

2. R. Bejtlich, *The Tao of Network Security Monitoring: Beyond Intrusion Detection* (Boston, MA: Addison-Wesley, 2004).

3. K. Fall and R. Stevens, *TCP/IP Illustrated, Volume 1: The Protocols*, 2nd ed. (Boston, MA: Addison-Wesley, 2011).

4. R. Perlman, *Interconnections: Bridges, Routers, Switches, and Internetworking Protocols*, 2nd ed. (Boston, MA: Addison-Wesley, 1999).

5. P. Goransson, C. Black, and T. Culver, *Software Defined Networks: A Comprehensive Approach* (Burlington, MA: Morgan Kaufmann, 2016).

## CHAPTER 3

Sensors in the Network Domain

This chapter is concerned with the data generated by network sensors. These are sensors that collect data directly from network traffic without the agency of an intermediary application, making them service or host domain sensors. Examples include NetFlow sensors on a router and sensors that collect traffic using packet capture, most notably tcpdump. This also includes middlebox services such as VPNs or NATs, which contain log data critical to identifying users.

The challenge of network traffic is the challenge you face with all log data: actual security events are rare, and data costs analysis time and storage space. Where available, log data is preferable because it's clean (a high-level event is recorded in the log data) and compact. The same event in network traffic would have to be extracted from millions of packets, which can often be redundant, encrypted, or unreadable. At the same time, it is very easy for an attacker to manipulate network traffic and produce legitimate-looking but completely bogus sessions on the wire. An event summed up in a 300-byte log record could easily be megabytes of packet data, wherein only the first 10 packets have any analytic value.

That's the bad news. The good news is that network traffic's "protocol agnosticism," for lack of a better term, means that it is also your best source for identifying blind spots in your auditing. Host-based collection systems require knowing that the host *exists* in the first place, and there are numerous cases where you're likely not to know that a particular service is running until you see its traffic on the wire. Network traffic provides a view of the network with minimal assumptions—it tells you about hosts on the network you don't know existed, backdoors you weren't aware of, attackers already inside your borders, and routes through your network you never considered. At the same time, when you face a zero-day vulnerability or new malware, packet data may be the only data source you have.

The remainder of this chapter is structured into discussions of various data formats. We will begin with an overview of Ethernet and IP packets, and the process of collecting this data using tcpdump and sensors derived from tcpdump. We will then discuss *NetFlow*, which provides a compact summary of network traffic generated by a number of different tools, including NetFlow reporting capabilities on routers and specialized software sensors that derive NetFlow from tcpdump output. We will then examine IDS and its use as a sensor, and end the chapter by discussing logs from middleboxes.

Packet and Frame Formats

On almost any modern system, tcpdump will be capturing IP over Ethernet, meaning that the data actually captured by libpcap consists of Ethernet frames containing IP packets. While the IP suite contains over 80 unique protocols, on any operational network the overwhelming majority of traffic will originate from just 3 of these: TCP (protocol 6), UDP (protocol 17), and ICMP (protocol 1).

While TCP, UDP, and ICMP make up the overwhelming majority of IP traffic, a number of other protocols may appear in networks, in particular if VPNs are used. The Internet Assigned Numbers Authority (IANA) has a complete list (*http://bit.ly/ protocol-numbers*) of IP suite protocols. Some notable ones to expect include IPv6 (protocol number 41), GRE (protocol number 47), and ESP (protocol number 50). GRE and ESP are used in VPN traffic.

Full packet capture is often impractical. The sheer size and redundancy of the data means that it's difficult to keep any meaningful fraction of network traffic for a reasonable time. There are three major mechanisms for filtering or limiting packet capture data: the use of rolling buffers to keep a timed subsample, manipulating the snap length to capture only a fixed-size packet (such as headers), and filtering traffic using Berkeley Packet Filter (BPF) or other filtering rules. Each approach is an analytic trade-off that provides different benefits and disadvantages.

While tcpdump is the oldest and most common packet capture tool, there are many alternatives. In the purely software domain, Google's Stenographer project (*https:// github.com/google/stenographer*) is a high-performance capture solution, and AOL's Moloch (*https://github.com/aol/moloch*) combines packet capture and analysis. There are also a number of hardware-based capture tools that use optimized NICs to capture at higher line speeds.

Rolling Buffers

A *rolling buffer* is a location in memory where data is dumped cyclically: information is dropped linearly, and when the buffer is filled up, data is dumped at the beginning of the buffer, and the process repeats. Example 3-1 gives an example of using a rolling buffer with `tcpdump`: in this example, the process writes approximately 128 MB to disk (specified by the -C switch), and then rotates to a new file. After 32 files are filled (specified by the -W switch), the process restarts.

Example 3-1. Implementing a rolling buffer in tcpdump

```
$ tcpdump -i en1 -s 0 -w result -C 128 -W 32
```

Rolling buffers implement a time horizon on traffic analysis: data is available only as long as it's in the buffer. For that reason, working with smaller file sizes is recommended, because when you find something aberrant, it needs to be pulled out of the buffers quickly. If you want a more controlled relationship for the total time recorded in a buffer, you can use the -G switch to specify that a file should be dumped at a fixed interval (specified by -G) rather than a fixed size.

Limiting the Data Captured from Each Packet

An alternative to capturing the complete packet is to capture a limited subset of the payload, controlled in `tcpdump` by the snaplen (-s) argument. Snaplen constrains packets to the frame size specified in the argument. If you specify a frame size of at least 68 bytes, you will record the TCP or UDP headers.[1] That said, this solution is a poor alternative to NetFlow, which is discussed later in this chapter.

Filtering Specific Types of Packets

An alternative to filtering at the switch is to filter after collecting the traffic at the spanning port. With `tcpdump` and other tools, this can be easily done using BPF. BPF allows an operator to specify arbitrarily complex filters, and consequently the possibilities are fairly extensive. Some useful options are described in this section, along with examples. Figure 3-1 provides a breakdown of the headers for Ethernet frames, IP, UDP, ICMP, and TCP.

As we walk through the major fields, I'll identify BPF macros that describe and can be used to filter on these fields. On most Unix-style systems, the `pcap-filter` manpage provides a summary of BPF syntax. Available commands are also summarized in the FreeBSD manpage for BPF (*http://bit.ly/bsd-manpages*).

---

[1] The snaplen is based on the Ethernet frame size, so 20 additional bytes have to be added to the size of the corresponding IP headers.

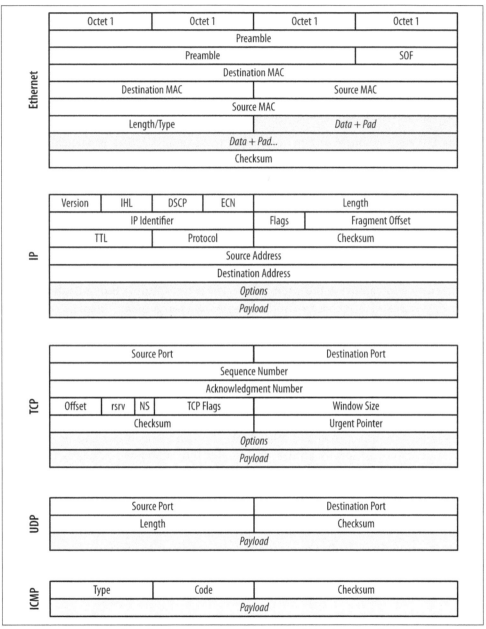

Figure 3-1. Frame and packet formats for Ethernet, IP, TCP, UDP, and ICMP

In an Ethernet frame, the most critical fields are the two MAC addresses: *destination MAC* and *source MAC*. These 48-bit fields are used to identify the hardware addresses of the interfaces that sent and will receive the traffic. MAC addresses are restricted to a single collision domain, and will be modified as a packet traverses multiple networks (see Figure 2-5 for an example). MAC addresses are accessed using the `ether src` and `ether dst` predicates in BPF.[2]

Within an IP header, the fields you are usually most interested in are the IP addresses, the length, the TTL, and the protocol. The IP identifier, flags, and fragment offset are used for attacks involving packet reassembly—however, they are also largely a historical artifact from before Ethernet was a nearly universal transport protocol. You can get access to the IP addresses using the `src host` and `dst host` predicates, which also allow filtering on netmasks.

Address Filtering in BPF

Addresses in BPF can be filtered using the various `host` and `net` predicates. To understand how these work, consider a simple `tcpdump` output:

```
host$ tcpdump -n -r sample.pcap  | head -5
reading from file sample.pcap, link-type EN10MB (Ethernet)
20:01:12.094915 IP 192.168.1.3.56305 > 208.78.7.2.389: Flags [S],
  seq 265488449, win 65535, options [mss 1460,nop, wscale 3,nop,
  nop,TS val 1111716334 ecr 0,sackOK,eol], length 0
20:01:12.094981 IP 192.168.1.3.56302 > 192.168.144.18.389: Flags [S],
  seq 1490713463, win 65535, options [mss 1460,nop,wscale 3,nop,
  nop,TS val 1111716334 ecr 0,sackOK,eol], length 0
20:01:12.471014 IP 192.168.1.102.7600 > 192.168.1.255.7600: UDP, length 36
20:01:12.861101 IP 192.168.1.6.17784 > 255.255.255.255.17784: UDP, length 27
20:01:12.862487 IP 192.168.1.6.51949 > 255.255.255.255.3483: UDP, length 37
```

`src host` or `dst host` will filter on exact IP addresses, filtering for traffic to or from 192.168.1.3 as shown here:

```
host$ tcpdump -n -r sample.pcap  src host 192.168.1.3 | head -1
reading from file sample.pcap, link-type EN10MB (Ethernet)
20:01:12.094915 IP 192.168.1.3.56305 > 208.78.7.2.389: Flags [S],
  seq 265488449, win 65535, options [mss 1460,nop,wscale 3,nop,
  nop,TS val 1111716334 ecr 0,sackOK,eol], length 0
host$ tcpdump -n -r sample.pcap  dst host 192.168.1.3 | head -1
reading from file sample.pcap, link-type EN10MB (Ethernet)
20:01:13.898712 IP 192.168.1.6.48991 > 192.168.1.3.9000: Flags [S],
  seq 2975851986, win 5840, options [mss 1460,sackOK,TS val 911030 ecr 0,
  nop,wscale 1], length 0
```

`src net` and `dst net` allow filtering on netblocks. The following example shows how we can progressively filter addresses in the 192.168.1 network using just the address or CIDR notation:

---

2 Most implementations of `tcpdump` require a command-line switch before showing link-level (i.e., Ethernet) information. In macOS, the -e switch will show the MAC addresses.

```
# Use src net to filter just by matching octets
host$ tcpdump -n -r sample.pcap  src net 192.168.1 | head -3
reading from file sample.pcap, link-type EN10MB (Ethernet)
20:01:12.094915 IP 192.168.1.3.56305 > 208.78.7.2.389: Flags [S],
 seq 265488449, win 65535, options [mss 1460,nop,wscale 3,nop,nop,
 TS val 1111716334 ecr 0,sackOK,eol], length 0
20:01:12.094981 IP 192.168.1.3.56302 > 192.168.144.18.389: Flags [S],
 seq 1490713463, win 65535, options [mss 1460,nop,wscale 3,nop,
 nop,TS val 1111716334 ecr 0,sackOK,eol], length 0
# Match an address
host$ tcpdump -n -r sample.pcap  src net 192.168.1.5 | head -1
reading from file sample.pcap, link-type EN10MB (Ethernet)
20:01:13.244094 IP 192.168.1.5.50919 > 208.111.133.84.27017: UDP, length 84
# Match using a CIDR block
host$ tcpdump -n -r sample.pcap  src net 192.168.1.64/26 | head -1
reading from file sample.pcap, link-type EN10MB (Ethernet)
20:01:12.471014 IP 192.168.1.102.7600 > 192.168.1.255.7600: UDP, length 36
```

To filter on protocols, use the ip proto predicate. BPF also provides a variety of protocol-specific predicates, such as tcp, udp, and icmp. Packet length can be filtered using the less and greater predicates, while filtering on the TTL requires more advanced bit manipulation, which is discussed later.

The following snippet filters out all traffic except that coming within this block (hosts with the netmask /24):

```
host$ tcpdump -i en1 -s 0 -w result src net 192.168.2.0/24
```

Example 3-2 demonstrates filtering with tcpdump.

Example 3-2. Examples of filtering using tcpdump

```
# Filtering out everything but internal traffic
host$ tcpdump -i en1 -s 0 -w result src net 192.168.2.0/24 && dst net \
     192.168.0.0/16
# Filtering out everything but web traffic, identified by port
host$ tcpdump -i en1 -s 0 -w result ((src port 80 || src port 443) && \
     (src net 192.168.2.0))
```

In TCP, the port number and flags are the most critical for investigation, analysis, and control. TCP flags are used to maintain the TCP state machine, while the port numbers are used to distinguish sessions and for service identification. Port numbers can be filtered using the src port and dst port switches, as well as the src portrange and dst portrange switches, which filter across a range of port values. BPF supports a variety of predicates for TCP flags, including tcp-fin, tcp-syn, tcp-rst, tcp-push, tcp-ack, and tcp-urg.

As with TCP, the UDP port numbers are the most important information for analyzing and controlling the traffic. They are accessible using the same `port` and `portrange` switches as TCP.

Because ICMP is the internet's error message–passing protocol, ICMP messages tend to contain extremely rich data. The ICMP type and code are the most useful for analysis because they define the syntax for whatever payload (if any) follows. BPF provides a variety of type- and code-specific filters, including `icmp-echoreply`, `icmp-unreach`, `icmp-tstamp`, and `icmp-redirect`.

What If It's Not Ethernet?

For the sake of brevity, this book focuses exclusively on IP over Ethernet, but you may well encounter a number of other transport and data protocols. The majority of these protocols are highly specialized and may require additional capture software besides the tools built on `libpcap`. A few of the more common ones are:

ATM
> *Asynchronous Transfer Mode*, the great IP slayer of the '90s. ATM is now largely used for ISDN and PSTN transport, and some legacy installations.

Fibre Channel
> Primarily used for high-speed storage, Fibre Channel is the backbone for a variety of SAN implementations.

CAN
> *Controller area network*. Primarily associated with embedded systems such as vehicular networks, CAN is a bus protocol used to send messages in small isolated networks.

These protocols are scratching the surface. In particular, if you're dealing with industrial control systems, you can expect to find a maze of proprietary protocols. When dealing with industrial systems, find their manuals first—it's likely to be the only way you can do anything akin to packet capture.

Any form of filtering imposes performance costs. Implementing a spanning port on a switch or a router sacrifices performance that the switch or router could be using for traffic. The more complicated a filter is, the more overhead is added by the filtering software. At nontrivial bandwidths, this will be a problem.

NetFlow

NetFlow is a traffic summarization standard developed by Cisco Systems and originally used for network services billing. While not intended for security, NetFlow is fantastically useful for that purpose because it provides a compact summary of network traffic sessions that can be rapidly accessed and contains the highest-value information that you can keep in a relatively compact format. NetFlow has been increasingly used for security analysis since the publication of the original *flow-tools* package in 1999, and a variety of tools have been developed that provide NetFlow with additional fields, such as selected snippets of payload.

The heart of NetFlow is the concept of a *flow*, which is an approximation of a TCP session. Recall that TCP sessions are assembled at the endpoint by comparing sequence numbers. Juggling all the sequence numbers involved in multiple TCP sessions is not feasible at a router, but it is possible to make a reasonable approximation using timeouts. A flow is a collection of identically addressed packets that are closely grouped in time.

NetFlow v5 Formats and Fields

NetFlow v5 is the earliest common NetFlow standard, and it's worth covering the values in its fields before discussing alternatives. NetFlow v5's fields (listed in Table 3-1) fall into three broad categories: fields copied straight from IP packets, fields summarizing the results of IP packets, and fields related to routing.

Table 3-1. NetFlow v5 fields

Bytes	Name	Description
0–3	srcaddr	Source IP address
4–7	dstaddr	Destination IP address
8–11	nexthop	Address of the next hop on the router
12–13	input	SNMP index of the input interface
14–15	output	SNMP index of the output interface
16–19	packets	Packets in the flow
20–23	dOctets	Number of layer 3 bytes in the flow
24–27	first	sysuptime at flow start[a]
28–31	last	sysuptime at the time of receipt of the last flow's packet
32–33	srcport	TCP/UDP source port
34–35	dstport	TCP/UDP destination port, ICMP type, and code
36	pad1	Padding
37	tcp_flags	Cumulative OR of all TCP flags in the flow
38	prot	IP protocol
39	tos	IP type of service
40–41	src_as	Autonomous system number (ASN) of source
42–43	dst_as	ASN of destination
44	src_mask	Source address prefix mask

Bytes	Name	Description
45	dst_mask	Destination address prefix mask
46–47	pad2	Padding bytes

[a] This value is relative to the router's system uptime.

The srcaddr, dstaddr, srcport, dstport, prot, and tos fields of a NetFlow record are copied directly from the corresponding fields in IP packets. Flows are generated for *every* protocol in the IP suite, however, and that means that the srcport and dstport fields, which strictly speaking are TCP/UDP phenomena, don't necessarily always mean something. In the case of ICMP, NetFlow records the type and code in the dstport field. In the case of other protocols, the value is meaningless; depending on the collection system you may end up with a previously allocated value, zeros, or other data.

The packets, dOctets, first, last, and tcp_flags fields all summarize traffic from one or more packets. packets and dOctets are simple totals, with the caveat that the dOctets value is the layer 3 total of octets, meaning that IP and protocol headers are added in (e.g., a one-packet TCP flow with no payload will be recorded as 40 bytes, and a one-packet UDP flow with no payload as 28 bytes). The first and last values are, respectively, the first and last times observed for a packet in the flow.

tcp_flags is a special case. In NetFlow v5, the tcp_flags field consists of an OR of all the flags that appear in the flow. In well-formed flows, this means that the SYN, FIN, and ACK flags will always be high for any valid TCP session.

The final set of fields—nexthop, input, output, src_as, dst_as, src_mask, and dst_mask—are all routing-related. These values can be collected only at a router.

NetFlow v9 and IPFIX

Cisco developed several versions of NetFlow over its lifetime, with NetFlow v5 ending up as the workhorse implementation of the standard. But v5 is a limited and obsolete standard, focused on IPv4 and designed before flows were commonly used. Cisco's solution to this was NetFlow v9, a template-based flow reporting standard that enabled router administrators to specify what fields were included in the flow.

Template-based NetFlow has since been standardized by the IETF as IPFIX.[3] IPFIX provides several hundred potential fields for flows, which are described in RFC 5102 (*http://bit.ly/rfc-5102*).

The main focus of the standard is on network monitoring and traffic analysis rather than information security. To address optional fields, IPFIX has the concept of a

---

3 See RFCs 5101 (*http://bit.ly/rfc-5101*), 5102 (*http://bit.ly/rfc-5102*), and 5103 (*http://bit.ly/rfc-5103*).

"vendor space." In the course of developing the SiLK toolkit, the CERT Network Situational Awareness Group at Carnegie Mellon University developed a set of security-sensitive fields that are in their IPFIX vendor space and provide a set of useful fields for security analysis.

NetFlow Generation and Collection

NetFlow records are generated directly by networking hardware appliances (e.g., a router or a switch), or by using software to convert packets into flows. Each approach has different trade-offs.

Appliance-based generation means using whatever NetFlow facility is offered by the hardware manufacturer. Different manufacturers use similar-sounding but different names than Cisco, such as JFlow by Juniper Networks and NetStream by Huawei. Because NetFlow is offered by so many different manufacturers with a variety of different rules, it's impossible to provide a technical discussion about the necessary configurations in the space provided by this book. However, the following rules of thumb are worth noting:

- NetFlow generation can cause performance problems on routers, especially older models. Different companies address this problem in different ways, ranging from reducing the priority of the process (and dropping records) to offloading the NetFlow generation task to optional (and expensive) hardware.

- Most NetFlow configurations default to some form of sampling in order to reduce the performance load. For security analysis, NetFlow should be configured to provide unsampled records.

- Many NetFlow configurations offer a number of aggregation and reporting formats. You should collect raw NetFlow, not aggregations.

The alternative to router-based collection is to use an application that generates NetFlow from pcap data, such as CERT's Yet Another Flowmeter (YAF) tool (*http://tools.netsa.cert.org*), softflowd (*http://bit.ly/softflowd*), or the extensive flow monitoring tools provided by QoSient's Argus (*http://bit.ly/qo-argus*) tool. These applications take pcap as files or directly off a network interface and aggregate the packets as flows. These sensors lack a router's vantage, but are able to devote more processing resources to analyzing the packets and can produce richer NetFlow output, incorporating features such as deep packet inspection.

Data Collection via IDS

Intrusion detection systems (IDSs) are network-vantage event-action sensors that operate by collecting data off of the interface and running one or more tests on the data to generate alerts. IDSs are not really built as sensors, instead being part of family of expert systems generally called *binary classifiers.*

A binary classifier, as the name implies, classifies information. A classifier reads in data and marks it as belonging to one of two categories: either the data is normal and requires no further action, or the data is characteristic of an attack. If it is deemed an attack, then the system reacts as specified; an IDS operates as an event sensor, generating an event. *Intrusion prevention systems* (IPSs), the IDS's more aggressive cousins, block traffic.[4]

There are several problems with classification, which we can term the *moral*, the *statistical*, and the *behavioral*. The moral problem is that attacks can be indistinguishable from innocuous, or even permitted, user activity. For example, a DDoS attack and a flash crowd can look very similar until some time has passed. The statistical problem is that IDSs are often configured to make hundreds or millions of tests a day—under those conditions, even low false positive rates can result in far more false positives in a day than true positives in a month. The behavioral problem is that attackers are intelligent parties interested in evading detection, and often can do so with minimal damage to their goals.

In later sections of the book, we will discuss the challenges of IDS usage in more depth. In this section, we will focus on the general idea of using IDSs as a sensing tool.

Classifying IDSs

We can divide IDSs along two primary axes: the IDS domain, and the decision-making process. On the first axis, IDSs are broken into *network-based IDSs* (NIDSs) and *host-based IDS* (HIDSs). On the second axis, IDSs are split between *signature-based* systems and *anomaly-based* systems. Relating these terms back to our earlier taxonomy, NIDSs operate in the network domain, HIDSs in the host domain. The classic IDS is an event sensor; there are controller systems, IPSs, which will control traffic in response to aberrant phenomena. This section focuses on NIDSs—network-domain event-action sensors.

A NIDS is effectively any IDS that begins with pcap data. For open source IDSs, this includes systems such as Snort, Bro, and Suricata. NIDSs operate under the constraints discussed for network sensors in Chapter 2, such as the need to receive traffic through port mirroring or direct connection to the network and an inability to read encrypted traffic.

---

4 Theoretically, nobody in their right minds trusts an IPS with more than DDoS prevention.

For the purposes of simplicity, in this section we will treat all IDSs as *signature-based*. A signature-based system uses a set of rules that are derived independently from the target in order to identify malicious behavior.

IDS as Classifier

All IDS are applied exercises in *classification*, a standard problem in AI and statistics. A classifier is a process that takes in input data and classifies the data into one of at least two categories. In the case of IDS, the categories are usually "attack" and "normal."

Signature and anomaly-based IDSs view attacks in fundamentally different ways, and this impacts the types of errors they make. A signature-based IDS is calibrated to look for specific weird behaviors such as malware signatures or unusual login attempts. Anomaly-based IDSs are trained on normal behavior and then look for anything that steps outside the norm. Signature-based IDSs have high false negative rates, meaning that they miss a lot of attacks. Anomaly-based IDSs have high false positive rates, which means that they consider a lot of perfectly normal activity to be an attack.

IDSs are generally binary classifiers, meaning that they break data into two categories. Binary classifiers have two failure modes:

False positives

> Also called a *Type I error*, this occurs when something that doesn't have the property you're searching for is classified as having the property—for instance, when email from the president of your company informing you about a promotion is classified as spam.

False negatives

> Also called a *Type II error*, this occurs when something that has the property you're searching for is classified as *not* having the property. This happens, for instance, when spam mail appears in your inbox.

Sensitivity refers to the percentage of positive classifications that are correct, and *specificity* refers to the percentage of negative classifications that are correct. A perfect detection has perfect sensitivity and specificity. In the worst case, neither rate is above 50%: the same as flipping a coin.

Most systems require some degree of trade-off; generally, increasing the sensitivity means also accepting a lower specificity. A reduction in false negatives will be accompanied by an increase in false positives, and vice versa.

To describe this trade-off, we can use a visualization called a *receiver operating characteristic* (ROC) curve (discussed in more depth in Chapter 11). A ROC curve plots the specificity against the false positive rates, using a third characteristic (the *operating characteristic*) as a control. Figure 3-2 shows an example of a ROC curve.

In this case, the operating characteristic is the number of packets in a session and is shown on the horizontal lines in the plot. At this site, HTTP traffic (falling at the very left edge) has a good ratio of true to false positives, whereas SMTP is harder to classify correctly, and FTP even harder.

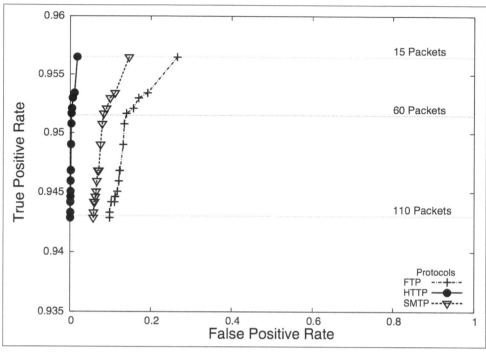

Figure 3-2. ROC curve showing packet size of messages sent for BitTorrent detection

Now, let's ask a question. Suppose we have an ROC curve and we calibrate a detector so it has a 99% true positive rate and a 1% false positive rate. We receive an alert. What is the probability that the alert is a true positive? It *isn't* 99%; the true positive rate is the probability that *if* an attack took place, the IDS would raise an alarm.

Let's define a *test* as the process that an IDS uses to make a judgment call about data. For example, a test might consist of collecting 30 seconds' worth of network traffic and comparing it against a predicted volume, or examining the first two packets of a session for a suspicious string.

Now assume that the probability of an actual attack taking place during a test is 0.01%. This means that out of every 10,000 tests the IDS conducts, one of them will be an attack. So out of every 10,000 tests, we raise one alarm *due to an attack*—after all, we have a 99% true positive rate. However, the false positive rate is 1%, which means that 1% of the tests raise an alarm even though nothing happened. This means that for 10,000 tests, we can expect roughly 101 alarms: 100 false positives and 1 true positive, meaning that the probability that an alarm is raised *because* of an attack is 1/101 or slightly less than 1%.

This *base-rate fallacy* explains why doctors don't run every test on every patient. When the probability of an actual attack is remote, the false positives will easily overwhelm the true positives. This problem is exacerbated because nobody in their right mind trusts an IDS to do the job alone.

Consider the data flow in Figure 3-3, which is a simple representation of how an IDS is normally used in defense.

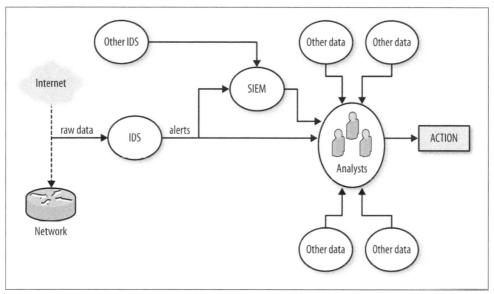

Figure 3-3. Simple detection workflow

Figure 3-3 breaks alert processing into three steps: IDS receives data, raises an alert, and that alert is then passed to analysts either directly or through a security information and event manager (SIEM) console.

Once an IDS generates an alert, that alert must be forwarded to an analyst for further action. Analysts begin by examining it and figuring out what it means. This may be a relatively simple process, but often it becomes wider-ranging and may involve a number of queries. Simple queries will include looking at the geolocation, ownership, and past history of the address the attack originates from (see Chapter 10), by examining the payload of the event using tcpdump or Wireshark. With more complex attacks, analysts will have to reach out to Google, news, blogs, and message boards to identify similar attacks or real-world events precipitating the attack.

With the exception of IPSs, which work on very crude and obvious attacks (such as DDoS attacks), there is always an interim analytical step between alert and action. At this point, analysts have to determine if the alert is a threat, if the threat is relevant to them, and whether or not there's anything they can do about it. This is a nontrivial problem. Consider the following scenarios:

- The IDS reports that an attacker is exploiting a particular Internet Information Services (IIS) vulnerability. Are there any IIS servers on the network? Have they been patched so they're not subject to the exploit? Is there evidence from other sources that the attacker succeeded?

- The IDS reports that an attacker is scanning the network. Can we stop the scan? Should we bother given that there are another hundred scans going on right now?

- The IDS reports that a host is systematically picking through a web server and copying every file. Is the host a Google spider, and would stopping it mean that our company's primary website would no longer be visible on Google?

Note that these are not actually failures on the part of detection. The first two scenarios represent actual potential threats, but those threats may not *matter*, and that decision can only be made through a combination of context and policy decisions.

Verifying alerts takes time. An analyst might be able to seriously process approximately one alert an hour, and complex events will take days to investigate. Consider how that time is spent given the false positive rates discussed earlier.

Improving IDS Performance

There are two approaches to improving how IDSs work. The first is to improve the IDS as a classifier; that is, increase the sensitivity and specificity. The second way is to reduce the time an analyst needs to process an alert by fetching additional information, providing context, and identifying courses of action.

There are no perfect rules to this process. For example, although it's always a good (and necessary) goal to minimize false positives, analysts will take a more nuanced approach to this problem. For example, if there's a temporary risk of a nasty attack, an analyst will often tolerate a higher false positive rate in order to more effectively defend against that attack.

There's a sort of Parkinson's law problem here. All of our detection and monitoring systems provide only partial coverage because the internet is weird, and we don't really have a good grasp of what we're missing. As any floor improves its detection process, it will find that there are newer and nastier alerts to consider. To paraphrase Donald Rumsfeld: we do have a problem with unknown unknowns.

This problem of unknown unknowns makes false negatives a particular headache. By definition, a signature-based IDS can't alert on anything it isn't configured to alert on. That said, most signature matching systems will be configured to identify only a limited subset of all the malicious behaviors that a particular host uses. By combining signature- and anomaly-detecting IDSs together, you can at least begin to identify the blind spots.

Enhancing IDS Detection

Improving an IDS as a classifier involves reducing the false positive and false negative rates. This is generally best done by reducing the scope of the traffic the IDS examines. In the same way that a doctor doesn't run a test until he has a symptom to work with, we try to run the IDS only when we have an initial suspicion that something odd is going on. A number of different mechanisms are available based on whether you're using a signature- or an anomaly-based IDS.

Inconsistent Notification: A Headache with Multiple IDSs

A special category of false negative involves inconsistent IDS rulesets. Imagine that you run a network with the access points A and B, with IDSs running on both. If you don't keep the ruleset on IDS A consistent with the ruleset on IDS B, you will find that A sends you alerts that B doesn't recognize, and vice versa.

The easiest way to manage this problem is to treat the rulesets as any other source code. That is, put the rules in a version control system, make sure that you commit and comment them, and then install the rules from your version control system. Keeping the rules under version control's a good idea anyway because if you're doing a multimonth traffic investigation, you really will want to look at those old rulesets to figure out exactly what you were blocking last April.

There is a class of IDS that makes this type of management particularly problematic, however. AV and some other detection systems are usually black-box systems. A black-box system provides ruleset updates as a subscription service, and the rulesets are usually completely inaccessible to an administrator. Inconsistent identification can be particularly problematic with black-box systems where, at the best, you must keep track of what the current rulebase is and identify systems that are behind.[5]

One mechanism common to both signature- and anomaly-based IDSs is using inventory to create whitelists. Pure whitelists, meaning that you implicitly trust all traffic from a host, are *always* a risk. I don't recommend simply whitelisting a host and never checking it. A better approach, and one that is going to appear in various forms throughout this discussion, is to use whitelisting as a guide for less or more extensive instrumentation.

For example, I create an inventory of all the web servers on my network. A host that is not a web server is suspicious if I see it serving HTTP traffic. In that case, I want to

---

5 This has the nice bonus of identifying systems that may be compromised. Malware will disable AV as a matter of course.

capture a representative cut of traffic and figure out *why* it's now a web server. At the same time, for actual web servers, I will use my standard signatures.

In signature-based IDSs, the signature base can usually be refined so that the rule triggers only for specific protocols or in tandem with other indicators. For example, a rule to detect the payload string "herbal supplement" on port 25 will track spam emails with that title, but also internal mail containing comments such as "we're getting a lot of herbal supplement spam lately." Reducing the false positive rate in this case involves adding more constraints to the match, such as tracking only mail from outside the network (filtering on addresses). By refining the rule to use more selective expressions, an operator can reduce the false positive rate.

Configuring Snort

For a Snort system, these signatures are literally handcrafted and user-maintained rules. For example:

```
alert tcp 192.4.1.0/24 any -> $HOME_NET 80 (flow:to_server,established; \
    content:"admin";)
```

This alert is raised when traffic from a suspicious network (192.4.1.0/24) attempts to contact any host on the internal network and tries to connect using an admin account. Ruleset creation and management is a significant issue for signature-based IDSs, and well-crafted rules are often the secret sauce that differentiates various commercial packages.

A signature-based IDS will only raise alerts when it has a rule specifying to do so. This limitation means that signature-based IDSs usually have a high false negative rate, meaning that a large number of attacks go unreported by them. The most extreme version of this problem is associated with vulnerabilities. AV systems primarily, but also NIDSs and HIDSs, rely on specific binary signatures in order to identify malware (see "On Code Red and Malware Evasiveness" on page 53 for a more extensive discussion on this). These signatures require that some expert have access to an exploit; these days, exploits are commonly "zero-day," meaning that they're released and in the wild *before* anyone has the opportunity to write a signature. Good IDS signature development will focus on the vulnerability rather than the exploit—a signature that depends on a transient feature of the exploit will quickly become obsolete.[6]

---

6 Malware authors test against AV systems, and usually keep current on the signature set.

On Code Red and Malware Evasiveness

Read the original papers on NIDSs by Paxson and Roesch (see "Further Reading" on page 61) and you'll see that they were thinking about handcrafted attacks on systems that they'd be able to defend by looking for people trying to log in as *root* or *admin*. There was a functionality change around 2001, which was the beginning of a very nasty worm-heavy era in defense. Worms like Code Red and Slammer caused widespread havoc by spreading actively and destructively choking bandwidth.

The Code Red v1 and v2 worms both exploited a buffer overflow in Microsoft IIS in order to subvert IIS processes and launch an attack against the White House. The original Code Red worm contained a payload looking like the following:

```
.......... GET
/default.ida?NNNNNNNNNNNNNNNNNNNNNNNNNNNNNNNNNNNNNNNNNNNNNNNNNNNNNNNNNNNNN
NNNNNNNNNNNNNNNNNNNNNNNNNNNNNNNNNNNNNNNNNNNNNNNNNNNNNNNNNNNNNNNNNNNNNNNNNNN
NNNNNNNNNNNNNNNNNNNNNNNNNNNNNNNNNNNNNNNNNNNNNNNNNNNNNNNNNNNNNNNNNNNNNNNNNNN
NNNNNNNNNNNNNNNNNNNNNNN%u9090%u6858%ucbd3%u7801%u9090%u6858%ucbd3%u7801
%u9090%u6858%ucbd3%u7801%u9090%u9090%u8190%u00c3%u0003%u8b00%u531b%u53ff
%u0078%u0000%u00=a HTTP/1.0 ..........
```

IDSs at the time detected Code Red by looking for that specific payload, and a couple of weeks later, an updated version of the worm using the same exploit was launched. The payload for Code Red II looked like this:

```
.......... GET
/default.ida?XXXXXXXXXXXXXXXXXXXXXXXXXXXXXXXXXXXXXXXXXXXXXXXXXXXXXXXXXXXXX
XXXXXXXXXXXXXXXXXXXXXXXXXXXXXXXXXXXXXXXXXXXXXXXXXXXXXXXXXXXXXXXXXXXXXXXXXXXX
XXXXXXXXXXXXXXXXXXXXXXXXXXXXXXXXXXXXXXXXXXXXXXXXXXXXXXXXXXXXXXXXXXXXXXXXXXXX
XXXXXXXXXXXXXXXXXXXXXXXXX%u9090%u6858%ucbd3%u7801%u9090%u6858%ucbd3%u7801
%u9090%u6858%ucbd3%u7801%u9090%u9090%u8190%u00c3%u0003%u8b00%u531b%u53ff
%u0078%u0000%u00=a HTTP/1.0 ..........
```

As a buffer overflow, the Code Red worms needed to pad their contents in order to reach a specific memory location; the worms were often differentiated by the presence of an X or an N in the buffer. The thing is, the buffer contents are *irrelevant* to the execution of the worm; an attacker could change them at will without changing the functionality.

This has been a problem for IDSs ever since. As originally conceived, intrusion detection systems were looking for anomalous and suspicious *user* behavior. These types of long-term hacks could be detected and stopped because they'd be happening over the course of hours or days, which is enough time for analysts to examine the alert, vet it, and take a course of action. Modern attacks are largely automated, and the actual subversion and control of a host can take place instantaneously if the right conditions are met.

The problem of binary signature management has gotten significantly worse in the past decade because it's easy for attackers to modify payload without changing the functionality of the worm. If you examine threat databases such as Symantec's, you will find that there are hundreds or more variants of common worms, each of them with a different binary signature.

As for the explosive, destructive worms like Slammer, they basically calmed down for what I will best describe as evolutionary reasons. Much like it doesn't pay a physical virus to kill its host until it's had a chance to spread, modern worms are generally more restrained in their reproduction. It's better to own the internet than to destroy it.

As an example, consider the following (oversimplified for clarity) rule to determine whether or not someone is logging on as *root* to an SSH server:

```
alert tcp any any -> any 22 (flow:to_server, established;)
```

A Snort rule consists of two logical sections: the header and the options. The header consists of the rule's *action* and addressing information (protocol, source address, source port, destination address, destination port). Options consist of a number of specific keywords separated by semicolons.

In the example rule, the action is `alert`, indicating that Snort generates an alert and logs the packet. Alternative actions include `log` (log the packet without alerting), `pass` (ignore the packet), and `drop` (block the packet). Following the action is a string naming the protocol: `tcp` in this case, with `udp`, `icmp`, and `ip` being other options. The action is followed by source-to-destination information separated by the arrow (->) digraph. Source information can be expressed as an address (e.g., 128.1.11.3), a net-block (118.2.0.0/16) as in the example, or `any` to indicate all addresses. Snort can also define various collections of addresses with macros (e.g., $HOME_NET to indicate the home network for an IDS). You can use these macros to define inventories of hosts within the network, and use that information for more finely tuned whitelisting or blacklisting.

This rule raises an alert when anyone successfully connects to an SSH server, which is far too vague. In order to refine the rule, we have to add additional constraints. For example, we can constrain it to only raise an alert if the traffic comes from a specific network, and if someone tries to log on specifically as *root*:

```
alert tcp 118.2.0.0/16 any -> any 21
    (flow:to_server,established; \ content:"root";
    pcre:"/user\s_root/i";)
```

Following the addressing information are one or more *rule options*. Options can be used to refine a rule, fine-tuning the information the rule looks for in order to reduce the false positive rate. Options can also be used to add additional information to an alert, to trigger another rule, or to complete a variety of other actions.

Snort defines well over 70 options for various forms of analysis. A brief survey of the more useful rules:

content

> content is Snort's bread-and-butter pattern matching rule; it does an exact match of the data passed in the content option against the packet payload. content can use binary and text data, enclosing the binary data in pipes. For example, content:|05 11|H|02 23| matches the byte with contents 5, then 11, then the letter H, then the byte 2, then the byte 23. A number of other options directly impact content, such as depth (specifying where in the payload to stop searching) and offset (specifying where in the payload to start searching).

HTTP options

> A number of HTTP options (http_client_body, http_cookie, http_header) will extract the relevant information from an HTTP packet for analysis by content.

pcre

> The pcre option uses a PCRE (Perl-Compatible Regular Expressions) regular expression to match against a packet. Regular expressions are expensive; make sure to use content to prefilter traffic and skip applying the regular expression against every packet.

flags

> This checks to see whether or not specific TCP flags are present.

flow

> The flow keyword specifies the direction traffic is flowing in, such as from a client, to a client, from a server, or to a server. The flow keyword also describes certain characteristics of the session, such as whether or not it was actually established.

Snort's rule language is used by several other IDSs, notably Suricata. Other systems may differentiate themselves with additional options (for example, Suricata has an iprep option for looking at IP address reputation).

Unlike signature-based systems, where you can't really go wrong by discussing Snort rules, anomaly-detection systems are more likely to be built by hand. Consequently, when discussing how to make an anomaly detector more effective, we have to operate at a more basic level. Throughout Part III, we discuss a number of different numerical and behavioral techniques for implementing anomaly-detection systems, as well as cases for false positives. However, this is an appropriate place to discuss general criteria for building good anomaly-detection systems.

In their simplest forms, anomaly-detection systems raise alarms via thresholds. For example, I might decide to build anomaly detection for a file server by counting the number of bytes downloaded from the server every minute. I can do so using rwfilter to filter the data and rwcount to count it over time. I can then use R to generate a histogram showing the probability that the value is above x. The nice thing about histograms and statistical anomaly detection is that I control this nominal false positive rate. A test every minute and a 95% threshold before raising alarms means that I create three alarms an hour; a 99% threshold means one alarm every two hours.

The problem lies in picking a threshold that is actually useful. For example, if an attacker is aware that I'll raise an alarm if he's too busy, he can reduce his activity below the threshold. This type of evasiveness is really the same kind we saw with Code Red in "On Code Red and Malware Evasiveness" on page 53. The attacker in that case could change the contents of the buffer without impacting the worm's performance. When you identify phenomena for anomaly detection, you should keep in mind how it impacts the attacker's goals; detection is simply the first step.

I have four of rules of thumb I apply when evaluating phenomena for an anomaly-detection system: predictability, manageable false positives, disruptibility, and impact on attacker behavior.

Predictability is the most basic quality to look for in a phenomenon. A predictable phenomenon is one whose value effectively converges over time. "Convergence" is something that I have to be a bit hand-wavy about. You may find that 9 days out of 10, a threshold is x, and then on the tenth day it rises to *10x* because of some unexplained weirdness. Expect unexplained weirdness; if you can identify and describe outliers behaviorally and whatever remains has an upper limit you can express, then you've got something predictable. False positives will happen during investigation, and true positives will happen during training!

The second rule is manageable false positives. Look at a week of traffic for any publicly available host and you will see something weird happen. Can you explain this weirdness? Is it the same address over and over again? Is it a common service, such as a crawler visiting a web server? During the initial training process for any anomaly detector, you should log how much time you spend identifying and explaining outliers, and whether you can manage those outliers through whitelisting or other behavioral filters. The less you have to explain, the lower a burden you impose on busy operational analysts.

A disruptible phenomenon is one that the attacker must affect in order to achieve his goals. The simpler, the better. For example, to download traffic from a web server, the attacker must contact the web server. He may not need to do so from the same address, and he may not need authentication, but he needs to pull down data.

Finally, there's the impact of a phenomenon on attacker behavior. The best alarms are the ones that the attacker *has* to trigger. Over time, if a detector impacts an attacker, the attacker will learn to evade or confuse it. We see this in antispam efforts and the various tools used to trick Bayesian filtering, and we see it consistently in insider threats. When considering an alarm, consider how the attacker can evade it, such as:

By moving slower
> Can an attacker impact the alarm if she reduces her activity? If so, what's the impact on the attacker's goal? If a scanner slows her probes, how long does it take to scan your network? If a file leech copies your site, how long does it take to copy the whole site?

By moving faster
> Can an attacker confuse the system if he moves faster? If he risks detection, can he move faster than your capability to block him by moving as fast as possible?

By distributing the attack
> If an attacker works from multiple IP addresses, can the individual addresses slip under the threshold?

By alternating behaviors
> Can an attacker swap between suspicious and innocent behavior, and confuse the IDS that way?

Many of the techniques discussed previously imply a degree of heterogeneity in your detection system. For example, anomaly-detection systems might have to be configured individually for different hosts. I have found it useful to push that idea toward a subscription model, where analysts choose which hosts to monitor, decide on the thresholds, and provide whitelisting and blacklisting facilities for every host they decide to monitor. Subscriptions ensure that the analyst can treat each host individually, and eventually build up an intuition for normal behavior on that host (for example, knowing that traffic to the payroll server goes bonkers every two weeks).

The subscription model acknowledges that you can't monitor everything, and consequently the next question about any subscription-based approach is precisely *what* to monitor. Chapter 15 and Chapter 19 discuss this issue in more depth.

Enhancing IDS Response

IDSs, particularly NIDSs, were conceived of as real-time detection systems—the assumption was that there would be enough of a gap between the time the attack began and the final exploit that, armed with the IDS alerts, the defenders could stop the attack before it caused significant damage. This concept was developed in a time when attackers might use two computers, when attacks were handcrafted by experts, and when malware was far more primitive. Now, IDSs are too often a recipe for annoyance. It's not simply a case of misclassified attacks; it's a case of attackers attacking hosts that aren't there in the hopes that they'll find something to take over.

At some point, you will make an IDS as effective a detector as you can, and you'll still get false positives because there are normal behaviors that look like attacks—and the only way you'll figure this out is by investigating them. Once you reach that point, you're left with the alerting problem: IDSs generate simple alerts in real time, and analysts have to puzzle them out. Reducing the workload on analysts means aggregating, grouping, and manipulating alerts so that the process of verification and response is faster and conducted more effectively.

When considering how to manipulate an alert, first ask what the response to that alert will be. Most Computer Security Incident Response Teams (CSIRTs) have a limited set of actions they can take in response to an alert, such as modifying a firewall or IPS rules, removing a host from the network for further analysis, or issuing policy changes. These responses rarely take place in real time, and it's not uncommon for certain attacks to not merit any response at all. The classic example of the latter case is scanning: it's omnipresent, it's almost impossible to block, and there's very little chance of catching the culprit.

If a real-time response isn't necessary, it's often useful to roll up alerts, particularly by attacker IP address or exploit type. It's not uncommon for IDSs to generate multiple alerts for the same attacker. These behaviors, which are not apparent with single real-time alerts, become more obvious when the behavior is aggregated.

Prefetching Data

After receiving an alert, analysts have to validate and examine the information around the alert. This usually involves tasks such as determining the country of origin, the targets, and any past activity by this address. Prefetching this information helps enormously to reduce the burden on analysts.

In particular with anomaly-detection systems, it helps to present options. As we've discussed, anomaly detections are often threshold-based, raising an alert after a phenomenon exceeds a threshold. Instead of simply presenting an aberrant event, configure the reporting system to return an ordered list of the most aberrant events at a fixed interval, and explanations for why these events are the most concerning.

Providing summary data in visualizations such as time series plots helps reduce the cognitive burden on the analyst. Instead of just producing a straight text dump of query information, generate relevant plots. Chapter 11 discusses this issue in more depth.

Most importantly, consider monitoring assets rather than simply monitoring attacks. Most detection systems are focused on attacker behavior, such as raising an alert when a specific attack signature is detected. Instead of focusing on attacker behavior, assign your analysts specific hosts on the network to watch and analyze the traffic to and from those assets for anomalies. Lower-priority targets should be protected using more restrictive techniques, such as aggressive firewalls. With hypervisors and virtualization, it's worth creating low-priority assets entirely virtually from fixed images, then destroying and reinstantiating them on a regular basis to limit the time any attacker can control those assets.

Assigning analysts to assets rather than simply having them react to alerts has another advantage: analysts can develop expertise about the systems they're watching. False positives often a rise out of common processes that aren't easily described to the IDS, such as a rise in activity to file servers because a project is reaching crunch time, regular requests to payroll, or a service that's popular with a specific demographic. Expertise reduces the time analysts need to sift through data, and helps them throw out the trivia to focus on more significant threats.

Middlebox Logs and Their Impact

As discussed in Chapter 2, middleboxes introduce significant challenges to the validity of network data analysis. Mapping middleboxes and identifying what logs you can acquire from them is a necessary step in building up actionable network data. In this section, I will discuss some general qualities of network middlebox logs, some recommendations for configuration, and strategies for managing the data.

When using middlebox data, I recommend storing the data and then applying it on a case-by-case basis. The alternative approach to this is to annotate other data (such as your flow or pcap) with the middlebox information on the fly. Apart from the computational complexity of doing so, my experience working with forensic middlebox data is that there are always fiddly edge cases, such as load balancing and caching, that make automated correlation inordinately complex.

As for what data to collect and when, I recommend finding VPN logs first, then moving onto proxies, NATs, and DHCP. VPN logs are critical not only because they provide an encrypted and trusted entry point into your network, but because your higher-quality attacker is intimately aware of this. The other classes of data are organized roughly in terms of how much additional information they will uncover—proxy logs, in addition to the problems of correlating across proxies, often serve as a convenient substitute for service logs.[7]

---

7 It's not a bad idea to consider proxies in front of embedded devices with critical web interfaces *just* to take advantage of the logging.

VPN Logs

Always get the VPN logs. VPN traffic is incomprehensible without the VPN logs—it is encrypted, and the traffic is processed at concentrators, before reaching its actual destination. The VPN logs should, at the minimum, provide you with the identity, credentials, and a local mapping of IP addresses after the concentrator.

VPN logs are session-oriented, and usually multiline behemoths containing multiple interstitial events. Developing a log shim to summarize the events (see Chapter 4) will cut down on the pain. When looking at VPN logs, check for the following data:

Credentials
> VPNs are authenticated, so check to see the identities that are being used. Linking this information with user identity and geolocation are handy anomaly-detection tricks.

Logon and logoff times
> Check when the sessions initiate and end. Enterprise users, in particular, are likely to have predictable session times (such as the workday).

External IP address
> The external IP address, in particular its geolocation, is a useful anomaly hook.

Assigned internal IP address
> Keeping track of the address the VPN assigns is critical for cross-correlation.[8]

Proxy Logs

Proxies are application-specific, replace the server address with their own, and often contain caching or other load balancing hacks that will result in causality problems. After VPNs, keeping track of proxies and collecting their logs is the next best bang for the buck.

In addition to the need to acquire proxy logs because proxies mess with traffic so creatively, proxy logs are generally *very* informative. Because proxies are application-specific, the log data may contain service information—HTTP proxy logs will usually include the URL and domain name of the request.

While proxy log data will vary by the type of proxy, it's generally safe to assume you are working with event-driven service log data. Squid, for example, can be configured to produce Common Log Format (CLF) log messages (see "HTTP: CLF and ELF" on page 78 for more information on this).

---

8 As with other material, I'm very fond of assigning fixed addresses to users, just so I have less information I need to cross-correlate.

NAT Logs

You can partially manage NATing validity by placing a sensor between the clients and the NAT. This will provide the internal addresses, and the external addresses should remain the same. That said, you will not be able to coordinate the communications between internal and external addresses—theoretically you should be able to map by looking at port numbers, but NATs are usually sitting in front of clients talking to servers. The end result is that the server address/port combinations are static and you will end up with multiple flows moving to the same servers. So, expect that in either case you will want the NAT logs.

Whether NAT logging is available is largely a question of the type of device performing the NATing. Enterprise routers such as Cisco and Juniper boxes provide flow log formats for reporting NAT events. These will be IPFIX messages with the NAT address contained as an additional field.[9] Cheaper embedded routers, such as ones for home networks, are less likely to include this capability.

As for the data to consider, make sure to record both the IP addresses *and* the ports: source IP, source port, destination IP, destination port, NAT IP, NAT port.

Further Reading

1. M. Fullmer and S. Romig, "The OSU Flow-tools Package and CISCO NetFlow Logs," *Proceedings of the 2000 USENIX Conference on System Administration (LISA)*, New Orleans, LA, 2000.

2. M. Lucas, *Network Flow Analysis* (San Francisco, CA: No Starch Press, 2010).

3. QoSient's Argus database (*https://qosient.com/argus/*).

4. C. Sanders, *Practical Packet Analysis: Using Wireshark to Solve Real-World Problems* (San Francisco, CA: No Starch Press, 2011).

5. Juniper Networks, "Logging NAT Events in Flow Monitoring Format Overview," available at *http://juni.pr/2uynYcw*.

6. Cisco Systems, "Monitoring and Maintaining NAT," available at *http://bit.ly/2u57dF6*.

7. S. Sivakumar and R. Penno, "IPFIX Information Elements for Logging NAT Events," available at *http://bit.ly/nat-logging-13*.

8. B. Caswell, J. Beale, and A. Baker, *Snort IDS and IPS Toolkit* (Rockland, MA: Syngress Publishing, 2007).

---

9 This is, as of this writing, very much a work in progress; see the references in the next section.

9. M. Roesch, "Snort: Lightweight Intrusion Detection for Networks," *Proceedings of the 1999 USENIX Conference on System Administration (LISA)*, Seattle, WA, 1999.

10. V. Paxson, "Bro: A System for Detecting Network Intruders in Real Time," *Proceedings of the 1998 USENIX Security Symposium*, San Antonio, TX, 1998.

## CHAPTER 4

Data in the Service Domain

This chapter is concerned with the practical problem of collecting data moderated by a service, which is to say *service domain* data. At the conclusion of this chapter, you will be able to identify the sources for service domain data and understand how vantage impacts this data and the challenges to its validity.

What and Why

Practically speaking, service domain data consists of log data generated by various services operating on a host. Service domain data is characterized by the service's moderation of things—where network data deals in packets which may or may not do anything, service data deals in events that are defined by the service. While data in the host domain consists of the host's current state, the service domain contains the events that caused a state change.

Service data is therefore distinguished from the other categories by the impact of a service moderating the information you receive. To understand how this moderation impacts use, consider the scenario shown in Figure 4-1. This figure shows how data in two domains is generated for two different phenomena.

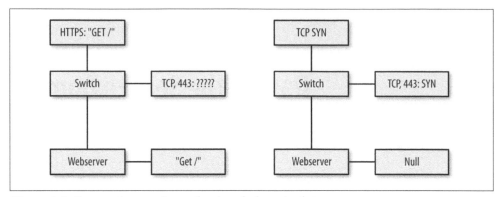

Figure 4-1. Comparing service and network domain data

On the left is a simple GET request via HTTPS. In this example, data is collected from two points: a span port on a switch collecting raw pcap, and the logs from the web server. Since the HTTPS packets are encrypted, the only information the span port can provide is header-based—ports, protocol, and nothing else. Meanwhile, the web server can decrypt and process the data, recording that information.

While encryption is the most obvious challenge to the validity of inferences using packet capture, *all* network-based instrumentation faces challenges to its internal validity because TCP/IP design is built on the *end-to-end* principle. Systems designed around this principle push more functionality to the endpoints, while keeping the network itself relatively simple.

The practical impact of the end-to-end principle on network monitoring is that nothing seen on the network can be taken at face value, especially once you allow for perverse and creative packet crafting. For example, an attacker can send perfectly valid DNS request packets or a realistic-looking half of a TCP session, and from the network traffic alone, the observer cannot guarantee that this wasn't real traffic. In the network domain, the best the defender can do is guess something happened, while in the service domain, the defender can find out what happened.

Instrumenting at the service domain is not a panacea, however, as shown in the right-hand side of the figure. In this case, a scanner is hitting the network with half-open scans, and the pcap sensor can see this information. But the web server *has never received an HTTPS session from this*, and doesn't record the information.

The net result of this is that no single collection point will address all of the potential phenomena you can face. Understanding the strength of each domain, and the data you can effectively collect in each case, is critical to determining what data to collect.

Logfiles as the Basis for Service Data

The foundational data you deal with when working with service information is *service-specific logfiles*. A service-specific logfile is a record of the *transactions* that the service engages in.

The concept of a transaction is critical here. A transaction is an interaction with the service *as defined by the service*. Example transactions may include fetching a web page (for a web server), sending out a DNS query (for a DNS server), or listing all the mail in a folder (for an IMAP server). Transactions are service-specific, and determining what transactions the service provides will require diving into its documentation and relevant standards.

Accessing and Manipulating Logfiles

Operating systems have dozens of processes generating log data at any time. In Unix systems, these logfiles are usually stored as text files in the */var/log* directory. Example 4-1 shows this directory for macOS (the ellipses indicate where lines were removed for clarity).

Example 4-1. A /var/log directory from a macOS system

```
drwxr-xr-x   2 _uucp       wheel       68 Jun 20  2012 uucp
...
drwxr-xr-x   2 root        wheel       68 Dec  9  2012 apache2
drwxr-xr-x   2 root        wheel       68 Jan  7 01:47 ppp
drwxr-xr-x   3 root        wheel      102 Mar 12 12:43 performance
...
-rw-r--r--   1 root        wheel      332 Jun  1 05:30 monthly.out
-rw-r-----   1 root        admin     6957 Jun  5 00:30 system.log.7.bz2
-rw-r-----   1 root        admin     5959 Jun  6 00:30 system.log.6.bz2
-rw-r-----   1 root        admin     5757 Jun  7 00:30 system.log.5.bz2
-rw-r-----   1 root        admin     5059 Jun  8 00:30 system.log.4.bz2
-rw-r--r--   1 root        wheel      870 Jun  8 03:15 weekly.out
-rw-r-----   1 root        admin    10539 Jun  9 00:30 system.log.3.bz2
-rw-r-----   1 root        admin     8476 Jun 10 00:30 system.log.2.bz2
-rw-r-----   1 root        admin     5345 Jun 11 00:31 system.log.1.bz2
-rw-r--r--   1 root        wheel   131984 Jun 11 18:57 vnetlib
drwxrwx---  33 root        admin     1122 Jun 12 00:23 DiagnosticMessages
-rw-r-----   1 root        admin     8546 Jun 12 00:30 system.log.0.bz2
-rw-r--r--   1 root        wheel   108840 Jun 12 03:15 daily.out
-rw-r--r--   1 root        wheel    22289 Jun 12 04:51 fsck_hfs.log
-rw-r-----   1 root        admin   899464 Jun 12 20:11 install.log
```

Note several features of this directory. The *system.log* files are started daily at 00:30 and are differentiated numerically. There are a number of subdirectories for handling various services. Check the configuration of each individual service you want to acquire logfiles for, but it's not uncommon for Unix systems to dump them to a sub-directory of */var/log* by default.

Unix logfiles are almost always plain text. For example, a brief snippet of a system log reads as follows:

```
$ cat system.log
Jun 19 07:24:49 local-imac.home loginwindow[58]: in pam_sm_setcred(): Done
    getpwnam()
Jun 19 07:24:49 local-imac.home loginwindow[58]: in pam_sm_setcred(): Done
    setegid() & seteuid()
Jun 19 07:24:49 local-imac.home loginwindow[58]: in pam_sm_setcred():
    pam_sm_setcred: krb5 user admin doesn't have a principal
Jun 19 07:24:49 local-imac.home loginwindow[58]: in pam_sm_setcred(): Done
    cleanup3
```

The majority of Unix system logs are text messages created by filling in templates with specific event information. This kind of *templated text* is easy to read, but doesn't scale very well.

As of Vista, Windows has extensively revamped its logging structure. Windows logs are further subdivided into several classes, notably:

Application log
Contains messages from individual applications. Note that services such as IIS may use auxiliary logs to contain additional information.

Security log
Contains security events, such as logon attempts and audit policy changes.

System log
Contains messages about system status, such as driver failures.

Forwarded events log
Stores events from remote hosts.

These logs are recorded in *%SystemRoot%\System32\Config* by default on most Windows installs; however, the more effective mechanism for accessing and reading the files is to use the Windows Event Viewer, as seen in Figure 4-2.

Note the use of the event ID in Figure 4-2; as with Unix systems, the Windows event messages are templated text, though Windows explicitly identifies the type of event using a unique numeric code. These messages are accessible from Microsoft's website.

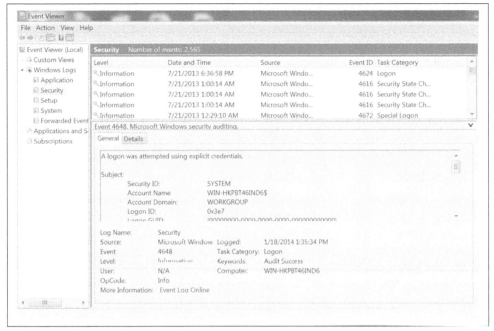

Figure 4-2. The Windows event log

On Linux, application logfiles are much less consistently located. As seen in the */var/log* directory, administrative structure may be set up to record a logfile in a fixed location, but almost every application has the ability to move around logfiles as necessary. When working with a particular application, consult its documentation to find out where it drops logs.

The Contents of Logfiles

Logs are usually designed to provide debugging and troubleshooting information for an administrator on the host. Because of this, you will often find that host-based logs require both some degree of parsing and some degree of reorganization to make them satisfactory security logs. In this section, we discuss mechanisms for interpreting, troubleshooting, and converting host log data.

The Characteristics of a Good Log Message

Before discussing how to convert a log message, and before complaining about how bad most log messages are, it behooves us to describe what a good security message should look like. A good security log should be *descriptive*, it should be *relatable* to other data, and it should be *complete*.

A descriptive message is one that contains enough information for an analyst to identify all necessary accessible resources for the event described by the message. For example, if a host log records that a user attempted to illegally access a file, it should contain the user's ID and the file accessed. A host log recording a change in group permissions for a user needs to record the user and the group. A log recording a failed remote login attempt should include the ID that attempted the login and the address that attempted the login.

For example, consider a log message about a failed login attempt on host 192.168.2.2, local name *myhost*. A nondescriptive message would look like this:

```
Mar 29 11:22:45.221 myhost sshd[213]: Failed login attempt
```

This message doesn't tell me anything about why the failure occurred and doesn't provide any information to differentiate between this and any other failed login attempts. I have no information on the target of the attack; is it against the *admin* account or some user? Analysts with only this information will have to reconstruct the attempt solely from timing data, and they can't even be sure what host was contacted because the name of the host is nondescriptive and there is no addressing information.

A more descriptive message would look like this:

```
Mar 29 11:22:45.221 myhost (192.168.2.2) sshd[213]: Failed
    login attempt from host 192.168.3.1 as 'admin',
    incorrect password
```

A good mental exercise for building a descriptive message is to fall back to the "five Ws and one H" approach from investigation and journalism: who, what, when, where, why, and how. The nondescriptive log message provides the what (failed login) and when, and a partial answer to where (*myhost*). The descriptive log message provides the who (192.168.3.1 as *admin*), why, and how (incorrect password), and a better where.

A relatable message is one where the event is easily related to information from other sources. For host-based events this requires IP address and timing information, including whether an event was remote or physically local, the IP address and port of the event if it was remote, and the IP address and port of the host. Relatability is a particular headache when dealing with service logs, as these types of logs often introduce additional addressing schemes on top of IP. For example, here's an unrelatable mail log message:

```
Mar 29 11:22:45.221 myhost (192.168.2.2) myspamapp[213]:
    Message <21394.283845@spam.com> title 'Herbal Remedies and Tiny Cars'
    from 'spammer@spam.com' rejected due to unsolicited commercial content
```

The message has a lot of information, but there's no way to relate the message sent back to the particular IP address that sent the message. When looking at log messages, consider how you will relate this information to other sources, *particularly* network traffic. A more relatable message would be as follows:

```
Mar 29 11:22:45.221 myhost (192.168.2.2) myspamapp[213]:
    Message <21394.283845@spam.com> title 'Herbal Remedies and Tiny Cars'
    from 'spammer@spam.com' at SMTP host 192.168.3.1:2034 rejected due
    to unsolicited commercial content
```

This example includes client port and addressing information, so we can now relate it to network traffic.

A complete log message is one that contains all the information about a particular event within that single log message. Completeness reduces the number of records an analyst has to search through and provides the analyst with a clear indicator that there is no further information to acquire from this process. Incomplete messages are usually a function of complicated process. For example, an antispam tool might run several different filters on a message, with each filter and the final decision being a separate log line:

```
Mar 29 11:22:45.221 myhost (192.168.2.2) myspamapp[213]:
    Received Message <21394.283845@spam.com> title
    'Herbal Remedies and Tiny Cars' from 'spammer@spam.com' at
    SMTP host 192.168.3.1:2034
Mar 29 11:22:45.321 myhost (192.168.2.2) myspamapp[213]:
    Message <21394.283845@spam.com> passed reputation filter
Mar 29 11:22:45.421 myhost (192.168.2.2) myspamapp[213]:
    Message <21394.283845@spam.com> FAILED Bayesian filter
Mar 29 11:22:45.521 myhost (192.168.2.2) myspamapp[213]:
    Message <21394.283845@spam.com> Dropped
```

With incomplete messages, you have to track state across multiple messages, each of which gives a snippet of information and which you're going to have to group together to do any useful analysis. Consequently, I prefer the message to be aggregated at the start, like this:

```
Mar 29 11:22:45.521 myhost (192.168.2.2) myspamapp[213]:
    Received Message <21394.283845@spam.com> title
    'Herbal Remedies and Tiny Cars' from 'spammer@spam.com' at
    SMTP host 192.168.3.1:2034 reputation=pass Bayesian=FAIL decision=DROP
```

Log messages are often only minimally modifiable directly. Instead, to build an effective message you might have to write some kind of logging shim. For example, if the log system outputs syslog messages, you can receive and parse those messages, convert them to a friendlier format, and then forward them on. When considering converting logfiles, in addition to the rules just mentioned, consider the following:

Convert time to epoch time
    Almost all record correlation involves identifying the same phenomenon from different sensors, meaning that you need to look for records that are close in time. Converting all time values to epoch time reduces parsing complexity,

throws out the nightmare of time zones and daylight saving time, and ensures a consistent treatment for a consistent value.

Make sure sensors are synchronized
A corollary to the first note, make sure that when sensors report the same event, they are reporting the same time. Trying to correct for this after the fact is terribly difficult, so make sure that all the sensors are coordinated, that they all report the same time, and that the clocks are corrected and resynchronized regularly.

Include addressing information
Wherever possible, include the flow five-tuple (source IP, destination IP, source port, destination port, protocol). If some of the values can be inferred from the record (e.g., HTTP servers are running TCP), they can be dropped.

Ensure that delimiters are understood by the logger
On several occasions, I have encountered helpful administrators reconfiguring HTTP logs to use pipes rather than spaces as delimiters. A worthy sentiment, except when the logging module doesn't know to escape the pipe when it occurs in text. If the logger can change its delimiter and understands that the change requires escaping the character, let the logger do it.

Use error codes rather than text if possible
Text doesn't scale well—it's bulky, difficult to parse, and often repetitive. Logging systems that generate template messages can also include an error code of some kind as a compact representation of the message. Use this rather than text to save space.

Existing Logfiles and How to Manipulate Them

We can break logfiles into three major categories: *columnar*, *templated*, or *stateful*. Columnar logs record records in discrete columns that are distinguishable by delimiters or fixed text width. Templated logfiles look like English text, but the text comes from a set of document templates and is enumerable. Stateful logfiles use multiple text records to describe a single event.

Columnar data, such as NCSA HTTPd's CLF format, records one message per event. This message is a summary of the entire event, and consists of a fixed set of fields in columnar format. Columnar logs are relatively easy to deal with as the fields are cleanly delineated and the format is rigid; every message has the same columns and the same information.

When dealing with columnar data, keep in mind the following:

- Is the data delimited or fixed-width? If it's fixed-width, are there fields that could conceivably exceed that width, and if so, are the results truncated or is the column expanded?

- If the data is delimited, is the delimiter escaped when used in the fields? Customizable formats (such as HTTP logs) may use a default delimiter and automatically escape it; if you decide to use your own delimiter, it probably won't be automatically escaped.

- Is there a maximum record length? If there is a maximum record length, you may encounter truncated messages with missing fields.

ELF and CLF logfiles, discussed in the next chapter, are good examples of columnar formats.

Templated text messages record one message per event, but the events are recorded as unformatted English text. The messages are *templated* in the sense that they come from a fixed and enumerable set of templates. Where possible, it's best to convert templated text messages into some kind of indexed numeric format. In the best case, this is at least partly done. For example, the Windows event log shown in Figure 4-2 has an event ID that describes the type of event and can be used to determine the other arguments that will be provided.

When dealing with templated text, keep in mind the following:

- Can you get a complete list of the log messages? As an example, consider the Windows logfile in Figure 4-2. Each of these messages is text, but it has a unique integer ID for the message. Check the documentation for a list of all potential log messages.

Converting Text to Columns

Templated text can be parsed; the messages belong to an enumerable set and can conceivably be converted into a columnar format. Creating such a system, however, requires developing an intermediary application that can read the text, parse each individual message, and deposit the result in a schema. Doing so is a nontrivial development task (and will have to be updated when new messages are developed), but it also can reduce the amount of space required and increase the readability of the data. Here are specific steps to take when creating a system to convert templated text into columns:

1. From whatever documentation you can find on the text format, identify and select the messages most relevant to security. Any conversion script is going to consist of a bunch of regular expressions, and the fewer expressions you have to maintain, the happier you'll be.

2. For each message, identify the parameters it contains. As an example, consider the following made-up templated messages: "Antispam tool SPAMKILLER identifies email <*12938@yahoo.com*> as Spam," "Antispam tool SPAMKILLER identi-

---

fies email *<12938@yahoo.com>* as Commercial," "Antispam tool SPAMKILLER identifies email *<12938@yahoo.com>* as Legitimate." There are three potential parameters here: the name of the antispam tool (enumerable), the message ID (a string), and the output (enumerable).

3. Once you've identified parameters for each potential message, merge the parameters to create a superset. The goal is to create a schema representation of all the parameters that a message may potentially have; a particular message may not have all of them.

4. Try to generate at least one event record for every templated message the application can generate, and then compare that to the output from the documentation. Documentation is often inaccurate, and you may be assuming a templated output that doesn't actually appear. This type of work is best done by setting up a small lab to actually generate each event.

5. Check absurdly long string lengths, delimiters, and control characters. Templates will often truncate output strings without clearly specifying them, and may also escape special characters. Since you will be laying multiple layers of parsers on top of each other, you need to be sure of what happens with those corner cases.

6. Fail conservatively when generating columnar data. You may not be able to realistically convert more than 9 out of every 10 messages; if that's the case, drop the unparsed messages into a separate error feed for the analysts to check as needed.

Stateful Logfiles

In a stateful logfile, a single transaction is split across multiple messages.[1] Stateful logfiles are extremely frustrating for operational analysis—you spend time and cycles reconstructing the event that happened.

Again, some kind of shim is the usual solution here. In general, a shim for a stateful logfile will be some kind of cache holding partially formed records. As it receives signals that a new transaction is happening, it pushes a new record into the cache. When it receives a signal that the transaction completed, or it times out (a critical step), it removes the relevant records from the cache. In between, it will fill each record with the appropriate messages, and by doing so converts the logfiles into a stateless format. In practice, building these shims requires managing a number of different failure modes based around when the message terminates.

This is the kind of work where, to generate a quality logfile, you're going to have to run the system through its paces and see whether there are hidden errors. To help

---

1 In the previous edition of the book, I referred to stateful logfiles as annotative. I've switched in order to focus on the major source of trouble in dealing with these files: state.

prep for these errors, consider stateful logs in three categories: stateful with delimiters, stateful with identifiers, and interleaved.

If a logfile is *stateful with identifiers*, then the messages have individual ID numbers that link together the transaction. The following truncated IronPort example is a good example of a stateful message with IDs:

```
Thu Mar 24 16:58:31 2016 Info: Start MID 452 ICID 98
Thu Mar 24 16:58:31 2016 Info: MID 452 ICID 98 From: <alerts@fakecompany.org>
Thu Mar 24 16:58:31 2016 Info: MID 452 ICID 98 RID 0 To: \
    <elvis.presley@graceland.int>
Thu Mar 24 16:58:31 2016 Info: MID 452 Subject 'Sent to elvis presley to test \
    regexps in filtering'
Thu Mar 24 16:58:31 2016 Info: MID 452 ready 665 bytes from \
    <alerts@fakecompany.org>
Thu Mar 24 16:58:31 2016 Info: MID 452 matched all recipients for per-recipient \
    policy DEFAULT in the inbound table
Thu Mar 24 16:58:31 2016 Info: Delivery start DCID 151 MID 452 to RID [0]
Thu Mar 24 16:58:31 2016 Info: Message done DCID 151 MID 452 to RID [0] \
    [('x-customheader', '192.168.1.1')]
Thu Mar 24 16:58:31 2016 Info: MID 452 RID [0] Response 'Ok'
Thu Mar 24 16:58:31 2016 Info: Message finished MID 452 done
Thu Mar 24 16:58:33 2016 Info: Start MID 453 ICID 98
```

When working with these types of logs, check for the following pitfalls:

- Determine the format of the identifiers, and how they are assigned. If identifiers are assigned linearly, (e.g., ID 1, ID 2, ID 3), be prepared for gaps in ID numbers and have contingencies ready, such as a secondary alert.

- Determine messages for creating and destroying the identifiers. Expect to have a timeout or other mechanism for dealing with messages that don't close.

- When creating a shim, fill in all the fields you will report on with a default *unreported* value, then update those fields as you encounter their values in the logfile. This way you can ship the record even if you don't have all the fields, and it will be clear which fields were omitted.

A logfile is *stateful with delimiters* if it uses some kind of discrete begin/end messages to indicate the beginning and ending of a transaction, and the entire transaction is contained within those begin and end messages. Example 4-2 shows a representative format; as this example shows, each individual event is prefaced with a timestamp, and then there are a variable number of fields. Also of note is that there is no *explicit* delimiter for ending the message—the `Request-Authenticator` field may be a delimiter, but given the differences in the fields shown in both entries, it can't be verified.

Example 4-2. An example of a delimited log: GNU RADIUS packets[2]

```
Fri Dec 15 18:00:24 2000
        Acct-Session-Id = "2193976896017"
        User-Name = "e2"
        Acct-Status-Type = Start
        Acct-Authentic = RADIUS
        Service-Type = Framed-User
        Framed-Protocol = PPP
        Framed-IP-Address = 11.10.10.125
        Calling-Station-Id = "+15678023561"
        NAS-IP-Address = 11.10.10.11
        NAS-Port-Id = 8
        Acct-Delay-Time = 0
        Timestamp = 976896024
        Request-Authenticator = Unverified

Fri Dec 15 18:32:09 2000
        Acct-Session-Id = "2193976896017"
        User-Name = "e2"
        Acct-Status-Type = Stop
        Acct-Authentic = RADIUS
        Acct-Output-Octets = 5382
        Acct-Input-Octets = 7761
        Service-Type = Framed-User
        Framed-Protocol = PPP
        Framed-IP-Address = 11.10.10.125
        Acct-Session-Time = 1905
        NAS-IP-Address = 11.10.10.11
        NAS-Port-Id = 8
        Acct-Delay-Time = 0
        Timestamp = 976897929
        Request-Authenticator = Unverified
```

When working with log data, expect to run into common problems, in particular with how log messages are delimited. From experience, I recommend checking the following:

- Verify that logs have both start and end delimiters. It's not uncommon for these log formats to explicitly start a log message, and then never end it.

- Verify that a single transaction happens between delimiters. If at all possible, test this empirically by running a long transaction and, while that is running, running a simultaneous short transaction. If messages overlap, you have an interleaved log.

---

2 From *https://www.gnu.org/software/radius/manual/html_mono/radius.html#SEC182*

- Determine the format of starting and ending messages, and be prepared to deal with incomplete messages.

The most problematic cases are *stateful interleaved* logfiles; these are logfiles where events take multiple lines, and multiple events happen simultaneously. In an interleaved logfile, you will see messages from event A, messages from event B, and then more messages from event A.

Stateful interleaved logfiles have serious internal validity problems and should, when encountered, be considered a secondary source of data—acceptable for debugging, terrible for forensics. Your best solution when encountering this type of message is to keep it in the original format, since you can't trust that you're seeing events in sequence

Further Reading

1. The OSSEC Log Samples page (*http://bit.ly/ossec-log-samp*).

2. A. Chuvakin and K. Schmidt, *Logging and Log Management: The Authoritative Guide to Dealing with Syslog, Audit Logs, Alerts, and other IT "Noise"* (Rockland, MA: Syngress Publishing, 2012).

3. J. Turnbull, *The Art of Monitoring*, available at *http://www.artofmonitoring.com*.

## CHAPTER 5

Sensors in the Service Domain

This chapter discusses specific sensors in the service domain. Service sensors, including HTTP server logs and mail transfer logs, describe the activity of a particular service: who sent mail to whom, what URLs were accessed in the last five minutes, activity that's moderated through a particular service.

As we saw in the previous chapter, service domain data is *log data*. Where available, logs are often preferable to other sources because they are generated by the affected process, removing the interpretation and guesswork often needed with network data. Service logs provide concrete information about events that, viewed from the network perspective, are hard to reconstruct.

Logs have a number of problems, the most important one being a management headache—in order to use a log, you have to know it exists and get access to it. In addition, host-based logs come in a large number of formats, many of them poorly documented. At the risk of a sweeping generalization, the overwhelming majority of logs are designed for debugging and troubleshooting individual hosts, not for evaluating security across networks. Where possible, you'll often need to reconfigure them to include more security-relevant information, possibly needing to write your own aggregation programs. Finally, logs are a target; attackers will modify or disable logging if possible.

Logs complement network data. Network data is good at finding blind spots, confirming phenomena reported in logs and identifying things that the logs won't pick up. An effective security system combines both: network data for a broad scope, service logs for fine detail.

The remainder of this chapter is focused on data from a number of host logs, including system logfiles. We begin by discussing several varieties of log data and preferable message formats. We then discuss specific host and service logs HTTP server log formats, email log formats, and Unix system logs.

Representative Logfile Formats

This section discusses common logfile formats, including ELF and CLF, the standard log formats for HTML messages. The formats discussed here are customizable, and I will provide guidelines for improving the log messages in order to provide more security-relevant information.

HTTP: CLF and ELF

HTTP is the modern internet's reason for existence, and since its development in 1991, it has metamorphosed from a simple library protocol into the internet's glue. Applications where formerly a developer would have implemented a new service are now routinely offloaded to HTTP and REST APIs.

HTTP is a challenging service to nail down. The core is incredibly simple, but any modern web browsing session involves combining HTTP, HTML, and JavaScript to create ad hoc clients of immense complexity. In this section, we briefly discuss the core components of HTTP with a focus on the analytical aspects.

HTTP is fundamentally a very simple file access service. To understand how simple it is today, try the exercise in Example 5-1 using `netcat`. `netcat` (which can also be invoked as `nc`, perhaps because administrators found it so useful that they wanted to make it easy to invoke) is a flexible network port access tool that can be used to directly send information to ports. It is an ideal tool for quickly bashing together clients with minimal scripting.

Example 5-1. Accessing an HTTP server using the command line

```
host$ echo 'GET /' | nc www.google.com 80 > google.html
```

Executing the command in this example should produce a valid HTML file. In its simplest, most unadorned form, an HTTP session consists of opening up a connection, passing a method and a URI, and receiving a file in return.

HTTP is simple enough to be run at the command line by hand if need be—however, that also means that an enormous amount of functionality is handed over to optional headers. When dealing with HTTP logs, the primary challenge is deciding which headers to include and which to ignore. If you try the very simple command in Example 5-1 on other servers, you'll find it tends to hang—without additional information such as the `Host` or `User-Agent`, the server will wait.

There are two standards for HTTP log data: Common Log Format (CLF) and Extended Log Format (ELF). Most HTTP log generators (such as Apache's mod_log) provide extensive configuration options.

CLF is a single-line logging format developed by the National Center for Supercomputing Applications (NCSA) for the original HTTP server; the W3C provides a minimal definition of the standard (*http://bit.ly/CLF-format*). A CLF event is defined as a seven-value single-line record in the following format:

```
remotehost rfc931 authuser [date] "request" status bytes
```

Where *remotehost* is the IP name or address of the remote host, *rfc931* is the remote login account name of the user, *authuser* is the user's authenticated name, *date* is the date and time of the request, *request* is the request, *status* is the HTTP status code, and *bytes* is the number of bytes.

Pure CLF has several eccentricities that can make parsing problematic. The *rfc931* and *authuser* fields are effectively artifacts; in the vast majority of CLF records, these fields will be set to -. The actual format of the date value is unspecified and can vary between different HTTP server implementations.

A common modification of CLF is *Combined Log Format*. The Combined Log Format adds two additional fields to CLF: the HTTP Referer field and the User-Agent string.

ELF is an expandable columnar format that has largely been confined to Microsoft's Internet Information Server (IIS), although tools such as Bluecoat also use it for logging. As with CLF, the W3C maintains the standard on its website (*http://bit.ly/log-file-format*).

An ELF file consists of a sequence of *directives* followed by a sequence of *entries*. Directives are used to define attributes common to the entries, such as the date of all entries (the `Date` directive), and the fields in the entry (the `Fields` directive). Each entry in ELF is a single HTTP request, and the fields that are defined by the directive are included in that entry.

ELF fields come in one of three forms: *identifier, prefix-identifier*, or *prefix(header)*. The prefix is a one- or two-character string that defines the direction the information took (`c` for client, `s` for server, `r` for remote). The identifier describes the contents of the field, and the *prefix(header)* value includes the corresponding HTTP header. For example, `cs-method` is in the *prefix-identifier* format and describes the method sent from client to server, while `time` is a plain *identifier* denoting the time at which the session ended.

Example 5-2 shows simple outputs from CLF, Combined Log Format, and ELF. Each event is a single line.

Example 5-2. Examples of CLF and ELF

```
#CLF
192.168.1.1 - - [2012/Oct/11 12:03:45 -0700] "GET /index.html" 200
1294

# Combined Log Format
192.168.1.1 - - [2012/Oct/11 12:03:45 -0700] "GET /index.html" 200 1294
"http://www.example.com/link.html" "Mozilla/4.08 [en] (Win98; I ;Nav)"

#ELF
#Version: 1.0
#Date: 2012/Oct/11 00:00:00
#Fields: time c-ip cs-method cs-uri
12:03:45 192.168.1.1 GET /index.html
```

Most HTTP logs are some form of CLF output. Although ELF is an expandable format, I find the need to carry the header around problematic in that I don't expect to change formats that much, and would rather that individual log records be interpretable without this information. Based on principles I discussed earlier, here is how I modify CLF records:

1. Remove the *rfc931* and *authuser* fields. These fields are artifacts and waste space.

2. Convert the date to epoch time and represent it as a numeric string. In addition to my general disdain for text over numeric representations, time representations have never been standardized in HTTP logfiles. You're better off moving to a numeric format to ignore the whims of the server.

3. Incorporate the server IP address, the source port, and the destination port. I expect to move the logfiles to a central location for analysis, so I need the server address to differentiate them. This gets me closer to a five-tuple that I can correlate with other data.

4. Add the duration of the event, again to help with timing correlation.

5. Add the host header. In case I'm dealing with virtual hosts, this also helps me identify systems that contact the server *without* using DNS as a moderator.

Creating Logfiles

Log configuration in Apache is handled via the mod_log_config module, which provides the ability to express logs using a sequence of string macros. For example, to express the default CLF format, you specify it as:

```
LogFormat "%h %l %u %t \"%r\" %>s %b"
```

Combined Log Format is expressed as:

```
LogFormat "%h %l %u %t \"%r\" %>s %b \"%{Referer}i\" \"%{User-Agent}i\""
```

This extended format contains the hostname, local IP address, server port, epoch time, request string, request status, response size, response time, Referer, User-Agent string, and host from the request:

```
LogFormat "%h %A %p %{msec}t \"%r\" %>s %b %T \"%{Referer}i\"
  \"${User-Agent}i\" \"${Host}i\""
```

Logging in nginx is controlled with HttpLogModule, which uses a similar log_format directive. To configure CLF, specify it with:

```
log_format clf $remote_addr - $remote_user [$time_local] "$request"
  $status $body_bytes_sent;
```

Combined Log Format is defined as follows:

```
log_format combined $remote_addr - $remote_user [$time_local] "$request"
  $status $body_bytes_sent "$http_referer" "$http_user_agent";
```

My extended format is defined as:

```
log_format extended $server_addr $remote_addr $remote_port $msec
  "$request$" $status $body_bytes_sent $request_time $http_referer
  $http_user_agent $http_host
```

Simple Mail Transfer Protocol (SMTP)

SMTP log messages vary by the mail transfer agent (MTA) used and are highly configurable. In this section, we discuss two log formats that are representative of the major Unix and Windows families: sendmail and Microsoft Exchange.

We focus on logging the transfer of email messages. The logging tools for these applications provide an enormous amount of information about the server's internal status, connection attempts, and other data that, while enormously valuable, requires a book of its own.

Sendmail

Sendmail moderates mail exchange through syslog, and consequently is capable of sending an enormous number of informational messages besides the actual email transaction. For our purposes, we are concerned with two classes of log messages: messages describing connections to and from the mail server, and messages describing actual mail delivery.

By default, sendmail will send messages to */var/maillog*, although the logging information it sends is controlled by sendmail's internal logging level. The logging level ranges from 1 to 96; a log level of *n* logs all messages of severity 1 to *n*. Notable log levels include 9 (all message deliveries logged), 10 (inbound connections logged), 12 (outbound connections logged), and 14 (connection refusals logged). Of note is that anything above log level 8 is considered an informational log in *syslog*, and anything above 11 a debug log message.

A sendmail log line consists of five fixed values, followed by a list of one or more *equates*:

```
<date> <host> sendmail[<pid>]: <qid>: <equates>
```

where *<date>* is the date, *<host>* is the name of the host, sendmail is a literal string, *<pid>* is the sendmail process ID, and *<qid>* is an internal queue ID used to uniquely identify messages. Sendmail sends at least two log messages when sending an email message, and the only way to group those messages together is through the *qid*. Equates are descriptive parameters given in the form *<key>=<value>*. Sendmail can send a number of potential equates, listed in Table 5-1 for messages.

Table 5-1. Relevant sendmail equates

Equate	Description
arg1	Current sendmail implementations enable internal filtering using rulesets; arg1 is the argument passed to the ruleset.
from	The from address of the envelope.
msgid	The message ID of the email.

Equate	Description
`quarantine`	If sendmail quarantines a mail, this is the reason it was held.
`reject`	If sendmail rejects a mail, this is the reason for rejection.
`relay`	This is the name and address of the host that sent the message; in recipient lines, it's the host that sent it, and in sender lines, the host that received it.
`ruleset`	This is the ruleset that processed the message, and provides the justification for rejecting, quarantining, or sending the message.
`stat`	The status of a message's delivery.
`to`	The email address of a target; multiple `to` equates can appear in the same line.

For every email message received, sendmail generates at least two log lines. The first line is the *receipt* line, and describes the message's point of origin. The final line, the *sender* line, describes the disposition of the mail, such as whether it was sent, quarantined, rejected, or bounced.

Sendmail will take one of four basic actions with a message: reject it, quarantine it, bounce it, or send it. Rejection is implemented by message filtering and is used for spam filtering; a rejected message is dropped. Quarantined messages are moved off the queue to a separate area for further review. A bounce means the mail was not sent to the target, and results in a nondelivery report being sent back to the origin.

Managing Email Rules and Filtering

Email traffic analysis is complicated, largely because email is attacked constantly (via spam), and there's a constantly escalating war between spammers and defenders. Even in a relatively small enterprise, it's easy to build a complex defensive infrastructure with relatively little work. In addition to the spam and defensive issues, email operates in its own little world—the IP addresses logged by email infrastructure are pretty much exclusively used by the email infrastructure.

As usual, the first step in email instrumentation is figuring out how email is routed. Is there some kind of dedicated antispam hardware at the gateway, such as a Barracuda or an IronPort box? How many SMTP servers are there, and how do they connect to the actual email servers (POP, IMAP, Exchange)? Figure out where a mail message will be sent if it's correctly routed, quarantined, rejected, or bounced. If webmail is available, figure out where it actually is; where is the webmail server, what's the route to SMTP, etc.

Once you've identified the hardware, figure out what blocking is going on. Blocking techniques include black-box sources (such as AV or IronPort's reputation service), public blacklists such as SpamHaus's SBL, and internal rules. Each requires a little different treatment.

Since black-box detection systems are basically opaque, it's important to track what version of the system's knowledge base is being used and when the system is updated;

verifying updates with network monitoring is a good idea. If you have multiple instances of the same detector, make sure that their updates are coordinated.

Most blacklist services are publicly accessible. Knowing which organization runs the blacklist, the frequency of its updates, and the delivery mechanisms are all good things. As with AV, verifying communications (particularly if its a DNS block list) is also a good thing.

Internal monitoring should be identified, audited, and kept under version control. Because these are the rules that you have the most control over, it's also a good idea to compare them to the rest of your blocking infrastructure and see what can be pushed out of the email system. If you're blocking a particular address, for example, you might be better off blocking at the router or the firewall.

Email works within its own universe, and the overwhelming majority of IP addresses recorded in email logs are the addresses of other email servers. To that end, while SMTP tracking is important, it's often the case that to fully figure out what happened with a message, you also need to track the IMAP or POP3 servers.

Microsoft Exchange: Message Tracking Logs

Exchange has one master log format for handling messages, the Message Tracking Log (MTL). Table 5-2 describes the fields.

Table 5-2. MTL fields

Field name	Description
date-time	The ISO 8601 representation of the date and time.
client-ip	The IP address of the host that submitted the message to the server.
client-hostname	The client_ip's fully qualified domain name (FQDN).
server-ip	The IP address of the server.
server-hostname	The server_ip's FQDN.
source-context	Optional information about the source, such as an identifier for the transport agent.
connector-id	The name of the connector.
source	Exchange enumerates a number of source identities for defining the origin of a message, such as an inbox rule, a transport agent, or DNS. The source field will contain this identity.
event-id	The event type. This is also an enumerable quantity, and includes a number of status messages about how the message was handled.
internal-message-id	An internal integer identifier used by Exchange to differentiate messages. The ID is not shared between Exchange servers, so if a message is passed around, this value will change.
message-id	The standard SMTP message ID. Exchange will create one if the message does not already have one.

Field name	Description
network-message-id	This is a message ID like internal-message-id except that it is shared across copies of the message and created when a message is cloned or duplicated, such as when it's sent to a distribution list.
recipient-address	The addresses of the recipients; this is a semicolon-delimited list of names.
recipient-status	A *per-recipient* status code indicating how each recipient was handled.
total-bytes	The total size of the message in bytes.
recipient-count	The size of recipient-address in terms of number of recipients.
related-recipient-address	Certain Exchange events (such as redirection) will result in additional recipients being added to the list; those addresses are added here.
reference	This is message-specific information; the contents are a function of the type of message (defined in event-id).
message-subject	The subject found in the Subject: header.
sender-address	The sender, as specified in the Sender: header; if Sender: is absent, From: is used instead.
return-path	The return email address, as specified in Mail From:.
message-info	Event type–dependent message information.
directionality	The direction of the message; an enumerable quantity.
tenant-id	No longer used.
original-client-ip	The IP address of the client.
original-server-ip	The IP address of the server.
custom-data	Additional data dependent on the type of event.

Additional Useful Logfiles

A number of additional useful services may or may not be present on your network, and as part of mapping and situational awareness, you should identify them and determine what logging is possible. In this section, I provide a small list of the services I consider most critical to keep track of.

These are largely enterprise services, and any discussion on the proper generation and configuration of logs will be a function of the application's configuration. In addition, for several of these services, you may need to reconfigure them to log the data you need. Many of these services will provide logging through syslog or the Windows Event Manager.

Staged Logging

Turning on all the logging mentioned here is going to drown analysts in a lot of data, which is primarily going to be used for rare, high-risk events. Consequently, when developing a logging plan, you should consider policies and processes for increasing or decreasing targeted logging as needed.

The process of staging up or staging down logging will be a function of events or a criticality. In the former case, you may increase logging because a particular event or trigger has raised concerns—for example, if a new exploit is in the wild, you may stage up logging for services vulnerable to that exploit. In the latter case, you may always keep high-information logging for critical services—monitoring fileshares for your IP, for example.

LDAP and Directory Services

If you have any form of active directory or other user management (Microsoft Active Directory, OpenLDAP), this information should be available. Directory services will generally consist of a database of users, events that update the database itself (addition, removal, or updates of users), as well as login and logoff events.

Consider collecting a complete, periodic dump of the directory and keeping it somewhere where the ops and analysis teams can get their hands on it quickly, such as storing it in Redis. You can expect that analysts will regularly access this data for context.

Logon and logoff data should be sent as a low-priority stream directly to your main console. It is useful for annotating where users are in the system at any time, and will often be cross-referenced with other actions.

File Transfer, Storage, and Databases

Besides HTTP, file transfer and file storage includes services such as SharePoint, NFS Mounts, FTP, anything using SMB, any code repositories (Git, GitHub, GitLab, SourceSafe, CVS, SVN), as well as web-based services such as Confluence. In the case of these services, you are most interested in monitoring users and times—who accessed the system, when they accessed the system, and how much they accessed.

Volumes are a good, if coarse, indicator of file transfer. A good companion metric is to check for locality anomalies (see Chapter 14). Fileshares inside of an enterprise are accessed by people who have a job—the majority of them are going to visit the same files over and repeatedly, working with a limited subset.[1]

Databases, including SQL servers such as Oracle, Postgres, and MySQL and NoSQL systems such as HDFS, should be tracked for data loss prevention and bulk transfer, just as with the file transfer systems. In addition, if possible, log the queries and check for anomalous query strings. In an enterprise environment, you should expect to see users rarely interacting with the console; rather, they should be using predictable sequences of SQL statements run through a form. Distance metrics (see Chapter 12

---

[1] Keep track of systems that do file transfers, and internal search engines. Both will be false positives.

for more information) can be used to match these strings to look for anomalous queries such as a SELECT *.

Logfile Transport: Transfers, Syslog, and Message Queues

Host logs can be transferred off their hosts in a number of ways, depending on how the logs are generated and on the capabilities of the operating system. The most common approaches involve using regular file transfers or the syslog protocol. A newer approach uses *message queues* to transport log information.

Transfer and Logfile Rotation

Most logging applications write to a rotating logfile (see, for example, the rotated system logs in "Accessing and Manipulating Logfiles" on page 65). In these cases, the logfile will be closed and archived after a fixed period and a new file will be started. Once the file is closed, it can be copied over to a different location to support analytics.

File transfer is simple. It can be implemented using SSH or any other copying protocol. The major headache is ensuring that the files are actually complete when copied; the rotation period for the file effectively dictates your response time. For example, if a file is rotated every 24 hours, then you will, on average, have to wait a day to get hold of the latest events.

Syslog

The grandfather of systematic system logging utilities is *syslog*, a standard approach to logging originally developed for Unix systems that now comprises a standard, a protocol, and a general framework for discussing logging messages. Syslog defines a fixed message format and enables messages to be sent to logger daemons that might reside on the host or be remotely located.

All syslog messages contain a time, a *facility*, a *severity*, and a text message. Tables 5-3 and 5-4 describe the facilities and priorities encoded in the syslog protocol. As Table 5-3 shows, the facilities referred to by syslog comprise a variety of fundamental systems (some of them largely obsolete). Of more concern is what facilities are *not* covered DNS and HTTP, for example. The priorities (in Table 5-4) are generally more germane, as the vocabulary for their severity has entered into common parlance.

Table 5-3. Syslog facilities

Value	Meaning
0	Kernel
1	User level
2	Mail
3	System daemons
4	Security/authorization
5	`syslogd`
6	Line printer
7	Network news
8	UUCP
9	Clock daemon
10	Security/authorization
11	`ftpd`
12	`ntpd`
13	Log audit
14	Log alert
15	Clock daemon
16–23	Reserved for local use

Table 5-4. Syslog priorities

Value	Meaning
0	Emergency: system is unusable
1	Alert: action must be taken immediately
2	Critical: critical conditions
3	Error: error conditions
4	Warning: warning conditions
5	Notice: normal but significant condition
6	Informational: informational messages
7	Debug: debugging information

Syslog's reference implementations are UDP-based, and the UDP standard results in several constraints. Most importantly, UDP datagram length is constrained by the MTU of the layer 2 protocol carrying the datagram, effectively imposing a hard limit of about 1,450 characters on any syslog message. The syslog protocol itself specifies that messages should be less than 1,024 characters, but this is erratically enforced, while the UDP cutoff *will* affect long messages. In addition, syslog runs on top of UDP, which means that when messages are dropped, they are lost forever.

The easiest way to solve this problem is to use TCP-based syslog, which is implemented in the open source domain with tools such as `syslog-ng` (*https://syslog-ng.org/*) and `rsyslog` (*http://www.rsyslog.com*). Both of these tools provide TCP transport, as well as a number of other capabilities such as database interfaces, the ability to rewrite messages en route, and selective transport of syslog messages to different receivers. Windows does not support syslog natively, but there exist a number of commercial applications that provide similar functionality.

CEF: Common Event Format

Syslog is a transport protocol—it doesn't specify anything about the actual contents of a message. A number of different organizations have attempted to develop interoperability standards for security applications, such as the Common Intrusion Detection Framework (CIDF) and Intrusion Detection Message Exchange Format (IDMEF). None of them have achieved serious industry acceptance.

What *has* been accepted widely is CEF. Originally developed by ArcSight (now part of Hewlett-Packard) to provide sensor developers with a standard format in which to send messages to their console, CEF is a record format that specifies events using a numeric header and a set of key/value pairs. For example, a CEF message for an attack from host 192.168.1.1 might look like this:

```
CEF:0|My Attack Detector|Test|1.0|1000|Attack|5|src=192.168.1.1
```

CEF is transport-agnostic, but the majority of CEF implementations use syslog as their transport of choice. The actual specification and key/value assignments are available from HP.

As of the new edition of this book, threat intelligence formats such as Structured Threat Information eXchange (STIX) have gained traction. See Chapter 17 for more information.

Further Reading

1. M. O'Leary, *Cyber Operations: Building, Defending, and Attacking Modern Computer Networks* (New York: Apress, 2015).

## CHAPTER 6

Data and Sensors in the Host Domain

This chapter is concerned with the practical problem of collecting data from a host. The *host domain* refers to any information that can be collected on the host without the moderation of a service; this includes information about the processes running on the host, the host's filesystem, its configuration, and to some extent information that overlaps the network and service domains.

Given the complexity of hosts, and the varieties of operating systems and configurations available, it is not possible to address all the information that can be collected from hosts in a single book, let alone a chapter. Rather, the network analyst needs a focused approach to determine what information is required to supplement the network data. For our purposes, this focused approach is comprised of four questions:

1. What hardware is behind this IP address?
2. How is it messing up my network?
3. Who owns this hardware?
4. Who do I yell at about it?

This chapter is predicated around figuring out how to answer those questions. Unfortunately, this requires navigating a maze of complicated and proprietary configuration data. Compared to service and network domain data, host domain data is all over the place. Windows and Unix systems have radically different ideas of where to keep this information, and even individual Unix variants can keep the same information in very different locations.

Note that host collection is intimately tied up with host configuration and inventory. The wider the variety of hosts you manage, the larger the number of different configurations that exist, the more legacy systems you have, the harder the problem of data collection will be. Automated provisioning and management, especially if you're navigating over to a cloud-based infrastructure, will save you an enormous amount of pain and effort. Host data collection is a last-mile problem in network security.

In order to address this problem, I have broken hosts into a collection of relevant data buckets. Figure 6-1 shows how these buckets are interrelated, and how we will link them together to answer questions. The remainder of this structure is broken into the major data domains discussed previously.

A Host: From the Network's View

Figure 6-1 shows a representation of the data I consider useful when talking about a host. Throughout this chapter, I will refer to elements of this abstraction as *buckets of useful data*—the information that I feel is most useful for security analysis that can be extracted from this abstraction. In the following chapter, I will discuss a portfolio of utilities that can extract this information from a host.

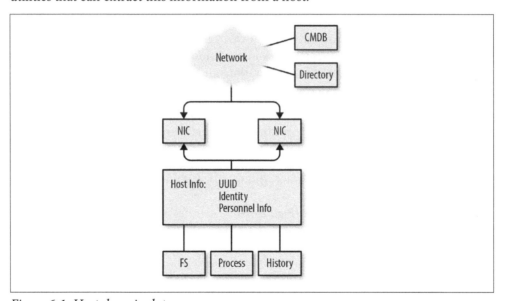

Figure 6-1. Host domain data

As Figure 6-1 shows, the host, in abstract, is composed of several discrete elements:

Network interfaces
> The host communicates with the network through one or more network interfaces. Modern hosts will have multiple interfaces, making them effectively mini-routers: laptops have WiFi and wired interfaces, mobile devices will have cellular radios and WiFi available.

Host

For our purposes, the host information refers to any unique identifiers you have for the host. This includes tags such as UUIDs, inventory management, users who actively touch the host, etc.—any information that will help you identify who is responsible for the host and what the host has done over time.

Filesystem

The files that make up the host. This is a list of all the files and their locations in the filesystem, as well as potential indicators of tampering such as access times, ownership, and hashes of file contents.

Process

The processes that are running on the host. This includes the host processes' IDs, their parent process IDs running back to the startup process, the ownership of the processes, and the processes' current state.

History

The history of a host is a log of all the commands that have been executed by a host: the start time of every process, the end time, the command-line parameters, and every command at the shell prompt.

The breakdown in Figure 6-1 is intended to model how a network analyst will generally progress through a host. As network security people, we generally begin with a network-based trigger—traffic. From the traffic, we attempt to get an identifier such as the IP address. From the IP address, we can associate the IP/port combination (hopefully) with a distinct process. From the process, we can figure out what is running on the port, which tells us where to look on disk and who is responsible. This information should all be available, on Unix systems, through common command-line tools.

The Network Interfaces

Hosts communicate with a network through one or more *network interfaces* (NIs). From the network's vantage, an NI is a distinct set of addresses it forwards packets to —the physical device is invisible to the network. From a host's vantage, the NI is a stream to which the host reads and writes information—the network addresses are an attribute of that stream.

Note that an NI does *not* have to be a device, and it may only exist as a process. Loopback addresses should not connect to the network, and most virtual machines will create a virtual interface to communicate with their host.

There are two core tools for checking network processes on a host: `ifconfig` and `netstat`. `ifconfig` provides information on the interfaces, `netstat` on the currently used ports; there is a fair amount of functional overlap between the two.

ifconfig, as the name implies, is actually a tool for *configuring* network interfaces. ifconfig is old but omnipresent; most modern Unixes provide their own configuration and setup tools, including ip for Linux variants and networksetup on macOS. The advantage of ifconfig is that it's available on almost all Unix variants and will provide you with an inventory of network interfaces and their status. Note that on modern systems you can expect to have *many* more interfaces than you have devices. Some of these are there for basic networking support (e.g., the loopback interface), while others are set up for specialized services (virtual machines have virtual interfaces, VPNs will have their own). The standard output from ifconfig is a block of network interface controller information, an example of which is shown here:

```
en1: flags=8863 UP,BROADCAST,SMART,RUNNING,SIMPLEX,MULTICAST mtu 1500
    ether fe:1c:29:33:f0:00
    inet6 fe80::407:d8a1:7085:f803 en1 prefixlen 64 secured scopeid 0x5
    inet 192.168.1.13 netmask 0xffffff00 broadcast 192.168.1.255
    nd6 options=201 PERFORMNUD,DAD
    media: autoselect
    status: active
```

In this example, the first field is the interface's *name*. Each unique active network interface on the system will have a unique name. Device names in Unix systems are heavily encoded with different information about the interface type. Table 6-1 provides a list of common interface names across different Unix flavors. Unfortunately, there is no real registry or central source for device names—it's a matter of convention, and the same type of device can have radically different names even in different versions of the same operating system.

Table 6-1. Useful device names

Name	Description
en, eth	Generic Ethernet interface names
p2p	New Ethernet names on Linux systems
wlan, iw	Wireless interfaces
lo	Loopback interface
tun, utun	VPN interfaces

ifconfig output will differ somewhat based on the version of the OS you're using. The preceding example is fairly standard for BSD variants (such as the macOS terminal I cribbed it from). You can expect to see variations that show packets transmitted and received, and different address fields.

So, this brings up the other fields. Most of the information that ifconfig dumps is addressing data—how the particular interface connects to a network. This is where you can find the NIC addresses (which you should be able to see from network vantage). In our example, you can see that the interface has three addresses: a 48-bit MAC address (ether), an IPv6 address (inet6), and an IPv4 addresses (inet). The additional fields are for neighbor discovery (part of IPv6), and a description of the interface's media (the type of device) and the current status (whether or not it's active).

Over time, ifconfig output tends to get messier—in a Unix system, interfaces are often added, rarely deleted. Consequently, when you look at a long-standing system, you're likely to see multiple legacy interfaces. Also, keep in mind that ifconfig is an interface on top of the actual configuration system used by your Unix variant.

Whereas ifconfig is about what the interfaces *are*, netstat is what about what the interfaces *are doing*. The best way to start with netstat is with a per-interface dump, such as netstat -i:

```
$ netstat -i
Name  Mtu    Network     Address             Ipkts  Ierrs   Opkts  Oerrs  Coll
lo0   16384  <Link#1>                        166486     0   166486     0    0
lo0   16384  127         localhost           166486     -   166486     -    -
lo0   16384  localhost   ::1                 166486     -   166486     -    -
lo0   16384  localhost   fe80:1::1           166486     -   166486     -    -
en0   1500   <Link#4>    10:dd:b1:ab:cc:fb        0     0        0     0    0
```

As with ifconfig, outputs will be operating system–specific, but the basic breakdown here illustrates what kind of information nestat will generally dump.

As this example shows, there's some overlap with the information from ifconfig—each interface is listed by its separate addresses, and the device name is present. In addition, this netstat implementation shows traffic to the various interfaces—in this case incoming and outgoing packets, as well as errors.

To find the status of individual sockets, use netstat -a. This yields output like the following:

```
$ netstat -a
Proto Recv-Q Send-Q  Local Address        Foreign Address        (state)
tcp4       0      0  192.168.1.13.62856   iad30s08-in-f14..https  ESTABLISHED
tcp4       0      0  192.168.1.13.62676   50.57.31.206.http       FIN_WAIT_2
tcp4       0      0  192.168.1.13.62461   cdn-208-111-161-.https  FIN_WAIT_2
tcp4       0      0  192.168.1.13.62381   75.98.58.181.https      FIN_WAIT_2
```

The output from this -a dump is a list of active sockets; -a should dump *all* active sockets, as opposed to just the ones associated with the current user. The fields are the protocol (Proto) queue sizes (bytes in the send and receive queues), the addresses, and the state. Note that the foreign addresses are actually FQDNs—netstat versions will automatically look up domain names and port numbers. This behavior is, in my experience, largely useless—the process takes time, and the port/service assignments are usually less useful than the straight port numbers. Look for an option to avoid looking up names (usually -n) and use that instead.

Note the (state) column. For TCP sockets, this column will correspond to the state of the TCP state machine (see Figure 13-3 for further information). Of note for us are sockets in the LISTEN state, which are waiting for connections from the outside world. netstat output will wildcard IP addresses in the output for servers, indicating that the socket will accept incoming connections from anywhere:

```
$netstat -an | grep LISTEN
tcp4       0        0    *.8000           *.*          LISTEN
tcp6       0        0    *.53             *.*          LISTEN
tcp4       0        0    *.53             *.*          LISTEN
tcp4       0        0    *.445            *.*          LISTEN
tcp6       0        0    *.445            *.*          LISTEN
tcp4       0        0    127.0.0.1.8021   *.*          LISTEN
```

The *.8000 here means that the TCP socket on port 8000 will accept connections from any working interface pointing to the host—in this case that includes 127.0.0.1 (localhost) and 192.168.1.13 (the address for the host). Conversely, the 127.0.0.1.8021 listener will *only* accept connections through the localhost interface.

Note that UDP is stateless—if there is an open UDP port on your system, it will be listed in the netstat output, but it won't have a value in the LISTEN column. A UDP listener, however, should list . in the Foreign Address column.

Once you have a port, the next question is what process is running it and who owns the process. Depending on your version of netstat, there may be a -o or -p command that will provide this information. Alternatively (as in macOS), you can find this information using lsof -i; lsof is a command that lists open files, and interfaces in Unix's "everything is a file" philosophy, are files. lsof -i lists open interfaces, providing information like in this dump:

```
$ lsof -i | grep 8000
python2.7 51121 mcollins 3u IPv4 0x7c0d6f5bfcc7ff3b 0t0 TCP *:8000 (LISTEN)
```

The Host: Tracking Identity

The host itself refers to the process that ties network interfaces to disks, files, memory, and users. For the network analyst, the host is a handle all the other data hangs on. Practically speaking, what we really need when we refer to a "host" is a mechanism to distinguish hosts from *each other*. Since any serious enterprise network runs on top of an ocean of virtual images, old handles for identity such as MAC IDs have basically become useless. Instead, I think it's preferable to grasp the nettle and deal straight with universally unique identifiers (UUIDs).

A UUID[1] is a 128-bit integer intended to serve as a distinct and unique identifier for the host. UUIDs are an old idea, and there are consequently a number of different techniques for generating them. The intent of the UUID is to remain unique throughout the lifetime of a host, regardless of changes in the name, the IP address, or any other shift. Implementation of this uniqueness is a mechanical task, and different manufacturers address the problem differently.

RFC 4122 (*https://tools.ietf.org/html/rfc4122*) specifies five different UUID versions:

- Version 1 combines the 48-bit MAC address, the time of creation (60 bits), and a 14-bit click sequence value. This version will generate similar UUIDs on the same host, and encodes the MAC address. Encoding the MAC address is, in my opinion, of limited value with multi-interface hosts.

- Version 2 is intended to provide a more secure version of the Version 1 UUID, but in practice isn't implemented. Most UUID generators will skip this version.

- Versions 3 and 5 generate a UUID by hashing a namespace (examples include DNS, URLs, OID, and X.500) and a name. The intent is that the UUID should be consistent for hosts with the same name. Version 3 uses a truncated MD5, Version 5 uses a truncated SHA1.

- Version 4 generates the UUID randomly.

The 128-bit UUID has structure, and you will often see UUIDs (particularly Microsoft and Apple ones) provided in an XXXXXXXX-XXXX-AXXX-BXXX-XXXXXXXXXXXX format, where each X is a hexadecimal digit. This format follows the structure of the original Version 1 UUID, although the separators are meaningless outside of Version 1—with one notable exception. UUIDs encode their version in the digits specified as A and B in this format. A is the UUID version, and the high three bits of B are the variant of that version. B should always be 8 or higher.

For Linux installations, the UUID is usually found in */etc/machine_id/*; BSD may use */etc/hostid*, but you should check the installation. UUIDs are generated on installation; an important caveat when working with virtual images is that duplicates of the same image will have the same UUID. macOS provides a hardware-generated UUID. You can find it in the Hardware Overview panel of the System Information app, or at the command line by invoking the system_profiler command; it's in the SPHardwareDataType field.

All of this is convention, and prone to operating system, platform, and designer fiat. For analysis, the point of the UUID is to provide you with a universal handle—a way of connecting other inventory information while things that might change (software

---

1 GUID in Microsoftian.

configuration, domain name, versions) shift around you. However, unless the UUID is tied to other data sources, the UUID serves no purpose.

Which brings us to the other problem. What you really need is a way to tie all of this information into an inventory. What you really want is a way to go from network observable (e.g., IP address) to UUID to software profile. This type of information is generally best handled by a configuration management database (CMDB); even if all you have is a spreadsheet containing UUIDs, operating systems, and IP addresses, it will save you a lot of pain later on.

Processes

A host's process information refers to the processes that are running on the host at sample time. As with most information in the host domain, process information is most useful for ascertaining damage done by changes to system state. If new processes appear, or standard processes (such as AV) stop running, that's an indication of anomalous behavior. If a system is under DDoS attack, then processes will react to that.

Structure

On Unix and Windows systems (considering macOS to be a Unix variant), processes are organized in a tree descending from a root processes. Every process posseses a unique process ID (PID), a numeric ID identifying the process during the time of execution. PIDs are assigned sequentially, beginning with an ID of 0 (for the system idle process in Windows) or 1 (for most Unixes). Every process except the root process has a parent process ID (PPID), which is the PID of the process that spawned it. By using the PID/PPID relationships, you can plot out processes as a tree and trace each back to its origin at the root process.

On Unix systems, the basic application for checking process status is ps. ps is a command-line utility that prints a list of current processes controlled by the invoking user's UID at the time of invocation. This is, on any system, the smallest and least interesting set of processes to look at.[2]

An example ps dump for a macOS system is shown here (formatted to fit the page):

```
$ ps -faxcel | head -10
  UID   PID  PPID  C STIME    TTY            TIME CMD
    0     1     0  0 16Feb17  ??         46:46.47 launchd
    0    51     1  0 16Feb17  ??          1:01.35 syslogd
    0    52     1  0 16Feb17  ??          2:18.75 UserEventAgent
    0    54     1  0 16Feb17  ??          0:56.90 uninstalld
```

---

2 Unless you control an attacker's account, in which case, good for you!

```
    0   55   1   0 16Feb17 ??        0:08.61 kextd
    0   56   1   0 16Feb17 ??        2:04.08 fseventsd
   55   61   1   0 16Feb17 ??        0:03.61 appleeventsd
    0   62   1   0 16Feb17 ??        0:07.72 configd
    0   63   1   0 16Feb17 ??        0:17.60 powerd

        F PRI NI       SZ     RSS WCHAN       S         ADDR              0
     4004  37  0  2537628   13372 -          Ss
     4004   4  0  2517212    1232 -          Ss             0              0
     4004  37  0  2547704   40188 -          Ss             0
     4004  20  0  2506256    5256 -          Ss             0
     4004  37  0  2546132   13244 -          Ss             0
  1004004  50  0  2520544    6244 -          Ss             0
     4004   4  0  2542188   11320 -          Ss             0
     400c  37  0  2545392   13288 -          Ss             0
     4004  37  0  2540644    8016 -          Ss
```

Table 6-2 summarizes the type of information that I generally find useful when monitoring processes.

Table 6-2. Useful process fields

Name	Type	ps options	Notes
PID	Integer		The process ID for a process
PPID	Integer	-f	The parent process ID of a process; i.e., the PID of the process that spawned it
UID	Integer	-f	The ID of the user who spawned the process
Command	String		The name of the process
Path	String	-E	The path of the process's executable
Memory	Integer(s)	-l	The memory used by the application
CPU	Numeric	-O cpu	The amount of CPU consumed
Terminal	String	-f	The ID of the terminal the process is attached to
Start Time	Date	-f	The time the process was invoked

Because the default ps invocation is so limited, you will invariably invoke it with a number of switches. The major switches are listed in Table 6-2, but be wary that ps options are platform-specific. For that reason, I'll talk about the provided options in more depth, and the corresponding fields.

PID and PPID

The PID is the most basic identifier available for a process. Operating systems organize processes into a tree, with a root process spawning children, those children spawning children, and so on. Process IDs are assigned linearly, in increasing order, but will loop if you reach whatever the maximum PID is for the operating system.

Consequently, it's possible but rare that you'll see a process with a PID lower than its parent process ID (PPID).

During bootup, systems spawn an enormous number of processes for I/O, disk management, and other housekeeping tasks. As a result of this, you can expect any system to run a number of long-lived processes in the lower ranks.

For the network security analyst, particular attention should be paid to network-facing processes (such as servers) and their spawn patterns. If a long-lived server process recently respawned, why did this happen? What are the children of network-facing processes? What processes are spawning command-line interfaces, shells, or other administrative tools?

UID

A process's UID is the numeric ID assigned to the user owning the process. Classically, Unix systems maintain this information in */etc/passwd*, and depending on configuration issues, it may still be possible to find that information there. However, odds are that's not going to be less valuable on any modern system. If you're running a system using LDAP for management, you can find the UID using ldapsearch; for macOS, it's currently managed by id.

For the network security analyst, UID questions often involve going back to identifying the history of a particular user. Is this user expected to administer the process? (I prefer to see daemons run by dedicated, chrooted daemon accounts, not individual users.) Is the user new?

Command and path

The command and the path refer to the command-line options used to invoke the process, and the path to the process's executable. This information is particularly critical for checking the links between a process, the filesystem, and the users.

For the network security analyst, command and path questions often involve checking to see if any unusual or unexpected commands have been called. Unusual commands may include evidence of an anomalous location for the command—if a command that is normally located in */usr/bin* has been executed from a local directory, for example. It may also include evidence of a command that the user does not normally execute based on past command history. Particular attention should be paid to administrative and network commands—anything that can access a socket or reconfigure a host.

Memory, CPU, terminal, and start time

Memory and CPU refer to the amount of memory and CPU resources consumed by a process, respectively. Keeping track of this information can help an analyst identify whether the process is going berserk (e.g., due to trying to process a DDoS attack). The terminal information refers to what terminal a process is connected to, and the start time is when the process started.

Alternatives to ps and Alternative Systems

ps is the go-to utility because it's command-line, bounded, and omnipresent—even if the individual system variants can be frustrating. Windows PowerShell even includes a ps command. However, there are a couple of other utilities of note.

top is the other major process sampling tool for Unix systems. top is a display rather than a sample—it provides a continuously updated sample that the operator can interact with. That said, top isn't really a sampling tool—it's supposed to be attached to a terminal and monitored continuously.

pstree is a handy Unix utility that displays the output of ps as a tree structure, explicitly visualizing the implicit relationship between PID and PPID.

On Windows systems, the go-to command for listing processes is tasklist.

For actually *managing* systems, however, you should be familiar with process monitoring tools such as nagios.

Filesystem

File information refers to the files on disk, and includes the following information:

- Path—the path to the file (i.e., the directory containing the file)
- Filename—the name of the file
- Creation time
- Modification time
- Size
- Hash—an MD5 hash of the file's contents
- UID—the ID of the owner of the file
- Permissions—the permissions on the file

Filesystem monitoring is usually about change notification, in particular whether protected system files have changed for no discernible reason (e.g., outside of system updates or, in some cases, ever).

Fallback for file comparisons: check the creation time, check the modification time, check the file size, check the permissions, check a hash. Hashing, in particular, is critical for working with threat intelligence, and given the diversity of indicators of compromise (IOC) information out there, you should expect to have a bunch of hashes on hand.

A *hash* is a mathematical function that converts data of arbitrary size into a fixed-length representation. This fixed-length representation is ideally *much* smaller—the ones we'll talk about here are intended to reduce files from megabytes down to dozens of bytes.

There's an extensive taxonomy of hashes with different attributes, so the *cryptographic hashes* we're interested in here are just a subcategory with specific properties. In particular, these hashes show an "avalanche effect": a small change in the data hashed results in a large change in the hash value. The point of using a secure hash, for filesystems, is to make tampering difficult—an attacker trying to alter a file without changing the hash will have to spend a *lot* of effort to do so undetectably.

The basic hash algorithms to know of are MD5, SHA-1, and SHA-256. On most systems you'll have command-line tools available to invoke them. Almost all IOCs are going to use one of these three, and you can always call them straight from Python (with `hashlib`, specifically). Of the three, MD5 is the shortest and SHA-256 the longest, and MD5 is the least and SHA-256 the most secure.

When Is a Hash More Secure?

Conventional wisdom is that MD5 is an insecure hash compared to, say, SHA-256; conventional wisdom is correct, but it's helpful to understand *why* this is an issue. Hashes are mathematical functions applied to a large input to produce a shorter, fixed-length output. Secure hashes are a class of hashes (there are many classes) with a specific goal: to make the likelihood of a collision (two inputs yielding the same output) low. The lower limit for "low" is a function of the hash's length. For example, in MD5, the attacker should have to explore on the order of 2^{128} values to find a collision.

Given two hash functions, the more secure one is the one that requires the attacker to search through a larger space. So, if the hash function provides a smaller space, it's less secure than one with a larger space, all other factors being equal. In the case of MD5, it's not the case that all factors are equal—collision attacks that effectively reduce the size of the MD5 space have been known since 2005.[3] If you want some practical examples of this, look at the *HashClash* project (*https://marc-stevens.nl/p/hashclash/*).

---

3 W. Xiaoyun and Y. Hongbo, "How to Break MD5 and Other Hash Functions," *Proceedings of the 2005 EURO-CRYPT Conference*, Aarhus, Denmark, 2005.

The practical impact of this is as follows: if you use an MD5 hash, it's feasible for someone with modern resources to generate a collision for the hashed file in a couple of seconds. If collision security is a priority, then you don't use MD5 and you don't trust MD5s. If what you're looking for is a quick-and-dirty way to compare two files, MD5 is tolerable, but the performance benefit you get from using an MD5 is less justifiable.

This is a race against time. New attacks are found against hashing algorithms all the time—as I am writing this entry, feasible collisions for SHA-1 have now entered the mainstream as well.[4]

Historical Data: Commands and Logins

When tracking lateral movement, you will often cross-reference network activity with user activity—specifically, actions like when a particular user connected to a particular service, when users logged on to the same system multiple times, or when users logged on to multiple services. This requires keeping track of the history of a server.

We're really talking about two separate pieces of information here: user logins and command history.

On Unix systems, the basic information on user logins and logouts is maintained in three files: *utmp*, *wtmp*, and *btmp*. *utmp* maintains current system status—uptime, logged-in users, and the like. *wtmp* is a historical record, and *btmp* is a list of failed logins. The standard interface to this file is the `lastlog` command, which when invoked will read the contents of the file and dump a chronological list of logons.

As for command history, that's basically maintained only in the individual user directories. This is maintained in a *_history* file specific to the user's shell (e.g., *bash_history*, *tcsh_history*).

Directory Services and You

The way I'm talking about hosts in this chapter is very much focused on the idea of data on the host; however, a reasonably well-managed modern network should be using directory services for user management. If you are concerned about issues involving user logins or multiple logins, check what your directory services say. Also, and this is important to check out, see if an account is registered on the host that isn't present in the directory services.

---

4 See *http://tcrn.ch/2mbEOdR*

Other Data and Sensors: HIPS and AV

Host-based data collection can be simplified through the use of various endpoint collection tools and host-based agents. The granddaddy of these systems is the antivirus (AV) systems, and the odds are good you're running one of those right now.

A caveat as we discuss what these systems are: the end state of almost all security companies is as a threat intelligence provider (more on this in Chapter 17). While there are some open source tools in this domain (notably ClamAV), most tools for data loss prevention, host intrusion prevention, and the like are proprietary. What you are *really* buying is a subscription to a threat intelligence feed, moderated through the tool.

Host intrusion prevention system (HIPS) is the general term for any system that monitors local host behavior and takes remedial action in the case of compromise or policy violation. A HIPS is effectively a boosted form of AV system, the workhorse of host-based defense. For the analyst, a HIPS is a new event feed focused on the endpoint—the HIPS will provide events based on a combination of signatures and heuristics, which it then feeds back into the console.

When considering HIPSs, keep track of the following issues:

- How deep into an endpoint can the HIPS go? With a HIPS, you're looking for something that will provide you with deeper information than you can quickly cobble together with a script. Does the HIPS hook into OS calls? Does it monitor memory, or is it just monitoring the filesystem?

- When considering that, note that these systems will have their own vulnerabilities and modify fundamental capabilities of your system. Disabling and manipulating AV has been a fundamental malware task for a very long time.

- How are updates delivered? In particular, will you have to deal with uneven updates (e.g., where half your system gets signature updates on Monday and half on Tuesday, so all of a sudden you get a spike in alerts on Monday afternoon)?

- How configurable is the HIPS? In particular, can you write custom signatures, and can you turn off irrelevant signatures?

- What constraints can you impose on the system? Is the HIPS going to come down on every violation like a meat-axe, or can you stage up or down detection?

- How does the HIPS differentiate assets? Is it going to provide its own ID? Can you map it to UUIDs? Does the HIPS require you to individually identify each asset?

- How much coverage will the HIPS provide? If you run a network consisting of heterogeneous assets (some Macs, some PCs, the occasional BeBox...), you need to keep track of which systems are running the HIPS and which systems aren't supported.

Further Reading

1. For host-based analysis, the most fundamental resources are good books on system administration for the individual operating systems. These include the Apple Pro training series (published by PeachPit), Microsoft's training manuals (from Microsoft Press), and the Windows Internals series (by Pearson).

2. S. Garfinkel, G. Spafford, and A. Schwartz, *Practical UNIX and Internet Security*, 3rd ed. (Sebastopol, CA: O'Reilly Media, 2011).

## CHAPTER 7

Data and Sensors in the Active Domain

In this chapter, we will discuss the *active domain*. Active domain data refers to data that the analyst specifically initiates the generation and collection of. Active data will involve the use of probing tools (e.g., ping, traceroute) and scanners (e.g., nmap). It is polled and triggered; as opposed to the continuous collection of the network and service domains, active analysis is done as a specific event or in response to specific anomalies.

Active work is client-focused, informative, and expensive. The analyst takes on the perspective of a client of an application (or, alternatively, an attacker) and is able to gather a lot of information about what a host does, although not necessarily much about what the host is for. But this fine-grained information doesn't come cheaply; intensive scanning is expensive, it interferes with the target, and it can take an enormous amount of resources to process all the data received.

Chapters related to this one include Chapter 2, on the basics of network traffic, Chapter 13, which discusses the observation of fumbling, and Chapter 17, which is about the use of threat intelligence data.

Discovery, Assessment, and Maintenance

The foundation of operational information security is inventory management. The less you know about the assets you're protecting—both what they *are* and what they're *for*—the more any security plan is filled with guesswork. Some amount of guesswork is inevitable; networks change minute by minute as wireless devices appear and disappear, users reconfigure hosts, and the workday progresses. However, a well-executed network monitoring strategy will manage this guesswork and point out how to reduce it.

It's in that context that we consider the interaction of active domain information and the information we've discussed elsewhere in this book. Active domain data is too expensive to collect universally and constantly, and the issues of vantage affect active data collection profoundly. Effective network monitoring will use network data to guide active collection. I'll be referring throughout this chapter to three key actions: *discovery*, *assessment*, and *maintenance*.

In the context of this book, *discovery* refers to identifying the existence of assets within a network. Discovery can range from knowing that a particular IP address is active, to a complete inventory of the asset. *Assessment*, after discovery, applies security knowledge to that information to determine risks and courses of action. Assessment depends heavily on expertise, and with many commercial assessment products you're paying primarily for that expertise. *Maintenance* is the ongoing process of checking an asset to ensure that it hasn't changed. In the conclusion of this chapter, I will discuss how to combine active and passive monitoring to conduct an inventory.

Discovery: ping, traceroute, netcat, and Half of nmap

Discovery is the process of discovering and inventorying assets on your network. Discovery is progressive, and I can break it into two broad steps: determining something is there, and then determining what that something is.

The first step begins with a list of IP addresses, and involves determining which addresses within your network are *dark* (routable, but no host) and which addresses are *lit*. The basic tools for doing so are ping, traceroute, and nc. Once you've determined something is there, you have to figure out what that something is—this generally involves working with nmap and a collection of service clients built with nc and other tools to figure out what services are visible on the host.

Checking Connectivity: Using ping to Connect to an Address

Given an IP address, the most basic command-line tool for determining something is present is ping. ping works by using ICMP (see "Packet and Frame Formats" on page 36) messages. ping sends an ICMP echo request (type 8, code 0) to the target. On receiving an echo request message, the target should respond with an echo reply (type 0, code 0). Example 7-1 shows sample output of ping and a pcap of the contents.

Example 7-1. ping output

```
$ ping -c 1 nytimes.com
PING nytimes.com (170.149.168.130): 56 data bytes
64 bytes from 170.149.168.130: icmp_seq=0 ttl=252 time=29.388 ms
```

```
$ tcpdump -Xnr ping.pcap
reading from file ping.pcap, link-type EN10MB (Ethernet)
20:38:09.074960 IP 192.168.1.12 > 170.149.168.130:
        ICMP echo request, id 44854, seq 0, length 64
    0x0000:  4500 0054 0942 0000 4001 5c9b c0a8 010c  E..T.B..@.\.....
    0x0010:  aa95 a882 0800 0fb8 af36 0000 5175 d7f1  .........6..Qu..
    0x0020:  0001 24a6 0809 0a0b 0c0d 0e0f 1011 1213  ..$.............
    0x0030:  1415 1617 1819 1a1b 1c1d 1e1f 2021 2223  .............!"#
    0x0040:  2425 2627 2829 2a2b 2c2d 2e2f 3031 3233  $%&'()*+,-./0123
    0x0050:  3435 3637                                4567
20:38:09.104250 IP 170.149.168.130 > 192.168.1.12:
        ICMP echo reply, id 44854, seq 0, length 64
    0x0000:  4500 0054 0942 0000 fc01 a09a aa95 a882  E..T.B..........
    0x0010:  c0a8 010c 0000 17b8 af36 0000 5175 d7f1  .........6..Qu..
    0x0020:  0001 24a6 0809 0a0b 0c0d 0e0f 1011 1213  ..$.............
    0x0030:  1415 1617 1819 1a1b 1c1d 1e1f 2021 2223  .............!"#
    0x0040:  2425 2627 2829 2a2b 2c2d 2e2f 3031 3233  $%&'()*+,-./0123
    0x0050:  3435 3637                                4567
```

Note first the size of the packet and the `ttl` value. These values are usually set by default by the TCP stack. In the case of macOS, the ICMP packet has a 56-byte payload, which results in an 84-byte packet (20 bytes of IP header, 8 bytes of ICMP header, and 56 bytes of payload). The type and code are at 0x0014–0x0015 (08 for the request, 00 for the response). After the ICMP header, note that the contents of the packet are echoed. ICMP has a concept of a session, and in many cases, messages are sent in response to packets from entirely different protocols. Different ICMP messages use different techniques to indicate their point of origin; in the case of `ping`, this is done by echoing the packet's original contents.

`ping` is a simple application: it sends an echo request with an embedded sequence identifier. The application then waits until a specified timeout (usually on the order of 4,000 ms); if the response is received in that time, the response is printed and the next packet is sent. `ping` is a diagnostic tool, and any serious implementation will provide a number of command-line switches for manipulating packet composition.

Sweeping Pings and Ping Sweeping

These are actually different terms, although Google gets confused when you enter a search for them. A *ping sweep* (or *ping sweeping*) is a scanning technique that systematically pings all the IP addresses assigned to a network to determine which ones are present and which ones are not. Ping sweeping is supported by `nmap` and a number of other scanning tools, although you can write a script to do it in about 20 seconds.

A *sweeping ping*, in contrast, is a sequence of ping messages that undergo size increases with each packet. Sweeping pings are intended to diagnose channels by identifying traffic manipulation or MTU issues. Sweeping pings are enabled by a command-line option on most modern `ping` implementations.

It's not uncommon to find networks blocking ICMP messages. Ping sweeping is consequently a middling tool for finding hosts on a network; direct TCP or UDP scanning will generally be more effective.

Tracerouting

traceroute is a tool and technique to identify the routers that forward packets from point A to point B. traceroute produces a sequential list of routers by manipulating packet TTLs.

The TTL (time-to-live) field of an IP packet is a mechanism developed to prevent packets from bouncing through the internet forever. Every time a packet is forwarded by a router, its TTL value decreases by one. When the TTL reaches zero, the forwarding router drops the packet and sends an ICMP time exceeded (type 11) message to the source IP address of the dropped packet.

Here is an example of a traceroute command in action:

```
$ traceroute www.nytimes.com
traceroute to www.nytimes.com (170.149.168.130), 64 hops max, 52 byte packets
 1  wireless_broadband_router (192.168.1.1)  1.189 ms  0.544 ms  0.802 ms
 2  l100.washdc-vfttp-47.verizon-gni.net (96.255.98.1)  2.157 ms  1.401 ms
    1.451 ms
 3  g0-13-2-7.washdc-lcr-22.verizon-gni.net (130.81.59.154)  3.768 ms  3.751 ms
    3.985 ms
 4  ae5-0.res-bb-rtr1.verizon-gni.net (130.81.209.222)  2.029 ms  2.314 ms
    2.314 ms
 5  0.xe-3-1-1.br1.iad8.alter.net (152.63.37.141)  2.731 ms  2.759 ms  2.781 ms
 6  xe-2-1-0.er2.iad10.us.above.net (64.125.13.173)  3.313 ms  3.706 ms  3.970 ms
 7  xe-4-1-0.cr2.dca2.us.above.net (64.125.29.214)  3.741 ms  3.668 ms
    xe-3-0-0.cr2.dca2.us.above.net (64.125.26.241)  4.638 ms
 8  xe-1-0-0.cr1.dca2.us.above.net (64.125.28.249)  3.677 ms
    xe-7-2-0.cr1.dca2.us.above.net (64.125.26.41)  3.744 ms
    xe-1-0-0.cr1.dca2.us.above.net (64.125.28.249)  4.496 ms
 9  xe-3-2-0.cr1.lga5.us.above.net (64.125.26.102)  24.637 ms
    xe-2-2-0.cr1.lga5.us.above.net (64.125.26.98)  10.293 ms  9.679 ms
10  xe-2-2-0.mpr1.ewr1.us.above.net (64.125.27.133)  20.660 ms  10.043 ms
    10.004 ms
11  xe-0-0-0.mpr1.ewr4.us.above.net (64.125.25.246)  15.881 ms  16.848 ms
    16.070 ms
12  64.125.173.70.t01646-03.above.net (64.125.173.70)  30.177 ms  29.339 ms
    31.793 ms
```

As the next code block shows, traceroute sends an initial 52-byte message, and then proceeds to receive sequential information about each address it contacts en route to 170.149.168.130. Let's look at the payload in more depth:

```
$ tcpdump -nXr traceroute.pcap | more
21:06:51.202439 IP 192.168.1.12.46950 > 170.149.168.130.33435: UDP, length 24
```

```
0x0000:  4500 0034 b767 0000 0111 ed85 c0a8 010c   E..4.g..........
0x0010:  aa95 a882 b766 829b 0020 b0df 0000 0000   .....f..........
0x0020:  0000 0000 0000 0000 0000 0000 0000 0000   ................
0x0030:  0000 0000                                 ....
21:06:51.203481 IP 192.168.1.1 > 192.168.1.12: ICMP time exceeded in-transit,
    length 60
0x0000:  45c0 0050 a201 0000 4001 548e c0a8 0101   E..P....@.T.....
0x0010:  c0a8 010c 0b00 09fe 0000 0000 4500 0034   ............E..4
0x0020:  b767 0000 0111 ed85 c0a8 010c aa95 a882   .g..............
0x0030:  b766 829b 0020 b0df 0000 0000 0000 0000   .f..............
0x0040:  0000 0000 0000 0000 0000 0000 0000 0000   ................
21:06:51.203691 IP 192.168.1.12.46950 > 170.149.168.130.33436: UDP, length 24
0x0000:  4500 0034 b768 0000 0111 ed84 c0a8 010c   E..4.h..........
0x0010:  aa95 a882 b766 829c 0020 b0de 0000 0000   .....f..........
0x0020:  0000 0000 0000 0000 0000 0000 0000 0000   ................
0x0030:  0000 0000                                 ....
21:06:51.204191 IP 192.168.1.1 > 192.168.1.12: ICMP time exceeded in-transit,
    length 60
0x0000:  45c0 0050 a202 0000 4001 548d c0a8 0101   E..P....@.T.....
0x0010:  c0a8 010c 0b00 09fe 0000 0000 4500 0034   ............E..4
0x0020:  b768 0000 0111 ed84 c0a8 010c aa95 a882   .h..............
0x0030:  b766 829c 0020 b0de 0000 0000 0000 0000   .f..............
0x0040:  0000 0000 0000 0000 0000 0000 0000 0000   ................
```

Note that traceroute sends out UDP messages, starting at port 33435 and incrementing the port number by one with each additional message. The port number is incremented so that it's possible later to reconstruct the order in which the packets are sent. Note that the ICMP packet from offset 0x001C onward contains the original UDP packet. As noted earlier, ICMP messages need to use a number of different techniques to provide context—error messages such as "TTL exceeded" include the IP header and the first 8 bytes of the original packet. This includes the UDP source port number. traceroute uses the included UDP source port to reconstruct the order in which these ICMP messages were sent.

While traceroute uses UDP by default, the same technique can be used by TCP or any other protocol where there is a controllable value (such as an ephemeral port number) in the first 8 bytes of the IP payload.

ping and traceroute are more useful if you can use them from different locations. To that end, a number of internet service providers and other organizations provide *looking-glass servers*. A looking-glass server is a publicly accessible (generally via the web) interface to any of a number of common internet applications. Most looking glasses are managed by NOCs or ISPs, and provide access to multiple routers. There is no standard for implementation, and different looking glasses will provide different services. A comprehensive list is available at *www.traceroute.org*.

Using nc as a Swiss Army Multitool

`ping` and `traceroute` represent traffic on the network proper; if you want to communicate with a specific service, you have to have a service client available to you. Alternatively, you can use `netcat`. In Chapter 5, I touched briefly on this tool: let's talk about what it can do in more depth.

Basic `netcat` invocation is simply `netcat` (or `nc`) with the destination address and port. If this connects to an open port, then `netcat` will operate like the `cat` command. If you know what the targeted service operates like, you can then send a request and get a response. For example, you can run an HTTP request by hand:

```
$ echo "GET /" | nc www.google.com 80 | head -4
HTTP/1.0 200 OK
Date: Mon, 20 Feb 2017 16:51:48 GMT
Expires: -1
Cache-Control: private, max-age=0
```

You can quickly implement a fast horizontal scan by using `netcat`'s *zero I/O* mode (`-z`). Zero I/O simply tries to open a port and, if it succeeds, immediately closes the session. On its own, this results in `netcat` providing zero information, so you need to up the output using `netcat`'s verbose option (`-v`):

```
$ netcat -vz localhost 8000
localhost [127.0.0.1] 8000 (irdmi) open
$ netcat -vz localhost 122
localhost [127.0.0.1] 122 (smakynet): Connection refused
```

A Brief Scanning Digression

Scanning is covered in more detail in Chapter 13, but the basic vocabulary should be mentioned here. Imagine that the space of IP addresses and ports in your network is arranged on a grid, with IP addresses on the horizontal axis, and ports on the vertical axis. A *horizontal* scan touches each address once and moves on (on the horizontal axis); a *vertical* scan touches all the ports on an address (on the vertical axis).

As a rule of thumb, scanners scan horizontally, defenders vertically. Scanners scan horizontally because they have a limited number of exploits to use and are focused on those. Defenders scan vertically because they don't know which exploits the attacker will use.

In the absence of other tools, `netcat` *can* be used to scan horizontally or vertically. The short and sour way to do this is just to iterate at the command line, possibly using the `-w` option to slow down consecutive invocations. For example, if I want to scan a local /24, I can do:

```
i=0; while [ ${i} -le 256 ];
do
    netcat -vz -w 2 192.168.1.${i} 8000
    i=$[ ${i} + 1 ]
done
```

Which results in:

```
192.168.1.1 8000 (irdmi): Connection refused
192.168.1.2 8000 (irdmi) open
192.168.1.3 8000 (irdmi): Operation timed out
```

and so on. Note the refusals and timeouts—a refusal means a host was present and the port was closed, while a timeout means that no successful communication took place (which is usually a good indicator that there is nothing on the other side). You can swap in a vertical scan by changing the IP address to the port number. netcat will take ranges:

```
$ netcat -vz 192.168.1.13 7990-8080
192.168.1.13 7990-8080 192.168.1.13 8000 (irdmi) open
```

Note that netcat will only provide output for open ports.

nmap Scanning for Discovery

nc is versatile, but not specialized. nmap integrates both discovery and assessment roles into an open source package.

Let's start our nmap exercises by doing some simple horizontal scanning for discovery (we'll get to assessment in the next section). These nmap commands are equivalent to the scans we did by hand with nc. Let's start with a horizontal scan on a /24; this is done using -p to specify a port, and then an address range. nmap can take CIDR notation (as seen here) as well as using a dash, so I could express this as 192.168.1.0-255:[1]

```
# Scanning a /24 with nmap; some addresses removed for brevity
$ nmap -p 8000 192.168.1.0/24

Starting Nmap 7.40 ( https://nmap.org ) at 2017-02-13 12:08 EST
Nmap scan report for 192.168.1.1
Host is up (0.0024s latency).
PORT     STATE  SERVICE
8000/tcp closed http-alt

Nmap scan report for 192.168.1.2
Host is up (0.015s latency).
PORT     STATE  SERVICE
8000/tcp closed http-alt
```

---

[1] nmap also recognizes that port 8000 may not be IRDMI; I weep with joy.

```
Nmap scan report for 192.168.1.13
Host is up (0.00021s latency).
PORT      STATE SERVICE
8000/tcp open  http-alt

Nmap done: 256 IP addresses (8 hosts up) scanned in 2.89 seconds
```

By default, nmap scans privileged TCP ports (1–1024), and reports anything open. For example:

```
$ nmap 192.168.1.13

Starting Nmap 7.40 ( https://nmap.org ) at 2017-02-13 12:17 EST
Nmap scan report for 192.168.1.13
Host is up (0.00046s latency).
Not shown: 813 closed ports, 182 filtered ports
PORT      STATE SERVICE
53/tcp    open  domain
445/tcp   open  microsoft-ds
548/tcp   open  afp
631/tcp   open  ipp
8000/tcp  open  http-alt
```

You can specify ports using the -p option, as shown here:

```
$ nmap -p 53,445,546-550  192.168.1.13

Starting Nmap 7.40 ( https://nmap.org ) at 2017-02-13 12:25 EST
Nmap scan report for 192.168.1.13
Host is up (0.00050s latency).
PORT      STATE  SERVICE
53/tcp    open   domain
445/tcp   open   microsoft-ds
546/tcp   closed dhcpv6-client
547/tcp   closed dhcpv6-server
548/tcp   open   afp
549/tcp   closed idfp
550/tcp   closed new-rwho
```

Note that when you specify the ports, the output will include only open ports. The default scan and nmap's fast scan (-F, it only scans the 100 most commonly used ports) both only show open ports.

That's the basics of horizontal and vertical TCP scanning with nmap. At this point, simple discovery scanning mostly involves knowing a couple of other options: in particular, -sU (scan UDP), -n (drop DNS resolution), and -sn (simple ping, akin to the netcat zero I/O mode).

Assessment: nmap, a Bunch of Clients, and a Lot of Repositories

Following discovery is assessment: figuring out what a host is vulnerable to. Effectively assessing a host's vulnerabilities requires inventory data and expertise—inventory to know what services and versions are running on a host, and expertise to know how someone can exploit this.

In this section, I will discuss a number of inventory techniques to support assessment. We will begin with using nmap to identify version numbers and operating systems, then discuss the general process of figuring out what a host is running. Finally, we will discuss the problem of determining what services are running on an open port when you have no idea what's there.

Basic Assessment with nmap

The basic command-line arguments for assessment are -O (check the operating system) and -sV (check the service and version on open ports). These options are frontends to what is, effectively, an expert system: a decision tree that passes different combinations of packets and flags in order to determine how your system responds and what that implies.

Running -O will provide you with an OS profile. If nmap knows the OS (and it knows a lot), you'll get a simple output like this one:

```
$ nmap -O
Nmap scan report for 192.168.1.13
Host is up (0.000070s latency).
Not shown: 995 closed ports
PORT     STATE SERVICE
53/tcp   open  domain
445/tcp  open  microsoft-ds
548/tcp  open  afp
631/tcp  open  ipp
8000/tcp open  http-alt
Device type: general purpose
Running: Apple OS X 10.10.X|10.11.X
OS CPE: cpe:/o:apple:mac_os_x:10.10 cpe:/o:apple:mac_os_x:10.11
OS details: Apple OS X 10.10 (Yosemite) - 10.11 (El Capitan) (Darwin 14.0.0 -
    15.4.0)
```

Most of the report was discussed earlier—the new fields are "Device type," "Running," and the OS information. The device type refers to what type of device nmap *thinks* it is; "general purpose" indicates that it's a general-purpose computing machine (i.e., a laptop or desktop), while other types include terminals, networking hardware (routers and switches), and various types of enterprise hardware.[2] "Running" simply refers to nmap's guess as to what type of operating system is running; nmap makes this guess with an ordered table of probabilities.

The next line of note is the *CPE* (Common Platform Enumeration). The OS information includes the Common Platform Enumeration (CPE), discussed in "The NVD and MITRE Standards" on page 117, and details on the operating system in use.

An Example: Finding an Embedded System

When nmap doesn't recognize what a particular system is, it sends back a *lot* of information. For example, suppose I run an nmap scan and get this back:

```
Nmap scan report for 192.168.1.6
Host is up (0.0011s latency).
Not shown: 999 closed ports
PORT    STATE SERVICE
80/tcp open  http
MAC Address: 00:17:88:11:22:47 (Philips Lighting BV)
No exact OS matches for host (If you know what OS is running on it, see
https://nmap.org/submit/ ).
TCP/IP fingerprint:
OS:SCAN(V=7.40%E=4%D=2/21%OT=80%CT=1%CU=35895%PV=Y%DS=1%DC=D%G=Y%M=001788%T
OS:M=58ACE89C%P=x86_64-apple-darwin16.3.0)SEQ(SP=A2%GCD=1%ISR=DC%TI=I%CI=I%
OS:II=RI%SS=S%TS=U)SEQ(SP=AB%GCD=1%ISR=DC%TI=I%II=RI%SS=O%TS=U)OPS(O1=M218%
OS:O2=M218%O3=M218%O4=M218%O5=M218%O6=M218)WIN(W1=860%W2=860%W3=860%W4=860%
OS:W5=860%W6=860)ECN(R=Y%DF=N%T=FF%W=860%O=M218%CC=N%Q=)T1(R=Y%DF=N%T=FF%S=
OS:O%A=S+%F=AS%RD=0%Q=)T2(R=N)T3(R=N)T4(R=Y%DF=N%T=FF%W=860%S=A%A=S%F=AR%O=
OS:%RD=0%Q=)T4(R=N)T5(R=Y%DF=N%T=FF%W=860%S=A%A=S+%F=AR%O=%RD=0%Q=)T6(R=Y%D
OS:F=N%T=FF%W=860%S=A%A=S%F=AR%O=%RD=0%Q=)T6(R=N)T7(R=N)U1(R=Y%DF=N%T=FF%IP
OS:L=38%UN=0%RIPL=G%RID=G%RIPCK=G%RUCK=G%RUD=G)IE(R=Y%DFI=N%T=FF%CD=S)

Network Distance: 1 hop

OS detection performed. Please report any incorrect results at
https://nmap.org/submit/ .
```

This is actually a fingerprint that nmap creates to feed back into its knowledge base (*https://nmap.org/submit*). This is actually a packed, fixed-length format.[3] While it's great for nmap (and you should submit it if you're comfortable sharing—this profiling will improve only if you share!), there's still the question of what it means for *us*.

First, note the MAC address. The MAC address is registered to a Philips lighting device; a network interface that isn't from a company specializing in network interfaces is likely to be some kind of IoT thing.

---

2 Check *https://nmap.org/book/osdetect-device-types.html* for a list of device types in the current version.

3 A description of what's in the format is at *https://nmap.org/book/osdetect-fingerprint-format.html*.

Next, note that the scan also includes a list of open ports, and `tcp/80` is open for business. Given that, I go and run `nc` on port 80:

```
$ echo "GET /" | nc 192.168.1.6 80 HTTP/1.1 200 OK
Content-type: text/html

<html><head><title>hue personal wireless lighting</title></head><body>
<b>Use a modern browser to view this resource.</b></body></html>
```

And yeah, it's a hub for a Philips Hue wireless lighting system. As a rule of thumb, running a quick `GET /` on an open port can't hurt—it's obvious on port 80, but odds are good you'll get a meaningful response on other ports as well. Most servers these days are modified web servers of some variety, so you're likely to find something speaking HTTP on the other end.

The NVD and MITRE Standards

For years, the US government contracted the MITRE Corporation to maintain a number of different repositories on attacks, platforms, vulnerabilities, and other information on security. The most well-known of these is the Common Vulnerability Enumeration (CVE), a living repository of software vulnerabilities. MITRE has produced a number of other standards as well, with the CPE mentioned earlier following just behind the CVE in exposure. The value of all of these standards is that they provide a common point of reference. In a field where people can get possessive about nomenclature, this is not to be underestimated.

As a rule, the most common and important standards are now managed by NIST under the header of the National Vulnerability Database (NVD). Here's a closer look at these standards:

- The Common Vulnerability Enumeration (CVE) is an index of software vulnerabilities. CVE indices are of the form CVE-YYYY-NNNN, where YYYY is the year of assignment and NNNN is a numeric index. CVEs are maintained as part of the NVD, and are accessible at *https://web.nvd.nist.gov/view/vuln/search*.

- The Common Platform Enumeration (CPE) is a hierarchical name structure that begins with the identifier "cpe", followed by one or more values separated by colons; these values are, in order, the part, the vendor, the product, the version, the update, the edition, the language, the software edition, the target software, the target hardware, and anything else. Some fields are optional, as seen in the `cpe:/o:apple:mac_os_x:10.10` string in the `nmap -O` output shown earlier (part: operating system, vendor: Apple, product: Mac OS X, version: 10.10; everything else dropped). CPEs are also part of the NVD; the standard and dictionaries are at *https://nvd.nist.gov/cpe.cfm*.

- The Security Content Automation Protocol (SCAP) is an umbrella term encompassing the CVE and CPE as well as the Common Weakness Enumeration

(CWE), the Common Vulnerability Scoring System (CVSS), and a number of other standards.

Vulnerability assessment involves taking a very specific inventory (down to platform and version numbers), consulting intelligence sources such as the NVD to determine which vulnerabilities exist, and then determining the response—patching, blocking, taking systems down, or whatever other action is deemed appropriate.

Unpatchable Vulnerabilities

An important note here: while we usually talk about vulnerabilities as flaws in software design, a flaw can also appear in policy or be embedded in the design of the protocol, and it may *not* be fixable. Some examples:

- Mediocre password management, in particular the use of default passwords for administration accounts, is a universal headache. The recent Mirai botnet exploited this across multiple embedded systems.

- Reflection attacks are a common problem with UDP-based protocols such as NTP and DNS. Reflection attacks leverage UDP's statelessness and the willingness of these protocols to send back "I dunno" packets when receiving uncertain messages.

- Administrative tools are often embedded into default installations with minimal, if any, permissions to execute them. The entire field of malware free intrusions depends on this. Finally, when dealing with embedded and IoT systems, expect that you often won't be able to *fix* the vulnerability, because patching and maintenance isn't part of the design.

The most advanced assessment tool that `nmap` provides is a full Lua-based flexible scripting capability, the *Nmap Scripting Engine* (NSE). The NSE commands `nmap`'s capabilities using Lua scripts that can write complex, sequential analyses of particular hosts and enable authors to identify vulnerabilities and traffic features that are outside the capabilities of vanilla `nmap`. The NMAP project maintains a constantly updated list of NSE scripts (*https://nmap.org/nsedoc/*); it's worth checking on a regular basis for specific and current vulnerabilities.

What's important to recognize about *all* of these tools is that the mechanical components are less important than the expertise. It's critical to pay attention to what features and scripts appear that are relevant to your particular organization. Similarly, if you buy a vulnerability scanner, you're paying for the company to keep up-to-date on current vulnerabilities. In Chapter 17 we discuss these issues in more detail.

Heartbeat Signals

The first thing to do in any measurement is check your ruler[4]; when you see an asset disappear on a network, your first step, before all the probing and pinging, is to ensure that the asset is the problem and not your data collection system. With critical assets, it's better to make this process proactive, by including some kind of beacon. A heartbeat signal is a process that periodically sends out a packet simply to remind you that the host is alive and kicking.

Heartbeat signals do not have to be particularly elaborate, but there are a couple of notes on setting them up properly that can help. When setting up heartbeat signals, pay attention to inventory and instrumentation, minimize secondary network effects, and pick a useful time interval.

Regarding inventory: the goal of the heartbeat signal is to provide an analyst with a quick heads up within a data feed. Since you can craft the packet to your needs within the constraints of the feed, feel free to leverage that—embed UUIDs in the packet, send packets to nonexistent hosts (the goal is for your detection systems to recognize it, not necessarily any target in the network).

That said, limit the secondary effects if possible. For defenders who are unaware what the signals are, heartbeat signals are going to be a deliciously obvious anomaly, a problem exacerbated if they generate a lot of noise due to TCP or ICMP responses. I prefer sending UDP packets because they limit the amount of noise that TCP or ICMP echo requests will send out.

Using Active Vantage Data for Verification

Because analysts have limited resources, the most effective use for active domain data is as a concentrated, limited-scope and high-information complement to broader passive data collection. Probe actively when the passive system can't figure out what's going on.

To make this more concrete, consider a scenario where you passively collect inventory to guide incident response. Using the techniques discussed in Chapter 19, you can passively collect information on hosts within the network. However, when doing so you will find that there are sites you cannot passively examine—examples include HTTPS servers (encrypted content) and services on unidentified ports. In this case, you can set up an automated watch for the presence of these services and, when identified, automatically scan them to find out more about what they are doing.

---

4 L. Grossman, "Nov. 10, 1999: Metric Math Mistake Muffed Mars Meteorology Mission." (*https://www.wired.com/2010/11/1110mars-climate-observer-report/*)

Passive and active discovery complement each other. Passive discovery is very handy when you don't know much about your network, and will identify hosts that you don't know about. Active discovery will help you find out what hosts are actually running.

Another example of how to combine active and passive mapping uses dropouts to identify diagnostic concerns. In this case, you use passive detection to monitor hosts within the network. For example, you may monitor the outgoing traffic from your servers and establish a lower limit for volume before you're concerned that that server is not communicating (e.g., if there's less than 5 MB every 10 minutes, or the heartbeat signal is not present). When you encounter a disruption in those timeouts, you initiate an active check.

In both cases, you rely on a large flow-based collection system to trigger a specific, fine-grained probe. This is, in my experience, the best way to combine active and passive probing—use the passive techniques to determine the network's population, and where you encounter ambiguity or uncertainty, probe actively.

Further Reading

1. G. Lyon, *Nmap Network Scanning: The Official Nmap Project Guide to Network Discovery and Security Scanning* (NMAP Project, 2009). Also check out the nmap project website (*https://www.nmap.org*).

2. Z. Durumeric, E. Wustrow, and J. A. Halderman, "ZMap: Fast Internet-Wide Scanning and Its Security Applications," *Proceedings of the 2013 USENIX Security Symposium*, Washington, DC, 2013.

3. The SANS Netcat Cheat Sheet (*https://www.sans.org/security-resources/sec560/netcat_cheat_sheet_v1.pdf*).

## PART II

Tools

This section is about a number of tools for use in data analysis. The primary focus of this section is on two particular tools: SiLK and R. The System for Internet-Level Knowledge (SiLK) is a NetFlow analysis toolkit developed by the CERT Division at Carnegie Mellon University that enables analysts to develop sophisticated flow analysis systems quickly and efficiently. R, a statistical analysis package developed at the University of Auckland, enables exploratory data analysis and visualization.

At this time, there is no killer app for network analysis. Analysis requires using many tools, often in ways they weren't really designed for. The tools covered in this section form what I believe to be a basic functional toolkit for an analyst. Combining them with a light scripting language such as Python empowers analysts to explore data and develop operationally useful products.

The remainder of this section is divided into three chapters. Chapter 8 discusses tools and techniques for analyzing the data. Chapter 9 describes the SiLK suite. Chapter 10 discusses tools to identify the ways in which hosts are connected to the internet, including reverse DNS lookups and looking glasses you collect.

Getting Data in One Place

Once you collect all your data, you have to have an environment where you can process it and produce results. In this chapter, I provide some notes on an architecture to facilitate the rapid development and operational deployment of security analysis software (*analytics*[1]).

There are a number of ways to implement this; the version you'll see in Figure 8-1 is a high-level diagram for a basic environment. In general, these environments should have the following attributes:

- Robust, universal access to all sensor data. The term "universal" here is used in lieu of "centralized"—it's not critical that the data be in one place, but it is critical that anyone implementing analytical code have uniform access to all the data.

- Access to a Turing-complete language. This differentiates an analysis environment from the classic security console. Complex analytics require access to a general-purpose programming language and the ability to build constructs that rely on in-place memory manipulation—so, Python good, R good, SQL bad.

- Performance. Any analytic system will have to deal with resource contention; it is better to overprovision for multiple simultaneous queries early on rather than have your analysts fighting to get results in a crisis.

---

1 Pedantry compels me to point out that "analytic" is an adjective, but I've lost that particular battle and will treat it as a noun. Also, it's "hieroglyph."

A Brief History of Security Analysis Tools, and Why They Don't Play Well with Each Other

Work on an operational floor, and you'll inevitably see analysts working on dual-monitor setups where they have one console in one window, another console in another window, and are manually passing information between the two consoles. These "chair-swivel" situations add stress and errors into an already stressful environment.

Before launching into the architectural walkthrough, I need to provide some context to explain the history of security analysis tools, and in particular, why security analysis tools generally don't do interoperations well (if at all).

For the purposes of this discussion, we can break security tools into three "generations," shown in the attached figure. The earliest generation, until the early 2000s, is characterized by isolated *inline* tools. Examples of these tools include IDSs, firewalls, AV systems, and the like. These tools were characterized by their simplicity and their isolation. IDS tools, running inline, could only manage a limited number of rules.

90s-2000s IDS, Firewalls	2003- Present	Present Prototyping
- Isolated sources - Data collection is ad hoc - Processing on hardware - Packages are assumed to be only defense - Analytics doesn't really exist - **Hardware performance limits complexity**	- Multiple sources - Collected results are processed in a data warehouse - Beginnings of working reporting standards (CEF, STIX) - Analytics tend towards dashboards - **Business logic limits complexity**	- Collection and storage is solved, big data increasingly turnkey - Problem is now too much data - More tools that share with each other - **Software crisis limits complexity**

The second generation, which really took off in the early 2000s, is characterized by *security information management* (SIM) or *security information and event management* (SIEM) tools and dashboards, particularly ArcSight and Splunk. These tools don't generate data; they are databases that other systems dump their security information into.

This second generation is defined largely by the first successful adoption of intercommunications standards, in particular rough-and-ready interfaces such as CEF. Still, systems in this generation are often run alone with nonstandardized output. Often, these systems repackage threat intelligence as part of their services.

We're in the midst of a third generation right now, which is characterized by two major factors: the adoption of big data architectures (which for the purposes of this discussion I describe as non-CRUD databases and the use of MapReduce operations) for analysis, and the increased reliance on annotative and third-party data such as threat intelligence.

For developers working with analysis teams, I recommend the following actions as rules of thumb:

- Develop command line–accessible APIs for every tool you build. System integration will be much easier if everything has a REST API, and analysts often work off the command line.[2] Keep the API current to the UI at all times.

- Include the ability to dump any and all output to CSV format. If it exists, someone is going to shove it into Excel.

- If you need authentication, work on single sign-on and keep discrete domains to a minimum.

- Work to the SIM; if the ops floor lives off ArcSight, Splunk, or an ELK stack, build your requirements backward from that, and maintain consistent terminology and interfaces with whatever tool they are using.

- Do not ignore reliability. Security analysis is usually done in a high-stress environment. Big data tools are, as of this writing, far more wonky than monotonous enterprise databases.

As a developer, design your tools to interoperate from the start. As a purchaser, check to see what the service level and data agreements are for the tool, *particularly at end of life*. There's nothing as painful as depending on a tool for five years and then finding out that you can't extract data from it.

High-Level Architecture

Figure 8-1 shows a high-level view of a security analysis environment. This environment is envisioned as assisting in the rapid prototyping and deployment of new analytics; security is a constantly moving target, and analysts will need to experiment with new analytics on a regular basis. I will briefly walk through the architectural goals and then discuss each component in more depth.

---

2 Where grep lives.

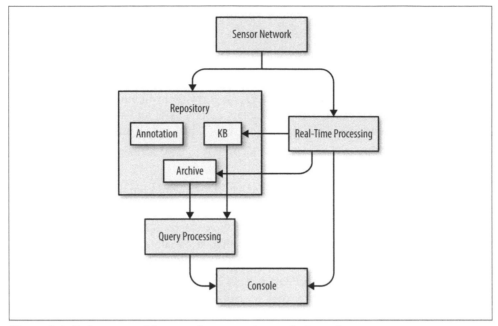

Figure 8-1. Reference architecture for a security analysis environment

The Sensor Network

The *sensor network* consists of all the data-gathering devices inside your observed network. This includes network sensing (e.g., IDS, firewall, flow sensing), host-based sensing (e.g., AV, HIDS, DLP), and service sensing (syslog, HTTP logs, and the like). Active sensing, being done on an ad hoc basis, is not embedded within the sensor network.

When designing a sensor network, consider the following questions and issues:

- Will the data be transported in band or out of band? If you are generating a large amount of sensor data, consider setting up dedicated VLANs for transporting this information so it is not reported within the sensor network.

- Will you store data on the sensors and fetch on demand, or will you forward all data? Summary data (such as NetFlow or constructed events) may be best stored centrally, while raw data is recorded at the sensors proper and pulled as needed.

- How will you measure the sensors themselves? The integrity of the sensor network will be an ongoing concern. Make sure that you have analytics available to verify that a sensor is correctly installed, to onboard new sensors, and to identify when a sensor has dropped off the network.

The Repository

The *repository* is a location for any nonstreaming data. As Figure 8-1 shows, this is subdivided into three components: an *archive*, *annotation data*, and the *knowledge base*.

The repository is the component of the system that is accessed most often and most randomly. As such, performance issues hit the repository more than any other part of the system. When building the repository, consider the following issues:

- How much information do you expect to maintain? This question may be determined by regulation within your sector. In the absence of that, I like being able to go back at least 90 days (a quarter), and longer if at all possible.

- How will you access immediate (say, the last two weeks) versus longer-term information? Longer queries will be rarer than ones over the last week or so, so if you intend to use high-performance, expensive storage, focus on the last week to two weeks.

- How often will you update your storage estimates? Network traffic volume will increase steadily over time, so updating the estimates of how much information you can store is a process you should consider at least quarterly.

Archive

The archive is a location for event data. Examples of this data include:

- Network traffic data (e.g., NetFlow logs, packet captures; see Chapter 3 for more information)
- System information (e.g., process statistics, filesystem stats, AV reports)
- System log data (e.g., server logs, syslog information)

Archive data is event data, meaning that it happens at a specific time and it doesn't update. This is the place in your analysis environment to build a humongous HDFS system and then pump queries through it constantly.

In addition to the general repository issues discussed earlier, issues to consider with the archive include:

- How will you manage queries involving aged-out data? If storage space is finite, you can bet that there will eventually be an investigation requiring going back to tape archives.

- Consider postprocessing summarization. Events such as scans take up a large amount of records for little value. You may want to consider storing raw data for a day, then start splitting out and summarizing high-level phenomena (scanning, legitimate interactions, dark space interaction) to improve access speed.

- How much data in the archive is redundant? Can you place the redundant or similar data in one location? For example, you might put all HTTP flows and weblogs in one repository.

Annotation

Annotation data refers to information that you use to supplement your archive data. This includes threat intelligence, geolocation data, network reputation, and other forms of mapping such as DNS repositories. Annotation data differs from event data in that it has a valid time—for example, the owner of an IP address may be one organization from March 5th to 10th, and another on the 11th onward. Coordinating this timing information is critical when considering annotation.

In addition to the general repository issues, specific questions to consider with annotation include:

- How do you combine annotation with archive data? Will you pay a performance cost and integrate them as needed, or pay a storage cost and update the archive records with annotations?

- If you have multiple redundant annotation sources (e.g., two different geolocation databases), how do you represent this?

Geolocation: You Get What You Pay For

Third-party geolocation software is primarily intended for web services companies to provide real-time geofencing information—for example, targeted advertising or rights management. Consequently, geolocation licensing agreements are usually a "per-lookup" style of license.

When buying geolocation software, keep the following rules in mind:

- Country-level location is generally pretty good, but once you try to get down to cities or metropolitan statistical areas (MSAs, geographic regions defined by the US government), you're going to find the accuracy goes downhill.

- Be aware of the location process's failure mode; a common problem has been geolocation software defaulting to the center of a region, leading to things like all the world's malware appearing to originate from Potwin, Kansas.

- Accuracy is generally best within the RIPE and ARIN regions (see "The RIRs and IP Address Allocation" on page 178), and tends to fall off outside of those areas.

- Check the licensing and see if the vendor will directly ship you a database, rather than buying a per-query license. A good day's worth of scan traffic may cost you your monthly query limit.

Knowledge base

The knowledge base (KB) consists of information and judgments that the organization has built up itself over time, and consists of information that is specifically relevant to the target enterprise. Examples of critical information in the KB include asset inventories (a CMDB if you have one), personnel data, and internal calendars. Unlike the other information here, KB data is unstructured and usually relatively small, as it's largely person-moderated.

Query Processing

The *query processing* system is a development environment that supports rapid prototyping, data synthesis, and providing contextual data. The system can process data from multiple locations to synthesize it.

Questions to ask when determining query processing requirements include:

- How do developers or analysts touch the query processing system? Limit the number of languages as much as possible, down to two if you can get away with it.

- How do they touch data? The great achievement of SIEM is to provide a developer access to all the data in one database cursor. However you store or hide the data, ensure that the analysts have one access point and consistently named tables (a source IP is a source IP everywhere).

- How will you manage queue contention? Figure out a query that takes about 5 minutes to run, then run it once, 4 times simultaneously, 10 times simultaneously, and 20 times simultaneously.[3] Many query systems will gracefully degrade, allowing x number of queries to process simultaneously, then holding off on $x+1$ until a query finishes. During times of stress, you can expect that analysts will be beating the system constantly, and queue contention is going to kill you.

---

3 Make sure you're doing this with similar-sized but different datasets so you can compensate for caching effects.

Real-Time Processing

Real-time processing consists of any analyses that are done *à la minute*, which may include straight signature matching, specifically crafted high-performance analytics, and logfile generation. As a rule, real-time processing should be distinct from query processing—real-time data should ideally summarize or process data to reduce the amount of query processing needed.

A Question of Timing

The term "real-time" in intrusion detection and network security is vaguely defined. The general sense of the term is that the system detects attacks "while the attack takes place"; this doesn't help because "while an attack takes place" is itself vaguely defined and may involve a number of short bursts over several months.

When discussing real-time detection, there are a couple of issues to keep in mind. First, there's a limiting case: without a real-time response, real-time detection is pointless. As a corollary to that, most self-respecting defenders aren't going to trust a real-time defense system since an attacker is going to see it as a "please DoS me kit."

Second, there's the problem of false positive rate. The base-rate problem impacts all detection systems. Effectively limiting the impact of false positives is going to involve correlating data and providing context, which isn't a real-time action.

Put another way, whatever you can do in real-time should be done because it *has* to be real-time, not because it can be. These include dealing with obvious threats such as DDoS attacks; things where the attack is obvious *and the consequences of an immediate response are manageable.*

There is one particular area where real-time data collection, if not detection, is critical: correlating transient lookup data. If something has a short lifetime, then collect it while it's alive. The most prominent example is the relationship between DNS names and IP addresses, but this also includes things such as address/port combinations across proxies and MAC/IP address relations in DHCP networks.

Source Control

I can't emphasize the importance of a source code repository enough—just make sure everyone knows how to use Git, even if they're not developers. In particular, the following information should be maintained in the repository:

- Analytics
- Signature sets

- Firewall and IDS configurations[4]

Analytics are obvious, since they are code executed on data. The others are less obvious, but as a rule, anything that is mechanically processed by a detection system or other middlebox in your network should be recorded and changes maintained in the archive. This is a necessity when reconstructing past events—if a change in traffic occurs on a network, the first question the analyst should ask is whether the change is due to the internet or due to the collection system.

Log Data and the CRUD Paradigm

The CRUD (create, read, update, and delete) paradigm describes the basic operations expected of a persistent storage system. Relational database management systems (RDBMSs), the most prevalent form of persistent storage, expect that users will regularly and asynchronously update existing contents. Relational databases are primarily designed for data integrity, not performance.

Ensuring data integrity requires a significant amount of the system's resources. Databases use a number of different mechanisms to enforce integrity, including additional processing and metadata on each row. These features are necessary for the type of data that RDBMSs were designed for. That data is not log data.

This difference is shown in Figure 8-2. In RDBMSs, users add and query data from a system constantly, and the system spends resources on tracking these interactions. Log data does not change, however; once an event has occurred, it is never updated. This changes the data flow as shown in the figure on the right. In log collection systems, the only things that write to disk are the sensors; users only *read* from disk.

This separation of duties between users and sensors means that, when working with log data, the integrity mechanisms used by databases are wasted. For log data, a properly designed flat file collection system will often be just as fast as a relational database.

---

4 Note that the converse is true as well—if you are managing a system with multiple firewalls, IDSs, and the like, make sure that you are also consistently pushing *out* your configurations.

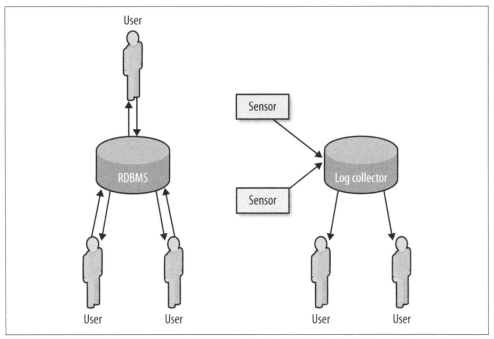

Figure 8-2. Comparing RDBMSs and log collection systems

Creating a Well-Organized Flat File System: Lessons from SiLK

In Chapter 9, we discuss SiLK, the analysis system CERT developed to handle large NetFlows. SiLK was a very early big data system. While it doesn't use current big data technologies, it was designed around similar principles, and understanding how those principles work can inform the development of more current systems.

Log analysis is primarily I/O bound, meaning that the primary constraint on performance is the number of records read, as opposed to the complexity of the algorithms run on the records. For example, in the original design of SiLK, we found that it was considerably faster to keep compressed files on disk—the performance hit from reading the records off of disk was much higher than the performance hit of decompressing a file in memory.

Because performance is I/O bound, a good query system will read the minimum number of relevant records possible. In log collection systems, the most effective way to reduce the records read is to index them by time and *always* require a user to specify the time queried. In SiLK, log records are stored in hourly files in a daily hierarchy; for example, */data/2013/03/14/sensor1_20130314.00* to */data/2013/03/14/sensor1_20130314.23*. SiLK commands include a globbing function that hides the actual filenames from the user; queries specify a start date and an end date, which in turn is used to derive the files.

This partitioning process does not have to stop with time. Because network traffic (and log data) is usually dominated by a couple of major protocols, those individual protocols can be split off into their own files. In SiLK installations, it's not unusual to split web traffic from all other traffic because web traffic makes up 40–80% of the traffic on most networks.

As with most data partitioning schemes, there's more art than science in deciding when to stop subdividing the data. As a rule of thumb, having no more than three to five further partitions after the time partition is acceptable because as you add additional partitions, you increase complexity for users and developers. In addition, determining the exact partitioning scheme usually requires some knowledge of the traffic on the network, so you can't do it until *after* you've acquired a better understanding of the network's structure, composition, and the type of data it encounters.

A Brief Introduction to NoSQL Systems

The major advance in big data in the past decade has been the popularization of NoSQL big data systems, particularly the MapReduce paradigm introduced by Google. MapReduce is based around two concepts from functional programming: *mapping*, which is the independent application of a function to all elements in a list, and *reducing*, which is the combination of consecutive elements in a list into a single element. Example 8-1 clearly shows how these elements work.

Example 8-1. Map and reduce functions in Python

```
>>> # map works by applying a function to every element in an array.
... # For example, we create a sample array of 1 to 10.
>>> sample = range(1,11)
>>> # We now define a doubling function.
...
>>> def double(x):
...     return x * 2
...
>>> # We now apply the doubling function to the sample data.
... # This results in a list whose elements are double the
... # original's.
...
>>> map(double, sample)
[2, 4, 6, 8, 10, 12, 14, 16, 18, 20]
>>> # Now we create a 2-parameter function that adds two elements.
...
>>> def add(a, b):
...     return a + b
...
>>> # We now run reduce with add and the sample; add is applied
... # to every element in turn, so we get add(1,2), which produces
... # 3. The list now looks like [3,3,...] as opposed to
```

```
... # [1,2,3....], and the process is repeated: 3 is added to 3,
... # and the list now looks like [6,4,...], until everything is
... # added.
...
>>> reduce(add, sample)
55
```

MapReduce is a convenient paradigm for parallelization. Map operations are implicitly parallel because the mapped function is applied to each list element individually, and reduction provides a clear description of how the results are combined. This easy parallelization enables the implementation of any of a number of big data approaches.

For our purposes, a big data system is a distributed data storage architecture that relies on massive parallelization. Recall the previous discussion about how flat file systems can enhance performance by intelligently indexing data. But now, instead of simply storing the hourly file on disk, we split it across multiple hosts and run the same query on those hosts in parallel. The finer details depend on the type of storage, for which we can define three major categories:

Key stores

Including MongoDB, Accumulo, Cassandra, Hypertable, and LevelDB. These systems effectively operate as a giant hashtable in that a complete document or data structure is associated with a key for future retrieval. Unlike the other two options, key store systems don't use schemas; structure and interpretation are dependent on the implementer.

Columnar databases

Including MonetDB, Sensage, and Paraccel. Columnar databases split each record across multiple column files with the same index.

Relational databases

Including MySQL, Postgres, Oracle, and Microsoft's SQL Server. RDBMSs store complete records as individually distinguishable rows.

Figure 8-3 explains these relations graphically. In a key store, the record is stored by its key while the relationship between the recorded data and any schema is left to the user. In a columnar database, rows are decomposed into their individual fields and then stored, one field per file, in individual column files. In an RDBMS, each row is a unique and distinguishable entity. The schema defines the contents of each row, and rows are stored sequentially in a file.

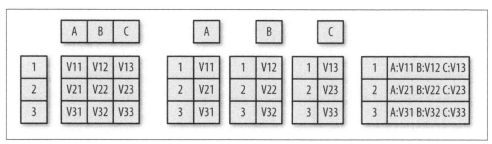

Figure 8-3. Comparing data storage systems

Key stores are a good choice when you have no idea what the structure of the data is, when you have to implement your own low-level queries (e.g., image processing and anything not easily expressed in SQL), or even if the data has structure. This reflects their original purpose of supporting unstructured text searches across web pages. Key stores will work well with web pages, tcpdump records containing a payload, images, and other datasets where the individual records are relatively large (on the order of 60 KB or more, around the size of the HTML on a modern web page). However, if the data possesses some structure, such as the ability to be divided into columns, or extensive and repeated references to the same data, then a columnar or relational model may be preferable.

Columnar databases are preferable when the data is easily divided into individual log records that don't need to cross-reference each other, and when the contents are relatively small, such as the CLF and ELF record formats discussed in "HTTP: CLF and ELF" on page 78. Columnar databases can optimize queries by picking out and processing data from a subset of the columns in each record; their performance improves when they query on fewer columns or return fewer columns. If your schema has a limited number of columns (for example, an image database containing a small date field, a small ID field, and a large image field), then the columnar approach will not provide a performance boost.

RDBMSs were originally designed for information that's frequently replicated across multiple records, such as a billing database where a single person may have multiple bills. RDBMSs work best with data that can be subdivided across multiple tables. In security environments, they're usually best suited to maintaining personnel records, event reports, and other knowledge—things that are produced after processing data or that reflect an organization's structure. RDBMSs are good at maintaining integrity and concurrency; if you need to update a row, they're the default choice. The RDBMS approach is possibly unwarranted if your data doesn't change after creation, individual records don't have cross-references, or your schemas store large blobs.

Further Reading

1. M. Kleppmann, *Designing Data-Intensive Applications* (Sebastopol, CA: O'Reilly Media, 2017).

2. M. Hausenblas and N. Bijnens, *The Lambda Architecture*, available at *http://www.lambda-architecture.net*.

## CHAPTER 9

The SiLK Suite

SiLK, the System for Internet-Level Knowledge, is a toolkit originally developed by Carnegie Mellon's CERT to conduct large-scale NetFlow analysis. SiLK is now used extensively by the US Department of Defense, academic institutions, and technical companies as a basic analytical toolkit.

This chapter focuses primarily on using SiLK as an analytical tool. The CERT Network Situational Awareness (NetSA) Group has published extensive references (*http://tools.netsa.cert.org/*) on using SiLK, installing collectors, and setting up the suite.

What Is SiLK and How Does It Work?

SiLK is a suite of tools for querying and analyzing NetFlow data. The SiLK suite enables an analyst to rapidly and efficiently query very large volumes of network traffic in order to identify complex aggregate phenomena or extract individual events.

SiLK is effectively a database at the command line. Each tool performs a specific query, manipulation, or aggregation of data, and commands are chained together to produce results. By chaining together multiple records along pipes, SiLK enables the analyst to create complex commands that field data along multiple channels simultaneously. For example, the sequence of SiLK queries in Example 9-1 pulls HTTP (port 80) traffic from flow data, producing a time series and a list of activity by busiest address. This example illustrates the basics of SiLK operation: commands are passed through a series of pipes, which can be stdin, stdout, or FIFOs (named pipes).

Example 9-1. Some overly complicated rwfilter voodoo

```
$ mkfifo out2
$ rwfilter --proto=6 --aport=80 data.rwf --pass=stdout |
     rwfilter --input=stdin  --proto=6 --pass=stdout
   --all=out2 | rwstats --top --count=10 --fields=1 &
   rwcount out2 --bin-size=300
```

Data is maintained in an efficient binary representation up until the last moment, until commands that produce text (or some optional/outputs) are called to produce output.

SiLK is very much an old-school Unix application suite: a family of tools tied together with pipes and using a lot of optional arguments. By using this approach, it's possible to create powerful analytic scripts with SiLK, because the tools have well-defined interfaces that will efficiently handle binary data. Effectively using SiLK involves connecting the appropriate tools together in order to process binary data and produce text only at the very end of the process.

This chapter also uses some basic Unix shell commands, such as `ls`, `cat`, and `head`, but doesn't require you to know the shell on an expert level.

Acquiring and Installing SiLK

The SiLK package is available as a free download on the CERT NetSA Security Suite web page (*http://tools.netsa.cert.org/silk/download.html*), and can be installed on most Unix systems without much difficulty. CERT also provides a live CD image that can be used on its own.

The SiLK live CD comes with a training dataset called LBNL-05, containing anonymized header traces from Lawrence Berkeley National Labs in 2005. If you install the live CD, the data will be immediately accessible. If not, you can fetch the data from the LBNL-05 reference data page (*http://bit.ly/lbnl-ref*).[1]

In addition to the live CD, SiLK is available in several package managers, including homebrew.

---

1 You'll notice that there are two datasets, one with scans and one without. To understand why, read R. Pang et al., "The Devil and Packet Trace Anonymization," ACM SIGCOMM *Computer Communication Review* 36:1 (2006): 29–38.

The Datafiles

The LBNL datafiles are stored in a file hierarchy; Example 9-2 shows the results of downloading and unarchiving them.

Example 9-2. Downloading the SiLK archives

```
$ gunzip -c SiLK-LBNL-05-noscan.tar
$ gunzip -c SiLK-LBNL-05-scanners.tar
$ cd SiLK-LBNL-05
$ ls
README-S0.txt in     out    silk.conf
README-S1.txt inweb      outweb
$ ls in/2005/01/07/*.01
in/2005/01/07/in-S0_20050107.01 in/2005/01/07/in-S1_20050107.01
```

When collecting data, SiLK partitions the data into subdirectories that divide traffic by the type of traffic and the time the event occurred. This provides scalability and speeds up analysis. However, it's also generally a black box, and one we're breaking right now simply to have some files to work with. For the purposes of demonstration and education, we're going to work with four specific files:

- *inweb/2005/01/06/iw-S0_20050106.20*
- *inweb/2005/01/06/iw-S0_20050106.21*
- *in/2005/01/07/in-S0_20050107.01*
- *in/2005/01/07/in-S1_20050107.01*

These files are not special in any way. I chose them just to provide examples of scan and nonscan traffic. The following section discusses how to partition data and what the filenames mean.

Choosing and Formatting Output Field Manipulation: rwcut

SiLK records are stored in a compact binary format. They can't be read directly, and are instead accessed using the rwcut tool (see Example 9-3). In the following example, and any other examples with an output longer than 80 characters, the lines are manually broken for clarity.

Example 9-3. Simple file access with rwcut

```
$ rwcut inweb/2005/01/06/iw-S0_20050106.20 | more
            sIP|                dIP|sPort|dPort|pro|   packets|      bytes|\
   flags|                stime|   dur|                    eTime|sen|
```

```
 148.19.251.179|    128.3.148.48| 2497|    80|  6|        16|      2631|\
 FS PA    |2005/01/06T20:01:54.119| 0.246|2005/01/06T20:01:54.365|   ?|
 148.19.251.179|    128.3.148.48| 2498|    80|  6|        14|      2159|\
  S PA    |2005/01/06T20:01:54.160| 0.260|2005/01/06T20:01:54.420|   ?|
 ...
```

In its default invocation, rwcut outputs 12 fields: source and destination IP addresses and ports, protocol, number of packets, number of bytes, TCP flags, start time, duration, end time, and sensor of a flow. These values were discussed previously in Chapter 2, except for the sensor field. SiLK can be configured to identify individual sensors, which is useful when you're trying to figure out where traffic came from or where it's going. The sensor field is whatever ID is assigned during configuration. In the default data there are no sensors, so the value is set to a question mark (?).

All SiLK commands have built-in documentation. Typing **rwcut --help** brings up an enormous help page. We will cover the basic options. A fuller description of options can be found in the SiLK documentation for rwcut (*http://bit.ly/silk-rwcut*).

The most commonly used rwcut commands select the fields displayed during invocation. rwcut can actually print 29 different fields, in arbitrary order. A list of these fields is in Table 9-1.

rwcut fields are specified using the --fields= option, which takes the numeric values in Table 9-1 or the string values and prints the requested fields in the order specified, as in Example 9-4.

Table 9-1. rwcut fields

Field	Numeric ID	Description
sIP	1	Source IP address
dIP	2	Destination IP address
sPort	3	Source port
dPort	4	Destination port: if ICMP, the ICMP type and code is encoded here also
protocol	5	Layer 3 protocol
packets	6	Packets in the flow
bytes	7	Bytes in the flow
flags	8	OR of TCP flags
sTime	9	Start time in seconds
eTime	10	End time in seconds
dur	11	Duration (eTime–sTime)
sensor	12	Sensor ID
in	13	SNMP ID of the incoming interface on the router
out	14	SNMP ID of the outgoing interface on the router

Field	Numeric ID	Description
nhIP	15	Next hop address
sType	16	Classification of the source address (internal, external)
dType	17	Classification of the destination address (internal, external)
scc	18	Country code of the source IP
dcc	19	Country code of the destination IP
class	20	Class of the flow
type	21	Type of the flow
sTime +msec	22	sTime in milliseconds
eTime +msec	23	eTime in milliseconds
dur +msec	24	Duration in milliseconds
icmpTypeCode	25	ICMP type and code
initialFlags	26	Flags in the first TCP packet
sessionFlags	27	Flags in all packets *except* the first
attributes	28	Attributes of the flow observed by the generator
application	29	Guess as to the application in the flow

Example 9-4. Some examples of field ordering

```
# Show a limited set of fields
$ rwcut --field=1-5 inweb/2005/01/06/iw-S0_20050106.20 | head -2
           sIP|            dIP|sPort|dPort|pro|
 148.19.251.179|    128.3.148.48| 2497|   80|  6|
$#Note the -, now explicitly enumerate
$ rwcut --field=1,2,3,4,5 inweb/2005/01/06/iw-S0_20050106.20 | head -2
           sIP|            dIP|sPort|dPort|pro|
 148.19.251.179|    128.3.148.48| 2497|   80|  6|
# Field order is based on what you enter in --field
$ rwcut --field=5,1,2,3,4 inweb/2005/01/06/iw-S0_20050106.20 | head -2
pro|            sIP|            dIP|sPort|dPort|
  6| 148.19.251.179|    128.3.148.48| 2497|   80|
# We can use text instead of numbers
$ rwcut --field=sIP,dIP,proto inweb/2005/01/06/iw-S0_20050106.20 |head -2
           sIP|            dIP|pro|
 148.19.251.179|    128.3.148.48|  6|
```

rwcut supports a number of other output formatting and manipulation tools. Some particularly useful ones, which let you control the lines that appear in the output, include:

--no-title

Commonly used with SiLK commands that produce tabular output. Drops the title from the output table.

--num-recs

Outputs a specific number of records, eliminating the need for the head pipe in Example 9-4. The default value is 0, which makes rwcut dump the entire contents of whatever file it's reading.

--start-rec-num *and* --end-rec-num

Can be used to fetch a range of records in the file.

Example 9-5 shows a few ways to manipulate record numbers and headers.

Example 9-5. Manipulating record numbers and headers

```
# Drop the title
$ rwcut --field=1-9 --no-title inweb/2005/01/06/iw-S0_20050106.20 | head -5
 148.19.251.179|    128.3.148.48| 2497|   80|  6|       16|     2631|FS PA
    |2005/01/06T20:01:54.119|
 148.19.251.179|    128.3.148.48| 2498|   80|  6|       14|     2159| S PA
    |2005/01/06T20:01:54.160|
 148.19.251.179|    128.3.148.48| 2498|   80|  6|        2|       80|F   A
    |2005/01/06T20:07:07.845|
  56.71.233.157|    128.3.148.48|48906|   80|  6|        5|      300| S
    |2005/01/06T20:01:50.011|
   56.96.13.225|    128.3.148.48|50722|   80|  6|        6|      360| S
    |2005/01/06T20:02:57.132|
# Drop the head statement
$ rwcut --field=1-9 inweb/2005/01/06/iw-S0_20050106.20 --num-recs=5
            sIP|          dIP|sPort|dPort|pro|  packets|    bytes|   flags
   |            sTime|
 148.19.251.179|    128.3.148.48| 2497|   80|  6|       16|     2631|FS PA
 |2005/01/06T20:01:54.119|
 148.19.251.179|    128.3.148.48| 2498|   80|  6|       14|     2159| S PA
 |2005/01/06T20:01:54.160|
 148.19.251.179|    128.3.148.48| 2498|   80|  6|        2|       80|F   A
 |2005/01/06T20:07:07.845|
  56.71.233.157|    128.3.148.48|48906|   80|  6|        5|      300| S
 |2005/01/06T20:01:50.011|
   56.96.13.225|    128.3.148.48|50722|   80|  6|        6|      360| S
 |2005/01/06T20:02:57.132|
# Print only the third through fifth records
$ rwcut --field=1-9 inweb/2005/01/06/iw-S0_20050106.20 --start-rec-num=3
   --end-rec-num=5
            sIP|          dIP|sPort|dPort|pro|  packets|    bytes|   flags
   |            sTime|
 148.19.251.179|    128.3.148.48| 2498|   80|  6|        2|       80|F   A
 |2005/01/06T20:07:07.845|
  56.71.233.157|    128.3.148.48|48906|   80|  6|        5|      300| S
 |2005/01/06T20:01:50.011|
   56.96.13.225|    128.3.148.48|50722|   80|  6|        6|      360| S
 |2005/01/06T20:02:57.132|
```

A number of options manipulate output format. Tabulation is controllable with the --column-separator, --no-final-column, and --no-columns switches. --column-separator will change the character used to distinguish columns, while --no-final-column drops the delimiter at the end of the line. --no-columns removes any space padding between columns. The --delimited switch combines all three: it takes a character as an argument, uses that character as a column separator, removes all padding in the columns, and drops the final column separator.

In addition, there are a variety of switches for changing column content:

--integer-ips
  Converts IP addresses to integers rather than dotted quads. This switch is deprecated as of SiLK v3, and users should now use --ip-format=decimal.

--ip-format
  The updated version of --integer-ips, --ip-format specifies how addresses are rendered. Options include canonical (dotted quad for IPv4, canonical IPv6 for IPv6), zero-padded (canonical, except zeros are expanded to the maximal value for each format, so 127.0.0.1 is 127.000.000.001), decimal (prints as the corresponding 32-bit or 128-bit integer), hexadecimal (prints the integer in hexadecimal format), and force-ipv6 (prints all addresses in canonical IPv6 format, including IPv4 addresses mapped to the ::ffff:0:0/96 netblock).

--epoch-time
  Prints timestamps as epoch values with floating-point millisecond precision.

--integer-tcp-flags
  Converts TCP flags to their integer equivalents.

--zero-pad-ips
  Pads the dotted quad IP address format with zeros, so that 128.2.11.12 is printed as 128.002.011.012. Deprecated in favor of --ip-format in SiLK v3.

--icmp-type-and-code
  Places the ICMP type in the source port and the ICMP code in the destination port.

--pager
  Specifies the program to use for paging output.

Example 9-6 shows some of the preceding options.

Example 9-6. Other formatting examples

```
# Change from fixed-width columns to delims
$ rwcut --field=1-5 inweb/2005/01/06/iw-S0_20050106.20 --no-columns --num-recs=2
```

```
sIP|dIP|sPort|dPort|protocol|
148.19.251.179|128.3.148.48|2497|80|6|
148.19.251.179|128.3.148.48|2498|80|6|
# Change the column separator
$ rwcut --field=1-5 inweb/2005/01/06/iw-S0_20050106.20 --column-sep=:
  --num-recs=2
            sIP:          dIP:sPort:dPort:pro:
 148.19.251.179:    128.3.148.48: 2497:    80:   6:
 148.19.251.179:    128.3.148.48: 2498:    80:   6:
$# Use --delim to change everything at once
$ rwcut --field=1-5 inweb/2005/01/06/iw-S0_20050106.20 --delim=: --num-recs=2
sIP:dIP:sPort:dPort:protocol
148.19.251.179:128.3.148.48:2497:80:6
148.19.251.179:128.3.148.48:2498:80:6
# Convert IP addresses to integers
$ rwcut --field=1-5 inweb/2005/01/06/iw-S0_20050106.20 --integer-ip --num-recs=2
      sIP|        dIP|sPort|dPort|pro|
2484337587|2147718192| 2497|    80|  6|
2484337587|2147718192| 2498|    80|  6|
# Use epoch time
$ rwcut --field=1-5,9 inweb/2005/01/06/iw-S0_20050106.20 --epoch --num-recs=2
            sIP|              dIP|sPort|dPort|pro|          sTime|
 148.19.251.179|    128.3.148.48| 2497|    80|  6|1105041714.119|
 148.19.251.179|    128.3.148.48| 2498|    80|  6|1105041714.160|
# Zero-pad IP addresses
$ rwcut --field=1-5,9 inweb/2005/01/06/iw-S0_20050106.20 --zero-pad --num-recs=2
            sIP|              dIP|sPort|dPort|pro|                  sTime|
148.019.251.179|128.003.148.048| 2497|    80|  6|2005/01/06T20:01:54.119|
148.019.251.179|128.003.148.048| 2498|    80|  6|2005/01/06T20:01:54.160|
```

You will note that, as the command lines get more complex, I have truncated the
longer options. SiLK uses GNU-style long options universally, so the only requirement for specifying an option is to type enough characters to make the name unam-
biguous. Expect more and more truncation as we build more and more complex
commands.

Basic Field Manipulation: rwfilter

The most basic SiLK command with analytical value is rwcut paired with rwfilter
through a pipe. Example 9-7 shows a simple rwfilter command.

Example 9-7. A simple rwfilter command

```
$ rwfilter --dport=80 inweb/2005/01/06/iw-S0_20050106.20 --pass=stdout
  | rwcut --field=1-9 --num-recs=5
            sIP|              dIP|sPort|dPort|pro|  packets|        bytes|    flags
  |              sTime|
 148.19.251.179|    128.3.148.48| 2497|    80|  6|       16|        2631|FS PA
  |2005/01/06T20:01:54.119|
```

```
148.19.251.179|    128.3.148.48| 2498|   80|  6|       14|      2159| S PA
  |2005/01/06T20:01:54.160|
148.19.251.179|    128.3.148.48| 2498|   80|  6|        2|        80|F   A
  |2005/01/06T20:07:07.845|
 56.71.233.157|    128.3.148.48|48906|   80|  6|        5|       300| S
  |2005/01/06T20:01:50.011|
 56.96.13.225|    128.3.148.48|50722|   80|  6|        6|       360| S
  |2005/01/06T20:02:57.132|
```

rwfilter with a single filter (the --dport option in this case) and a single redirect (the --pass=stdout) is about as simple as you can get. rwfilter is the workhorse of the SiLK suite: it reads input (directly from a file, using a set of globbing specifications, or through a pipe), applies one or more filters to each record in the data, and then redirects the records based on whether a record matches the filters (passes) or doesn't match (fails).

SiLK's rwfilter documentation (*http://bit.ly/rwfilter-doc*) is humongous, but primarily consists of repetitively describing the filter specifications for every field, so don't be intimidated. rwfilter options basically do one of three things: they specify how to filter data, how to read data, or how to direct the results of those filters.

Ports and Protocols

The easiest filters to start with are --sport, --dport, and --protocol. As the names imply, they filter on the source port, destination port, and protocol, respectively (see Example 9-8). These values can filter on a specific value (e.g., --sport=80 will pass any traffic where the source port is 80), or a range specified with a dash or commas (so --sport=79-83 will pass anything where the source port is between 79 and 83 inclusive, and could be expressed as --sport=79,80,81,82,83).

Example 9-8. Examples of filtering by ports and by protocol

```
$ rwfilter --dport=4350-4360  inweb/2005/01/06/iw-S0_20050106.20
  --pass=stdout | rwcut --field=1-9 --num-recs=5
          sIP|          dIP|sPort|dPort|pro|  packets|   bytes|  flags
  |          sTime|
218.131.115.42| 131.243.105.35|  80| 4360|  6|        2|        80|F   A
  |2005/01/06T20:24:21.879|
148.19.96.160|131.243.107.239|  80| 4350|  6|       27|   35445|FS PA
  |2005/01/06T20:59:42.451|
148.19.96.160|131.243.107.239|  80| 4352|  6|        4|      709|FS PA
  |2005/01/06T20:59:42.507|
148.19.96.160|131.243.107.239|  80| 4351|  6|       15|   16938|FS PA
  |2005/01/06T20:59:42.501|
148.19.96.160|131.243.107.239|  80| 4353|  6|        4|      704|FS PA
  |2005/01/06T20:59:42.544|
$ rwfilter --sport=4000-  inweb/2005/01/06/iw-S0_20050106.20
  --pass=stdout | rwcut --field=1-9 --num-recs=5
```

```
          sIP|                dIP|sPort|dPort|pro|    packets|       bytes|   flags
|                   sTime|
 56.71.233.157|    128.3.148.48|48906|    80|  6|          5|        300|  S
|2005/01/06T20:01:50.011|
 56.96.13.225|    128.3.148.48|50722|    80|  6|          6|        360|  S
|2005/01/06T20:02:57.132|
 56.96.13.225|    128.3.148.48|50726|    80|  6|          6|        360|  S
|2005/01/06T20:02:57.432|
 58.236.56.129|   128.3.148.48|32621|    80|  6|          3|        144|  S
|2005/01/06T20:12:10.747|
 56.96.13.225|    128.3.148.48|54497|   443|  6|          6|        360|  S
|2005/01/06T20:09:30.124|
$ rwfilter --dport=4350,4352  inweb/2005/01/06/iw-S0_20050106.20
--pass=stdout | rwcut --field=1-9 --num-recs=5
          sIP|                dIP|sPort|dPort|pro|    packets|       bytes|   flags
|                   sTime|
148.19.96.160|131.243.107.239|   80| 4350|  6|         27|      35445|FS PA
|2005/01/06T20:59:42.451|
148.19.96.160|131.243.107.239|   80| 4352|  6|          4|        709|FS PA
|2005/01/06T20:59:42.507|
148.19.96.160|131.243.107.239|   80| 4352|  6|          1|         40|   A
|2005/01/06T20:59:42.516|
$ rwfilter --proto=1 in/2005/01/07/in-S0_20050107.01 --pass=stdout
| rwcut --field=1-6 --num-recs=2
          sIP|                dIP|sPort|dPort|pro|    packets|
 35.223.112.236|    128.3.23.93|    0| 2048|  1|          1|
 62.198.182.170|    128.3.23.81|    0| 2048|  1|          1|
$ rwfilter --proto=1,6,17 in/2005/01/07/in-S0_20050107.01 --pass=stdout
| rwcut --num-recs=2 --fields=1-6
          sIP|                dIP|sPort|dPort|pro|    packets|
 116.66.41.147|131.243.163.201| 4283| 1026| 17|          1|
 116.66.41.147|131.243.163.201| 3131| 1027| 17|          1|
$ rwfilter --proto=1,6,17 in/2005/01/07/in-S0_20050107.01 --fail=stdout
| rwcut --num-recs=2 --fields=1-6
          sIP|                dIP|sPort|dPort|pro|    packets|
 57.120.186.177|    128.3.26.171|    0|    0| 50|         70|
 57.120.186.177|    128.3.26.171|    0|    0| 50|         81|
```

Note the use of --fail in the last example. Because there are 255 potential protocols, specifying "everything but TCP, ICMP, and UDP" could be expressed in two ways: either by specifying everything you want (--proto=0,2-5,7-16,18-), or by using the --fail option. I'll discuss more advanced manipulation of --pass and --fail in the next chapter.

Size

Size options (e.g., bytes and packets) are similar to the protocol and port options in that you express them numerically. Unlike the enumerations (ports and protocols), these numeric values can be expressed only as single digits or ranges, not as comma-separated values. So, --packets=70-81 is acceptable, but --bytes=1,2,3,4 is not.

IP Addresses

The simplest form of IP address filtering simply expresses the IP address directly (see Example 9-9). The following examples show strict filtering on the source (--saddress) and destination (--daddress) address, and the --any-address option. --any-address will match *either* source or destination addresses.

Example 9-9. Filtering on IP addresses

```
$ rwfilter --saddress=197.142.156.83 --pass=stdout
   in/2005/01/07/in-S0_20050107.01 | rwcut --num-recs=2
         sIP|             dIP|sPort|dPort|pro|    packets|     bytes|   flags|
               sTime|      dur|                    eTime|sen|
 197.142.156.83|   224.2.127.254|44510| 9875| 17|        12|      7163|         |
2005/01/07T01:24:44.359|   16.756|2005/01/07T01:25:01.115|  ?|
 197.142.156.83|   224.2.127.254|44512| 9875| 17|         4|      2590|         |
2005/01/07T01:25:02.375|    5.742|2005/01/07T01:25:08.117|  ?|
$ rwfilter --daddress=128.3.26.249 --pass=stdout
   in/2005/01/07/in-S0_20050107.01 | rwcut --num-recs=2
         sIP|             dIP|sPort|dPort|pro|    packets|     bytes|   flags|
               sTime|      dur|                    eTime|sen|
211.210.215.142|   128.3.26.249| 4068|   25|  6|         7|      388|FS PA   |
  2005/01/07T01:27:06.789|    5.052|2005/01/07T01:27:11.841|  ?|
 203.126.20.182|   128.3.26.249|51981| 4587|  6|        56|      2240|F   A   |
  2005/01/07T01:27:04.812|   18.530|2005/01/07T01:27:23.342|  ?|
$ rwfilter --any-address=128.3.26.249
   --pass=stdout in/2005/01/07/in-S0_20050107.01 | rwcut --num-recs=2
         sIP|             dIP|sPort|dPort|pro|    packets|     bytes|   flags|
               sTime|      dur|                    eTime|sen|
211.210.215.142|   128.3.26.249| 4068|   25|  6|         7|      388|FS PA   |
  2005/01/07T01:27:06.789|    5.052|2005/01/07T01:27:11.841|  ?|
 203.126.20.182|   128.3.26.249|51981| 4587|  6|        56|      2240|F   A   |
  2005/01/07T01:27:04.812|   18.530|2005/01/07T01:27:23.342|  ?|
```

Address options accept a variety of range descriptors. Each quad in an IP address can be expressed using the same comma-dash format that protocols and ports use. IP addresses will also accept the character x to mean 0–255. This expression can be used within each quad; SiLK will match each quad separately. In addition to this comma-dash format, SiLK can match on CIDR blocks.

SiLK supports IPv6 by using IPv6's colon-based notation. The following are all examples of valid IPv6 filters in SiLK, and Example 9-10 shows how to filter them:

```
::ffff:x
::ffff:0:aaaa,0-5
::ffff:0.0.5-130,1,255.x
```

Example 9-10. Filtering on IP ranges

```
# Filtering on the last quad
$ rwfilter --daddress=131.243.104.x inweb/2005/01/06/iw-S0_20050106.20
  --pass=stdout | rwcut --field=1-5 --num-recs=5
          sIP|            dIP|sPort|dPort|pro|
 150.52.105.212|131.243.104.181|   80| 1262|   6|
 150.52.105.212|131.243.104.181|   80| 1263|   6|
  59.100.39.174| 131.243.104.27|   80| 3188|   6|
  59.100.39.174| 131.243.104.27|   80| 3191|   6|
  59.100.39.174| 131.243.104.27|   80| 3193|   6|
# Filtering a range of specific values in the third quad
$ rwfilter --daddress=131.243.104,107,219.x inweb/2005/01/06/iw-S0_20050106.20
  --pass=stdout | rwcut --field=1-5 --num-recs=5
          sIP|            dIP|sPort|dPort|pro|
  208.122.23.36|131.243.219.201|   80| 2473|   6|
 205.233.167.250|131.243.219.201|   80| 2471|   6|
  58.68.205.40| 131.243.219.37|   80| 3433|   6|
 208.233.181.122| 131.243.219.37|   80| 3434|   6|
  58.68.205.40| 131.243.219.37|   80| 3435|   6|
# Using CIDR blocks
$ rwfilter --saddress=56.81.0.0/16 inweb/2005/01/06/iw-S0_20050106.20
  --pass=stdout | rwcut --field=1-5 --num-recs=5
          sIP|            dIP|sPort|dPort|pro|
  56.81.19.218|131.243.219.201|   80| 2480|   6|
   56.81.16.73|131.243.219.201|   80| 2484|   6|
   56.81.16.73|131.243.219.201|   80| 2486|   6|
   56.81.30.48|131.243.219.201|  443| 2490|   6|
  56.81.31.159|131.243.219.201|  443| 2489|   6|
```

Time

There are three time options: `--stime`, `--etime`, and `--active-time`. These fields require a time range, which in SiLK is written in the format:

```
YYYY/MM/DDTHH:MM:SS-YYYY/MM/DDTHH:MM:SS
```

Note the T separating the day and hour. The `--stime` and `--etime` fields filter exactly what it says on the can, which can be a bit counterintuitive; specifying `--stime=2016/11/08T00:00:00-2012/11/08T00:02:00` filters any record whose *start time* is between midnight and two minutes after midnight on November 8, 2016. Records that started *before* midnight and are still being transmitted during that range will not pass. To find records that occurred within a particular period, use the `--active-time` filter.

TCP Options

Flows are aggregates of packets, and in the majority of cases, this aggregation is relatively easy to understand. For example, the number of bytes in a flow is the sum of the number of bytes in all the packets that comprise the flow. TCP flags, however, are a bit more problematic. In NetFlow v5, a flow's flags are the bitwise OR of the flags in its constituent packets—meaning that a flow indicates that a flag was present or absent in the *entire* flow, but not *where*. A flow could conceivably consist of a gibberish sequence of flags such as a FIN, then an ACK and SYN. Monitoring software such as Yet Another Flowmeter (YAF) expands NetFlow to include additional flag fields, which SiLK can take advantage of.

The core flag filtering switches are `--flags-initial`,`--flags-all`, and `--flags-session`. These options accept flags in the form *<high flags>/<mask flags>*. If a flag is listed in the mask, SiLK always parses it. If a flag is listed in the high flags, SiLK passes it *only* if the value is high. The flags themselves are expressed using the characters in Table 9-2.

Table 9-2. Expressing TCP flags in rwfilter

Character	Flag
F	FIN
S	SYN
R	RST
P	PSH
A	ACK
U	URG
E	ECE
C	CWR

The combination of high flags and mask flags tends to confuse people, so let's review some examples. Remember that the basic rule is that for a flag to be evaluated, it *must* be in the mask. A flag specified as high but not specified in the mask will be ignored. So:

- Setting the value to `S/S` will pass any record where the SYN flag is high, regardless of what the other flags are set to.

- Setting the value to `S/SA` will pass any record where the SYN flag is high *and* the ACK flag is low.

- Setting the value to `SA/SA` will pass any record where *both* the SYN and ACK flags are high.

- A combination like `SAF/SAFR` will return any record where the SYN, ACK, and FIN flags are high *and* the RST flag is low, which would be expected of a normal TCP connection.

In addition to these options, SiLK provides a set of flag-specific options in the form of `--syn-flag`, `--fin-flag`, and so on for each potential flag. These options take a 1 or 0 as an argument: setting the value to 1 will pass records where the flag is high, 0 will pass records where the flag is low, and not including the option will pass all records.

> # What Should TCP Flags Look Like?
>
> The combination of TCP flags in any particular flow can be a useful indicator of the flow's behavior, and there are certain flag combinations that raise suspicion.
>
> Almost all TCP flows should pass *either* SAF/SAFR or SAR/SAFR, *without* passing SAFR/SAFR. This is because most sessions will end in a FIN, with aberrations ending in an RST. If both FIN and RST are seen, that *should* be suspicious; I've seen servers that intentionally terminated sessions with RST, but that's bad practice.
>
> A TCP session without an ACK flag is curious, *especially* if that session has four or more packets. Stacks are usually hardcoded to give up after *n* packets, where *n* tends to be in the neighborhood of three.
>
> For a client, the initial flag should be a SYN, while a server should have a SYN+ACK. You should never see a SYN after the initial flag. Resynchronization would mean a new session started using the same ephemeral port, which is weird for TCP.
>
> The PSH and URG flags are, in my mind, the universal indicators of boring sessions. If I see a session *without* PSH, especially if the session is long, it strikes me as curious. In my mind, a "normal" TCP session will have FSPA high. A flow with just PA high is usually a keepalive and an indication of a broken flow—look in the repository for the same address combination and you'll probably find a SAP flow occurring before it.
>
> Backscatter/response messages include A, SA, and RA flows. A good number of RA packets will arrive on any large network due to backscatter from spoofed DDoS attacks. There isn't really anything you can do about these packets; they're not even directly aimed at your network.
>
> The "new flags" (ECE and CWR) are used to manage congestion notification, and fit into the same category as PSH and URG in my mind—indicators of tedious normality. However, they are new flags, and are only partially adopted at this time—Apple has been aggressively using these flags, but they still show up only in a minority of traffic.

Helper Options

If you compare `rwfilter`'s option-based filtering against `tcpdump`'s BPF filtering, it's immediately obvious that `rwfilter`'s approach is much more primitive. This was an intentional decision: `rwfilter` is focused on processing large volumes as quickly as possible, and the overhead involved in processing some kind of parseable language was deemed too expensive.

What usually trips people up is the lack of obvious not and or operators. For example, if you want to filter out all web sessions, you may try to filter traffic where one port is 80, and the other is ephemeral. The initial attempt might be:

```
$ rwfilter --sport=80,1024-65535 --dport=80,1024-65535 --pass=stdout
```

The problem is that this will also pass any flows where the source and destination port are both 80, and flows where the source and destination port are both ephemeral. To deal with such issues, rwfilter has a collection of helper functions that, combined with the --fail option and multiple filters, should be able to address any of these problems.

In the case of ports, the --aport option refers to either the source *or* the destination port. Using --aport and two filters, you can identify the appropriate sessions as follows:

```
$ rwfilter --aport=80 --pass=stdout | rwfilter --input-pipe=stdin
    --aport=1024-65535 --pass=stdout
```

The first filter identifies anything engaged in port 80 traffic, and the second takes that set and identifies anything that also used an ephemeral port.

A number of IP address helper options are available. --anyaddress filters across source and destination addresses simultaneously. --not-saddress and --not-daddress pass records with addresses that *don't* match the option specification.

Miscellaneous Filtering Options and Some Hacks

rwfilter has a couple of direct text output options: --print-stat (see Example 9-11) and --print-volume-stat. These can be used to print a summary of the traffic without having to resort to cut, count, or other display tools. They also will print volumes of records that did *not* pass a filter.

Example 9-11. Using --print-stat

```
$ rwfilter --print-volume-stat in/2005/01/07/in-S0_20050107.01 --proto=0-255
    |              Recs|          Packets|            Bytes|     Files|
Total|           2019|          2730488|        402105501|         1|
 Pass|           2019|          2730488|        402105501|          |
 Fail|              0|                0|                0|          |
$ rwfilter --print-stat in/2005/01/07/in-S0_20050107.01 --proto=0-255
Files    1.  Read     2019.  Pass     2019. Fail        0.
```

Note in Example 9-11 the use of the --proto=0-255 option. In almost all invocations, rwfilter expects *some* form of filtering applied to it, so when you need a filter that passes everything, the easiest approach is just to specify all the protocols. `--print-stat` and `--print-volume-stat` output to `stderr`, so you can still use `stdout` for pass, fail, and all channels.

Like `rwcut`, `rwfilter` has record-limiting commands. `--max-pass-records` and `--max-fail-records` can be used to limit the number of records passed through a pass or fail channel.

rwfileinfo and Provenance

SiLK filter files contain a fair amount of metadata, which can be accessed using the `rwfileinfo` command (see Example 9-12). `rwfileinfo` can work with files, as seen in the examples here, or directly on `stdin` by using `stdin` or - as an argument.

Example 9-12. Using rwfileinfo

```
$ rwfileinfo in/2005/01/07/in-S0_20050107.01
in/2005/01/07/in-S0_20050107.01:
  format(id)          FT_RWAUGMENTED(0x14)
  version             2
  byte-order          littleEndian
  compression(id)     none(0)
  header-length       28
  record-length       28
  record-version      2
  silk-version        0
  count-records       2019
  file-size           56560
  packed-file-info    2005/01/07T01:00:00 ? ?
$ rwfilter --print-stat in/2005/01/07/in-S0_20050107.01 --proto=6
  --pass=example.rwf
Files      1.  Read     2019.  Pass      1353. Fail          666.
$ rwfileinfo example.rwf
example.rwf:
  format(id)          FT_RWGENERIC(0x16)
  version             16
  byte-order          littleEndian
  compression(id)     none(0)
  header-length       156
  record-length       52
  record-version      5
  silk-version        2.1.0
  count-records       1353
  file-size           70512
  command-lines
                  1  rwfilter --print-stat --proto=6 --pass=example.rwf
  in/2005/01/07/in-S0_20050107.01
$ rwfilter --aport=25 example.rwf --pass=example2.rwf --fail=example2_fail.rwf
$ rwfileinfo example2.rwf
```

```
example2.rwf:
  format(id)          FT_RWGENERIC(0x16)
  version             16
  byte-order          littleEndian
  compression(id)     none(0)
  header-length       208
  record-length       52
  record-version      5
  silk-version        2.1.0
  count-records       95
  file-size           5148
  command-lines
                1  rwfilter --print-stat --proto=6 --pass=example.rwf
  in/2005/01/07/in-S0_20050107.01
                2  rwfilter --aport=25 --pass=example2.rwf
  --fail=example2_fail.rwf example.rwf
```

The fields reported by rwfileinfo are as follows:

example2.rwf

> The first line of every rwfileinfo dump is the name of the file.

format(id)

> SiLK files are maintained in a number of different optimized formats; the format value is a C macro describing the type of the file, followed by the hexadecimal ID of that type.

version

> The version of the file format.

byte-order

> The order in which bytes are stored on disk; SiLK maintains distinct little- and big-endian formats for faster reading.

compression(id)

> Whether the file is natively compressed, again for faster reading.

header-length

> The size of the file header; a SiLK file with no records will be just the size of the header.

record-length

> The size of individual file records. This value will be 1 if records are variable length.

record-version

> The version of the records (note that record versions are distinct from file versions and SiLK versions).

`silk-version`
> The version of the SiLK suite used to create the file.

`count-records`
> The number of records in the file.

`file-size`
> The total size of the file; if the file is uncompressed, this value should be equivalent to the header length added to the product of the record length and record count.

`command-lines`
> A record of the SiLK commands used to create the file.

Example 9-13 shows how to use the `--note-add` command.

Example 9-13. Using --note-add

```
$ rwfilter --aport=22 example.rwf --note-add='Filtering ssh' --pass=ex2.rwf
$ rwfileinfo ex2.rwf
ex2.rwf:
  format(id)          FT_RWGENERIC(0x16)
  version             16
  byte-order          littleEndian
  compression(id)     none(0)
  header-length       260
  record-length       52
  record-version      5
  silk-version        2.1.0
  count-records       10
  file-size           780
  command-lines
                  1  rwfilter --print-stat --proto=6 --pass=example.rwf
  in/2005/01/07/in-S0_20050107.01
                  2  rwfilter --aport=22 --note-add=Filtering ssh
  --pass=ex2.rwf example.rwf
  annotations
                  1  Filtering ssh
```

Combining Information Flows: rwcount

`rwcount` can produce time series data from the output of an `rwfilter` command. It works by placing counts of bytes, packets, and flow records into fixed-duration *bins*, which are equally sized time periods specified by the user. `rwcount` is a relatively straightforward application. Most of its complexity comes from relating the flows, which themselves have a duration, to the bins.

The simplest invocation of rwcount is shown in Example 9-14. The first thing to notice is the use of the `--bin-size` option. In this example, the bins are half an hour, or 1,800 seconds. If `--bin-size` isn't specified, rwcount will default to 30-second bins. Bin sizes don't have to be integers; floating-point specifications with a resolution down to the millisecond are acceptable for people who like *lots* of bins in their output.

Example 9-14. Simple rwcount invocation

```
$ rwfilter in/2005/01/07/in-S0_20050107.01 --all=stdout |
   rwcount --bin-size=1800
              Date|      Records|             Bytes|          Packets|
2005/01/07T01:00:00|       257.58|       42827381.72|        248724.14|
2005/01/07T01:30:00|      1589.61|      211453506.60|       1438751.93|
2005/01/07T02:00:00|       171.81|      147824612.67|       1043011.93|
```

As Example 9-14 shows, rwcount outputs four columns: a date column in SiLK's standard date format (YYYY/MM/DDTHH:MM:SS), followed by record, byte, and packet columns. The floating-point values are a function of rwcount interpolating how much traffic should be in each bin; rwcount calls this a *load scheme*.

The load scheme is an attempt by rwcount to approximate how much of a flow took place over the period specified by the bins. In the default load scheme, rwcount splits each flow proportionally across all the bins during which the flow was taking place. For example, if a flow takes place from 00:04:00 to 00:11:00, and bins are 5 minutes long, 1/7 of the flow will be added to the first (00:00:00–00:04:59) bin, 5/7 to the second bin (00:05:00–00:09:59), and 1/7 to the third (00:10:00–00:14:59) bin. rwcount takes an integer parameter in the `--load-scheme` option, with the following results:

0

Split the traffic evenly across all bins covered. In the example flow given in the previous paragraph, the flow would be split into thirds, and a third added to each bin.

1

Add the entire flow to the first bin covered by the flow: 00:00:00–00:04:59 in the above example.

2

Add the entire flow to the last bin covered by the flow: in the example above, 00:10:00–00:14:59.

3

Add the entire flow to the middle bin covered by the flow: in the example above, 00:05:00–00:09:59.

4
    The default load scheme.

rwcount uses the flow data provided to guess which time bins are required, but sometimes you have to explicitly specify the time, especially when coordinating multiple
files. This can be done using the --start-epoch and --end-epoch options to specify
starting and ending bin times. Note that these parameters can use the epoch time or
yyyy/mm/dd:HH:MM:SS format. rwcount also has an option to print dates using epoch
time: the --epoch-slots option.

The --skip-zero option (see Example 9-15) is one of a number of output format
options. Normally, rwcount prints every empty bin it has allocated, but --skip-zero
causes empty bins to be omitted from the output. In addition, rwcount supports
many of the output options mentioned for rwcut: --no-titles, --no-columns,
--column-separator, --no-final-delimiter, and --delimited.

Example 9-15. Using epoch slots and the --skip-zero option

```
$ rwfilter in/2005/01/07/in-S0_20050107.01 --all=stdout |
    rwcount --bin-size=1800.00 --epoch
            Date|     Records|            Bytes|          Packets|
      1105059600|      257.58|      42827381.72|        248724.14|
      1105061400|     1589.61|     211453506.60|       1438751.93|
      1105063200|      171.81|     147824612.67|       1043011.93|
$ rwfilter in/2005/01/07/in-S0_20050107.01 --all=stdout |
    rwcount --bin-size=1800.00 --epoch --start-epoch=1105057800
            Date|     Records|            Bytes|          Packets|
      1105057800|        0.00|             0.00|             0.00|
      1105059600|      257.58|      42827381.72|        248724.14|
      1105061400|     1589.61|     211453506.60|       1438751.93|
      1105063200|      171.81|     147824612.67|       1043011.93|
$ rwfilter in/2005/01/07/in-S0_20050107.01 --all=stdout |
    rwcount --bin-size=1800.00 --epoch --start-epoch=1105056000
            Date|     Records|            Bytes|          Packets|
      1105056000|        0.00|             0.00|             0.00|
      1105057800|        0.00|             0.00|             0.00|
      1105059600|      257.58|      42827381.72|        248724.14|
      1105061400|     1589.61|     211453506.60|       1438751.93|
      1105063200|      171.81|     147824612.67|       1043011.93|
$ rwfilter in/2005/01/07/in-S0_20050107.01 --all=stdout |
    rwcount --bin-size=1800.00 --epoch --start-epoch=1105056000 --skip-zero
            Date|     Records|            Bytes|          Packets|
      1105059600|      257.58|      42827381.72|        248724.14|
      1105061400|     1589.61|     211453506.60|       1438751.93|
      1105063200|      171.81|     147824612.67|       1043011.93|
```

rwset and IP Sets

IP sets are SiLK's most powerful capability, and something that distinguishes the toolkit from most other analytical tools. An IP set is a binary representation of an arbitrary collection of IP addresses. IP sets can be created from text files, from SiLK data, or by using other binary SiLK structures.

The easiest way to start with IP sets is to create one, as in Example 9-16.

Example 9-16. Creating IP sets with rwset

```
$ rwfilter in/2005/01/07/in-S0_20050107.01 --all=stdout |
  rwset --sip-file=sip.set --dip-file=dip.set
$ ls -l *.set
-rw-r--r-- 1 mcollins  staff    580 Jan 10 01:06 dip.set
-rw-r--r-- 1 mcollins  staff  15088 Jan 10 01:06 sip.set
$ rwsetcat sip.set | head -5
0.0.0.0
32.16.40.178
32.24.41.181
32.24.215.49
32.30.13.177
$ rwfileinfo sip.set
sip.set:
  format(id)         FT_IPSET(0x1d)
  version            16
  byte-order         littleEndian
  compression(id)    none(0)
  header-length      76
  record-length      1
  record-version     2
  silk-version       2.1.0
  count-records      15012
  file-size          15088
  command-lines
                  1  rwset --sip-file=sip.set --dip-file=dip.set
```

rwset takes flow records and produces up to four output files. The file specified with --sip-file will contain source IP addresses from the flow, --dip-file will contain destination addresses, --any-file will contain source and destination IP addresses, and nhip file will contain next hop addresses. The output is binary and read with rwsetcat, and as with all SiLK files, the file can be examined using rwfileinfo.

The power of IP sets comes when they're combined with rwfilter. rwfilter has eight commands that accept IP sets (--sipset, --dipset, --nhipset, --anyset, and their negations). Sets are explicitly designed so rwfilter can rapidly query using them, enabling a variety of useful queries, as seen in Example 9-17.

Example 9-17. Set manipulation and response

```
# First, we create IP sets; I use --aport=123 (NTP on UDP) to filter down
# to a reasonable set of addresses.  NTP clients and servers use the same
# port.
$ rwfilter in/2005/01/07/in-S0_20050107.01 --pass=stdout --aport=123 |
  rwset --sip-file=sip.set --dip-file=dip.set
# Now, let's see how many IP addresses are created.
$ rwsetcat --count-ip sip.set
15
# Generating output using rwfilter; note the use of the --dipset file as the
# sip set; this means that I'm now looking for messages that responded to
# these addresses.  This means that I've seen NTP going to and from the
# address, meaning it's likely to be a legitimate speaker, as opposed to a
# scan on port 123.
$ rwfilter out/2005/01/07/out-S0_20050107.01 --dipset=sip.set --pass=stdout
  --aport=123 | rwcut | head -5
          sIP|            dIP|sPort|dPort|pro|    packets|      bytes|  \
flags|               sTime|      dur|                   eTime|sen|
  128.3.23.152|    56.7.90.229|  123|  123| 17|          1|        76|  \
    |  2005/01/07T01:10:00.520|    0.083|2005/01/07T01:10:00.603|  ?|
  128.3.23.152|   192.41.221.11|  123|  123| 17|          1|        76|  \
    |  2005/01/07T01:10:15.519|    0.000|2005/01/07T01:10:15.519|  ?|
  128.3.23.231| 87.221.134.185|  123|  123| 17|          1|        76|  \
    |  2005/01/07T01:24:46.251|    0.005|2005/01/07T01:24:46.256|  ?|
  128.3.26.152| 58.243.214.183|  123|10123| 17|          1|        76|  \
    |  2005/01/07T01:27:08.854|    0.000|2005/01/07T01:27:08.854|  ?|
# Let's look at statistics; using the same file, I look at the hosts
# that responded.
$ rwfilter out/2005/01/07/out-S0_20050107.01 --dipset=sip.set  --aport=123
  --print-stat
Files     1.  Read     12393.  Pass          21. Fail       12372.
# Now I look at everyone else; --not-dipset means that I'm looking at everything
# on port 123 that doesn't go to these addresses.
$ rwfilter out/2005/01/07/out-S0_20050107.01 --not-dipset=sip.set  --aport=123
  --print-stat
Files     1.  Read     12393.  Pass         337. Fail       12056.
```

Sets can also be generated by hand using `rwsetbuild`, which takes text input and produces a set file as the output. The `rwsetbuild` specification takes any of the IP address specifications used by the `--saddress` option in `rwfilter`: literal addresses, integers, ranges within dotted quads, and netmasks. Example 9-18 demonstrates this.

Example 9-18. Building a set using rwsetbuild

```
$ cat > setsample.txt
# Comments in set files are prefaced with a hashmark
# Literal address
255.230.1.1
# Note that I'm putting addresses in some semi-random order; the output
```

```
# will be ordered
111.2.3-4.1-2
# Netmask
22.11.1.128/30
^D
$ rwsetbuild setsample.txt setsample.set
$ rwsetcat --print-ip setsample.set
22.11.1.128
22.11.1.129
22.11.1.130
22.11.1.131
111.2.3.1
111.2.3.2
111.2.4.1
111.2.4.2
255.230.1.1
```

Sets can also be manipulated using the `rwsettool` command, which provides a variety of mechanisms for adding and removing sets. `rwsettool` supports four manipulations:

`--union`
Creates a set that includes any address that appears in any of the sets.

`--intersect`
Creates a set that includes only addresses that appear in all the sets specified.

`--difference`
Removes addresses in the latter sets from the first set.

`--sample`
Randomly samples a set to produce a subset.

`rwsettool` is generally invoked using an output path (`--output=file`), but if nothing is specified, it will dump to `stdout`. As with `rwfilter`, `rwsettool` output is binary, so a pure terminal dump triggers an error. Example 9-19 shows a manipulation with `rwsettool`.

Example 9-19. Set manipulation with rwsettool

```
$ rm setsample2.set
$ cat > setsample2.txt
# Build a set that covers our original setsample file to
# see what happens with various functions
22.11.1.128/29
$ rwsetbuild setsample2.txt setsample2.set
$ rwsettool --union setsample.set setsample2.set | rwsetcat
22.11.1.128
22.11.1.129
```

```
22.11.1.130
22.11.1.131
22.11.1.132
22.11.1.133
22.11.1.134
22.11.1.135
111.2.3.1
111.2.3.2
111.2.4.1
111.2.4.2
255.230.1.1
$ rwsettool --intersect setsample.set setsample2.set | rwsetcat
22.11.1.128
22.11.1.129
22.11.1.130
22.11.1.131
$ rwsettool --difference setsample.set setsample2.set | rwsetcat
111.2.3.1
111.2.3.2
111.2.4.1
111.2.4.2
255.230.1.1
```

Finally, there's the `rwsetmember` command, which is effectively a set-based `grep`. Using `rwsetmember`, you can query multiple sets simultaneously about whether an IP address is present, as seen in the following examples:

```
$ rwsetcat x.set
4.8.2.1
92.11.3.15
128.2.1.1
$ rwsetcat y.set
44.3.17.2
99.3.5.5
128.2.1.1
$ rwsetmember 128.2.1.1 *.set
x.set
y.set
$ rwsetmember 99.3.5.5 *.set
y.set
```

Caching IP Sets

`rwsetmember` facilitates a very common and handy SiLK hack, generating periodic (usually hourly or daily) sets of IP addresses engaged in particular activity. For example, you may run a daily query creating a set of all the incoming IP addresses per day, storing the results as a distinct set. Then, in your directory of *day1.set* to *dayn.set*, you can run `rwsetmember` and get a list of every date where the IP address appeared.

Raw flow data has a very low signal-to-noise ratio, so caching information on a per-address basis via sets and bags saves you space and time. Useful information to save includes:

- IP address (incoming and outgoing)
- Scanners
- Visits from blacklists or other threat intelligence sources
- Traffic per host
- Legitimate (4+ packet TCP with SAF) traffic per host

rwuniq

rwuniq is the utility knife of counting tools. It allows an analyst to specify a key containing one or more fields, and will then count a number of different values, including total number of bytes, packets, flow records, or unique IP addresses matching the key.

rwuniq's default configuration counts the number of flows that occurred for a particular key. The key itself must be specified using the --field option, which accepts the field specifiers in Table 9-1. rwuniq can accept multiple fields, and the key will be generated in the order specified in the command line. Example 9-20 demonstrates the key features of the --field option. As it shows, field order in the option affects field ordering in the output.

Example 9-20. Various field specifiers using rwuniq

```
$ rwfilter out/2005/01/07/out-S0_20050107.01 --all=stdout |
  rwuniq --field=sip,proto | head -4
           sIP|pro|    Records|
 131.243.142.85| 17|         1|
131.243.141.187| 17|         6|
    128.3.23.41| 17|         4|
$ rwfilter out/2005/01/07/out-S0_20050107.01 --all=stdout |
  rwuniq --field=1,2 | head -4
           sIP|             dIP|  Records|
 128.3.174.158|     128.3.23.44|        2|
    128.3.191.1|239.255.255.253|        8|
   128.3.161.98|131.243.163.206|        1|
$ rwfilter out/2005/01/07/out-S0_20050107.01 --all=stdout |
  rwuniq --field=sip,sport | head -4
           sIP|sPort|  Records|
 131.243.63.143|53504|        1|
 131.243.219.52|61506|        1|
131.243.163.206| 1032|        1|
```

```
$ rwfilter out/2005/01/07/out-S0_20050107.01 --all=stdout |
  rwuniq --field=sport,sip | head -4
sPort|            sIP|   Records|
55876|   131.243.61.70|         1|
51864|131.243.103.106|         1|
50955| 131.243.103.13|         1|
```

Note that when fields' orders are changed, the order in which records are output also changes. rwuniq does *not* guarantee record ordering by default; sorting can be ordered by using the --sort-output option.

rwuniq provides a number of count switches that instruct it to count additional values (see Example 9-21). The counting switches are --bytes, --packets, --flows, --sip-distinct, and --dip-distinct. Each of these fields can be used on their own, or by specifying a threshold (e.g., --bytes, --bytes=10, or --bytes=10-100). A single-value threshold (--bytes=10) provides a minimum, while a two-value threshold (--bytes=10-100) provides a range with a minimum and maximum. If you don't specify an argument, then the switch returns all values.

Example 9-21. Field spec with rwuniq

```
$ rwfilter out/2005/01/07/out-S0_20050107.01 --all=stdout |
  rwuniq --field=sport,sip --bytes --packets | head -5
sPort|            sIP|        Bytes|   Packets|
55876|   131.243.61.70|          308|         4|
51864|131.243.103.106|          308|         4|
50955| 131.243.103.13|          308|         4|
56568|   128.3.212.145|          360|         5|
$ rwfilter out/2005/01/07/out-S0_20050107.01 --all=stdout |
  rwuniq --field=sport,sip --bytes --packets=8 | head -5
sPort|            sIP|        Bytes|   Packets|
    0| 131.243.30.224|         2520|        30|
  959|    128.3.215.60|          876|        19|
 2315|131.243.124.237|          608|         8|
56838| 131.243.61.187|          616|         8|
$ rwfilter out/2005/01/07/out-S0_20050107.01 --all=stdout |
  rwuniq --field=sport,sip --bytes --packets=8-20 | head -5
sPort|            sIP|        Bytes|   Packets|
  959|    128.3.215.60|          876|        19|
 2315|131.243.124.237|          608|         8|
56838| 131.243.61.187|          616|         8|
  514|    128.3.97.166|         2233|        20|
```

rwbag

The last set of tools to discuss in this chapter are *bag tools*. A *bag* is a form of storage structure. It contains a key (which can be an IP address, a port, the protocol, or an interface index), and a count of values for that key. Bags can be created from scratch or from flow data using the `rwbag` command (see Example 9-22).

Example 9-22. An rwbag call, creating an IP address bag

```
$ rwfilter out/2005/01/07/out-S0_20050107.01 --all=stdout |
  rwbag --sip-bytes=sip_bytes.bag
$ rwbagcat sip_bytes.bag | head -5
       128.3.2.16|          10026403|
       128.3.2.46|             27946|
       128.3.2.96|            218605|
       128.3.2.98|               636|
      128.3.2.102|              1568|
```

Like sets, bags are a second-order binary structure for SiLK, meaning that they have their own toolkit (`rwbagcat`, `rwbagtool`, and `rwbagbuild`), the data is binary (so it can't be read with `cat` or a text editor), and they can be derived from flow data or built from a datafile.

The basic bag generation tool is `rwbag`, which as seen in Example 9-22 takes flow data and produces a bag file from it. `rwbag` can generate 27 types of bags, simultaneously if you're so inclined. These 27 types comprise 3 types of counting (`bytes`, `packets`, and `flows`) and 9 types of key (`sip`, `dip`, `sport`, `dport`, `proto`, `sensor`, `input`, `output`, `nhip`). Combine the key and the counting type, and you have a switch that will create a bag. For example, to count all packets from source and destination IP addresses, call `rwbag --sip-packets=b1.bag --dip-packets=b2.bag`.

Advanced SiLK Facilities

In this section, we discuss more advanced SiLK facilities: in particular, the use of PMAPs and the collection and conversion of SiLK data.

PMAPs

A SiLK *prefix map* (PMAP) is a binary file that associates specific subnetworks (prefixes) with tags. PMAPs are used to record various mappings of a network, such as whether a network belongs to a particular organization or ASN, and for country code lookup. Using a source such as GeoIP (*http://www.maxmind.com*), you can build a PMAP that associates IP addresses with their country of origin.

The SiLK tool suite expects some basic PMAPs:

address_types.pmap

> Describes an address's type, conventionally indicating whether the address is inside or outside of the network you are monitoring. Specify the default filesys-

tem location for this PMAP using the SILK_ADDRESS_TYPES environmental variable.

country_codes.pmap

This PMAP describes the country code for an address. Specify the default location for this PMAP using the SILK_COUNTRY_CODES environmental variable.

PMAPs, like set files, can be created from text. Example 9-23 shows a simple PMAP file. Note the following attributes:

- The set of labels at the beginning. PMAPs do not store strings, but enumerable types identified by an integer. This enumeration is defined using the labels. You can see that the PMAP in Example 9-23, for instance, stores a 3 to mark normal traffic.

- The default key. Any value that doesn't match one of the network blocks listed in the map is given the default value.

- The actual declarations. Each declaration consists of a network specification, such as 192.168.0.0/16, followed by a label.

Example 9-23. PMAP input

```
# This is a simple PMAP file that tracks some of the standard RFC 1918
# reserved addresses
#
# First we create some labels
label 0 1918-reserved
label 1 multicast
label 2 future
label 3 normal
#
# Specify the mode; this must be either ip or proto-port. ip in this case
# refers to v4 addresses.
#
mode ip
#
# Everything otherwise not specified is normal
default normal
# Now the maps
192.168.0.0/16    1918-reserved
10.0.0.0/8        1918-reserved
172.16.0.0/12     1918-reserved
224.0.0.0/4       multicast
240.0.0.0/4    future
```

Once you've created a text representation of the PMAP, you can compile the binary PMAP file using the rwpmapbuild command. rwpmapbuild has two mandatory arguments: an input filename, with the file in the text format described previously, and a name for the output file. As with most SiLK commands, rwpmapbuild will not overwrite an existing output file. For example:

```
$ rwpmapbuild -i reserve.txt -o reserve.pmap
$ ls -l reserve.*
  -rw-r--r-- 1 mcollins staff 406 May 27 17:16 reserve.pmap
  -rw-r--r-- 1 mcollins staff 526 May 27 17:00 reserve.txt
```

Once a PMAP file is created, it can be added to rwfilter and rwcut using the pmap-file argument. Specifying the use of a PMAP file effectively creates a new set of fields in the filter and cut commands; since PMAP files are explicitly related to IP addresses, these new fields are bound to IP addresses.

Consider Example 9-24, which uses rwcut. In this example, the --pmap-file argument is colon-delimited; the value before the colon (reserve in the example) is a label, and the value after is a filename. rwcut binds the term reserve to the PMAPs for the source and destination IP address, creating two new fields: src-reserve (for the mapping of the source address to the PMAP) and dst-reserve (for the mapping of the destination address).

Example 9-24. Creating the src-reserve and dst-reserve fields

```
$ rwcut --pmap-file=reserve:reserve.pmap --fields=1-4,src-reserve,dst-reserve
  traceroute.rwf | head -5
           sIP|            dIP|sPort|dPort|   src-reserve|    dst-reserve|
  192.168.1.12|   192.168.1.1|65428|   53| 1918-reserved| 1918-reserved|
  192.168.1.12|   192.168.1.1|56126|   53| 1918-reserved| 1918-reserved|
  192.168.1.12|   192.168.1.1|52055|   53| 1918-reserved| 1918-reserved|
   192.168.1.1|   92.168.1.12|   53|56126| 1918-reserved| 1918-reserved|


# Using the pmap in filter; note that rwcut is not using the pmap
$ rwfilter --pmap-file=reserve:reserve.pmap --pass=stdout traceroute.rwf
    --pmap-src-reserve=1918-reserved  | rwcut --field=1-5
   | head -5
sIP| dIP|sPort|dPort|pro|
192.168.1.12| 192.168.1.1|65428| 53| 17|
192.168.1.12| 192.168.1.1|56126| 53| 17|
192.168.1.12| 192.168.1.1|52055| 53| 17|
192.168.1.1| 192.168.1.12| 53|56126| 17|
```

Collecting SiLK Data

There are a number of different tools for collecting data and pushing it into SiLK. The major ones are YAF, which is a flow collector, and rwptoflow and rwtuc, which convert other data into SiLK format.

YAF

Yet Another Flowmeter (YAF) is the reference implementation for the IETF IPFIX standard, and is the standard flow collection software for the SiLK toolkit. YAF can read pcap data from files or capture packets directly, which it then assembles into flow records and exports to disk. The tool itself can be entirely configured using command-line options, but the number of options is fairly daunting. At its simplest, a YAF command looks like this:

```
$ sudo yaf -i en1 --live=pcap -out /tmp/yaf/yaf
```

This reads data from interface `en1` and drops it to the file in the temporary directory. Additional options control how data is read and how it is converted into flow records and other output formats.

yaf output is specified via the `--out` switch in tandem with the `--ipfix` and `--rotate` switches. By default, `--out` outputs to a file; in the preceding example, the file is */tmp/yaf/yaf*, but any valid filename will do (if `--out` is set to -, then yaf will output to `stdout`).

When `--out` is specified with `--rotate`, yaf writes the output to files that are rotated at an interval specified by the `--rotate` switch (e.g., `--rotate 3600` will update files every hour). In this mode, yaf uses the name specified by `--out` as a base filename, and attaches a suffix specified in `YYYYMMDDhhmmss` format, along with a decimal serial number and a *.yaf* file extension.

When yaf is specified with the `--ipfix` switch, it communicates IPFIX data to a daemon located elsewhere on the network. In this case (the most complicated option), `--ipfix` takes a transport protocol as an argument, while `--out` takes the IP address of the host. The additional `--ipfix-port` switch takes a port number when needed. Consult the documentation (*http://tools.netsa.cert.org/yaf/yaf.html*) for more information.

The most important options are:

`--live`
: Specifies the type of data being read; possible values are `pcap`, `dag`, or `napatech`. `dag` and `napatech` refer to proprietary packet capture systems, so unless you have that hardware, just set `--live` to `pcap`.

`--filter`
: Applies a BPF filter to the pcap data.

`--out`
: The output specifier, discussed previously. This will be a file, a file prefix, or an IP address depending on whatever other switches are used.

`--ipfix`
> Takes a transport protocol (`tcp`, `udp`, `sctp`, or `spread`) as an argument, and specifies that output is IPFIX-transported over the network. Consult the `yaf` documentation for more information.

`--ipfix-port`
> Used only if `--ipfix` is specified. Specifies the port that the IPFIX data is sent to.

`--rotate`
> Used only with files. If present, the filename in `--out` is used as a prefix, and files are written with a timestamp appended to them. The `--rotate` option takes an argument and the number of seconds to wait before moving to a new file.

`--silk`
> Specifies output that can be parsed by SiLK's `rwflowpack` tools.

`--idle-timeout`
> Specifies the idle timeout for flows in seconds. If a flow is present in the flow cache and isn't active, it's flushed as soon as it's been inactive for the duration of the idle timeout. Defaults to 300 seconds (5 minutes).

`--active-timeout`
> Specifies the active timeout for flows, or the maximum amount of time an active flow will be stored in the cache before being flushed. Defaults to 30 minutes (1,800 seconds). Note that the active timeout determines the maximum observed duration of collected flows.

YAF has many more options, but these are the basic ones to consider when configuring flows. Consult the `yaf` manpage for more details.

A Few Handy YAF Examples

YAF has a ton of options, and how they operate together can be a bit confusing. Here are some examples of YAF invocations.

Read `yaf` from an interface (`en1`) and write to a file on disk:

```
$ sudo yaf -i en1 --live=pcap -o /tmp/yaf/yaf
```

Rotate the files every five minutes:

```
$ sudo yaf -i en1 --rotate 300 --live=pcap -o /tmp/yaf/yaf
```

Read a file from disk and convert it:

```
$ yaf <example.pcap >yafout
```

Run a BPF filter on the data, in this case for TCP data only:

```
$ sudo yaf -i en1 --rotate 300 --live=pcap -o /tmp/yaf/yaf --filter="tcp"
```

Export the YAF data over IPFIX to address 128.2.14.11:3059:

```
$ sudo yaf --live pcap --in eth1 --out 128.2.14.11 --ipfix-port=3059
  --ipfix tcp
```

rwptoflow

SiLK uses its own compact binary formats to represent NetFlow data that tools such as rwcut and rwcount present in a human-readable form. There are times when an analyst needs to convert other data into SiLK format, such as when taking packet captures from IDS alerts and converting them into a format where IP set filtering can be done on the data.

The go-to tool for this task is rwptoflow. rwptoflow is a packet data to flow conversion tool. It does *not* aggregate flows; instead, each flow generated by rwptoflow is converted into a one-packet flow record. The resulting file can then be manipulated by the SiLK suite like any other flow file.

rwptoflow is invoked relatively simply with an input filename as its argument. In Example 9-25, the pcap data from a traceroute is converted into flow data using rwptoflow. The resulting raw file is then read using rwcut, and you can see the correspondence between the traceroute records and the resulting flow records.

Example 9-25. Converting pcap data with rwptoflow

```
$ tcpdump -v -n -r traceroute.pcap  | head -6
reading from file traceroute.pcap, link-type EN10MB (Ethernet)
21:06:50.559146 IP (tos 0x0, ttl 255, id 8010, offset 0, flags [none],
    proto UDP (17), length 64)
    192.168.1.12.65428 > 192.168.1.1.53: 63077+ A? jaws.oscar.aol.com. (36)
21:06:50.559157 IP (tos 0x0, ttl 255, id 37467, offset 0, flags [none],
    proto UDP (17), length 86)
    192.168.1.12.56126 > 192.168.1.1.53: 30980+ PTR?
    dr._dns-sd._udp.0.1.168.192.in-addr.arpa. (58)
21:06:50.559158 IP (tos 0x0, ttl 255, id 2942, offset 0, flags [none],
    proto UDP (17), length 66)
    192.168.1.12.52055 > 192.168.1.1.53: 990+ PTR? db._dns-sd._udp.home. (38)
$ rwptoflow traceroute.pcap > traceroute.rwf
$ rwcut --num-recs=3 --fields=1-5 traceroute.rwf
   sIP|     dIP|sPort|dPort|pro|
 192.168.1.12|   192.168.1.1|65428|   53| 17|
 192.168.1.12|   192.168.1.1|56126|   53| 17|
 192.168.1.12|   192.168.1.1|52055|   53| 17|
```

rwtuc

When correlating data between different sources, you will occasionally want to convert it into SiLK's format. rwtuc is the default tool for converting data into SiLK representation, as it works with columnar text files. Using rwtuc, you can convert IDS alerts and other data into SiLK data for further manipulations.

The easiest way to invoke rwtuc is to use it as an inverse of rwcut. Create a file with columnar entries and make sure that the titles match those used by rwcut:

```
$ cat rwtuc_sample.txt
sIP        |dIP        |proto
128.2.11.4 | 29.3.11.4 | 6
11.8.3.15  | 9.12.1.4  | 17
$ rwtuc < rwtuc_sample.txt > rwtuc_sample.rwf
$ rwcut rwtuc_sample.rwf --field=1-6
 sIP| dIP|sPort|dPort|pro|   packets|
   128.2.11.4| 29.3.11.4|   0|   0|  6|         1|
    11.8.3.15|  9.12.1.4|   0|   0| 17|         1|
```

As the following fragment shows, rwtuc will read the columns, use the headers to determine column content, and stuff any unspecified fields with a default value if no column is provided. rwtuc can also take column specifications at the command line using the --fields and --column-separator switches, as so:

```
$ cat rwtuc_sample2.txt
128.2.11.4  x 29.3.11.4 x 6 x 5
7.3.1.1     x  128.2.11.4 x 17 x 3
$ rwtuc --fields=sip,dip,proto,packets --column-sep=x < rwtuc_sample2.txt
  > rwtuc_sample2.rwf
$ rwcut --fields=1-7 rwtuc_sample2.rwf
   sIP|  dIP|sPort|dPort|pro|   packets|     bytes|
   128.2.11.4| 29.3.11.4|   0|   0|  6|         5|         5|
     7.3.1.1| 128.2.11.4|   0|   0| 17|         3|         3|
```

SiLK's binary format requires values for every field, which means that rwtuc makes a best guess for field values that it doesn't have. For instance, the previous example specifies packets as a field but not bytes, so rwtuc just defines the packet value to be identical to the byte value.

If there exists a common default value (e.g., all traffic has the same protocol), this value can be defined using one of a number of field-stuffing options in rwtuc. These options are identical to the field filtering options in rwfilter, except they only take single values. For example, --proto=17 sets the protocol of every entry to 17.

In the following fragment, we use the field stuffing command --bytes=300 to set a value of 300 bytes for every entry in *rwtuc_sample2.txt*:

```
$ rwtuc --fields=sip,dip,proto,packets --column-sep=x --bytes=300 <
  rwtuc_sample2.txt > rwtuc_sample2.rwf
```

```
$ rwcut --fields=1-7 rwtuc_sample2.rwf
     sIP|    dIP|sPort|dPort|pro|     packets|      bytes|
  128.2.11.4|    29.3.11.4|    0|    0|  6|           5|        300|
    7.3.1.1|  128.2.11.4|    0|    0| 17|           3|        300|
```

The resulting RWF file will contain a value of 300 bytes, even though the byte value is not in the original text file. The packet values, which are specified in the file, are set to whatever was specified there.

rwrandomizeip

rwrandomizeip is a tool to shuffle IP addresses in order to anonymize data for public release. Anonymization is itself a complex process, and should be considered on a case-by-case basis. To that end, rwrandomizeip provides a number of different anonymization techniques, including pure randomization and consistent mapping.

The basic invocation of rwrandomizeip takes an input file and an output file, and generates random addresses for both sets:

```
$ cat rwtuc_sample3.txt
sIP        |dIP        |proto
128.2.11.4 | 29.3.11.4 | 6
11.8.3.15  | 9.12.1.4  | 17
128.2.11.4 | 29.3.99.8 | 6
9.88.4.17  | 29.3.11.4 | 6
$ rwtuc < rwtuc_sample3.txt | rwrandomizeip stdin stdout | rwcut --fields=1-7
  --ipv6=ignore
             sIP|             dIP|sPort|dPort|pro|     packets|      bytes|
    10.93.81.37|    10.85.44.118|    0|    0|  6|           1|          1|
   10.99.53.145|  10.130.150.112|    0|    0| 17|           1|          1|
   10.146.120.29|    10.31.222.59|    0|    0|  6|           1|          1|
    10.3.86.205|  10.206.186.249|    0|    0|  6|           1|          1|
$ rwtuc < rwtuc_sample3.txt | rwrandomizeip stdin stdout | rwcut --fields=1-7
  --ipv6=ignore
             sIP|             dIP|sPort|dPort|pro|     packets|      bytes|
  10.147.117.187|  10.161.218.135|    0|    0|  6|           1|          1|
   10.15.216.69|   10.85.128.237|    0|    0| 17|           1|          1|
   10.148.145.16|   10.231.231.13|    0|    0|  6|           1|          1|
   10.255.35.36|  10.240.107.198|    0|    0|  6|           1|          1|
```

Specifying a seed with the --seed switch (which takes an integer) will randomize addresses consistently between invocations:

```
$ rwtuc < rwtuc_sample3.txt | rwrandomizeip --seed=590 stdin stdout | rwcut
  --fields=1-7 --ipv6=ignore
             sIP|             dIP|sPort|dPort|pro|     packets|      bytes|
   10.147.108.49|   10.207.87.141|    0|    0|  6|           1|          1|
   10.193.249.8|  172.29.236.141|    0|    0| 17|           1|          1|
     10.3.188.2|    10.103.37.28|    0|    0|  6|           1|          1|
  10.40.122.115|  10.247.125.160|    0|    0|  6|           1|          1|
$ rwtuc < rwtuc_sample3.txt | rwrandomizeip --seed=590 stdin stdout | rwcut
```

```
--fields=1-7 --ipv6=ignore
            sIP|            dIP|sPort|dPort|pro|    packets|       bytes|
   10.147.108.49|   10.207.87.141|    0|    0|  6|          1|           1|
    10.193.249.8|  172.29.236.141|    0|    0| 17|          1|           1|
      10.3.188.2|    10.103.37.28|    0|    0|  6|          1|           1|
   10.40.122.115|  10.247.125.160|    0|    0|  6|          1|           1|
```

An alternative approach is to use the `--consistent` switch; this switch will generate a per-octet randomization that can be recorded in a distinct shuffle file. Once created, the shuffle file be reloaded and reused:

```
$ rwtuc < rwtuc_sample3.txt | rwrandomizeip --consistent --save-table=ipmap
  stdin stdout | rwcut --fields=1-7 --ipv6=ignore
            sIP|            dIP|sPort|dPort|pro|    packets|       bytes|
   47.116.224.20|   60.107.224.20|    0|    0|  6|          1|           1|
    211.8.97.234|  41.140.114.20|    0|    0| 17|          1|           1|
   47.116.224.20|   60.107.220.71|    0|    0|  6|          1|           1|
    41.24.235.32|   60.107.224.20|    0|    0|  6|          1|           1|
```

Note that in this example, the IP addresses in 29.3 are consistently mapped to 60.107.

Further Reading

1. The best source for information on applied SiLK use is CERT's FloCon web page (*https://resources.sei.cmu.edu/news-events/events/flocon/*). FloCon is CERT's annual conference for large-scale security analysis, and has regular presentations on applications of SiLK, Argus, and other flow analysis tools.

2. T. Shimeall et al., "Using SiLK for Network Traffic Analysis," Carnegie Mellon University Software Engineering Institute, Pittsburgh, PA, 2014, available at *http://tools.netsa.cert.org/silk/analysis-handbook.pdf*.

3. C. Gates et al., "More NetFlow Tools for Performance and Security," *Proceedings of the 2004 USENIX Conference on System Administration*, Atlanta, GA, 2004.

4. J. McHugh, "Sets, Bags, and Rock and Roll? Analyzing Large Data Sets of Network Data," *Proceedings of the 2004 European Symposium on Research In Computer Security*, Sophia Antipolis, France, 2004.

5. M. Thomas et al., "SiLK: A Tool Suite for Unsampled Network Flow Analysis at Scale," CERT Publication CERTCC-2014 24.

## CHAPTER 10

Reference and Lookup: Tools for Figuring Out Who Someone Is

Each alert or logfile line that reports an event provides some basic information about the source of the event. Just from the IP address, you can derive information about geographic location and do a reverse DNS lookup. This chapter covers tools that help you track the identity of a host.

This chapter is focused on the idea of "walking up" the OSI stack, mentioned in "The Basics of Network Layering" on page 19. I like to view the OSI layer as a sequence of lookup processes. Each layer offers a different piece of addressing information, such as the MAC address at layer 2, the IP address at 3, and the ports at 4. This information is moved between layers through the agency of various referencing systems: ARP maps IP addresses to MAC addresses, DNS maps domain names to IP addresses, and so on. Again, the abstraction isn't perfect—DNS translation doesn't move us up or down the OSI stack—but by walking up each layer, we can describe what the addresses *mean* and when they are relevant to investigation.

The remainder of this chapter is structured as follows: a section on MAC addresses, then IPv4 and IPv6, followed by internet-layer information, then DNS, then higher-level protocols. Finally comes a discussion of other important tools that don't fit into the layering model—in particular, reputation databases and malware repositories.

A general comment on the data discussed in this chapter: much of what is referenced here is maintained by a crazy quilt of entities with differing concepts of the information they should provide. Some do good jobs, some do bad jobs, some intentionally obfuscate everything they provide. In many cases, you will want to pull the same data from multiple sources to validate it, and take everything you read with a grain of salt.

MAC and Hardware Addresses

Chapter 2 discusses the basics of a media access control (MAC) address. MAC addresses are defined in the network hardware to provide a locally unique address for each host within a single layer 2 network. The majority of MAC addresses follow the 48-bit *Extended Unique Identifier* (EUI) standard: 6 bytes expressed hexadecimally (e.g., 08-21-23-41-FA-BB). More modern network hardware may use EUI-64, which adds an additional 16 bits. When a frame goes from a 48-bit system to a 64-bit system, the 48-bit address is padded to 64 bits.

Figure 10-1 shows how the EUI-48 and EUI-64 break down.

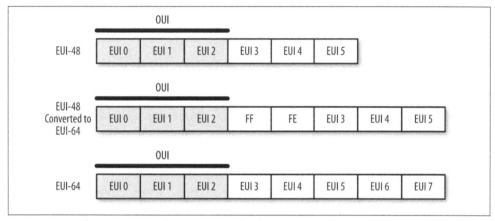

Figure 10-1. The EUI-48 and EUI-64 standards

Note two things in particular. First, if an EUI-48 is converted to an EUI-64, you can tell this by looking at bytes 3 and 4, which will be FFFE. More important is that the first 3 bytes are the *organizationally unique identifier* (OUI), which is a 24-bit value assigned by the IEEE to the hardware manufacturer. OUIs are fixed serial numbers, and if you know the OUI, you can find out who manufactured the card. The IEEE maintains a list of OUI assignments (*http://bit.ly/oui-guide*), where you can use a search engine to find OUIs by company, or companies by OUI.

For example, consider the following packet from a pcap:

```
$ tcpdump -c 1 -e -n -r web.pcap
reading from file web.pcap, link-type EN10MB (Ethernet)
00:37:56.480768 8c:2d:aa:46:f9:71 > 00:1f:90:92:70:5a, ethertype IPv4 (0x0800),
              length 78: 192.168.1.12.50300 > 157.166.241.11.80: Flags [S],
              seq 4157917085, win 65535, options [mss 1460,nop,wscale 4,nop,
              nop,TS val 560054289 ecr 0,sackOK,eol], length 0
```

The communication goes from 8c:2d:aa:46:f9:71 to 00:1f:90:92:70:5a. Looking these up tells us that 8c:2d:aa belongs to Apple, and 00-1f-90 belongs to Actiontec Electronics, which makes Verizon's FIOS routers.

There's Less Work Than You Think

A common analytical stumbling block comes when an analyst tries to build a complicated general solution to a problem when only a limited number of options are present. To use a military example, you don't have to develop a general solution for identifying aircraft carriers because there are only 20 of them in active service. Instead of working on one big problem, you can solve 20 problems that are considerably smaller and mostly similar.

When dealing with hardware systems and applications, it often helps to stop, step back, and do some market research. The problem often becomes smaller when you find out, for example, that while there are a bunch of systems with embedded web servers, most of them are using Allegro RomPager.

MAC addresses operate entirely within the scope of the local network. To communicate beyond the borders of a router, the host must have an IP address. The relationship between a local MAC and an IP address is managed through the *Address Resolution Protocol* (ARP). Individual hosts maintain *ARP tables* that contain mappings between IP addresses and MAC addresses on a network. For example, on my local host, I can query the ARP table using `arp -a`:

```
$ arp -a
wireless_broadband_router.home (192.168.1.1) at 0:1f:90:92:70:5a on en1 ifscope
/[ethernet]
new-host-2.home (192.168.1.3) at 0:1e:c2:a6:17:fb on en1 ifscope [ethernet]
new-host.home (192.168.1.4) at cc:8:e0:68:b8:a4 on en1 ifscope [ethernet]
apple-tv-3.home (192.168.1.9) at 7c:d1:c3:26:35:bf on en1 ifscope [ethernet]
? (192.168.1.255) at ff:ff:ff:ff:ff:ff on en1 ifscope [ethernet]
```

Do the lookups and you'll find that I *really* like Apple hardware.[1]

Analytically, MAC addresses (when you can get them, and you'll normally have them only for your local network, as already explained) are particularly useful for identifying and differentiating *hardware*, particularly networking hardware such as routers. IP addresses are considerably more fungible than MAC addresses, and if you need to track a mobile asset like a laptop or anything moderated through DHCP, the MAC address will be your best asset for doing so.

---

1 And I prefer to keep my Windows and Linux boxes physically wired.

IP Addressing

IP addresses are the most commonly accessed piece of information about a host, and often the only piece of data you will have about a host.

IP is slowly transitioning from IPv4 to IPv6. IPv6 corrects a number of design errors in IPv4, the most notable being IP address exhaustion. An IPv4 address is a 32-bit value, conventionally written in "dotted quad" format: four bytes, written decimally, separated by periods (like 192.168.1.1). At the time of IPv4's original design, nobody seriously expected that the 4 billion addresses provided would ever be exhausted, and many of the early allocations of IPv4 addresses are comically generous, as you can see from the master list of /8 allocations (*http://bit.ly/8-allocations*). A /8 is a collection of 16 million+ addresses (2^{24}), all of which have the same first octet, so 9.0.0.0 to 9.255.255.255 are all owned by IBM, for example. Looking at the list, you'll see that several of the blocks were assigned large and early to companies such as Xerox and Ford, which don't really use the space they have. The situation has actually improved over the past few years, as several drug companies that owned nearly empty /8s have returned them to IANA.

The majority of the English-speaking internet still runs on IPv4, while in Asia and elsewhere, IPv6 is increasingly prevalent. The uneven allocation of IPv4 addresses forces countries that have come to the internet historically later to build IPv6 infrastructure.

IPv4 Addresses, Their Structure, and Significant Addresses

IPv4 addresses can be expressed using a number of different notations. The most common is the dotted quad format discussed earlier: four integer values between 0 and 255, separated by periods. An address can also be referred to directly as a value, usually in hexadecimal. Consequently, the IP address 0xA1010203 is 161.1.2.3 as a dotted quad, and 2701197827 as a decimal integer.

Groups of IP addresses are usually described linearly (e.g., 128.2.11.3–128.2.3.14), or using a Classless Internet Domain Routing (CIDR) block. CIDR blocks are a mechanism for describing the addresses reachable by picking a particular route. Addresses in CIDR notation are represented by a *prefix*,[2] which is a dotted quad representation of the significant bits of an address, and then a *mask*, which indicates how many bits make up the prefix.

For example, the CIDR block 128.2.11.0/24 consists of all addresses whose first 24 bits are 128.2.11, so any address from 128.2.11.0 to 128.2.11.255 is in that block.

---

2 Note that the prefix is the equivalent to a subnet's netmask.

A number of IP addresses are either reserved or fixed by convention in network configuration. For an individual host on a network, the most important are the broadcast address, gateway, and netmask:

- IP networks are logically divided into *subnets*, collections of contiguous addresses that can all communicate with each other without the need for internal routing. When configuring an IP address, this range is specified using a *netmask*, which is an IP address with a certain number of its least significant bits zeroed out.

- To communicate outside its subnet, a host will have to talk to a router, and does so using a preconfigured *gateway address*. The gateway address is simply the IP address of the router's interface to the subnet. Gateway addresses are customarily assigned the lowest value in the subnet, but this is not a requirement.

- A network's *broadcast* address is set to the subnet mask, but with all the host bits high (e.g., for a network with subnet mask 192.168.1.0, the broadcast address is 192.168.1.255). Messages sent to the broadcast address are sent to every target within the network. The broadcast address is one of a number of addresses you should *never* see outside of local network traffic. Addresses ending in .255, for lack of a better term, smell funny.

A number of IPv4 addresses are reserved for specific networking functions. These addresses are specifically intended for local use and consequently should not be seen crossing networks. The most significant are:

Local identification addresses
These belong to the 0.0.0.0/8 CIDR block (0.0.0.0–0.255.255.255). Local identification addresses are used during the startup sequence for a host that doesn't have an IP address yet.

Loopback address
The loopback address of a host is 127.0.0.1. Traffic sent to the loopback address is sent back to the host without entering the network. IANA has reserved the entire 127.0.0.0/8 CIDR block (127.0.0.0–127.255.255.255) for loopback, so as with local identification, nothing from the 127.0.0.0/8 CIDR block should be seen crossing network boundaries.[3]

RFC 1918 netblocks
RFC 1918 defines a number of netblocks for private use. These addresses can be used within local networks with the intent that they never communicate directly with the global internet. The RFC netblocks are 10.0.0.0/8, 192.168.0.0/16, and

---

3 That doesn't mean you *won't* see it, just that you *shouldn't*, and if you *do*, you should figure out a way to *stop it*. The internet is weird.

172.16.0.0/12. Addresses within these blocks are often assigned automatically by local routing tools or DHCP.

Multicast addresses

Multicast addresses are used to classify specific groups of hosts within a subnet. For example, multicast address 224.0.0.2 is the "all routers" multicast address, and all routers within the subnet will receive traffic sent there. Multicast traffic is primarily the focus of routing and other internet control protocols.

IPv6 Addresses, Their Structure, and Significant Addresses

One of the most significant changes between IPv4 and IPv6 is the number of addresses they make available. IPv6 assigns 128 bits to each address; this ensures plenty of addresses, but introduces some problems in notation.

The default format for an address is eight 16-bit hexadecimal values separated by colons, such as 2001:0010:AF3A:FB31:09A8:08A1:1098:1101. Given that this is a long and clumsy representation, addresses are usually represented using a number of shorthand conventions. When writing IPv6 addresses, apply these rules:

- Leading zeros in any group are omitted, so 01AA:0002 can be written as 1AA:2.

- Consecutive groups of zeros may be replaced with a single pair of colons, so 2001:0:0:0:0:0:0:1 is written as 2001::1. The double-colon reduction can be used only once, so 2001:0:0:0:11:0:0:1 is written as 2001::11:0:0:1.

The RIRs and IP Address Allocation

Researching an IP address often means tracing the chain of ownership to a specific organization. The process of reservation is hierarchical; at the top level, IP address allocation is controlled by the Internet Assigned Numbers Authority (*http://www.iana.org*). IANA is a department of the Internet Corporation for Assigned Names and Numbers (ICANN), the US-based nonprofit in charge of managing IP address and DNS name assignment.

IANA delegates the control of blocks of numbers to the Regional Internet Registries (RIRs), continental organizations that manage the allocation of IP addresses and autonomous system numbers within their continents. RIRs are the intermediaries between IANA and the various national and top-level domain (TLD) registrars that actually deal with the allocation of addresses (see Table 10-1).

Table 10-1. The RIRs

RIR	Domain	URL
ARIN	US and Canada	*www.arin.net*
LACNIC	Central and South America, the Caribbean	*lacnic.net*
RIPE	Europe, Russia, and the Middle East	*www.ripe.net*
APNIC	Asia and Oceana	*www.apnic.net*
AfriNIC	Africa	*www.afrinic.net*

As with IPv4, multiple IPv6 blocks are reserved for specific functions. The most important reservation at this point is 2000::/3 (as with IPv4, CIDR block notation can be used with IPv6 addresses, and the mask can extend up to 128 bits). IPv6 space is *huge*, and to help keep routes reasonably close together, *all routable traffic in IPv6 should be in the 2000::/3 block*. IANA maintains further divisions within the 2000::/3 block, as it does with the /8 registry for IPv4. The master reference is available on the IPv6 Global Unicast Address Assignments page (*http://bit.ly/ipv6-add*).

Additional address blocks of note include the ::/128 and ::1/128 blocks, which are the unspecified and loopback addresses (the equivalent of 0.0.0.0 and 127.0.0.0 for IPv4).

Of particular interest are the utility address blocks 2001:758::/29 and 2001:678::/29. 2001:758::/29 is specifically assigned to *internet exchange points* (IXPs); an IXP is a physical location where multiple ISPs interconnect with each other. 2001:678::/29 represents a block of provider-independent addresses; users can contact their RIRs directly for these addresses.

For clarity, a summary of local and unroutable addresses is provided in Table 10-2.

Table 10-2. Notable addresses

IPv4 block	IPv6 block	Description
0.0.0.0/0	::/0	Default route; addresses from this block shouldn't be seen
0.0.0.0/32	::/128	Unspecified address
127.0.0.1/8	::1/128	Loopback
192.168.0.0/16	fc00::/7	Reserved for local traffic
10.0.0.0/8	fc00::/7	Reserved for local traffic
172.16.0.0/12	fc00::/7	Reserved for local traffic
224.0.0.0/4	ff00::/8	Multicast addresses

IP Intelligence: Geolocation and Demographics

A number of database and intelligence services provide further information about an IP address. This type of augmentation data includes ownership, geolocation, and demographic information.

It's important to distinguish this augmentation data from information such as autonomous system, domain name, and WHOIS data. The latter is necessary for the upkeep of the network, and is maintained by internet organizations related to ICANN. Geolocation, demographic data, and ownership are intelligence products. The companies that produce them use a variety of mechanisms including network scanning as well as shoe-leather investigation. This leads to several important qualities:

- The intelligence updates slowly, whereas DNS names can change very rapidly. Intelligence updates require calling up entities, checking public records, and other physical efforts to find out that, say, 128.2.11.214 is no longer involved in selling car parts and is now hosting malware.

- There is always some degree of approximation. As a rule of thumb, intelligence data gets less accurate as you delve down into finer detail. Country information is usually good, but I'm moderately skeptical about city information outside of the US and Western Europe, and I never trust physical location.

- You get what you pay for. The companies that produce this data have customers who need it. Most of the companies started out providing demographic data for large websites, and it's still common to find limits on the number of queries you can conduct per license. You pay for accuracy and you pay for precision. There are free intelligence databases, but if you want to get finer detail than country codes, prepare to crack open your wallet.

The most commonly used open source reference is MaxMind's GeoIP (*http://bit.ly/geo-ip*), which provides a number of databases for city, country, region, organization, ISP, and network speed. MaxMind also provides free services in the form of "lite" databases for identifying the city and country associated with an IP address. All of its products are downloadable databases and are updated regularly. MaxMind has been providing this service for years, along with a number of APIs in Python and other scripting languages that are available to access the database.

Applied Security (*http://www.appliedsec.com*) has produced a good GeoIP library in Python (`pygeoip` (*http://bit.ly/pygeoip*), also available in `pip`). `pygeoip` works with MaxMind's commercial and free database instances. The following sample script, *pygeoip_lookup.py*, shows how the API works:

```
#!/usr/bin/env python
#
```

```
# pygeoip_lookup.py
#
# Takes any IP addresses passed to it as input,
# runs them through the MaxMind GeoIP database, and
# returns the country code.
#
# Command-line arguments:
# argv[1]: Filename for a GeoIP database from MaxMind.

include sys,string,pygeoip

gi_handle = None
try:
    geoip_dbfn = sys.argv[1]
    gi_handle = pygeoip.GeoIP(geoip_dbfn,pygeoip.MEMORY_CACHE)
except:
    sys.stderr.write("Specify a database\n")
    sys.exit(-1)

for i in sys.stdin.readlines():
    ip = i[:-1]
    cc = gi_handle.country_code_by_addr(ip)
    print "%s %s" % (ip, cc)
```

For more extensive information, options include Neustar (*http://www.neustar.biz*) and Digital Envoy's Digital Element (*http://www.digitalenvoy.com*). Both provide more precise measurement, as well as additional demographic data such as MSA (metropolitan statistical areas, contiguous areas of high population density used by the US government for statistical analysis) and NAICS (North American Industry Classification System, a numerical identifier akin to a Dewey Decimal number for business type) codes. These services are *not* cheap, however.

DNS

In a just world, each IP address would have a single DNS name, and finding the DNS name associated with an IP address would be a simple matter of consulting a database. This world is not just.

DNS is the glue that makes the internet usable by human beings. As one of the older services making the internet work, DNS overlaps with a couple of other services (particularly mail). The Domain Name System is, at this point, a distributed database that provides lookup information for a number of different relationships: DNS name to IP address, DNS name to DNS name, email address to mail server, and so on.

DNS Name Structure

A *domain name* consists of a hierarchical sequence of labels separated by periods, such as *www.oreilly.com*. Domain names become more general as you read from left to right, ending at the root domain (the root domain is ., but it's almost always implicit). Domain names do have limits. The total length of a name cannot exceed 253 characters, and individual labels are limited to 63. Finally, domain names are limited to 127 distinct labels, although the character limit should affect that far earlier.

Historically, labels were limited to a restricted subset of ASCII characters. Since 2009, it has been possible to acquire *internationalized domain names*, which are encoded using character systems such as Chinese, Greek, and so on.[4] The mechanical limits of 253 characters per name still hold, though the encoding is more complex, as discussed in Chapter 12.

NICs and Domain Name Allocation

The authority to allocate domain names, as with IP addresses, begins with ICANN. ICANN controls the root zone and defines the top-level domains that lie just below the root of the tree. As with addresses, each TLD has a managing authority referred to as a *network information center* (NIC). Each NIC establishes different policies for name allocation—for example, anyone can get a *.com* address, but only accredited educational institutions qualify for a *.edu* address. Depending on NIC policy, registration authority may be further delegated to one or more *registrars*.

IANA defines two principal categories of TLD: the country-agnostic *generic TLDs* (gTLDs), and the *country code TLDs* (ccTLDs), which are two-letter top-level domains for individual countries (e.g., *.ie* for Ireland).

ccTLDs and gTLDs have their own subdivisions. In ccTLDs are a new set of *internationalized TLDs*; these allow non-Latin characters in the name. Under gTLDs are four groupings, currently with 21 TLDs:

- *Sponsored TLDs* (sTLDs) are managed and allocated by specific top-level organizations; they include many of the classic gTLDs (*.edu*, *.gov*, *.mil*), as well as new ones such as *.mobi* (mobile providers), *.museum* (museums), and *.xxx* (pornography).
- *Generic TLDs* are now limited to *.com*, *.info*, *.net*, and *.org*.
- *Generic restricted TLDs* are unsponsored but intended for specific purposes: *.biz* is for business, *.name* is for personal names, and *.pro* for professionals.
- The *infrastructure TLD* contains the *.arpa* domain used for reverse DNS lookups.

---

4 Internationalized domain names raise the risk of homoglyphic attacks, such as creating a domain name that looks like *oreilly.com* but uses a Cyrillic O; see Chapter 12 for more information on this.

As of this writing, there are new gTLDs in the pipeline: most notably *geographic TLDs* to group together cultures, languages, cities, or other regions that aren't well served by country codes.

Each TLD has its own NIC. Table 10-3 shows the NICs for a number of commonly consulted TLDs.

Table 10-3. Notable NICs

TLD	NIC	URL
.org	Public Interest Registry	www.pir.org
.biz	Neustar	www.neustar.biz/enterprise/domain-name-registry
.com	VeriSign	www.verisigninc.com
.net	VeriSign	www.verisigninc.com
.edu	Educause	www.educause.ed
.int	IANA	www.iana.org/domains/int
.fr	AFNIC	www.afnic.fr
.uk	Nominet	www.nominet.org.uk
.ru	Coordination Center for TLD RU	www.cctld.ru/en
.cn	CNNIC	www1.cnnic.cn
.kr	KISA	www.kisa.or.kr

This hierarchy of nameservers also serves to determine which servers are *authoritative*. Top-level registries assign authority to subregistries by granting them *zones*. Each zone has one master server that maintains its domain names and is authoritative when queried, but zones can be nested in order to give different servers authority.

Forward DNS Querying Using dig

The basic DNS query tool is the *domain information groper* (dig), a command-line DNS client that enables you to query DNS servers for all of the major records. We'll begin by conducting a simple dig query:

```
$ dig oreilly.com
dig oreilly.com

; <<>> DiG 9.8.3-P1 <<>> oreilly.com
;; global options: +cmd
;; Got answer:
;; ->>HEADER<<- opcode: QUERY, status: NOERROR, id: 29081
;; flags: qr rd ra; QUERY: 1, ANSWER: 2, AUTHORITY: 0, ADDITIONAL: 0

;; QUESTION SECTION:
;oreilly.com.                    IN      A
```

```
;; ANSWER SECTION:
oreilly.com.            383     IN      A       208.201.239.101
oreilly.com.            383     IN      A       208.201.239.100

;; Query time: 10 msec
;; SERVER: 192.168.1.1#53(192.168.1.1)
;; WHEN: Sat Jul 20 19:11:17 2013
;; MSG SIZE  rcvd: 61
$ dig +short oreilly.com
208.201.239.101
208.201.239.100
```

Let's examine dig's display options, and then the structure of the DNS response. As seen in the previous example, the basic dig command provides extensive information about the query, beginning with a list of options invoked, then a DNS header, and then several sections corresponding to the query. Note the QUERY, ANSWER, AUTHORITY, and ADDITIONAL fields in the header line, and how those correspond to the lines in the corresponding sections. Because this domain returned no AUTHORITY or ADDI TIONAL records, none are shown in the output. The query is followed by a set of statistics about the query: the server, the time it took, and the size of the message.

dig provides an enormous number of output options; the previous example showed the default display. Individual sections of that display can be turned off using +nocom ments (which kills all the comments beginning with a double semicolon), +nostats (killing the statistics at the end), and +noquestion and +noanswer (to eliminate the DNS responses). +short, as illustrated at the end of the previous example, will simply remove all the cruft and show the responses.

dig is a DNS client, so the majority of information seen is from the DNS server itself. dig enables you to query different servers by using @ in the command line. For example:

```
# 8.8.8.8 is Google's public DNS server; let's query a content
# distribution network using it
$ dig @8.8.8.8 www.foxnews.com
; <<>> DiG 9.8.3-P1 <<>> @8.8.8.8 www.foxnews.com
; (1 server found)
;; global options: +cmd
;; Got answer:
;; ->>HEADER<<- opcode: QUERY, status: NOERROR, id: 18702
;; flags: qr rd ra; QUERY: 1, ANSWER: 4, AUTHORITY: 0, ADDITIONAL: 0

;; QUESTION SECTION:
;www.foxnews.com.               IN      A

;; ANSWER SECTION:
www.foxnews.com.        282     IN      CNAME   www.foxnews.com.edgesuite.net.
www.foxnews.com.edgesuite.net. 21582 IN CNAME  a20.g.akamai.net.
```

```
a20.g.akamai.net.          2       IN      A       204.245.190.42
a20.g.akamai.net.          2       IN      A       204.245.190.8

;; Query time: 141 msec
;; SERVER: 8.8.8.8#53(8.8.8.8)
;; WHEN: Sat Jul 20 19:48:01 2013
;; MSG SIZE  rcvd: 135

# Query using my default server
$ dig www.foxnews.com


; <<>> DiG 9.8.3-P1 <<>> www.foxnews.com
;; global options: +cmd
;; Got answer:
;; ->>HEADER<<- opcode: QUERY, status: NOERROR, id: 47098
;; flags: qr rd ra; QUERY: 1, ANSWER: 4, AUTHORITY: 0, ADDITIONAL: 0

;; QUESTION SECTION:
;www.foxnews.com.                  IN      A

;; ANSWER SECTION:
www.foxnews.com.           189     IN      CNAME   www.foxnews.com.edgesuite.net.
www.foxnews.com.edgesuite.net. 9699 IN    CNAME   a20.g.akamai.net.
a20.g.akamai.net.          9       IN      A       23.66.230.160
a20.g.akamai.net.          9       IN      A       23.66.230.106

;; Query time: 97 msec
;; SERVER: 192.168.1.1#53(192.168.1.1)
;; WHEN: Sat Jul 20 19:48:09 2013
;; MSG SIZE  rcvd: 135
```

As you can see, querying a CDN-moderated site (Fox News uses Akamai) results in radically different IP addresses for the same name. CDNs manipulate the DNS to ensure that caches of published data are geographically close to their target. If you don't specify the server using @, dig will default to whatever server the system is configured to use (for example, in Unix systems this is maintained in */etc/resolv.conf*).

A CDN is a caching network that makes the internet viable. Before the web, a user might visit four to five hosts in an hour; after the web, a request to a web page might launch a hundred different HTTP requests. The majority of these requests are redirected via DNS to caching servers that are located geographically nearby. CDNs add an annoying wrinkle to web analysis, because a single CDN server may host multiple websites—if a host is identified as part of a CDN, the only organization that can tell you what's on that host is the CDN provider.

Now, let's look at the DNS data. DNS is a federated database system, so queries go first to a local DNS server, which sends a response if it possesses the answer to the query. If the server doesn't have the information, it uses the hierarchical structure of the name to figure out where to send the request, waits for a response, and sends the response back. DNS supports a number of different queries, termed *resource records*

(RRs), and the options sent as part of the query specify the resource record requested as well as options for querying additional servers. The values with As or CNAMEs in the preceding response are resource records.

Note that the DNS header lists eight fields:

opcode
> This field was intended to specify a number of different actions, such as queries, inverse queries, and server status. In practice, it should always be set to QUERY. A number of other opcodes exist, but they are used to communicate information between servers.

status
> The status of the response. Three messages appear most often: NOERROR indicates that the query was successful, NXDOMAIN indicates that no domain was available, and SERVFAIL indicates that authoritative servers for the domain were unreachable.

id
> The message ID. DNS is a UDP-moderated protocol and uses message IDs to track queries and responses.

flags
> These provide information on the response; they include qr (set high for a response), aa (set high when the answer is from an authoritative server), ra (recursion desired), and rd (recursion available).

QUERY
> This field indicates that the record is simply a copy of the original request; you can see in this case that the query is echoed in what dig refers to as the QUESTION section.

ANSWER
> Contains the response.

AUTHORITY
> Reserved for records that identify other servers.

ADDITIONAL
> Provides additional information, such as the expected responses to future queries.

Additional information is very much a function of the nameserver's administrators. A common example of its use follows, where the information provides a name lookup for the mail server identified by an MX query:

```
$ dig +nostats +nocmd mx cmu.edu
;; Got answer:
;; ->>HEADER<<- opcode: QUERY, status: NOERROR, id: 30852
;; flags: qr rd ra; QUERY: 1, ANSWER: 4, AUTHORITY: 0, ADDITIONAL: 3

;; QUESTION SECTION:
;cmu.edu.                        IN      MX

;; ANSWER SECTION:
cmu.edu.                20051   IN      MX      10 CMU-MX-02.ANDREW.cmu.edu.
cmu.edu.                20051   IN      MX      10 CMU-MX-03.ANDREW.cmu.edu.
cmu.edu.                20051   IN      MX      10 CMU-MX-04.ANDREW.cmu.edu.
cmu.edu.                20051   IN      MX      10 CMU-MX-01.ANDREW.cmu.edu.

;; ADDITIONAL SECTION:
CMU-MX-03.ANDREW.cmu.edu. 20412 IN      A       128.2.155.68
CMU-MX-01.ANDREW.cmu.edu. 20232 IN      A       128.2.11.59
CMU-MX-02.ANDREW.cmu.edu. 20051 IN      A       128.2.11.60
```

Now, let's discuss what those resource records actually mean. DNS has upward of 20 resource records for different functions. The major ones are:

A

An answer record, providing the IP address associated with a particular name.

AAAA

Like A, but provides an IPv6 address for a name.

CNAME

Relates two names, a canonical name and an alias.

MX

Returns the mail server for a domain.

PTR

Points to a canonical name; mostly used for DNS reverse lookups.

TXT

Contains arbitrary text data.

NS

Describes the nameserver for an address.

SOA

Provides information about the authoritative nameserver for an address.

dig starts all resource records with the same four values: a name, a time to live (TTL), a class, and an identifier for the RR (for example: cmu.edu, 20051, IN, MX). The name is passed with the query. The TTL indicates for how long (in seconds) the value of the name can be trusted; DNS relies heavily on caching and the TTL provides instructions on when to refresh the cache. The class will almost invariably be IN (internet); other class names are possible, but outside the scope of this book.

A and AAAA (address) provide basic DNS functionality: they associate the queried name with an IP address. A records provide IPv4 addresses, and AAAA records provide IPv6 addresses. By default, dig queries for A records, while other record types are specified by adding them to the command line, as seen here:

```
$ dig +nocomment +noquestion +nostats +nocmd www.google.com
www.google.com.        55       IN       A       74.125.228.81
www.google.com.        55       IN       A       74.125.228.83
www.google.com.        55       IN       A       74.125.228.84
www.google.com.        55       IN       A       74.125.228.80
www.google.com.        55       IN       A       74.125.228.82
$ dig +nocomment +noquestion +nostats +nocmd aaaa www.google.com
www.google.com.        18       IN       AAAA    2607:f8b0:4004:802::1014
```

Note that the query to Google responds with five A records. This is an example of *round robin DNS allocation*, a common load balancing technique. In round robin allocation, the same domain name is assigned to multiple IP addresses. Consequently, when a query chooses an IP address to contact for the name, it effectively picks the name randomly from the set of targets. Round robin DNS allocation is one of many DNS hacks that make reverse lookups (IP addresses from names) incredibly annoying.

Note also the short TTL values in the response. If a particular Google server goes down, the TTL guarantees that in 55 seconds, the user has good odds of contacting another server.

Canonical name (CNAME) records are used to associate an alias to a canonical name. For example, consider lookups for *www.oreilly.com*:

```
$ dig +nocomment +noquestion +nostats +nocmd www.oreilly.com
www.oreilly.com.       3563     IN       CNAME   oreilly.com.
oreilly.com.           506      IN       A       208.201.239.101
oreilly.com.           506      IN       A       208.201.239.100
```

As this shows, the name *www.oreilly.com* actually points to *oreilly.com*. *www.oreilly.com* does *not* have an IP address; it points to *oreilly.com*, and *that* name has an IP address. Canonical names are used for shortcuts (as in the previous example), and also to manage content distribution. The example using Fox News showed how Akamai first aliases all of Fox News's sites into its own network names using CNAME.

DNS provides lookup functions for email through the agency of the mail exchange (MX) record. MX records record the addresses of mail servers for a particular domain. For example, if I want to send mail to *jbro@andrew.cmu.edu*, I can find the mail server for doing so by looking up the MX records for *cmu.edu*:

```
$ dig  +noquestion +nostats +nocmd mx cmu.edu
;; Got answer:
;; ->>HEADER<<- opcode: QUERY, status: NOERROR, id: 49880
;; flags: qr rd ra; QUERY: 1, ANSWER: 4, AUTHORITY: 0, ADDITIONAL: 2

;; ANSWER SECTION:
cmu.edu.                        21560   IN      MX      10 CMU-MX-03.ANDREW.cmu.edu.
cmu.edu.                        21560   IN      MX      10 CMU-MX-04.ANDREW.cmu.edu.
cmu.edu.                        21560   IN      MX      10 CMU-MX-01.ANDREW.cmu.edu.
cmu.edu.                        21560   IN      MX      10 CMU-MX-02.ANDREW.cmu.edu.

;; ADDITIONAL SECTION:
CMU-MX-01.ANDREW.cmu.edu. 21519 IN      A       128.2.11.59
CMU-MX-02.ANDREW.cmu.edu. 21159 IN      A       128.2.11.60
```

MX records include a server name (such as CMU-MX-03.ANDREW.cmu.edu), as well as a priority value for the email server. The weighting value is used to choose a mail server: mail clients should pick mail servers in order of ascending priority (i.e., 1 should be chosen before 10).

Of note in this example are the A records shoved into the additional section. These records resolve the CMU-MX-01 and CMU-MX-02 addresses. This reflects a conscious decision by CMU's DNS administrators to include this information and reduce the number of lookups done.

Nameserver (NS) records are used to find the authoritative nameserver for a zone. For example, for O'Reilly Media:

```
$ dig +nostat ns oreilly.com

; <<>> DiG 9.8.3-P1 <<>> +nostat ns oreilly.com
;; global options: +cmd
;; Got answer:
;; ->>HEADER<<- opcode: QUERY, status: NOERROR, id: 32310
;; flags: qr rd ra; QUERY: 1, ANSWER: 2, AUTHORITY: 0, ADDITIONAL: 0

;; QUESTION SECTION:
;oreilly.com.                   IN      NS

;; ANSWER SECTION:
oreilly.com.            3600    IN      NS      nsautha.oreilly.com.
oreilly.com.            3600    IN      NS      nsauthb.oreilly.com.
```

Now look at the NS record for a site managed by a CDN, such as Fox News again:

```
$ dig +nostat ns foxnews.com

; <<>> DiG 9.8.3-P1 <<>> +nostat ns foxnews.com
;; global options: +cmd
;; Got answer:
;; ->>HEADER<<- opcode: QUERY, status: NOERROR, id: 38538
;; flags: qr rd ra; QUERY: 1, ANSWER: 8, AUTHORITY: 0, ADDITIONAL: 5
```

```
;; QUESTION SECTION:
;foxnews.com.                          IN      NS

;; ANSWER SECTION:
foxnews.com.            300     IN      NS      usc2.akam.net.
foxnews.com.            300     IN      NS      ns1.chi.foxnews.com.
foxnews.com.            300     IN      NS      ns1-253.akam.net.
foxnews.com.            300     IN      NS      dns.tpa.foxnews.com.
foxnews.com.            300     IN      NS      usw1.akam.net.
foxnews.com.            300     IN      NS      usw3.akam.net.
foxnews.com.            300     IN      NS      asia3.akam.net.
foxnews.com.            300     IN      NS      usc4.akam.net.

;; ADDITIONAL SECTION:
usw1.akam.net.          28264   IN      A       96.17.144.195
usw3.akam.net.          50954   IN      A       69.31.59.199
asia3.akam.net.         28264   IN      A       222.122.64.134
usc4.akam.net.          28264   IN      A       96.6.112.196
usc2.akam.net.          88188   IN      A       69.31.59.199
```

Note that in this case, the authoritative nameservers are largely owned by *akam.net* (Akamai). Fox News is hosted by Akamai's CDN, and Akamai modifies the names of the hosts as necessary in order to boost performance.

Start of Authority (SOA) records contain summary information about the authoritative server for a domain. These records are most commonly encountered during failed lookups. When an address isn't found, the SOA information for that zone's server is returned instead:

```
$ dig @8.8.4.4 +multiline +nostat zlkoriongomk.com

; <<>> DiG 9.8.3-P1 <<>> @8.8.4.4 +multiline +nostat zlkoriongomk.com
; (1 server found)
;; global options: +cmd
;; Got answer:
;; ->>HEADER<<- opcode: QUERY, status: NXDOMAIN, id: 11857
;; flags: qr rd ra; QUERY: 1, ANSWER: 0, AUTHORITY: 1, ADDITIONAL: 0

;; QUESTION SECTION:
;zlkoriongomk.com.      IN A

;; AUTHORITY SECTION:
com.                    899 IN SOA a.gtld-servers.net. nstld.verisign-grs.com. (
                        1374373035 ; serial
                        1800       ; refresh (30 minutes)
                        900        ; retry (15 minutes)
                        604800     ; expire (1 week)
                        86400      ; minimum (1 day)
                        )
```

The SOA field begins with the source host, followed by a contact email address (note that the email address uses a dot rather than an at-sign as a separator). After this address comes a serial number, which indicates how many times the source file has been modified, and then timeout statistics. Note the +multiline option for dig; this will provide a multiple-line, more human-readable output for the SOA record.

The TXT field is a wildcard field used for any text output that the server administrator feels like passing. For example, Google passes strings for managing Google Apps:

```
$ dig +short txt google.com
"v=spf1 include:_spf.google.com ip4:216.73.93.70/31 ip4:216.73.93.72/31 ~all"
```

The DNS Reverse Lookup

A *reverse lookup* is the process of reconstructing a DNS name from an IP address. For example, if I want to find out who owns 208.201.139.101, I do so using dig -x:

```
$ dig +nostat -x 208.201.139.101

; <<>> DiG 9.8.3-P1 <<>> +nostat -x 208.201.139.101
;; global options: +cmd
;; Got answer:
;; ->>HEADER<<- opcode: QUERY, status: NOERROR, id: 7519
;; flags: qr rd ra; QUERY: 1, ANSWER: 1, AUTHORITY: 0, ADDITIONAL: 0

;; QUESTION SECTION:
;101.139.201.208.in-addr.arpa.   IN      PTR

;; ANSWER SECTION:
101.139.201.208.in-addr.arpa. 21600 IN  PTR     host-d101.studley.com.
```

Reverse lookups are requests to get DNS names from IP addresses. Note that the question section does not request the IP address, 208.201.139.101, but 101.139.201.208.in-addr.arpa, which lists the fields of the IP address in reverse order. When DNS does a reverse lookup, it creates a special domain name to query in the *in-addr.arpa* TLD.[5] The string of digits and periods used for a reverse lookup is the original IP address reversed. This is because DNS names and IP addresses are defined in a contradictory fashion. A DNS name becomes more finely defined (from TLD to domain to individual host) by reading from right to left, while IP addresses are more finely defined reading from left to right.

Reverse lookups are a kludge. Note that the record returned in the answer is a pointer (PTR) record. PTR records are not automatically created with the canonical A

---

5 *.arpa* officially stands for Address and Routing Parameter Area. This name is a backronym, because the abbreviation initially meant Advanced Research Projects Agency, the DoD agency that originally funded internet development.

records, but are instead registered separately by the NIC. More important, there's no requirement that a PTR record be registered, and the relationships between names and IP addresses are tenuous at best.

For example, consider a CDN. If I look up one of Fox News's IP addresses, such as 23.66.230.66, I get this:

```
$ dig +nostat +nocmd -x 23.66.230.66
;; Got answer:
;; ->>HEADER<<- opcode: QUERY, status: NOERROR, id: 56379
;; flags: qr rd ra; QUERY: 1, ANSWER: 1, AUTHORITY: 0, ADDITIONAL: 0

;; QUESTION SECTION:
;66.230.66.23.in-addr.arpa.       IN        PTR

;; ANSWER SECTION:
66.230.66.23.in-addr.arpa. 290  IN
PTR      a23-66-230-66.deploy.static.akamaitechnologies.com.
```

The CDN becomes an informational dead end; the answer from the reverse lookup has no meaningful relation to the names in the original query.

In general, DNS information is best collected at the time of the original query. The uncertainty of reverse lookups is part of the reason for this. However, even if reverse lookups worked perfectly, attackers often use very short-lived names. Where possible, record domain names as they're used (such as the URL in HTTP logs) rather than trying to reconstruct them after the fact.

Using whois to Find Ownership

While DNS can provide information on a domain's name, the meat of ownership information is provided by WHOIS. This is a federated protocol (defined in RFC 3912 (*https://tools.ietf.org/html/rfc3912*)) that lists the putative owners of DNS names. The standard whois query on a domain will return ownership and contact information for a domain, as seen in Example 10-1.

Example 10-1. A whois query for oreilly.com

```
$ whois oreilly.com

<boilerplate>

  Domain Name: OREILLY.COM
  Registrar: GODADDY.COM, LLC
  Whois Server: whois.godaddy.com
  Referral URL: http://registrar.godaddy.com
  Name Server: NSAUTHA.OREILLY.COM
  Name Server: NSAUTHB.OREILLY.COM
  Status: clientDeleteProhibited
```

```
    Status: clientRenewProhibited
    Status: clientTransferProhibited
    Status: clientUpdateProhibited
    Updated Date: 26-may-2012
    Creation Date: 27-may-1997
    Expiration Date: 26-may-2013

<more boilerplate>

    Registered through: GoDaddy.com, LLC (http://www.godaddy.com)
    Domain Name: OREILLY.COM
        Created on: 26-May-97
        Expires on: 25-May-13
        Last Updated on: 26-May-12

    Registrant:
    O'Reilly Media, Inc.
    1005 Gravenstein Highway North
    Sebastopol, California 95472
    United States

    Administrative Contact:
        Contact, Admin  nic-ac@oreilly.com
        O'Reilly Media, Inc.
        1005 Gravenstein Highway North
        Sebastopol, California 95472
        United States
        +1.7078277000      Fax -- +1.7078290104

    Technical Contact:
        Contact, Tech  nic-tc@oreilly.com
        O'Reilly Media, Inc.
        1005 Gravenstein Highway North
        Sebastopol, California 95472
        United States
        +1.7078277000      Fax -- +1.7078290104

    Domain servers in listed order:
        NSAUTHA.OREILLY.COM
        NSAUTHB.OREILLY.COM
```

You'll note that a WHOIS entry for a domain returns an enormous amount of boiler-plate information. You will also find that the information returned has no particular fixed format—WHOIS information is the electronic equivalent of 3×5 index cards. Depending on who owns the card and how they decide to administer it, you may get phone numbers and biographies, or nothing at all.

A good way to get a feel for the differences in registration is to take a look at the registration files for different countries. There is no central WHOIS database—instead, depending on the top-level domain, WHOIS information may be maintained by any of a number of WHOIS servers. For example, Russian WHOIS data (the *.ru* domain) is maintained by *whois.ripn.net*, French by *lvs-vip.nic.fr*, and Brazilian by *registro.br*. Fortunately, the good folks at *whois-servers.net* provide aliases for every country and TLD, and depending on your whois implementation, the information may be baked into the executable for you already.

At the minimum, any whois implementation will provide the ability to specify a lookup server using the -h switch. So, whois -h ru.ripn.net will query that server directly. Several whois implementations offer a country-specific -c option, making whois -c RU identical to querying *whois.ripn.net*.

In addition to providing information on domain names, whois is also useful for providing information on address allocation and ownership. If whois is called with an IP address rather than a name, like in Example 10-2, it will provide information on the organization that owns that address, often in the form of a netblock. For example, if I look up the whois information for Voila, a French search engine, I get different information based on whether I look at RIPE (the European top-level registry) or the French NIC. RIPE is informative; the French NIC is considerably less so.

Example 10-2. Using whois with an IP address

```
$ dig +short voila.fr
193.252.148.80

$ whois -h whois.ripe.net 193.252.148.80
% This is the RIPE Database query service.
% The objects are in RPSL format.
%
% The RIPE Database is subject to Terms and Conditions.
% See http://www.ripe.net/db/support/db-terms-conditions.pdf

% Note: this output has been filtered.
%       To receive output for a database update, use the "-B" flag.

% Information related to '193.252.148.0 - 193.252.148.255'

% Abuse contact for '193.252.148.0 - 193.252.148.255' is 'gestionip.ft@orange.com'

inetnum:        193.252.148.0 - 193.252.148.255
netname:        ORANGE-PORTAILS
descr:          France Telecom
descr:          internet portals for multiple services
country:        FR
admin-c:        WPTR1-RIPE
tech-c:         WPTR1-RIPE
status:         ASSIGNED PA
remarks:        for hacking, spamming or security problems send mail to
remarks:        abuse@orange.fr
mnt-by:         FT-BRX
source:         RIPE # Filtered
```

```
role:           Wanadoo Portails Technical Role
address:        France Telecom - OPF/Portail/DOP/Hebex
address:        48, rue Camille Desmoulins
address:        92791 Issy Les Moulineaux Cedex 9
address:        FR
phone:          +33 1 5888 6500
fax-no:         +33 1 5888 6680
admin-c:        WPTR1-RIPE
tech-c:         WPTR1-RIPE
nic-hdl:        WPTR1-RIPE
mnt-by:         FT-BRX
source:         RIPE # Filtered

% This query was served by the RIPE Database Query Service version 1.60.2 (WHOIS4)

$ whois -h fr.whois-servers.net 195.152.120.129
%%
%% This is the AFNIC Whois server.
%%
%% complete date format : DD/MM/YYYY
%% short date format     : DD/MM
%% version               : FRNIC-2.5
%%
%% Rights restricted by copyright.
%% See http://www.afnic.fr/afnic/web/mentions-legales-whois_en
%%
%% Use '-h' option to obtain more information about this service.
%%
%% [96.255.98.126 REQUEST] >> 195.152.120.129
%%
%% RL Net [#########] - RL IP [#########.]
```

You will find that the situation is reversed with Asian information. The APNIC WHOIS is often fairly sparse, but the WHOIS entries at the country level are usually informative.

WHOIS information is particularly useful when you can't get much useful data out of a DNS reverse lookup. If you can't find the specific domain name, you can use `whois` to at least find the block of addresses that host the domain.

DNS Blackhole Lists

Reputation information such as *DNS blackhole lists* (DNSBLs) are generated by a number of organizations as a form of threat intelligence. A DNSBL is a DNS-based IP address database used primarily as an antispam technique. The first DNSBLs were actually implemented using the Border Gateway Protocol (BGP, see Chapter 19 for more information) and were intended to actively drop routes associated with spammer IP addresses. Modern DNSBLs are instead DNS-moderated, and serve as reputation databases for email software. For example, a mail transfer agent can consult a DNSBL to determine if the sending IP is a spammer and react accordingly.

DNSBLs work by providing a reverse lookup–style functionality on their DNS servers. For example, I can look up an echo address on a DNSBL using dig:

```
$ dig 2.0.0.127.sbl.spamhaus.org

; <<>> DiG 9.8.3-P1 <<>> 2.0.0.127.sbl.spamhaus.org
;; global options: +cmd
;; Got answer:
;; ->>HEADER<<- opcode: QUERY, status: NOERROR, id: 45434
;; flags: qr rd ra; QUERY: 1, ANSWER: 1, AUTHORITY: 0, ADDITIONAL: 0

;; QUESTION SECTION:
;2.0.0.127.sbl.spamhaus.org.     IN      A

;; ANSWER SECTION:
2.0.0.127.sbl.spamhaus.org. 300 IN      A       127.0.0.2

;; Query time: 39 msec
;; SERVER: 192.168.1.1#53(192.168.1.1)
;; WHEN: Sun Jul 28 15:10:23 2013
;; MSG SIZE  rcvd: 60
```

The address I intended to query was 127.0.0.2. Note that, as with a reverse lookup, I reversed the IP address. After reversing the address, I attached it to the name of the list and query. This process is effectively a reverse lookup without relying on the hardcoded *.arpa* TLD. Instead, the response is provided by an A record provided by Spamhaus's SBL server.

DNSBLs differ depending on the list and provider. Providers may provide several different forms of lists for different categories of traffic. Different providers will also provide different policies for adding or removing addresses to or from the DNSBL. How different organizations handle *delisting* (address removal) radically impacts the character of the list. Most automatically drop an address a fixed number of days after the last abuse; others require manual intervention.

Some notable DNSBLs include:

Spam and Open Relay Blocking System (SORBS) (http://www.sorbs.net)
SORBS provides over 15 different DNSBLs that categorize hosts into a number of different behaviors. It's particularly useful for categorizing dynamic addresses such as dialup and DSL addresses through a specialized list, the Dynamic User and Host List (DUHL).

Spamhaus (http://www.spamhaus.org)
A nonprofit private company that produces a number of distinct blacklists and whitelists, Spamhaus's most commonly used lists are the Policy Block List (PBL,

for end-user addresses), Spamhaus Block List (SBL, for known spam addresses), and Exploits Block List (XBL, for hijacked IP addresses and bots). These lists are accessible as a single combined service, ZEN.

SpamCop (https://www.spamcop.net/)
> Currently owned by Cisco Systems, SpamCop began as a private effort and eventually became part of IronPort's email reputation system. Currently, SpamCop provides one public list, the SpamCop Block List (SCBL).

DNSBLs are useful for identifying hostile activity. Using a DNSBL, an analyst can determine whether a particular address has been doing something hostile elsewhere on the internet and possibly what kind of activity it was. They supplement the more basic lookup information discussed earlier by providing some idea of a site's past history.

DNSBLs are designed to be real-time tools that work primarily with mail agents, not to support forensic analysis. Records will change quickly and unpredictably, so an address may be recognized by the DNSBL as hostile at the time of an event, but be delisted when an analyst examines it later. Most of the blacklists sell some kind of feed or data dump that, for forensic purposes, is preferable.

Search Engines

Never underestimate the value of just Googling something. A good hunk of internet traffic consists of people mapping out said traffic, and it's obviously of value for the rest of us to take advantage of it. Search engines, whether universal ones such as Google or specialized ones such as Shodan, can provide you with additional contextual information about an IP address.

General Search Engines

The two most useful general-purpose search engines are Google and the Internet Archive. In the case of Google, it's omnipresent, there are a number of powerful search predicates, and you have access to cached sites. If you're actively engaged in work outside of the English language/Roman alphabet, then it helps to be familiar with international search engines such as Naver (Korea), Yandex (Russia), or Baidu (China), as well as the various language-specific Googles.

Regardless of the search engine, you want to identify predicates that will help you refine the search to find specific sites or technical terms. For example, in Google, you can literalize a search by using quotes (e.g., Googling "the google" returns the exact phrase "the google" from the Google). Other predicates of note include `site:` (which will search only for a specific domain name—handy for identifying subdomains of the same domain), `inurl:` (which looks for a string in a URL), and `cache:` (which returns the latest version of a URL from Google's cache, avoiding directly contacting the site).

After Google, the Internet Archive (*https://www.archive.org*) is useful when you're looking for context or the history of a website. If a particular domain name appears that you've never seen before, it's useful to check the archive for a history of that domain. If a site changes radically, the Internet Archive has a reasonable chance of maintaining a pre-change version. The Alrwais paper mentioned at the end of this chapter is a good example of using the Internet Archive to track changes.

Scanning Repositories, Shodan et al

Not all scanners are malicious. A number of threat intelligence groups scan the Internet on a regular basis, providing information on vulnerabilities. Notable repositories include:

Censys (https://www.censys.io)
> Censys is a scanning team that provides a search engine hosted at the University of Michigan. Censys regularly scans the entire IPv4 address space, Alexa's million busiest hosts, and other hosts for a constantly updated list of vulnerabilities.

Shodan (https://www.shodan.io)
> Shodan is the oldest internet-wide vulnerability scanning system. Currently, it markets itself as the search engine for IoT, but historically it has scanned for everything.

Both of these engines scan for a specific set of vulnerabilities, and are pretty good about listing what they look for—be aware that, particularly as a defender, their primary value is in scanning *you* rather than looking at what other sites host.

Further Reading

1. S. Alrwais et al., "Catching Predators at Watering Holes: Finding and Understanding Strategically Compromised Websites," *Proceedings of the 2016 Annual Computer Security Applications Conference (ACSAC)*, Los Angeles, CA, 2016.

2. J. Long, B. Gardner, and J. Brown, *Google Hacking for Penetration Testers*, 3rd ed. (Rockland, MA: Syngress Publishing, 2015).

3. Bishop Fox Google Hacking Diggity Project (*http://www.bishopfox.com/resources/tools/google-hacking-diggity/*).

4. ICANNWiki (*https://www.icannwiki.org*).

## PART III

Analytics

In the previous two sections of the book, we've discussed the types of data you can collect, and tools for manipulating that data. In this section, we focus on taking that data and conducting analyses on this.

Each chapter in this section focuses on a different family of mathematical and analytical techniques that can be used on data, with an emphasis on providing information that is relevant to security and operations. Chapter 11 focuses on the process of exploratory data analysis (EDA), and should be read before anything else. Chapters 12, 13, 14, and 15 are focused on constructs that can support analysis: text analysis, fumbling, volume and time analysis, and graphs. Chapters 16 and 17 discuss specific applications of data for insider threat and threat intelligence, respectively, while Chapters 18 and 19 focus on the basic problems of inventory. Finally, Chapter 20 discusses how analysis teams can work with operations floors to improve performance.

An Overview of Attacker Behavior

We need some vocabulary for talking about how attackers behave. There are a number of papers and studies on *attack models* that try to break the hacking process into discrete steps. These models range from relatively simple linear affairs to extremely detailed *attack trees* that attempt to catalog each vulnerability and exploit. I'll start by laying out a simple but flexible model that contains steps common to a majority of attacks. These are:

Reconnaissance

The attacker scouts out the target. Depending on the type of attack, reconnaissance may consist of Googling, social engineering (posting on message boards to find and befriend users of a network), or active scanning using nmap or related tools.

Subversion

The attacker launches an exploit against a target and takes control. This may be done via a remote exploit, sending a Trojan file, or even password cracking.

Configuration

The attacker converts the target into a system more suitable for his own use. This may involve disabling antivirus packages, installing additional malware, taking inventory of the system and its capabilities, and/or installing additional defenses to prevent other attackers from taking over the target.

Exploitation

The attacker now uses the host for his own purposes. The nature of exploitation varies based on the attacker's original reason for being interested in the target (discussed shortly).

Propagation

The attacker will, if possible, use the host to attack other hosts. The host may serve as an expendable proxy, attacking neighbors (for example, other hosts behind a firewall on a 192.168.0.0/16 network).

This model isn't perfect, but it's a good general description of how attackers behave without getting bogged down in technical minutiae. There are always common tweaks; for example:

- Peer-to-peer worm propagation and phishing attacks rely on passive exploits and a bit of social engineering. These attacks rely on a target clicking a link or accessing a file, which requires that the bait (the filename or story surrounding it) be attractive enough to merit a click. As I was writing this, for example, I witnessed a spate of phishing attacks using credit ratings as the bait—the earliest informed me that my credit rating had risen, while the latest batch were more ominously warning me of the consequences of a recently dropped credit rating. On peer-to-peer networks, attackers will drop Trojans with the names of current games or albums in order to attract victims. Even in this case, "surveillance" is still possible. The phishing attacks done in many APT attacks often depend on scouting out the population and posting habits of a site before identifying victims likely to respond to a crafted mail.

- Worms often merge the reconnaissance and subversion stages into one step. Some examples of this are shown later in the book (notably, in Example 13-2, where an attacker just launches exploits against well-known PHP URLs without checking to see if they actually exist).

- Insider threat attacks will often conduct reconnaissance and subversion out of band, such as by stealing another employee's password or talking with a sysadmin to find out where assets are. Don't be surprised if an insider already has all the resources they need to jump straight to exploitation, and completely ignores propagation.

When we think about attackers, we tend to think of technically literate individuals figuring out specific weaknesses on a site in order to grab files or information off of it. This is the classic example of an *interested* attacker who wants to subvert and control a particular site in order to acquire cash, data, street cred, or who knows what. They make for great stories, and they are significant threats, but they are a small fragment of the attacker population.

The vast majority of attacks today are conducted by *uninterested* attackers who want to take over as many hosts as possible and don't care about the fine details of any particular one. Uninterested attacks are largely automated; they have to be in order to tolerate their inordinately high failure rate. Because of this, the reconnaissance and subversion steps are often merged together. An automated worm may simply launch its attack against every host it encounters, regardless of whether the host is vulnerable.

Uninterested attackers rely on tools and the expectation that someone, somewhere, will be vulnerable. In most cases, they won't even be aware that a host exists until they take it over. Early examples of uninterested attackers harvested robots for DDoS networks. Botmasters would take over a dozen or so machines, install DDoS software on them, and then launch SYN floods against targets. As connectivity increased, the scope and flexibility of botnets increased as well—attackers started to install software to work as proxies, rob images from attached webcams and sell them to porn sites, install spambots, and carry out a virtually limitless catalog of other abuses.

Uninterested attackers consequently operate more like harvesters than traditional targeted attackers. A uninterested attacker runs a script, then filters through the results of that script to see what she's pulled in. A host has a webcam, and it's located in a college dorm? Porn feed. A host has a lot of disk space and a fat pipe? File server. A host is a home machine? Keylogger.

This harvest-based approach means that attackers often have little to no idea what they're taking over. In the early days of SCADA exploits, it was apparent that the attackers had no idea what they were looking at: just a Windows host with some weird applications and extra directories. Even now, it's not uncommon to see medical hardware taken over and used as a botnet.

In recent years, a host's "configuration" also includes its role: who owns it, what it's used for, and what kind of bragging rights can be acquired by bagging it. For example, if two countries share a hostile border, resident hacker rings will deface sites in the opposing country. The US Department of Defense runs literally thousands of websites, ranging from intelligence servers to grade schools. It's not hard to find a vulnerable site and then announce to the world that you've "hacked the DoD!" after the fact.

Analysts need to be aware of this balance between common, stupid, automated attacks and rarer, intelligent, targeted attacks. Smart attackers will rely on the noise generated by stupid attackers. For analysts, this impacts an economy of attention—an analyst can only process so many alerts per shift, and there are only so many effective actions that can be taken. The analytics discussed in this section will help inform these decisions.

Further Reading

1. E. Hutchins, M. Cloppert, and R. Amin, "Intelligence-Driven Computer Network Defense Informed by Analysis of Adversary Campaigns and Intrusion Kill Chains," *Proceedings of the 2011 International Conference on I-Warfare and Security*, Washington, DC, 2006.

2. S. Caltagirone, A. Pendergast, and C. Betz, "The Diamond Model of Intrusion Analysis," United States Department of Defense Defense Technical Information Center, Fort Belvoir, VA, Tech. Report No. ADA586960, July 2013.

CHAPTER 11

Exploratory Data Analysis and Visualization

Exploratory data analysis (EDA) is the process of examining a dataset without preconceived assumptions about the data and its behavior. Real-world datasets are messy and complex, and require progressive filtering and stratification in order to identify phenomena that are worth using for alarms, anomaly detection, and forensics. Attackers and the internet itself are moving targets, and analysts face a constant influx of weirdness. For this reason, EDA is a constant process.

The point of EDA is to get a better grip on a dataset before pulling out the math. To understand why this is necessary, I want to walk through a simple statistical exercise. In Table 11-1, there are four datasets, each consisting of a vector X and a vector Y. For each dataset, calculate these values:

- The mean of X and Y
- The variance of X and Y
- The correlation between X and Y

Table 11-1. Four datasets

I		II		III		IV	
X	Y	X	Y	X	Y	X	Y
10.0	8.04	10.0	9.14	10.0	7.46	8.0	6.58
8.0	6.95	8.0	8.14	8.0	6.77	8.0	5.76
13.0	7.58	13.0	8.74	13.0	12.74	8.0	7.71
9.0	8.81	9.0	8.77	9.0	7.11	8.0	8.84
11.0	8.33	11.0	9.26	11.0	7.81	8.0	8.47
14.0	9.96	14.0	8.10	14.0	8.84	8.0	7.04

I		II		III		IV	
6.0	7.24	6.0	6.13	6.0	6.08	8.0	5.25
4.0	4.26	4.0	3.10	4.0	5.39	19.0	12.50
12.0	10.84	12.0	9.13	12.0	8.15	8.0	5.56
7.0	4.82	7.0	7.26	7.0	6.42	8.0	7.91
5.0	5.68	5.0	4.74	5.0	5.73	8.0	6.89

You will find that the mean, variance, and correlation are identical for each dataset, but simply looking at the numbers should make you suspect something fishy. A visualization will show just how diverse they are. Figure 11-1 plots these sets and shows how each dataset results in a radically different distribution. The *Anscombe Quartet* was designed to show the impact of outliers (such as in dataset IV) and visualization on data analysis.

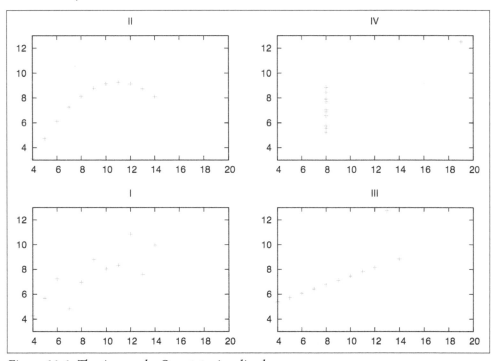

Figure 11-1. The Anscombe Quartet, visualized

As this example shows, simple visualization will identify significant features of the dataset that aren't identified by reaching for the stats. The classic mistake in statistical analysis involves pulling out the math before looking at the data. For example, analysts will often calculate the mean and standard deviation of a dataset in order to produce a threshold value (normally around 3.5 standard deviations from the mean).

This threshold is based on the assumption that the dataset is normally distributed; if it isn't (and it rarely is), then simple counting will produce more effective results.

The Goal of EDA: Applying Analysis

The point of any EDA process is to move toward a model; that model might be a formal representation of the data, or it might be as simple as "raise an alarm when we see too much stuff" (where "too much" and "stuff" are, of course, exquisitely quantified). For the purposes of information security, we have four goals: alarm construction, forensics, defense construction, and situational awareness.

When used as an alarm, an analytic process involves generating some kind of number, comparing it against a model of normal activity, and determining if the observed activity *requires an analyst's attention*. An anomaly isn't necessarily an attack, and an attack doesn't necessarily merit a response. A good alarm will be based on phenomena that are predictable under normal circumstances, that the defender can do something about, and which the attacker must disrupt to reach his goals.

The problem in operational informational security isn't *creating* alarms; it's making them manageable. The first thing an analyst has to do when she receives an alarm is provide context—validating that the threat is real, ensuring that it's relevant, determining the extent of the damage, and recommending actions to take. False positives are a significant problem, but they do not represent the whole scope of failure modes for alarms. Good analysis can increase the efficacy of alarms.

The majority of security analysis is forensic analysis, taking place after an event has occurred. Forensic analysis may begin in response to information from anywhere: alarms, IDS signals, user reports, or newspaper articles.[1]

A forensic analysis begins with some datum, such as an infected IP address or a hostile website. From there, the investigator has to find out as much as possible about the attack—the extent of the damage, other activities by the attacker, a timeline of the attack's major events. Forensic analysis is often the most data-intensive work an analyst can do, as it involves correlating data from multiple sources ranging from traffic logs to personnel interviews and looking through archives for data stored potentially years ago.

Alarms and forensic analysis are both reactive measures, but an analyst can also use data proactively and construct defenses. As analysts, we have a set of tools, such as policy recommendations, firewall rules, and authentication, that can be used to implement defenses. The challenge when doing so is that these measures are funda-

---

1 There's nothing quite like the day you start an investigation based on the attacker being written up in the *New York Times*.

mentally restrictive; from the users' perspective, security is a set of rules that limit their behavior now in order to prevent some abstract bad thing from happening later.

People are always the last line of defense in information security. If security is implemented poorly or arbitrarily, it encourages an adversarial relationship between system administrators and users, and before long, everything is moving on port 80. Analysis can be used to determine reasonable constraints that will limit attackers without imposing an undue burden on users.

Alarms, forensics, and remediation are all focused on the attack cycle—detecting attacks, understanding attacks, and recovering from attacks. Throughout this cycle, however, there is a constant dependence on knowledge management. Knowledge management in the form of inventories, past history, lookup data, and even phone books changes processes from rolling disasters into manageable disasters.

Knowledge management affects everything. For example, almost all intrusion detection systems (especially signature management systems) focus on packet contents without knowing, for example, that the IIS exploit they've helpfully identified was aimed at an Amiga 3000 running Apache.[2] In IDSs, a false positive is usually a sign that the IDS copped out early. Maintaining inventory and mapping information is a necessary first step toward developing effective alarms; many attacks are failures, and those failures can be identified through context and the alerts trashed before they annoy analysts.

Good inventory and past history data can also be used to speed up a forensic investigation. Many forensic analyses are cross-referencing different data sources in order to provide context, and this information is predictable. For example, if I have an internal IP address, I'll want to know who owns it and what software it's running.

Knowledge management requires pulling data from a number of discrete sources and putting it in one place. Information like ASNs, WHOIS data, and even simple phone numbers is often stored in dozens if not hundreds of variably maintained databases and subject to local restrictions and politics. Internal network status is often just as chaotic, if not more so, because almost invariably people are running services on the network that nobody knows about. Often, the very process of identifying assets will help network management and IT concerns in general.

As you look at data, keep in mind the goals of the data analysis. In the end, you have to figure out what the process is for—whether it's an alarm, timeline reconstruction, or figuring out whether you can introduce a firewall rule without dealing with pitchforks and torches.

---

2 It still exists.

EDA Workflow

Figure 11-2 is a workflow diagram for EDA in infosec. As this workflow shows, the core EDA process is a loop involving applying EDA techniques, extracting phenomena, and analyzing them in more depth. EDA begins with a question, which can be as open-ended as "What does typical activity look like?" The question drives the process of data selection. For example, addressing a question such as "Can BitTorrent traffic be identified by packet size?" could involve selecting traffic communicating with known BitTorrent trackers or traffic that communicated on ports 6881–6889 (the common BitTorrent ports).

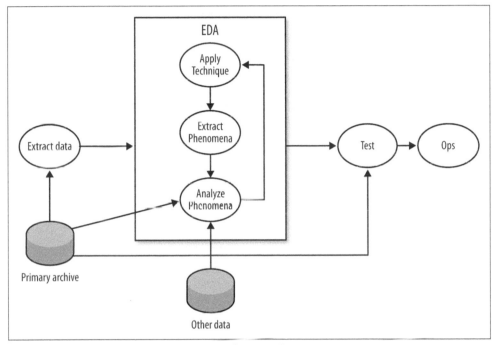

Figure 11-2. A workflow for exploratory data analysis

In the EDA loop, an analyst repeats three steps: summarizing and examining the data using a technique, identifying phenomena in the data, and then examining those phenomena in more depth. An *EDA technique* is a process for taking a dataset and summarizing it in some way that allows a *person* to identify phenomena worth investigating. Many EDA techniques are visualizations, and the majority of this chapter is focused on visual tools. Other EDA techniques include data-mining approaches such as clustering, and classic statistical techniques such as regression analysis.

EDA techniques provide behavioral cues that can then be used to go back to the original data, extract particular phenomena from that dataset and examine them in more depth. For example, looking at port 6881–6889 traffic, an analyst finds that hosts often have flows containing between 50 and 200 bytes of payload. Using that information, he goes back to the original data and uses Wireshark to find out that those packets are BitTorrent control packets.

This technique–extract–analyze process can be repeated indefinitely; finding phenomena and knowing when to stop are arts learned through experience. Analysis involves an enormous number of false positives because the most effective initial formulations are broad and prone to false positives. The EDA process will often require looking at multiple data sources. For example, an analyst looking at BitTorrent data could consult the protocol definition or run a BitTorrent client himself to determine whether the properties observed in the data hold true.

At some point, the EDA process has to stop. On the completion of EDA, an analyst will usually have multiple potential mechanisms for answering the initial question. For example, when looking for periodic phenomena such as dial-homes to botnet command and control (C&C) servers, it's possible to use autocorrelation, Fourier analysis, or simply count time in bins. Once an analyst has options, the real question is which one to use, which is determined by a process usually driven by testing and operational demand.

The testing process should take the techniques developed during EDA and determine which ones are most suitable for operational use. This phase of the process involves constructing alarms and reports.

Variables and Visualization

The most accessible and commonly approached EDA techniques are visualizations. Visualizations are tools, and based on the type of data examined and the goal of the analysis, there are a number of specific visualizations that can be applied to the task.

In order to understand data, we have to start by understanding *variables*. A variable is a characteristic of an entity that can be measured or counted, such as weight or temperature. Variables can change between entities or over time; the height of a person changes as he ages, and different people have different heights.

There are four categories of variables, which readers who have had an elementary statistics course will be familiar with. I'll review them briefly here, in descending order of rigor:

Interval

An interval variable is one where the difference between two values is meaningful, but the ratio between two values has no meaning. In network traffic data, the start time of an event is the most common form of interval data. For example, an event may be recorded at 100 seconds after midnight, and another one at 200 seconds after midnight. The second event takes place after the first one, but it isn't meaningful to talk about it taking place "twice as long" after the first one since there's no real concept of "zero start time."

Ratio

A ratio variable is like an interval variable, but also has a meaningful form of "zero," which enables us to discuss ratio variables in terms of multiplication and division. One form of a ratio variable is the number of bytes in a packet. For example, we can have a packet with 200 bytes, and another one with 400 bytes. As with interval variables, we can describe one as larger than the other, and we can also describe the second packet as "twice as large" as the second one.

Ordinal

Data is in numerical order, but does not have fixed intervals. Customer ratings fall in this category. A rating of 5 is higher than 4, and 4 is higher than 3, so you can be assured that 5 is also higher than 3. But you can't say that the degree of customer satisfaction goes up the same from 3 to 4 and from 4 to 5. (A common error is to base calculations on this, treating ratings as interval or ratio data.)

Nominal

This data is just named rather than numeric, as the term "nominal" indicates. There is no order to it. Data of this type that you commonly track includes your hosts and your services (web, email, etc.).

Data isn't necessarily ordinal just because it's designated by numbers. Your ports are nominal data. Port 80 is not "higher" in some way than port 25; it's best just to think of the numbers as alternative names for your HTTP port, your SMTP port, etc.

Interval, ratio, and ordinal variables are also referred to as *quantitative*, while nominal variables are also called *qualitative* or *categorical*. Interval and ratio variables can be further divided into *discrete* and *continuous* variables. A discrete variable has an indivisible difference between every value, while continuous variables have infinitely divisible differences. In network traffic data, almost all data collected is discrete. For example, a packet can contain 9 or 10 bytes of payload, but nothing in between. Even values such as start time are discrete, even if the subdivisions are extremely fine. Continuous variables are generally derived in some way, such as the average number of bytes per packet.

Univariate Visualization

Based on the type of variable measured, we can choose different visualizations. The most basic visualizations are applied to *univariate* data, which consists of one observed variable per unit measured. Examples of univariate measurements include the number of bytes per packet or the number of IP addresses observed over a period.

Histograms

A *histogram* is the fundamental plot for ratio and interval data; it is a count of how often a variable takes each possible value. A histogram consists of a set of *bins*, which are discrete ranges of values, and *frequencies*. Thus, if you can receive packets at any rate from 0 to 10,000 a second, you can create 10 bins for the ranges 0 to 999, 1,000 to 1,999, and so on. A frequency is the number of times that the observed value occurred within the range of the bin.

Generating a Histogram

The base material for a histogram is a set of quantitative observations. Using the Python analytic suite, we can generate and plot a quick histogram using the plt.hist function:

```
>>> sample = np.random.normal(25,5,size=10)
>>> samplearray([ 25.02265902,  25.7679
        597 ,  21.5888752 ,  29.71095039,
        22.02452105,  29.11490268,  24.28407423,  33.92459679,
        16.30043738,  24.05680052])
>>> h = plt.hist(sample)
>>> plt.show()
```

Random number generation is supported in numpy's random library, which provides a standard suite of random number generators for different distributions. Plotting a histogram is done through matplotlib using the hist function. hist does a fair amount of hand-holding, automatically generating bins and scaling.[3]

Optional arguments for matplotlib functions are usually passed as keyworded arguments. For histograms, be familiar with the normed (Boolean) argument, which will convert the counts to probabilities, and bins, which takes an integer and specifies the number of bins in the histogram.

A histogram is valuable for data analysis because it helps you find structure in a variable's distribution, and structure provides material for further investigation. In the case of the histogram, that structure is generally a *mode*, the most commonly occurring value in a distribution. In a histogram, modes appear as peaks. Histogram analysis almost invariably consists of two questions:

---

3 When looking at visualization tools, you should always pay attention to scanning, bins, outliers, and other algorithmic features that the tool may handle for you automatically. With EDA, hand-holding is a *good* thing; but when you start stacking and comparing plots, you will need to exert more fingernail-grip control in order to make sure, if nothing else, that your numbers line up.

---

1. Is the distribution normal or another one I know how to use?

2. What are the modes?

As an example of this type of analysis, take a look at the histogram in Figure 11-3. This is a histogram of flow size distributions for BitTorrent sessions, showing a distinctive peak between about 78–82 bytes. This peak is defined by the BitTorrent protocol: it's the result of a BitTorrent peer asking another peer if it has a particular piece of a file, and getting back "no" as an answer.

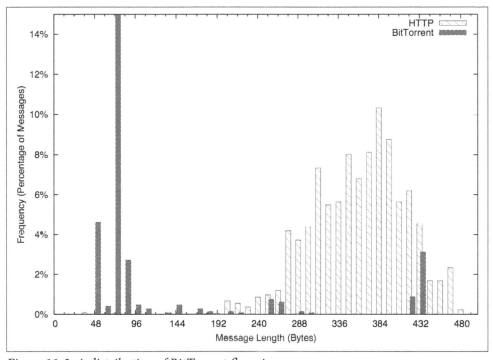

Figure 11-3. A distribution of BitTorrent flow sizes

Modes enable you to ask new questions. Once you've identified modes in a distribution, you can go back to the source data and examine the records that produced a mode. In the example in Figure 11-3, you could go back to the times in the 250–255 mode and see whether the traffic showed any distinctive characteristics—short flows, long flows, communications with empty addresses, and so on. Modes direct your questions.

This process of visualizing, then returning to the repository and pulling more detailed data is a good example of the iterative analysis shown in Figure 11-2. EDA is a cyclic process where analysts will return to the source (or multiple sources) repeatedly to understand why something is distinctive.

Bar Plots (Not Pie Charts)

A *bar plot* is the analog to a histogram when working with univariate qualitative data. Like a histogram, it plots the frequency of values observed in the dataset by using the heights of various bars. Figure 11-4 is an example of such a plot, in this case showing the counts of various services from network traffic data.

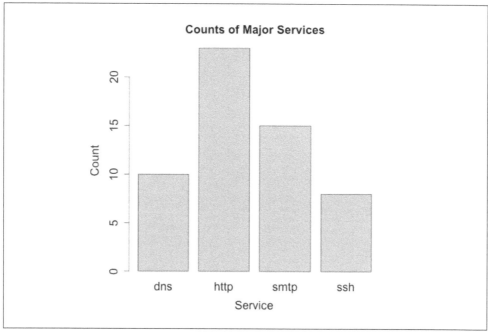

Figure 11-4. A bar plot showing the distribution of major services

The difference between bar plots and histograms lies in the binning. Qualitative data can be grouped into ranges, and in histograms, the bins represent those ranges. These bins are approximations, and the range of values they contain can be changed in order to provide a more descriptive image. In the case of bar plots, the different potential values of the data are discrete, enumerable, and often have no ordering. This lack of ordering is a particular issue when working with multiple bar plots—when doing so, make sure to keep the same order in each plot and to include zero values.

In scientific visualization, bar plots are preferred over pie charts. Viewers have a hard time differentiating fine variations in pie slice sizes—variations that are much more apparent in bar plots.

The Five-Number Summary and the Boxplot

The five-number summary is a standard statistical shorthand for describing a dataset. It consists of the following five values:

- The *minimum* value in a dataset
- The *first quartile* of the dataset
- The *second quartile* or *median* of the dataset
- The *third quartile* of the dataset
- The *maximum* value in the dataset

Quartiles are points that split the dataset into quarters, so the five numbers translate into the smallest value, the 25% threshold, the median, the 75% threshold, and the maximum. The five-number summary is a shorthand, and if you're looking at a lot of datasets very quickly, it can provide you with a quick feel for what the sets look like.

The five-number summary can be visualized using a *boxplot* (Figure 11-5), which is also called a *box-and-whiskers plot*. A boxplot consists of five lines, one for each value in the five-number summary. The center three lines are then connected as a box (the *box* of the plot), and the outer two lines are connected by perpendicular lines (the *whiskers*) of the plot.

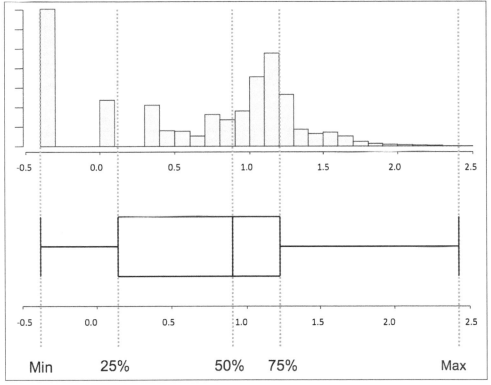

Figure 11-5. A boxplot and the corresponding histogram

Generating a Boxplot

Pandas directly provides a five-number summary via the `describe` method on a `Series`. For example:

```
>>> import numpy as np
>>> import pandas as pd
>>> data = pd.Series(np.random.normal(25,5,size=100))
>>> data.describe()
count    100.000000
mean      24.747831
std        4.905132
min       13.985350
25%       21.432594
50%       24.666327
75%       27.704180
max       36.785944
dtype: float64
```

`matplotlib` provides basic plotting functionality with `boxplot` (Figure 11-6):

```
> boxplot(data)
```

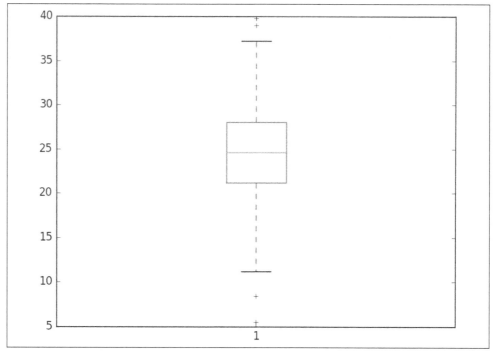

Figure 11-6. An example boxplot

Note that this plot produced a series of crosses outside the whiskers. These are *outliers*, meaning they are far outside the first and third quartiles. By default, a low value is considered an outlier if its distance to the first quartile is more than 1.5 times the interquartile range (the difference between the first and third quartiles). Similarly, a high value is considered an outlier if its distance to the third quartile is more than 1.5 times the interquartile range.

I rarely find boxplots to be useful on their own. If I'm dealing with a single variable, I'm going to get more information out of a histogram. Boxplots become more valuable when you start stacking bunches of them together—a situation where histograms are going to be just too busy to be meaningfully examined.

Bivariate Description

Bivariate data consists of two observed variables per unit measured. Examples of bivariate data include the number of bytes and packets observed in a traffic flow (which is an example of two quantitative variables), and the number of packets per protocol (an example of a quantitative and qualitative variable). The most common plots used for bivariate data are scatterplots (for comparing two quantitative variables), multiple boxplots (for comparing quantitative and qualitative variables), and contingency tables (for comparing two qualitative variables).

Scatterplots

Scatterplots are the workhorse of quantitative plots, and show the relationship between two ordinal, interval, or ratio variables. The primary challenge when analyzing scatterplots is to identify structure among the noise. Common features in a scatterplot are clusters, gaps, linear relationships, and outliers.

Let's start exploring scatterplots by looking at completely unrelated data. Figure 11-7 is an example of a noisy scatterplot, generated in this case by plotting two uniform distributions against each other. This is a boring plot.

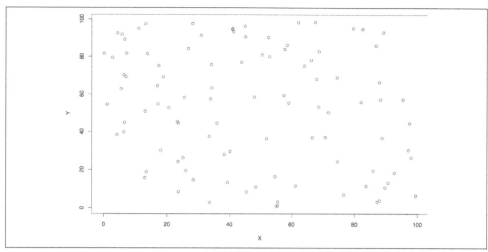

Figure 11-7. A boring scatterplot

Clusters and gaps are changes in the density of a scatterplot. The boring scatterplot in Figure 11-7 is a plot of uniform variables of unrelated density. If the two variables are related, then there should be a change in the density of the data somewhere on the plot. Figure 11-8 shows an example of clusters and gaps. In this example, there is a marked increase in activity in the lower-left quadrant, and a marked decrease in the upper-right quadrant.

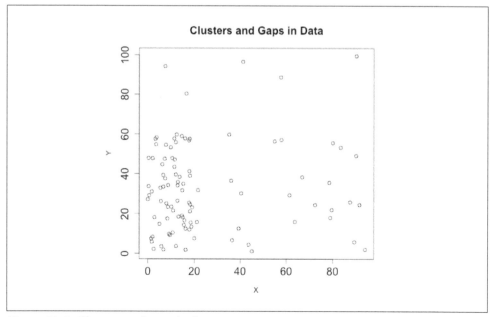

Figure 11-8. Clusters and gaps in data

Linear relationships, as the name indicates, appear in scatterplots as a line. The strength of the relationship can be estimated from the density of the points around the line. Figure 11-9 shows an example of three simple linear relationships of the form $y=kx$, but each relationship is progressively weaker and noisier.

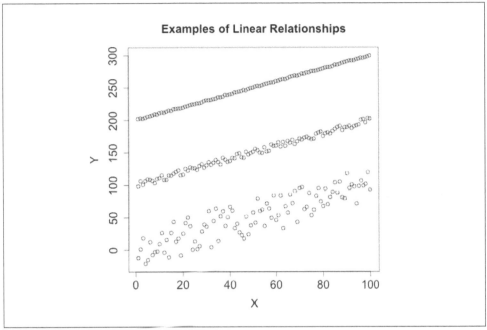

Figure 11-9. Linear relationships in data

Multivariate Visualization

A multivariate dataset is one that contains at least three variables per unit measured. Multivariate visualization is more of a technique rather than a specific set of plots. Most multivariate visualizations are built by taking a bivariate visualization and finding a way to add additional information. The most common approaches include colors or changing icons, plotting multiple images, and using animation.

Building good multivariate visualizations requires providing information from each of the datsets without drowning the reader in details. It's easy to plot a dozen different datasets on the same chart, but the results are often confusing.

The most basic approach for multivariate visualization is to overlay multiple datasets on the same chart, using different tick marks or colors to indicate the originating dataset. As a rule of thumb, you can plot about four series on a chart without confusing a reader. When picking the colors or symbols to use, keep the following in mind:

- Don't use yellow; it looks too much like white and is often invisible on printouts and monitors.

- Choose symbols that are very different from each other. I personally like the open circle, closed circle, triangle, and cross.

- Choose colors that are far away from each other on the color wheel: red, green, blue, and black are my preferred choices.

- Avoid complex symbols. Many plotting packages offer a variety of asterisk-like figures that are hard to differentiate.

- Be consistent with your color and symbol choices, and don't overlap their domains. In other words, don't decide that red is HTTP and triangles are FTP.

Animation is pretty much what it says on the tin: you create multiple images and then step through them. In my experience, animation doesn't work very well. It reduces the amount of information directly observable by an analyst, who has to correlate what's going on in her memory as opposed to visually.

Other Visualizations and Their Role

The visualizations discussed in this chapter are, so far, derived from the data represented. A number of specialized visualizations are also useful for the analyst; we will discuss them here.

Pairs plots and trellising

A *pairs plot* is a form of specialized multivariate visualization for data analysis and exploration. Given a data frame with a set of columns, a pairs plot is a stacked set of scatterplots representing every combination of columns. Pandas provides a scatterplot via its plotting tools, in the form of a `scatter_matrix` function:

```
>>> import pandas as pd
>>> import matplotlib.pyplot as plt
>>> data = pd.read_csv('voldata.csv')
>>> data.columns.values
array(['Time', 'Volume', 'Articles', 'Users'], dtype=object)
>>> axes = pd.tools.plotting.scatter_matrix(data)
>>> plt.show()
```

The result is shown in Figure 11-10. As this figure shows, the 4 columns in the array result in 16 plots, 1 for each variable pairing. Pairs plots vary in practice, and different tools will tweak the results in different ways—the default Pandas version in Figure 11-10 plots the diagonal (which consists of the variable plotted against itself) with a histogram, where other platforms may use the title, or remove the redundant plots and leave a stairstep-like visualization.

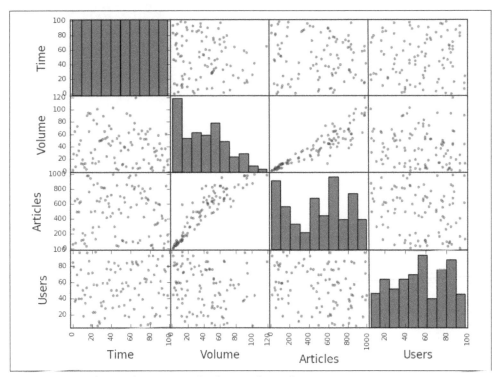

Figure 11-10. The resulting pairs plot from volume data

A pairs plot, like this one, is also a good example of *trellising*, a good technique for clearly visualizing multivariate data. A trellised plot consists of one or more small plots that are stacked adjacent to each other (horizontally, vertically, or both). Trellis plots are, in my experience, preferable to multicolor plots.

When developing trellis plots, you will have to consider how to coordinate information across multiple axes. Since trellis plots generally consist of multiple small plots, wasting space reprinting the same labels is confusing and expensive. Note that the plot in Figure 11-10 relies on the fact that the various pairs share axes in common and consequently only prints the axis labels on the outside of the plot. If you are plotting a trellis, align all the values on a common axis and provide a single label.

Spider plots

Spider plots (so called because they look like a spiderweb) are a specialized type of two-dimensional plot that plots information radially. Figure 11-11 shows an example of this type of plot: in this case, the number of active hours a host showed per day for a week.

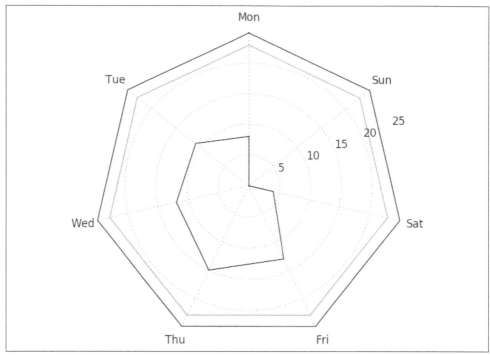

Figure 11-11. An example of a spider plot

I find spider plots most useful for visualizing cyclical data, such as activity over the course of the business cycle for several weeks, or activity per hour. Since the plot links the end of one cycle to the beginning of the next, common activity is more clearly represented than if you're looking at a set of linear plots. An alternative use of spider plots is to visualize attributes along multiple differing datasets. This approach lends itself well to trellising.

Building a spider plot in `matplotlib` requires a bit of work. An example of spider plot generation is available on the `matplotlib` website (*http://bit.ly/radar-chart*), but it requires more work than the other plots shown so far.

ROC curves

Receiver operating characteristic (ROC) curves are a form of specialized visualization associated with binary classification systems (such as most IDSs). Binary classifiers end up with one of four results when run: they either detect something that is there (a true positive), detect something that isn't there (false positive), don't detect something that is there (false negative), or don't detect something that isn't there (true negative). ROC curves evaluate the true positive and false positive rates of a detection system: the *sensitivity* of the system as a function of its (inverted) *specificity*.

Figure 11-12 shows an example of a ROC curve in action. Despite being on a two-dimensional field, ROC curves are actually three-value plots. These three values are the false positive rate, the true positive rate, and an *operating characteristic*, which is the variable you use to tune the ROC curve. In the example in Figure 11-12, the operating characteristic is the number of packets used for the threshold, and is expressed using lines pointing to the label. Depending on the plotter, ROC curves may individually label points with the operating characteristic or use pointers, as in this example.

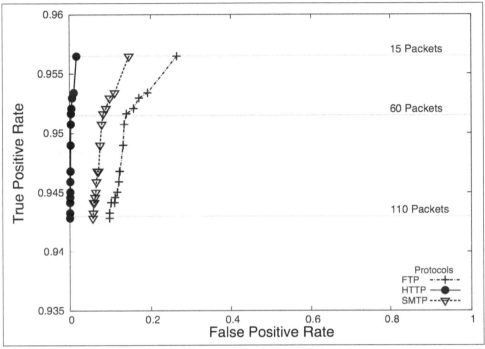

Figure 11-12. An example ROC curve

ROC curves are a common visualization technique for binary classification, but be aware that the rates used in ROC curves are conditional—the true positive rate is the probability of detecting an event *if the event happened*, and the false positive rate is the probability of detecting an event *if the event didn't happen*. Both of these rates are ultimately driven by the probability of the event happening in the first place,[4] which brings us back to the base rate problem, as discussed in Chapter 3.

---

4 This entire discussion is an exercise in conditional probabilities and Bayes' theorem.

Operationalizing Security Visualization

EDA and visualization are part of the exploratory process and, as such, are somewhat rough around the edges. The EDA process involves a large number of dead ends and false starts. During the operationalization phase of an analytic process, the visualizations will need to be modified in order to supplement action and response. Additional processing and modification are needed to polish a visualization sufficiently for it to work on the floor. The following subsections provide examples of good and bad visualizations and rules for addressing the problems of visualizing data for information security.

Rule one: Bound and partition your visualization to manage disruptions

When plotting security information, you need to expect and manage disruptions—after all, the whole point of looking for security events is to find disruptive activity. Plotting features like autoscaling can work against you by hiding data when something weird happens. For example, consider a count of anomalous events such as in Figure 11-13. This plot has two anomalies, but one is obscured by the need to plot the second.

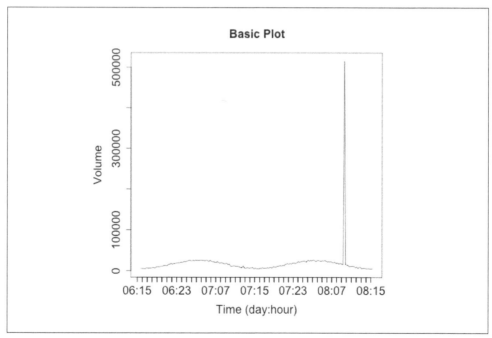

Figure 11-13. Autoscale's impact on disruptive event visualization

There are two strategies for dealing with these spikes. The first is to use *logarithmic scaling* on the dependent (y) axis. Log scaling replaces the linear scale with a logarithmic scale. For example, the ticks on the axis go from being 10, 20, 30, 40 to 10, 100, 1000, 10000. Figure 11-14 shows a logarithmic plot of the same phenomenon. Using a logarithmic scale will reduce the difference between the major anomaly and the rest of the data.

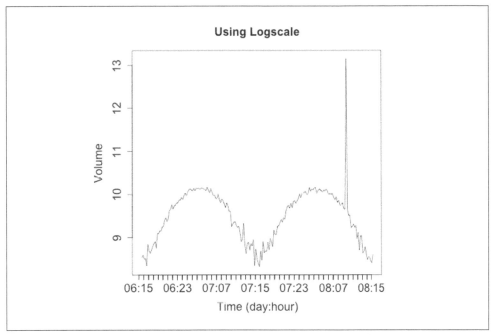

Figure 11-14. Using a log scale plot to limit the impact of large outliers

A logarithmic scale is suitable for EDA, and most tools provide an option to automatically plot data this way. With R, you pass in a `log` parameter to the plotting command to indicate which axis should be logarithmic (e.g., `log="y"`).

I don't like using logarithmic scales when developing an operational visualization, however. With logarithmic scales you tend to lose information about typical phenomena—the curve for typical traffic in Figure 11-14 is deformed by the logarithmic scale. Also, the explanation of what a logarithmic scale is a bit recondite; I don't want to have to explain logarithmic scaling over and over again. When somebody is looking at the same data repeatedly, I'd rather keep it linear.

For these reasons, I prefer to keep the scaling on a plot consistent and identify and remove outliers. When developing an operational plot, I estimate the range of the plot, and usually set the upper limit displayed to the 98th percentile of the observed data. Then, when an anomaly occurs, I plot it separately and differently from the other data to indicate that it is an anomaly. Figure 11-15 shows a simple example of this.

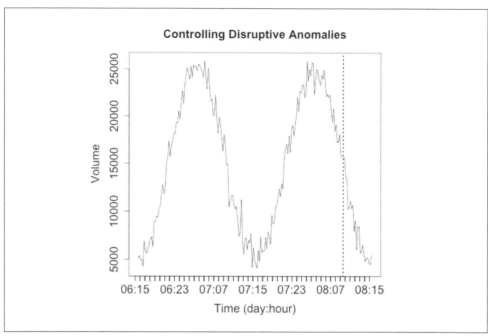

Figure 11-15. Partitioning anomalies out from normal data

The anomaly in Figure 11-15 is identified by the single line indicating that it's off the scale. The second anomaly (at 07:11) is not detected by that process, but the event is now obvious through visualization. That said, the anomaly marker is completely meaningless without further information and training, which leads into rule two.

Rule two: Label anomalies

If rule one is in place, then you've already established some basic rules for discerning anomalies from normal traffic. Now, apply those rules to identify the anomalies and modify the visualization to make them stand out for the reader.

An operational visualization is an aid to anomaly detection, so the same rules apply as for constructing IDSs (see "Prefetching Data" on page 58)—you should prefetch data to reduce the operator's response time. As an example, the anomaly in Figure 11-16 is annotated with information about what caused the anomaly as well as some statistics.

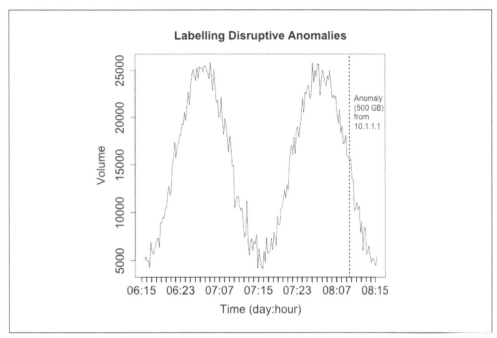

Figure 11-16. Labeling anomalies to aid investigation

Labeling anomalies on the plot can be useful for rapid reference, but if there are too many anomalies (and working off of rule one, you should expect that there will be too many anomalies), you will end up sacrificing clarity in the image. You can see this happening in Figure 11-16, where the label, while informative, is already consuming about a fifth of the horizontal space available. A better approach is to explain the anomalies in a separate table next to the visualization, which allows you to include as much data as necessary.

Rule three: Use trendlines, distinguish artifacts from observations

Operational visualizations need to balance summarization and smoothing techniques that can help the analyst process data without getting mired in details, while at the same time providing the analyst with the actual data and not thinking for him. As a result, when I operationally visualize data I prefer to include the raw data and some kind of smoothing trendline at the same time. Figure 11-17 is a simple example of this kind of visualization, where a moving average is used to smooth out the observed disruptions.

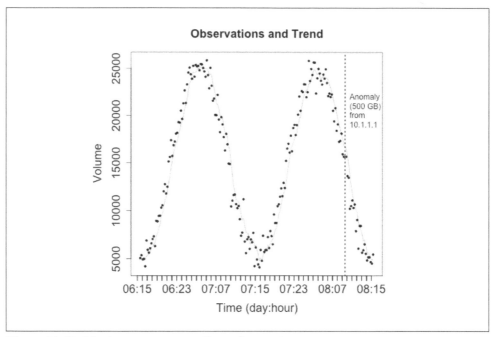

Figure 11-17. Moving average over direct observations

When creating visualizations like this, you need to ensure that the analyst can clearly differentiate between the data (the original information) and the artifacts you've created to aid analysis. You also need, as per rule one, to keep track of the impact of disruptive events—you don't want them interfering with your smoothing.

Rule four: Be consistent across plots

Visualization exploits our pattern matching capabilities. However, those capabilities just *love* to run rampant on the vaguest hint. For example, say you decide to pick a red line to represent HTTP traffic in a per-host activity. If you then decide to use a red line to represent incoming traffic in the same suite of visualizations, *somebody* is going to assume it's HTTP traffic again.

Rule five: Annotate with contextual information

In addition to labeling anomalies, it's good to include unobtrusive contextual data that can help facilitate analysis. The example shown in Figure 11-18 adds some gray bars to indicate whether activity is taking place during or outside business hours.

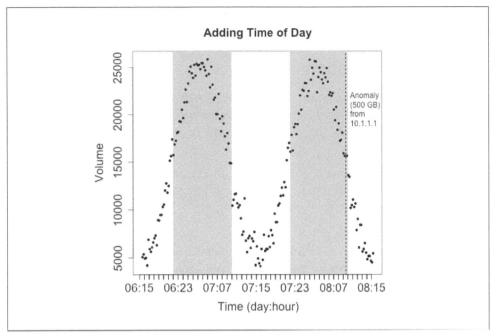

Figure 11-18. Adding some color to identify time of day

Rule six: Avoid flash in favor of expressiveness

Recognize that operational visualizations are intended to be processed quickly and repeatedly. They're not a showcase for innovative graphic representation. The goal of an operational visualization should be to express information quickly and clearly. Graphically excessive features like animation, unusual color choices, and the like will increase the time it takes to process the image without contributing information.

Be particularly careful about visualizations based on real-world or cyberspace metaphors. Whimsy wears thin *very* quickly, and we're not dealing with the physical world here. Metaphors such as "opening a desk" or "rattling all the doors in a building" (visualizations I've seen tried, and the less said about them the better) often look neat in concept, but they usually require complex interstitial animations (which take up time) and lose information because of the metaphor. Focus on simple, expressive, serious displays.

Rule seven: When performing long jobs, give the user some status feedback

When I run SiLK queries, I have a habit of running them with the `--print-file` switch active, not because I care about which files are being accessed, but in order to have an indicator of whether the process is running or the system is hung. When building visualizations, it's important to know how long it will take to complete one and to provide the user with some feedback that the visualization is actually being generated.

Fitting and Estimation

Once you've got some data, and you know how it's weird and have identified its outliers, the next step is generating some kind of estimate for it—a threshold. In this section, I'm going to discuss the general problem of estimating statistical data for information security.

The general problem is that the data doesn't fit common distributions particularly well. Data is heavy-tailed, and the results just aren't that precise.

Is It Normal?

There are a diverse family of techniques for determining whether or not a dataset is normally distributed, or, to be more precise, can be satisfactorily modeled using a normal distribution. Parametric distributions, if applicable, open up a number of tools to us. The problem is that in raw network data they're rare. Among the techniques discussed in this chapter are:

- Histograms, for visualizing the distribution
- Quantile-quantile (QQ) plots, for comparing the data against a normal distribution
- Goodness of fit tests, such as the K-S or S-W tests

Visualizations (histograms and QQ plots) are, in my opinion, the preferable option. My interest in acquiring a distribution is utilitarian. I'm looking for reasonable thresholds and something that matches a theoretical distribution well enough that I can use other tools, because I don't have the control to make very sensitive measurements. Attackers will usually be fairly easy to identify once you've picked the right metric.

The classic mistake with using means and standard distributions without looking at the data is that most network security datasets have a number of outliers. These outliers end up producing ridiculously large standard deviations, and the resulting threshold is triggered only for egregious events.

Simply Visualizing: Projected Values and QQ Plots

There are two ways to generate a visualization to test against a distribution. The first approach is to compare a histogram against a theoretical model (generally some distribution). There are a variety of ways to do this using Pandas, so I'm going to show one simple example. This example, using `matplotlib`'s `mlab` (MATLAB compatibility) module, is representative of the basic process: generate a histogram with a fixed set of bins that will serve as the x points, then generate the y values using the normpdf function, and plot the results:

```
>>> import matplotlib.pyplot as plt
>>> from scipy.stats import norm
>>> import matplotlib.mlab as mlab
>>> import numpy.random
# Generate a hundred points of normally distributed random data
# with a mean of 20 and a standard deviation of 5
>>> data = numpy.random.normal(20,5,100)
>>> n,bins,other = plt.hist(data,normed=1)
# Generate the mean and standard distribution for a model
>>> mean,sd = norm.fit(data)
>>> mean, sd
(20.596980651919221, 5.1886885182512357)
# You can just as easily do this 'by hand'
>>> yv = mlab.normpdf(bins,mean,sd)
>>> plt.plot(bins,yv,'r',linewidth=2)
[<matplotlib.lines.Line2D object at 0x113bc1990>]
>>> plt.xlabel('Value')
<matplotlib.text.Text object at 0x113f1e810>
>>> plt.ylabel('Probability')
<matplotlib.text.Text object at 0x114d8a710>
>>> plt.title('Comparison of Histogram and Model')
<matplotlib.text.Text object at 0x113f0e850>
>>> plt.show()
```

The resulting image is shown in Figure 11-19.

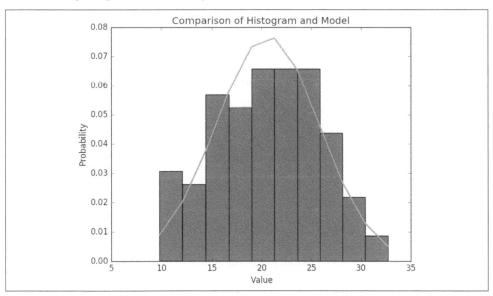

Figure 11-19. Example of comparing distributions

Straight comparison against an assumed distribution (that is, assuming a distribution is normal and plotting it just to eyeball it) is trivial. I do it by default, whatever toolkit I'm using, just so that I have some idea of what the data looks like; it's quick, but it's really just testing against one assumption. For more exploratory work, you need to use something like a QQ plot or the other visualizations discussed in this chapter.

A QQ plot compares the distributions of two variables against each other. It's a two-dimensional plot, with the x-axis being the values of one distribution normalized as quantiles, and the y-axis being values of the second distribution normalized as quantiles. For example, if I break each distribution into 100 centiles, the first point is the first percentile for each, the 50th point is the 50th percentile for each, and so on.

Figures 11-20 and 11-21 show two QQ plots, with the companion code following. These plots were generated using the `probplot` function found in the `scipy stats` library. The first plot, a normal distribution, shows the expected behavior when two similar distributions are plotted on a QQ plot—the values track the diagonal. There is some deviation but it isn't very severe. Compare the results with the uniform distribution in the second figure; in this one, significant deviations happen on the ends of the plot.

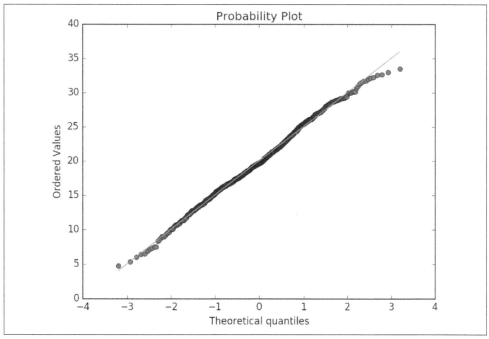

Figure 11-20. Example QQ plot against a normal distribution

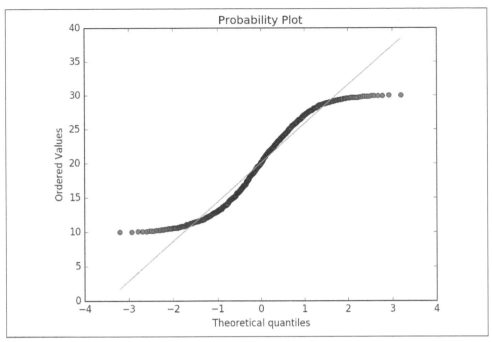

Figure 11-21. Example QQ plot against a uniform distribution

Here's the code that generates these plots:

```
# Generate normal and uniform distribution data
>>> normal = numpy.random.normal(20,5,1000)
>>> uniform = numpy.random.uniform(10,30,1000)
>>> results = stats.probplot(normal,dist='norm',plot=plt)
>>> plt.show()
>>> results = stats.probplot(uniform,dist='norm',plot=plt)
>>> plt.show()
```

The full pandas stack has QQ plotting stuffed away in a number of locations. In addition to the calls in stats, the statsmodels.qqplot function will provide a similar plot.

Fit Tests: K-S and S-W

Goodness of fit tests compare observed data against a hypothetical distribution in order to determine whether or not the data fits the distribution. Determining that a phenomenon can be satisfactorily modeled with a distribution enables you to use the distribution's characteristic functions to predict the values.

Everyone's standard approach for this is the *normal*, or *Gaussian*, distribution, also known as the bell curve. If data can be modeled by a normal distribution (and snarking aside, it's called normal because it's pretty normal), you can generate an estimate from a small sample of data and reasonably predict the probability of other values. Given a mean of μ and a standard deviation of σ, a normal distribution has a probability density function of the form:

$$\frac{1}{\sigma\sqrt{2\pi}}e^{-\frac{(x-\mu)^2}{2\sigma^2}}$$

If traffic can be satisfactorily modeled with a distribution, it provides us with a mathematical toolkit for estimating the probability of an occurrence happening. To get something that does behave that way, expect that you will have to run heavy heuristic filtering to remove the outliers, oddities, and other strange conditions.

This matters because if you use the mathematics for a model without knowing if the model *works*, then you run the risk of building a faulty sensor. There exist, and any toolkit provides, an enormous number of different statistical tests to determine whether you can use a model. For the sake of brevity, this text focuses on two tests, among a number provided by `scipy`'s stats library. These are:

Shapiro-Wilk (`shapiro.test`*)*
    The Shapiro-Wilk test is a goodness of fit test against the normal distribution. Use this to test whether or not a sample set is normally distributed.

Kolmogorov-Smirnov (`ks.test`*)*
    A goodness of fit test to use against continuous distributions such as the normal or uniform distribution.

All of these tests operate in a similar fashion: the test function is run by comparing two sample sets (either provided explicitly or through a function call). A test statistic describing the quality of the fit is generated, and a p-value produced.

The Shapiro-Wilk test is a normality test; the null hypothesis is that the data provided is normally distributed. See Example 11-1 for an example of running the test.

Example 11-1. Running the Shapiro-Wilk test

```
# Test to see whether a random normally distributed
# function passes the Shapiro test
>>> scipy.stats.shapiro(numpy.random.normal(100,100,120))
(0.9825371503829956, 0.12244515120983124)
# W = 0.98; p-value = 0.12
# We will explain these numbers in a moment
# Test to see whether a uniformly distributed function passes the Shapiro test
>>> scipy.stats.shapiro(numpy.random.uniform(1,100,120))
(0.9682766199111938, 0.006203929893672466)
```

All statistical tests produce a *test statistic* (W in the Shapiro-Wilk test), which is compared against its distribution under the null hypothesis. The exact value and interpretation of the statistic are test-specific, and the p-value should be used instead as a normalized interpretation of the value.

The Kolmogorov-Smirnov (KS) test is a simple goodness of fit test that is used to determine whether or not a dataset matches a particular continuous distribution, such as the normal or uniform distribution. It can be used either with a function (in which case it compares the dataset provided against the function) or with two datasets (in which case it compares them to each other). See the test in action in Example 11-2.

Example 11-2. Using the KS test

```
># The KS test in action; let's create two random uniform distributions
>>> scipy.stats.ks_2samp(
        numpy.random.normal(100,10,1000),
        numpy.random.normal(100,10,1000))
Ks_2sampResult(statistic=0.026000000000000023, pvalue=0.88396190167972111)
#----------------------------------------
```

The KS test has weak power. The power of an experiment refers to its ability to correctly reject the null hypothesis. Tests with weak power require a larger number of samples than more powerful tests. Sample size, especially when working with security data, is a complicated issue. The majority of statistical tests come from measurements in the natural sciences, where acquiring 60 samples can be a bit of an achievement. While it is possible for network traffic analysis to collect huge numbers of samples, the tests will start to behave wonkily with too much data; small deviations from normality will result in certain tests rejecting the data, and it can be tempting to keep throwing in more data, effectively crafting the test to meet your goals.

Further Reading

1. J. Tukey, *Exploratory Data Analysis* (London: Pearson Education, 1977).

2. E. Tufte, *The Visual Display of Quantitative Information* (Cheshire, CT: Graphics Press, 2001).

3. P. Bruce and A. Bruce, *Practical Statistics for Data Scientists* (Sebastopol, CA: O'Reilly Media, 2017).

4. R. Langley, *Practical Statistics Simply Explained* (Mineola, NY: Dover Publications, 1971).

5. W. McKinney, *Python for Data Analysis: Data Wrangling with Pandas, NumPy, and IPython*, 2nd ed. (Sebastopol, CA: O'Reilly Media, 2017).

## CHAPTER 12

On Analyzing Text

This chapter is about the general problem of analyzing security data consisting of text. Text analysis, particularly log and packet payload analysis, is a consistent unstructured task for security analysts. This chapter provides tools, techniques, and a basic workflow for dealing with the problem of semistructured text analysis.

I use the term *semistructured* to refer to data such as DNS records and logs. This contrasts with *unstructured* text (text for human consumption, like this book) in that there are well-defined rules for creating the text. With semistructured text, some enterprising developer wrote a series of logical statements and templates for generating every conceivable result. However, in comparison to fully structured data, those logical statements and templates are often opaque to the security analyst.

This chapter is divided into three main sections. The first section discusses text encoding and its impact on security data. The second section discusses basic skills that an analyst should expect to have for processing this data—this is primarily represented as a set of Unix utilities and the corresponding mechanisms in Python. The third section discusses techniques for analyzing and comparing text; these are standard text processing techniques, largely focused on the problem of finding similarity. This section also discusses security-specific text encoding problems: in particular, obfuscation and homoglyphs.

Text Encoding

Encoding refers to the rules that tell a computer that it should display the value 65 with the image *A*, and that the value 0x43E is displayed as *o*. Current systems rely heavily on the Unicode encoding standard, usually encoded as UTF-8, but in order to maintain backward compatibility, an enormous legacy infrastructure exists on top of this.

Text encoding requires managing a vast number of corner cases and legacy processing. The plethora of standards leads to ambiguity, and attackers thrive on ambiguity. Information passing between two hosts will be encoded multiple times, often implicitly. For example, HTTP supports implicit compression (usually with `gzip` or `deflate`); if your inline packet inspector isn't aware of that, then the attacker just has to kick in the right compression algorithm and continue onward. This is effectively an arms race, with the attacker looking for more obscure obfuscators and the defender looking for more defenses.[1]

Unicode is a character set—it is an index that associates each character with a single numerical value (a *code point*). An encoding is a mechanism for representing these numbers in a standardized binary form. A character is not an image; instead, it's the idea behind a family of images, the way a mathematical point is the idea behind the dot you draw on a blackboard. The equivalent of that blackboard dot is a *glyph*; glyphs are what you see on screen. A glyph is the representation of a character that is indexed by a code point.

The reason for the distinction between character and glyph is because different encoding schemes may handle the same representations very differently. Encoding schemes don't simply have to handle images—they contain control characters, possibly even sounds (the BEL character in ASCII is an example). In addition, the same glyph may be represented by radically different encodings; for example, a character such as *ä* may, depending on the encoding scheme, be represented by a code point for "a with umlaut," by an "a" followed by an umlaut, or by an "a", followed by a non-deleting backspace and an umlaut.

Finally, and this is a critical legacy issue, the distinction between a code point and its encoding is not necessarily as clear outside of the Unicode world. Unicode does not make an assumption about how code points are represented—that's a task for encoding schemes such as UTF-8 or UTF-16. Conversely, Windows code pages, macOS code pages, and the ISO standards make assumptions about numeric representation.[2]

History and legacy are important issues here. The encoding world's history is breakable into two epochs: before Unicode and after Unicode. In the pre-Unicode world, encoding standards developed within individual countries and proprietary platforms. This meant that communicating between hosts using different coding standards involved navigating multiple incompatible drivers and arcane character sets, sometimes chosen for intentional incompatibility.[3] Major computer companies also main-

---

1 The attacker will always win this race.

2 That said, UTF-8 = ASCII = ISO-Latin-1 if the value is below 128.

3 IBM, eternally content to make everyone march to its drummer, used a number of slightly different encoding schemes called EBCDIC while everyone else went toward ASCII.

tained their own standards—Apple and Microsoft have their own code page tables with distinct indices for different character sets. Incompatibilities were often so bad that software was forked just to handle a specific encoding scheme, because the assumptions of an ASCII-dominated world would cause buffer overflows when dealing with 16-bit code points. The Unicode standard was designed to deal with all of these problems. Unicode does for characters what IPv6 does for addresses—provide so many slots that everything from Amharic (U+1200) to Engsvanyali (U+E100[4]) is consistently represented.

Unicode supplanted, but did not replace, these legacy standards.[5] Today, for compatibility reasons Japanese systems and web pages will recognize JIS, Russian ones will recognize KOI8, and so on. To some extent, the world is divided into encoding standards—there are tools that Chinese-language users rely on that users who work with the Roman script will never know about, and there is malware specifically for those tools. Table 12-1 tries to unify this Babel into a coherent whole by providing a list of major character sets, their code pages, and legacy encoding schemes.

Table 12-1. Coding standards

Character set	Unicode code page	Legacy encodings	Notes
Roman	U+0000	ASCII, ISO-8859-XX, ISO-Latin-1, Mac OS Roman	ASCII isn't able to handle accent characters, so languages like French and Spanish had to move to other standards.
Chinese	U+4E00	GuoBiao, EUC-CN, Big5	The Unicode page is the CJK (Chinese-Japanese-Korean) set. GuoBiao is PRC, Big5 is Taiwan and HK.
Japanese	U+3040	JIS, EUC-JP	The code page is specifically for kana, while JIS standards include kana and kanji.
Cyrillic	U+0400	KOI8-X, Windows-1251, ISO-8859-5	This includes Russian, Ukrainian, and Tajik.
Korean	U+AC00, U+1100	EUC-KR, KS X 1001	U+AC00 is the syllabary, U+1100 is the individual jamo. North Korea has its own standard. [a]
Arabic	U+0600		U+0600 is the base set, but Arabic is scattered about the standard.

[a] KPS 9566-97.

---

4 Okay, so it's private space; it's the thought that counts.

5 You can trace the process of supplanting at *https://w3techs.com/technologies/history_overview/character_encoding/ms/y*.

Unicode, UTF, and ASCII

As noted previously, Unicode isn't an encoding scheme, it is a standard for relating code points to characters. The Unicode standard specifies up to 1,114,112 code points, each of which is stored in one of 16 65,536-point *code planes*. We care primarily about plane zero, which contains all the characters in the sets listed in Table 12-1.

Encoding, which is to say the process of actually representing the characters, is managed primarily via UTF-8 (Unicode Text Format, RFC 3629). UTF-8 is a variable-length encoding scheme specifically designed to handle a number of problems involved in transmission and in its predecessor standard, UTF-16. This means that Unicode encoding has a number of header and delimiter conventions that limit the efficiency of the system. The value 129, for instance, is going to stretch across 2 bytes. The following example shows this in action, as well as the germane Python commands:

```
# This is done in Python 2.7; the Python 3 version merges the uni*
# functions for ease of use.
>>> s=unichr(4E09)
# unichr is the Unicode equivalent of chr; note that I enter the
# hexadecimal index.  All it cares about is the index value.
>>> print(s)
三
>>> print(unichr(19977))
三
# print is important, direct text dump is going to give me the
# abstract Unicode encoding that Python uses.  Note the u and \u
# characters.  The u before the string indicates it's Unicode,
# the \u indicates it's an unsigned sixteen bit--Python effectively
# uses UTF-16 internally for representation.
>>> s
u'\u4e09'
# Now, let's convert from utf-16 to utf-8.
>>> s.encode('utf-8')
'\xe4\xb8\x89'
# Note that this is 3 bytes; a utf-8 representation includes
# overhead to describe the data provided.  Let's compare it
# with vanilla ASCII.
>>> s=u'a'
>>> print s
a
>>> s
a
# Note that we're in ASCIIland and it's treated as a default.
>>> s.encode('utf-8')
'a'
>>> ord(s)
97
```

Note that in the example, as soon as I went to the *a* character, the encoding function and everything else dropped all of the hexadecimal and integer encoding. UTF-8 is backward compatible with ASCII (American Standard Code for Information Interchange), the 7-bit[6] character encoding standard.

Encoding for Attackers

Having discussed the general role of encoding, now let's talk about the role of encoding for an attacker. For attackers, encoding is a tool for evasion, slipping information past filters intended to stop them, delaying defenders from figuring out that something is amiss. To that end, the attackers can rely on a number of different techniques to manipulate encoding, abetted by the implicit dependencies encoding strategies have.

Base64 encoding

Base encoding[7] is an encoding technique originally developed for email that currently serves as a workhorse for data transfer, including malware.

The goal of base64 encoding is to provide a mechanism for encoding arbitrary binary values using commonly recognized characters. To do so, it maps binary values to values between 0 and 63, assigns each code point a common, easily recognizable character, and then encodes the values using that character. The base64 encoding standard involves 64 code points representing the characters A–Z, a–z, and 0–9, and two characters that differ by standard—we'll say + and / for now.

Figure 12-1 shows the basic process of base64 encoding. Note that the process includes a padding convention; when working with bytes, base64 encoding neatly transfers 3 bytes into 4 characters. If your string isn't a multiple of three, you'll need to zero-pad up to three and then add equals signs at the end of the encoded string to indicate this.

---

6 Note that ASCII is a 7-bit representation. The high bit is always 0. 7 bits it shall be, and the number of bits shall be 7; if you don't believe me transfer a binary in text mode and wonder why.

7 RFC 3548 summarizes, but don't treat it like gospel; everybody tweaks.

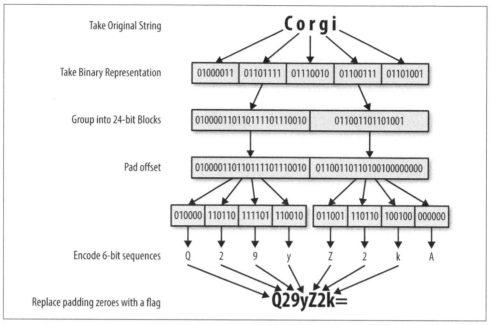

Figure 12-1. Base64 encoding in action

Base64 encoding is cheap and omnipresent; Python includes a standard library in the form of `base64`, and JavaScript has `btoa` and `atob` functions to handle it. This makes it a pretty easy and quick way to hide text directly.

In addition to base64, HTML natively supports a completely different encoding, called *numeric character references* (NCRs). Numeric character references encode values using the format &#DDDD;, where DDDD is the index of the corresponding code point in Unicode. NCRs can use decimal (e.g., 三) or hex (e.g., &#0x4E09;).

The fastest way to identify base64 is to look for characters that base64 *doesn't* cover, but which you expect to see: commas, spaces, periods, and apostrophes. Long sequences of text without those will be unusual. NCRs are recognizable by the use of ampersands.

Informal encoding/obfuscation

Introduce rules, and people are going to find ways around them. Informal encoding schemes pop up because people are looking for quick-and-dirty ways to evade a detection or filtering technique, then they become ossified and just part of a culture. There are no real rules here, just some rubrics I've seen over time that are worth at least noting.

The most common immediate tricks are simple reversals and appending. For example, it's been an old trick for years to rename *.zip* files with a *.piz* extension to trick filters into passing them. Similarly, I regularly see users just append numbers to strings.

Given enough time, substitutions can become more formal. The most common example of this is leetspeak and its cousins; whenever I see 1337 show up somewhere, I raise an eyebrow. It's not that leetspeak (properly 1337sp3ak, more properly l33tsp34k, even more properly 1337sp34|<) is an attack technique, but it's one of those forehead-slapping flags that I've run into too many times not to pay attention to. There aren't hard and fast rules for leetspeak, but there are common behaviors. 3, 4, 7, and 1 are used for *e*, *a*, *t*, and *l*; *z* is usually substituted for *s*. 0 is used to indicate *0*, *ah*, and *u* noises (as in hax0rz, pr0n, and n00bs).

Compression

An easy and robust mechanism for evading detection is to simply compress the files, maybe throwing in a garbage datafile with each instance to change the resulting compressed payload. This is not a new problem, and many deep packet inspection tools these days will include a half dozen common unpackers specifically to deal with it.

That said, the beauty of compression (for attackers) is that people are *constantly* building new compressors. It's easy for an attacker to go find a new archive format, harder for defenders to recognize that archived data is in a new format and figure out what the decompressor is. Table 12-2 is a list of common archiving formats.

Table 12-2. Common archiving formats

Name	Extension	Notes
ZIP	.zip	By far the most prevalent compression scheme, from PKZIP
GZIP	.gz	The GNU version of ZIP
TAR	.tar	TApe aRchive, not a compression scheme but a multifile archiving utility
TAR-GZIP	.tgz	TAR with GZIP, ubiquitous on Unix systems
CAB	.cab	A Microsoft archiving format including compression and certificates
ARC	.arc	ARChive format, antique but occasionally seen
UPX	.upx	Ultimate Packer for eXecutables; a PE compressor
7ZIP	.7z	An efficient but slow compression algorithm
RAR	.rar	Common on Windows systems (winRAR)
LZO	.lzo	Compact and fast

Of particular note when looking at compression algorithms are *executable compressors* such as UPX, Themida, and ASPack. These systems pack the datafile and the decompressor into a single executable package. Executable compressors are attractive because they're easily portable—the attacker can bring the whole shebang across the network rather than having to transfer a decompressor separately.

Encryption

Checking the entropy of a sample is a relatively quick-and-dirty way to identify that traffic is encrypted. Properly encrypted data should have a high entropy; there is a potential false positive in that the data may be compressed, but this should be identifiable by looking for the corresponding headers indicating the type of compression.

Basic Skills

In this section, I will review a basic set of skills for processing and manipulating text. In the field, analysts will usually work with a combination of command-line Unix tools and functions within a scripting language. Consequently, this section largely consists of examples within both environments. Both Unix and Python have an enormous number of text processing tools, and the references at the end of the chapter will provide additional reading material.

This section is skill-based rather than tool-based. That is, each subsection covers a specific problem and ways to handle it in Unix or Python.

Finding a String

The go-to tool for finding a particular string is `grep` (the generalized regular expression processor). When using `grep`, remember that its default input is regular expressions—consequently, when entering IP addresses, you can run into overmatches. For example:

```
$ grep 10.16 http_example.txt  | grep '10:16'
10.147.201.99 - - [17/Sep/2016:10:16:14 -0400] "HEAD / HTTP/1.1" 200 221 "-" "-"
10.147.201.99 - - [17/Sep/2016:10:16:16 -0400] "GET / HTTP/1.1" 200 2357 "-" "-"
$ grep 10.16 http_example.txt  | grep -v '10:16' | head -1
10.16.94.206 - - [18/Sep/2016:05:57:16 -0400] "GET
    /helpnew/faq/faq_simple_zh_CN.jsp HTTP/1.1" 404 437 "-"
    "Mozilla/5.0 (Macintosh; Intel Mac OS X 10_9_4) AppleWebKit/537.36
    (KHTML, like Gecko) Chrome/36.0.1985.125 Safari/537.36"
```

Since the . character is a wildcard in regular expressions, `grep` looks for both the address and the time signature. Ensure that you match a literal dot using the `\.` construct:

```
$ grep '10\.16' http_example.txt | head -1
10.16.94.206 - - [18/Sep/2016:05:57:16 -0400] \
    "GET /helpnew/faq/faq_simple_zh_CN.jsp HTTP/1.1" 404 437 "-" \
    "Mozilla/5.0 (Macintosh; Intel Mac OS X 10_9_4) AppleWebKit/537.36 \
        (KHTML, like Gecko) Chrome/36.0.1985.125 Safari/537.36"
```

Python strings support two searching methods: `find` and `index`. Of the two, I prefer `find` over `index` purely because `index` raises an exception when it fails to find a string. I'm intentionally avoiding discussing the `re` library for now; I'll discuss regular expressions a bit more later.

Manipulating Delimiters

The `tr` tool provides a number of handy utilities for splitting delimiters. Without other switches, `tr` will do an ordered substitution of the contents of one list with another list. Here's an example of how this works:

```
$ echo 'dog cat god' | tr 'dog' 'bat'
bat cat tab
```

As the example shows, `tr` transposes the individual characters, not the entire string. To do this in Python, you need to use a string's `.translate` method. This method takes a translation table, which is best generated using the `maketrans` function from the `string` library. Here's an example:

```
>>> from string import maketrans
>>> 'dog cat god'.translate(maketrans('dog','bat'))
'bat cat tab'
```

`tr` includes a number of other handy routines, the most important one being `-s`. The *squeeze* operation will reduce multiple copies of a specified character down to one, particularly important when working with spaces. For example:

```
$ echo 'a||b|c' | tr -s '|'
a|b|c
```

The most Pythonic way to do this is to split the series into a list, filter out empty elements, and then join the list using the original delimiter. For example:

```
>>> '|'.join(filter(bool, 'a||b|c'.split('|')))
'a|b|c'
```

Splitting Along Delimiters

`cut` is capable of splitting files along delimiters, characters, bytes, or other values as needed. To use delimiters, specify a `-d` argument and then a `-f` for the fields:

```
$ echo 'a|b|c' | cut -d '|' -f 3,1
a|c
```

Note that `-f` doesn't pay attention to the ordering—you get the fields in the order they appear in the file. Also note that the `-d` argument takes a single character.

In Python, the `.split` method converts strings to lists, after which you can manipulate them as normal. Given how Python slicing works, it's generally preferable to use the `itemgetter` function after that to get ordered elements:

```
>>> from operator import itemgetter
>>> itemgetter(2,1,5)('a|b|c|d|e|f'.split('|'))
('c', 'b', 'f')
```

In passing, NumPy arrays provide an arbitrary selection operator via double brackets
([[).

Regular Expressions

Regular expressions are the most powerful tool directly available for text analysis. In
this section, I will provide a very brief overview of their use, as well as some rules for
ensuring that they don't get out of hand. In general, my largest caution about using
regular expressions is that they are very expensive—regular expressions are effectively an interpreted programming language for matching text, and there are often
much more effective and faster mechanisms for achieving the same results, such as
tr.

A *regular expression* is a sequence of characters specifying how to match another
sequence of characters. In its simplest form, a regular expression is just a string. Here
is an example of regular expression matching in Python:

```
>>> import re
>>> re.search('foo','foobar')
<_sre.SRE_Match object at 0x100431cc8>
>>> re.search('foo','waffles')
```

Python regular expressions are implemented by the re library. As this example shows,
a successful regular expression search will return a match object; a failure of the
search function will return None.

The re library contains three key functions: search, match, and findall. search
searches through the target string and terminates on the first match; match succeeds
only on an exact match. Both search and match return match objects on success, or
None on failure. findall will search for every instance of a regular expression and
return a list of successful matches:

```
>>> re.match('foo','foobar')
<_sre.SRE_Match object at 0x100431cc8>
>>> re.match('foo','barfoo')
# Note the failure; this is because of the positioning of foo - the characters
# bar precede it.
>>> re.search('foo','foobar')
<_sre.SRE_Match object at 0x1004318b8>
>>> re.search('foo','barfoo')
<_sre.SRE_Match object at 0x100431cc8>
# Search works because it isn't an exact match
>>> re.findall('foo','foofoo')
['foo', 'foo']
```

Regular expressions provide a rich language for wildcarding. The most basic wild-cards involve the use of the ., ?, +, and * characters. . specifies a match for a single character, while the other three specify the order of the match. ? indicates zero or one instances, + one or more, and * zero or more:

```
>>> re.findall('foo.+','foo foon foobar')
['foo foon foobar']
>>> re.findall('foo.?','foo foon foobar')
['foo ', 'foon', 'foob']
>>> re.findall('foo.','foo foon foobar')
['foo foon foobar']
>>> re.findall('foo*','foo foon foobar')
['foo', 'foo', 'foo']
>>> re.findall('foo.*','foo foon foobar')
['foo ', 'foon', 'foob']
```

Instead of simply matching on one or more characters, regular expressions can be grouped into parentheses. The order characters can then be applied to the whole expression:

```
>>> re.findall('f(o)+','foo foooooo')
['o', 'o']
>>> re.findall('f(o)+','foo')
['o']
```

When you use a group, the matches will only return the characters in the group. This is handy for extracting specific terms. For example:

```
>>> re.findall('To: (.+)','To: Bob Smith <bob@smith.com>')
['Bob Smith <bob@smith.com>']
>>> re.findall('To: (.+) <','To: Bob Smith <bob@smith.com>')
['Bob Smith']
>>> re.findall('To: (.+) <(.*)>','To: Bob Smith <bob@smith.com>')
[('Bob Smith', 'bob@smith.com')]
```

Groups can also express a number of options, via a bar, and a specific number of instances by putting the range in curly braces:

```
>>> re.findall('T(a|b)','To Ta Tb To Tb Ta')
['a', 'b', 'b', 'a']
>>> re.findall('T(a){2,4}','To Ta Taa Taaa')
['a', 'a']
```

Square brackets are used to match a range of characters:

```
>>> re.findall('f[abc]','fo fa fb fo fc')
['fa', 'fb', 'fc']
```

Finally, a couple of special notes. The ^ and $ symbols are used to match the beginning and end of a string:

```
>>> re.findall('^f[o]+','foo fooo')
['foo']
```

```
>>> re.findall('f[o]+','foo fooo')
['foo', 'fooo']
>>> re.findall('f[o]+$','foo fooo fo')
['fo']
```

You can match any of the control characters (e.g., {, +, etc.) by slapping a \ in front of them:

```
>>> re.findall('a\+.','ab a+b')
['a+b']
```

That was a very basic introduction to regular expressions, but I'll also make some practical observations.

First, if you're using regular expression matching with a new tool, check to see how much regular expression parsing the tool does. At the minimum, regular expressions tend to be broken into a basic syntax, an extended syntax (ERE), and PCRE (Perl Compatible Regular Expression) syntax. The default grep tool, for example, doesn't recognize extended syntax, so the first command here produces no output:

```
$ echo 'foo' | grep 'fo.?'
$ echo 'foo' | egrep 'fo.?'
foo
```

Most modern environments will use ERE, and everything I've discussed in this chapter should work if the parser recognizes ERE. PCRE, yet more powerful, usually requires additional libraries, and there is a standard PCRE tool (pcregrep) for parsing those expressions. If you expect to be doing a lot of Unicode work, I suggest going straight to PCRE.

Second, keep notes. Outside of one-off parsing, you're most likely going to use regular expressions to repeatedly parse and normalize logfiles as part of the analysis infrastructure. The logfile format changes, regular expressions fail, and you're left trying to figure out what that string of line noise actually means. A useful aid to this documentation process is to use capture groups, to ensure that you can track what you're watching for.

Third, use regular expressions for what they're good for, and keep them simple. Matching string. is an expensive way to match string. As a rule of thumb, if I'm not doing something at least as complex as a conditional (e.g., (a|b)) or a sequence count (e.g., a{2,3}), I'm looking for a simpler approach. Regular expressions are expensive—many common tasks, such as squeezing spaces, are three to four times slower using REs.

Finally, if you're working in Python, make sure you're compiling, and know the difference between match and search and findall. Since match requires that you express the full string, it tends to necessitate a considerable amount more complexity and performance than search does.

Techniques for Text Analysis

In this section, I will discuss numerical techniques applying the tools and approaches discussed earlier in this chapter. The following techniques are a grab back of mechanisms for processing data, and are often used in combination with each other.

N-Gram Analysis

An *n-gram* is a sequence of *n* or more tokens. For example, when parsing characters in a text string, an *n*-gram will be *n* or more individual characters in sequence, such as turning "waffles" into the trigrams "waf", "aff", "ffl", "fle", and "les". The same principle can be used for words in a sentence ("I have", "have pwnd", "pwnd your", "your system") or any other token.

The key feature of *n*-gram decomposition is the use of this sliding window. *n*-gram decompositions produce a lot of strings from a single source, and the process of analyzing the *n*-grams is computationally expensive. However, *n*-gram analysis is, in my experience, a very good "I don't know what's in this data yet" technique when you're looking at previously unknown piles of text. With many of the following distance techniques, you may use them interchangeably with the original strings or with n-grams.

Jaccard Distance

Of the three comparison metrics I will discuss in this section, the Jaccard distance is the cheapest to implement, but also the least powerful. Given two strings, A and B, the Jaccard distance is calculated as the ratio of the *intersection* of A and B over the *union* of A and B. Jaccard distance is trivial to calculate using Python's set operators, as shown here:

```python
def jaccard(a,b):
    """
    Given two strings a and b, calculate the Jaccard distance
    between them as characters
    """
    set_a = set(a)
    set_b = set(b)
    return float(len((set_a.intersection(set_b))))/float(len(set_a.union(set_b)))
```

Jaccard distance is quick to implement, and it's easy to implement a very fast version of the set when you know all the potential tokens. It's also normalized: a value of 0 indicates no characters in common, and 1 indicates that all characters are in common. That said, it's not a very powerful distance metric—it doesn't account for duplicated characters, string ordering, or the presence of substrings, so the strings "foo" and "ofoffffoooo" are considered as identical as "foo" and "foo".

Hamming Distance

The Hamming distance between two strings of identical length is the total number of individual characters within those strings that differ. This is shown in Python in the following example:

```
def hamming(a,b):
    """
    Given two strings of identical length, calculate the Hamming
    distance between them.
    """
    if len(a) == len(b):
        return sum(map(lambda x:1 if x[0] == x[1] else 0, zip(a,b)))
    else:
        raise Exception, "Strings of different length"
```

Hamming distance is a powerful similarity metric. It's fast to calculate, but it's also restricted by string size, and the lack of normalization means that the values are a little vague. In addition, when you calculate a Hamming distance, you have to be very clear about what your definition of a different token is. For example, if you decide to use individual bits as a distance metric, you will find that UTF-16 encodings and UTF-8 encodings of the same strings will have different values due to the encoding overheads!

Levenshtein Distance

The Levenshtein distance between two strings is described as the minimum number of single character operations (insertions, deletions, or character substitutions) required to change one string to another string. For example, the strings "hax0r" and "hacker" have a Levenshtein distance of 3 (add a *c* before the *x*, change *x* to *k*, change *0* to *e*).

Levenshtein distance is one of those classic "let's learn dynamic programming" examples, and is a bit more complex than I want to dive into in this chapter. The leven shtein function in *text_examples.py* provides an example of how to implement this distance metric.

Levenshtein distance is sensitive to substrings and placement in ways that Hamming distance isn't. For example, the strings "hacks" and "shack" have a Hamming distance of 5 but a Levenshtein distance of 2 (add an *s* at the beginning, drop an *s* from the end). However, it's a considerably more computationally expensive algorithm to implement than Hamming distance, and you may end up paying a performance cost for identifying phenomena that are discernible using a cheaper algorithm.

An Example of Distance Metrics in Action: Fat-Fingering

A common deceptive technique involves exploiting *fat-fingering* in order to produce domains that look like well-used, legitimate domains: for example, substituting `steam community` with `sleamcommunity` or `steamcornmunity`. We should expect that different organizations will choose significantly different domain names, so if we see an excessively *similar* domain, we could expect it to be a result of intentional engineering.

To test this hypothesis, I sampled 30 domains I picked randomly from my web surfing. This isn't necessarily representative, but it's sufficient for initial exploration. I calculated the mutual Levenshtein, Hamming, and Jaccard distances for all 30 samples, plotting the distributions on the histograms in Figure 12-2.

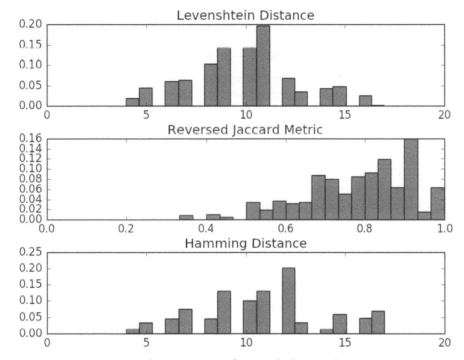

Figure 12-2. Comparative distance metrics for sample domain data

Figure 12-2 shows the Levenshtein distance, reversed Jaccard metric (i.e., 1 indicates no similarity, 0 indicates identical strings), and Hamming distance. As you can see, the figures are right-biased; if the strings aren't identical, then there are usually several characters' distance between them. By comparison, a single-character substitution such as we'd expect from fat-fingering will result in a distance *below* the observed thresholds.

Entropy and Compressibility

The *entropy* (properly, Shannon entropy) of a signal is the probability that a particular character will appear in a sample of that signal. This is mathematically formulated as:

$$H(X) = -\sum_{x \in X} P(x) \log_2 P(x)$$

That is, the sum over all the observed symbols of their probabilities by their information content (the log of their entropy).

The entropy as formulated here describes the number of bits required to describe all of the characters observed in a string. So, the entropy of the string "abcd" would be 2 (there are four unique symbols), and the entropy of the string "abcedfgh" would be 3 (8 unique symbols). Signals that are high-entropy are *noisy*—they look like the data is randomly generated, as the probability of seeing any particular token is largely even. Low-entropy signals are biased toward repeated patterns; as a rule of thumb, low-entropy data is structured, has repeated symbols, and is compressible.

Natural language is low-entropy, and most logfiles are low-entropy; compressed data is high-entropy (compression is about finding entropy and exploiting it), and encrypted data is high-entropy (because the goal is to look like noise). Figure 12-3 shows this phenomenon in more depth; this figure shows the results, respectively, of compressing and encrypting data (in this case, 10,000-character samples of the complete works of Shakespeare). As the example illustrates, the entropy of natural-language text hovers at around 5 bits/character, while that of compressed and encrypted data is approximately 8 bits/character.

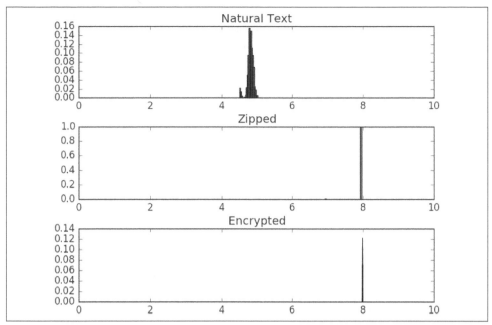

Figure 12-3. A comparison of entropy for different systems

Selectively sampling and approximating entropy is a good quick-and-dirty technique to check for compression or encryption on a dataset.

Homoglyphs

In *http_example.txt*, there's a line that reads:

```
10.193.9.88 - - [19/Sep/2016:19:36:11 -0400] "POST
/wp-loader.php HTTP/1.1" 404 380 "-" "Mozilla/5.0
(Windows NT 6.0; rv:16.0) Gecko/20130722 Firefox/16.0"
```

Let's look for it:

```
$ cat http_example.txt | grep loader
$ cat http_example.txt | grep 10.193.9.88
10.193.9.88 - - [19/Sep/2016:19:36:11 -0400] "POST
/wp-loader.php HTTP/1.1" 404 380 "-" "Mozilla/5.0
(Windows NT 6.0; rv:16.0) Gecko/20130722 Firefox/16.0"
```

What sorcery is this? The *a* in the logfile is actually the Unicode character 0x430, or the Cyrillic lowercase a. Thus, the first request returns no results. This is an example of a *homoglyph*—two code points with identical-appearing glyphs. Homoglyph attacks rely on this similarity; to the human eye the characters look identical, but they are encoded differently and an analyst grepping for the former will not find the latter.

Homoglyphs are a particular problem when dealing with the DNS. Internationalized domain names (IDNs) include mechanisms to ease the process of creating multi-code-page domain names, resulting in demonstrated attacks. Unfortunately, there's no fast and easy way to determine whether something is a homoglyph—they are literally fooling sight. Generally, the best rule of thumb is to try to work within a specific code page (such as in the US, catching anything with a character code above 127). Alternatively, there are tables of known homoglyphs (see the next section for more information) that can provide you with lists of characters to watch out for.

Further Reading

1. C. Weir, "Using Probabilistic Techniques to Aid in Password Cracking Attacks," PhD Dissertation, Dept. of Computer Science, Florida State University, Tallahassee, FL, 2010.

2. A. Das et al., "The Tangled Web of Password Reuse," *Proceedings of the 2014 Network and Distributed Security (NDSS) Symposium*, San Diego, CA, 2014.

3. W. Alcorn, C. Frichot, and M. Orru, *The Browser Hacker's Handbook* (Indianapolis, IN: John Wiley & Sons, 2014).

4. *http://www.homoglyphs.net.*

5. The Homoglyph Attack Generator (*http://www.irongeek.com/homoglyph-attack-generator.php*).

6. D. Sarkar, *Text Analytics with Python* (Berkeley, CA: Apress, 2016).

## CHAPTER 13

On Fumbling

Up to this point, we have discussed a number of techniques for collecting and analyzing data. We must now marry this with attacker behavior.

Recall from Chapter 3 the distinction between anomaly and signature detection. A focus of this book is on identifying viable mechanisms for detecting and dealing with anomalies, and to find these mechanisms, we must identify general attacker behaviors. *Fumbling*, which is the topic of this chapter, is the first of several such behaviors.

Fumbling refers to the process of systematically failing to connect to a target using a reference. That reference might be an IP address, a URL, or an email address. What makes fumbling *suspicious* is that a legitimate user should be given the references he needs. When you start at a new company, they *tell* you the name of the email server; you don't have to guess it.

Attackers don't have access to that information. They must guess, steal, or scout that data from the system, and they will make mistakes. Often, those mistakes are huge and systematic. Identifying these mistakes and differentiating them from innocent errors is a valuable first step for analysis.

In this chapter, we will look at models of normal user behavior that are violated by attackers. This chapter integrates a variety of results from previous chapters, including material on email, network traffic, and social network analysis.

Fumbling: Misconfiguration, Automation, and Scanning

We'll use the term *fumble* to refer generically to any failed attempt by a host to access a resource. A fumble in TCP means that a host wasn't able to reach a particular host address/port combination, whereas a fumble in HTTP refers to the inability to access a URL. Individual fumbles are expected and are not automatically suspicious. What's more of a concern is a tendency toward repeated fumbling. Fumbling as an aggregate behavior can happen for several reasons: an error in lookup or configuration, automated software, and scanning.

Lookup Failures

Fumbles usually happen because the destination doesn't exist in the first place. This can be a transient phenomenon due to misaddressing or movement, or it can be due to someone addressing a resource that never existed.

Keep in mind that people *rarely* enter addresses by hand. Most users will never directly enter an IP address, instead relying on DNS to moderate their communications. Similarly, apart from a TLD, users rarely enter URLs by hand, instead copying or clicking them from other applications. When someone does enter a faulty address or URL, it usually means that something further up the chain of lookup protocols that got him there failed.

When a target moves, *misaddressing* is a common phenomenon. In the case of a misaddress, the target *does* exist, but the source is misinformed about the address. For example, an attacker may enter the wrong name or IP address, or use an earlier IP address after a host moves.

Every site has unused IP addresses and port numbers. For instance, a /24 (class C) address space allows 254 addresses (2 more are reserved for special purposes), but the network usually uses only a fraction of them. An unused address or port number is called *dark space*. Legitimate users rarely try to access dark space, but attackers almost always do. However, knocking on the door of an unused IP address or port is not dangerous in itself, and is so common that tracking it isn't worthwhile.

Misaddressing is often a common mode failure, meaning that it will not be limited to one or two users, but to a large community. The classic example of a misaddress is somebody sending a message to a mailing list and mistyping a URL. When this happens, you don't see one or two errors, and you don't see individual errors. You see the exact same meaningless string occurring over and over again, coming from dozens if not hundreds of sites. If you see a large number of fumbles coming from different sites, all identical and all indicating a misspelling, then it's a good sign that the error has a common cause such as a misconfigured DNS server, a faulty redirect on the web server, or an email with the wrong URL.

Automation

People are impatient. Very often, when they can't actually reach a site, they may retry once, but then they'll go off and find something better to do with their time. Conversely, automated systems retry connections as a reliability measure, and will often return after a relatively short interval to see if the target is up and running.

On a network traffic feed, this means that a protocol that is human-driven (SSH, HTTP, Telnet) is likely to have a lower failure rate per connection than protocols that are largely automated (SMTP, peer-to-peer communications).

Scanning

Scanning is *the most common form of attack traffic observed on the network*. If you own a nontrivial chunk of IP space (say, a /24 or more), you will literally be scanned thousands of times a day.

Scanning is one of the great sources for bogus security figures. If you classify a scan as an attack, then you can claim to be dealing with thousands of attacks per day. Attacks you're going to do precisely nothing about, but still thousands. Scanning is easy, fun, and stupid amusement for script kiddies.

Imagine that your network is a two-dimensional grid, where the x-axis shows your IP addresses and the y-axis shows the ports. The grid will then have 65,536 by k cells, where k is the total number of IP addresses. Now, every time a scanner hits a target (an IP/port combination), mark a cell. If you're interested in all the capabilities of a single host, you may open up a connection to every port it has, resulting in a single vertical line on the grid: a *vertical scan*. The complement to a vertical scan is a *horizontal scan*, where the attacker communicates with every host on the network, but only on a specific port.

As a rule of thumb, defenders scan vertically and attackers horizontally. The difference is primarily opportunistic—attackers scan a network horizontally because they are uninterested in the targets *outside of the vulnerabilities they can exploit*. An attacker who *is* interested in a specific target may well scan it vertically. Defenders scan vertically because they can't predict what an attacker will hit.

If an attacker knows something about the structure of a network ahead of time, she may use a *hit list*, a list of IP addresses that she knows or suspects may be vulnerable. An example of a common hit-list attack is where the attacker begins by using a blind scan of a network to identify SSH hosts and then, sometime later, uses that list to begin password attacks.[1]

Identifying Fumbling

There are two stages to identifying the process of fumbling. The first is determining what, in a protocol, means that a user failed to correctly access a resource. In other words, what does a failed access "look" like?

---

[1] See E. Alata et al., "Lessons Learned from the Deployment of a High-Interaction Honeypot," *Proceedings of the Sixth European Dependable Computing Conference*, Coimbra, Portugal, 2006.

The second stage is determining whether the failure is consistent or transient, global or local. Fumbling false positives can include misconfigurations, transient changes to the network (such as a DNS record updating), and user mistakes. Fumbling identification requires differentiating a pattern of intent from random phenomena.

There are a number of different techniques for identifying fumbling. These include:

- Communication with dark addresses. If a host is trying to contact dark (nonexistent but routable) addresses, it's a good indication that the host doesn't know your network configuration.

- Address spread. Most hosts communicate with a small and disparate set of addresses internally. If you see hosts that are talking to a disproportionately large set of targets over a short time, that's a warning sign.

- Failed sessions. With TCP, you can examine flag combinations to see if the flow looks like a real session. If you have a payload, you can look to see if an actual service ran during the session. If a host doesn't engage in anything but the most cursory interaction, that's a good sign that it's fumbling through targets on the network.

- Spikes in ICMP alerts. If a host is contacting dark ports or hosts, odds are that you'll see a jump in ICMP traffic to the outside world providing error messages.

- Service-specific spikes. Depending on the service you're looking at, it may have "not found" messages—DNS NXDOMAIN messages, SMTP bounces, etc. A jump in these with a single source is a warning sign.

Example Data for This Chapter

This chapter will rely on the datasets *fumbling_flow.rwf* and *http_session.txt*, available in this book's GitHub repository (*https://github.com/mpcollins/nsda_examples*).

fumbling_flow.rwf is a raw file containing synthetic SSH data for a 10.128.5.0/24 network within an internal 10.0.0.0/8 network. The network contains one SSH server (10.128.5.24) and a small number of legitimate clients. All other hosts within the network are scanners using different approaches and operating systems.

http_session.txt is a collection of HTTP log data from a personal web server with some other attacks injected into it. This file will appear in multiple chapters. For the purposes of this chapter, the relevant parts are the failed attempts to touch various PHP and other services on the host.

IP Fumbling: Dark Addresses and Spread

Let us begin by considering fumbling at the IP level, without access to any other information provided by protocols such as TCP or services such as HTTP. At this level, there are two techniques for identifying fumbling: communication with dark addresses, and communication with excessive addresses (spread).

A dark address is any IP address within a network that does not currently host an asset. As discussed earlier, any nontrivial network will likely have dark addresses, and legitimate users have no reason to contact them. At the IP level, the best way to determine if communications were to a dark address is to maintain a network map; see Chapter 19 for an in-depth discussion on processes for doing so.

That said, a network map is not relying on actual network information—it's relying on a model of the network that was constructed some time before the event. At the most extreme end, a map of a DHCP network has a limited viable lifetime, but even a statically addressed network will see new services and hosts arrive on a regular basis. When using a network map, make sure to regularly test its integrity using one of the other techniques listed in this section.

Once you've constructed a map, it's a matter of combining the map with incoming traffic data to determine whether or not a host is communicating with a dark address. Example 13-1 shows this process using SiLK and the example datafile. In this example, we construct an IP set from the list of dark addresses, then use it to partition out legitimate users from hosts.

Example 13-1. Dark space and spread construction using SiLK

```
$ cat hosts.txt
10.128.5.8
$ rwsetbuild hosts.txt > light.set
$ cat > network.txt
10.128.5.0/24
$ rwsetbuild network.txt | rwsettool --difference - light.set > dark.set
$ rwsetcat --count-ip network.set light.set dark.set
network.set:256
light.set:1
dark.set:255
$ rwfilter --dipset=dark.set --pass=stdout fumbling_example.rwf | rwuniq --field=sip
--packets --dip-distinct | head -3
                        sIP|      Packets|dIP-Distin|
               10.3.64.3|          277|       254|
              10.45.9.23|          284|       254|
```

I use the term *spread* to refer to the number of distinct addresses a host communicates with. As a rule of thumb, individual users talk with a relatively limited number of addresses within a particular network. Figure 13-1 shows this behavior in action.

In this figure, there are seven dark and one lit addresses—the legitimate user only talks to the one lit address, while the scanners contact all eight addresses within the network. The end result is that the number of distinct IP addresses a legitimate host talks to hangs at around one address (plus or minus some error), while the scanners talk to a much higher ratio.

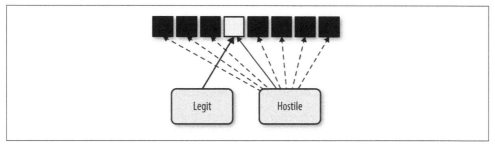

Figure 13-1. Communications with dark addresses and spread

In SiLK, you can calculate spread using `rwuniq --dip-distinct`, as shown in Example 13-1. Spread is easily estimated via histograms. The example shown in Figure 13-2 is a bit exaggerated for a legitimate network, but only in the sense that the number of scanners is too small—on large internet-facing networks, I expect SSH scanning to dwarf legitimate SSH traffic.

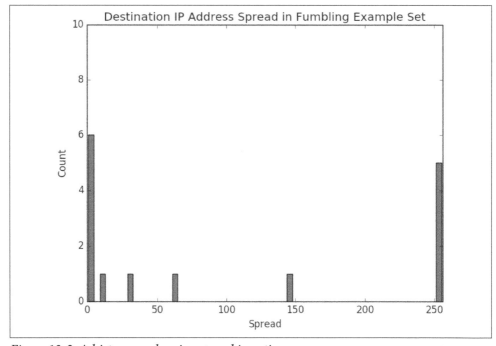

Figure 13-2. A histogram showing spread in action

TCP Fumbling: Failed Sessions

Identifying failed TCP connections requires some understanding of the TCP state machine and how it works. As we've discussed before, TCP imposes the illusion of a stream-based protocol on top of the packet-based IP. This simulation of a stream is produced using the TCP state machine, shown in Figure 13-3.

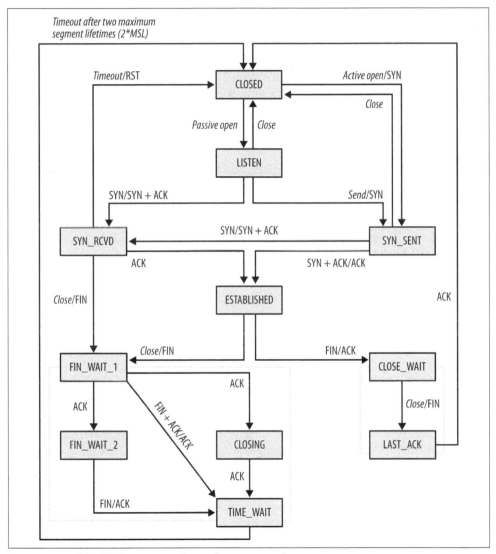

Figure 13-3. The TCP state machine, from texample.net

Under normal circumstances, a TCP session consists of a sequence of handshake packets that set up initial state:

- On the client side, the transition is from SYN_SENT (client sends an initial SYN packet) to ESTABLISHED (client receives a SYN|ACK packet from server, sends an ACK in response), and then to normal session operations.

- On the server side, the transition is from LISTEN to SYN_RCVD (receives a SYN, sends a SYN|ACK), and then to ESTABLISHED (receives an ACK).

- For either side, closure consists of at least two packets (CLOSE_WAIT to LAST_ACK or FIN_WAIT_1 to CLOSING/FIN_WAIT_2 to TIME_WAIT).

The net result of these transitions is that a well-behaved TCP/IP session requires *at least* three packets simply to set up the connection. This is overhead required by TCP, and does not include any communications done by the protocol itself. Throw in a standard MTU of 1,500 bytes, and most legitimate sessions are going to consist of at least several dozen packets.

Automated retry attempts add another layer of complexity to the problem. RFC 1122 establishes basic guidelines for TCP retransmission attempts and recommends a minimum of three retransmissions before giving up on a connection. The actual retry value is usually softcoded and stack-dependent; for example, in Linux systems, the number of retries generally defaults to three and is controlled by the `tcp_retries1` TCP variable. In Windows systems, the `TcpMaxConnectRetransmissions` registry value in *HKLM\SYSTEM\CurrentControlSet\Services\Tcpip\Parameters* governs this behavior.

An analyst can identify fumbling by looking at a variety of indicators, depending on the type of data the operator has available and the degree of accuracy necessary. I will discuss several here, such as unidirectional flow filtering, looking for dark ports, and seeing spikes in alert messages.

You Were Scanned, Here's Your Medal

At this point, scanning is so omnipresent, unstoppable, and obnoxious that it has ceased to be an attack and instead has become a form of internet weather. I can place a reasonable bet that you're mostly being scanned on TCP ports 80, 443, 22, 25, and 139 without looking at your network.

So, scanning in and of itself is uninteresting, but there is still *value* in scan detection. Primarily, this is an optimization issue. As discussed in Chapter 7, scanning data can be shunted off during postprocessing in order to reduce the number of records that an analyst encounters in the main data flow. As you monitor larger networks, the problem of scan data becomes increasingly important—a dumb scanner on a /16 will generate 65,535 flows for every port it hits. You may see eight flows for a long-lived SSH session, if you see them among all the scanning noise.

Scan removal is best done on an IP-by-IP basis, because if a host is scanning the network, it's likely not doing anything legitimate. Identify each scanning address and remove *all* traffic originating from that address. This traffic set can then be examined for trends by identifying the destination ports of the scans, determining the exploits used (if identified by your IDS), and comparing the types of scans conducted over time. Top-*n* lists are generally not particularly useful for scan trending because the top five positions have been fairly static for the past five years.

In operational environments, I generally haven't been too fussy about exactly identifying flow traffic, instead opting to use the high-pass filter approach to split TCP traffic into *short* and *long* files, and then using the long files as the default dataset for queries. On occasions when I really need to access the short files, the data is there, and the probability of a short communication actually being meaningful *and all traffic from that host being in the short file* is pretty much nonexistent.

Analytically, scan data is often more useful for identifying who *responded* to a scan than who sent it. Attackers are likely to scan your network far more actively and far more often than your own network management staff, meaning that by keeping track of the hosts that responded to scans, you will likely discover new systems and services long before your next audit.

Speculatively, there may be some value in scan trending. SANS, among other organizations, does keep track of current scanning statistics on the Internet Storm Center (*https://isc.sans.edu*). However, if there is value in trending, it has to get past the overwhelming dominance of the top five ports: ports 22, 25, 80, 443, and 139.

Unidirectional flow filtering

If you have access to both sides of a session (i.e., client to server, server to client), identifying complete sessions is simply a matter of joining the two sides together. In the absence of that information, it's still possible to guess whether packets are part of a whole session.

In my personal experience, I find flows to be more effective than individual packets for detecting fumbling. A fumbling attacker doesn't interact with a service proper because there is no payload to examine. At the same time, identifying fumbling involves looking for multiple identically addressed packets that occur around the same time, which is the textbook definition of a flow.

Depending on the amount of information needed and the precision required, a number of different heuristics can identify fumbles in TCP flows. The basic techniques involve looking at flags, packet counts, or payload size and packet count.

Flags are a good indicator of fumbling, but using them is complicated by a messy collection of corner cases happily exploited by scanners to differentiate different IP stack implementations. Recall from Figure 13-3 that a client sends an ACK flag only after receiving an initial SYN + ACK from the server. In the absence of a response, the client should not send an ACK flag; consequently, flows with a SYN and no ACK flag are a good indicator of a fumble. There exists the *potential* that a response came outside of the timeout of the flow collector, but that's rare in applied cases.

Attackers craft packets with odd flag combinations in order to determine stack and firewall configurations. The best known of these combinations is the "Christmas tree" packet (so called because all flags are lit up like a Christmas tree), setting SYN ACK FIN PUSH URG RST. Combinations of flags with both SYN and FIN high are common as well. When dealing with long-lived protocols (such as SSH), it's not uncommon to encounter a packet consisting solely of an ACK. These packets are TCP keep-alive packets and are not fumbling.

Another odd nonfumbling behavior is *backscatter*. Backscatter occurs when a host opens a connection to an existing server using a spoofed address, and the server sends the corresponding response to *the original* spoofed address. Figure 13-4 shows this in more detail, but here's a brief walkthrough of the process:

1. The host at 100.2.3.99 targets 11.65.80.99 and sends a spoofed packet claiming to be from 39.8.44.3.

2. 11.65.80.99 receives the spoofed packet and responds as normal to the IP address it sees the message originating from: 39.8.44.3.

3. 39.8.44.3 receives a packet acknowledging an open session from 11.65.80.99 and is now confused.

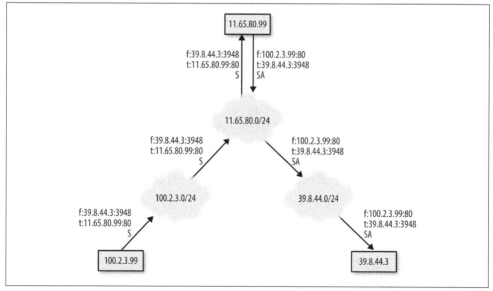

Figure 13-4. Backscatter in action

The larger a network is, the more backscatter it will receive—so much so that there are several organizations running *internet telescopes* around large dark spaces in order to estimate and characterize this network background radiation. On a large enough network, you will see enough backscatter that, at first glance, it will be confused with fumbling.

An easy, if rough, indicator of whether a flow shows a complete session is to simply look at the number of packets. A legitimate TCP session requires at least three packets of overhead before it considers transmitting service data. Furthermore, most stacks set their retry value to between three and five packets. These rules provide a simple filter: TCP flows that have five packets or less are likely to be fumbles.

Flow size can be complemented by looking at the ratio of packet size to number of packets. TCP SYN packets contain a number of TCP options (*http://bit.ly/tcp-para*) of variable length. During a failed connection, the host will send the same SYN packet options repeatedly. Consequently, if a flow is an n-packet SYN fumble, we can expect that the total number of bytes sent is $n \times (40 + k)$, where k is the total size of the options.

Dark ports and UDP fumbling

When working with TCP and UDP, you can expand the concept of dark space to include not only addresses, but ports. Scanners usually scan across a limited set of services—SSH, SMTP, anything that has a vulnerability to exploit. The number of hosts running these services is generally vanishingly small relative to the total number of addresses on the network. Using a network map, you can identify scanners using the same dark address techniques discussed for IP in general, just adding in port numbers.

Dark ports are more critical for UDP than TCP—the rubrics discussed earlier for identifying failed sessions make it possible to identify a failed TCP connection straight from the flow. It's rarely possible to identify a failed UDP connection from the UDP traffic itself. TCP has symmetry baked into the protocol, whereas UDP doesn't provide any guarantees of delivery. If a UDP *service* provides some form of symmetry or other reciprocity, that's a service-specific attribute. In order of preference, dark ports and ICMP traffic are the best ways to identify UDP fumbling.

Research Scanners

Not every small collection of packets is a scan, and not every scan is a threat. A small number of organizations regularly scan the entire internet for vulnerabilities, and they are going to show up whenever you run scan detection.[2]

---

[2] They'd better show up if you're doing scan detection!

The following is a relatively current list of such organizations. Some of these groups publish a list of their scanning addresses, and for the others those addresses will be discernible via reverse DNS lookup:

Censys
> Censys (*http://scans.io*) is a huge repository of scan data created and aggregated by the University of Michigan's Censys Group. In addition to conducting their own scans (and developing the primary internet-wide scanning tool, ZMap), the Censys site serves as a frontend for a number of other scanning repositories.

Shodan
> Shodan (*http://shodan.io*) is the oldest search engine on this list, having been in operation since 2009. It runs a scanning service that grabs host banners to determine what services are running on a host.

Project Sonar
> Run by Rapid7 (*http://www.rapid7.com*), Project Sonar is a bulk scanning effort that checks DNS records, SSL certificates, and a number of UDP vulnerabilities. Rapid7 contributes its results to Censys and maintains a wiki (*https://github.com/rapid7/sonar/wiki*) with its scanning addresses.

Shadowserver
> Shadowserver (*http://www.shadowserver.org*) is a network of volunteer computer security professionals who track botnets and other hostile internet-wide activity. They maintain a constantly updated list of what they are scanning for on their blog (*http://bit.ly/shadowserver-blog*).

ICMP Messages and Fumbling

ICMP is actually designed to inform a user that she has failed to make a connection. ICMP type 3 messages (destination unreachable) are supposed to be sent to a host to indicate that the target network (code 0), host (code 1), or port (code 3) cannot be reached by the client packet. ICMP also provides messages indicating that a route is unknown (code 7) or administratively prohibited (code 13).

With the exception of pings, ICMP messages appear in *response* to failures in other protocols. Several messages, such as host or net unreachable, originate from some point other than the destination address—generally the nearest router. ICMP messages may also be filtered, depending on the policies of the network in question, and consequently not received by your sensors.

This asymmetry means that when tracking fumbling from ICMP traffic, it is more productive to look for the responses. If you see a sudden spike in messages originating from a router, it's a good bet that the target it's sending the messages to has been probing that router's network. You can then look at the host's traffic to identify what it communicated with that might be suspicious.

Fumbling at the Service Level

Service-level fumbling commonly results from scanning, automated exploits, and a number of scouting tools. Unlike network-level fumbling, service-level fumbling is usually clearly identifiable as such because there are error codes in most major services that are logged and can be used to differentiate illegitimate connections from legitimate requests.

HTTP Fumbling

Recall that each HTTP transaction returns a three-digit status code, with the 4xx family of status codes reserved for client errors. In the 4xx family, the two most important and common access errors are 404 (not found) and 401 (unauthorized).

404 indicates that a resource was not available at the URL specified by the requestor, and is the most common HTTP error in existence. Users will often trigger 404 errors by hand, such as when they mistype a complex URL. Misconfiguration will often cause problems as well, such as when someone publicizes a URL that doesn't exist.

These types of errors, from a misconfigured URL announcement or fat-fingering, are relatively easy to identify. Fat-fingering should be relatively rare. Fat-fingered URLs will rarely repeat—if one user is mistyping, he'll mistype slightly differently each time. At the same time, since fat-fingering is an *individual* mistake, the same fat-fingering will not appear from multiple locations. If you see the same mistake coming from multiple discrete locations, that is more likely to be a result of a misconfigured URL announcement. Such an announcement may be identifiable by examining the HTTP Referer header. If the Referer points to a site you have control over, then you can identify and fix the error on that site.

The third common source for 404 errors is bots scanning HTTP sites for well-known vulnerabilities. Because most modern HTTP sites are built on top of a collection of other applications, they often carry vulnerabilities from one or more of their component applications. These vulnerabilities are well known, placed in common locations, and consequently hunted for by bots everywhere. The URLs referenced in Example 13-2 are all associated with phpMyAdmin, a common MySQL database management tool.

Example 13-2. Botnets attempting to fetch common URLs

```
223.85.245.54 - - [16/Feb/2013:20:10:12 -0500]
        "GET /pma/scripts/setup.php HTTP/1.1" 404 390 "-" "ZmEu"
223.85.245.54 - - [16/Feb/2013:20:10:15 -0500]
        "GET /MyAdmin/scripts/setup.php HTTP/1.1" 404 394 "-" "ZmEu"
188.230.44.113 - - [17/Feb/2013:16:54:05 -0500]
         "GET http://www.scanproxy.net:80/p-80.html HTTP/1.0" 404 378 "-"
194.44.28.21 - - [18/Feb/2013:06:20:07 -0500]
```

```
        "GET /w00tw00t.at.blackhats.romanian.anti-sec:) HTTP/1.1" 404 410
     "-" "ZmEu"
194.44.28.21 - - [18/Feb/2013:06:20:07 -0500]
        "GET /phpMyAdmin/scripts/setup.php HTTP/1.1" 404 397 "-" "ZmEu"
194.44.28.21 - - [18/Feb/2013:06:20:08 -0500]
        "GET /phpmyadmin/scripts/setup.php HTTP/1.1" 404 397 "-" "ZmEu"
194.44.28.21 - - [18/Feb/2013:06:20:08 -0500]
        "GET /pma/scripts/setup.php HTTP/1.1" 404 390 "-" "ZmEu"
194.44.28.21 - - [18/Feb/2013:06:20:09 -0500]
        "GET /myadmin/scripts/setup.php HTTP/1.1" 404 394 "-"
```

Unlike the 404 errors discussed earlier, 404 scanning is generally identifiable by being *completely unrelated* to the actual structure of a site. Attackers are *guessing* that something is there and are going by the documentation and common practice to try to reach a vulnerable target.

401 errors are authentication errors, and come from HTTP's basic access authentication mechanism—which you should never use. 401 authentication was baked into the HTTP standard early on,[3] and uses unencrypted base64-encoded passwords to authenticate a user's access to protected directories.

Basic access authentication is a disaster and should not be used by any modern web server. If you do see 401 errors in your system logs, you should identify and eliminate the source of them on your server. Unfortunately, basic authentication still occasionally pops up in embedded systems as the only form of authentication available.

Web Crawlers and Robots.txt

Search engines employ automated processes called, variously, *crawlers*, *spiders*, or *robots* to scout out websites and identify searchable content. These crawlers can be phenomenally aggressive in copying site contents. Website owners can define what the crawlers access using the *robot exclusion standard*, or *robots.txt*. The standard defines a common file (the aforementioned *robots.txt*), which is accessed by the crawler and provides instructions about which files it can and can't access.

A host that *doesn't* access *robots.txt* and immediately begins poking around the site is suspicious. However, *robots.txt* is a voluntary standard; there's nothing preventing a crawler from ignoring it, and it's not uncommon for unethical or new crawlers to ignore the instructions.

It's also not uncommon for scanners who want to probe a site to pretend to be a crawler. Crawlers are usually identifiable by two behaviors: they use a User-Agent

---

3 See RFC 1945 (*http://bit.ly/rfc-1945*) and RFC 2617 (*http://bit.ly/rfc-2617*).

string unique to the crawler, and they come from a fixed range of IP addresses.[4] Most search engines publish their address ranges to help stop masquerading; these address ranges can change, so regularly checking a site such as the Robots Database (*http://bit.ly/web-robots*) or List of User-Agents (*http://www.user-agents.org*) is a good idea.

SMTP Fumbling

For our purposes, SMTP fumbling occurs when a host sends mail to a nonexistent address. Depending on SMTP server configurations, this will result in one of three actions: a rejection, a bounce, or (in the case of a catch-all configuration) redirection to a catch-all account. All of these events should be logged by the SMTP server that makes the final routing decision.

Analyzing SMTP fumbles runs into the same problem that analyzing all SMTP traffic does: spam. There are a lot of failed addresses sent in SMTP messages because spammers will send mail to every conceivable address.[5] Fumbling (misaddressing) may exist, but these efforts are relatively innocuous and likely to be drowned in spam. At the same time, the reasons for attackers to fumble (reconnaissance) are effectively pointless because spammers don't probe to see whether an address exists; they spam it.

There may be one good reason to analyze failed SMTP addresses: uncovering deception. In several APT-type spear-phishing emails, I've seen the attackers seed the To: line with realistic-looking but fake addresses. I assume that the addresses are either out of date due to enterprise turnover or intentionally added to provide the mail with a veneer of legitimacy.

DNS Fumbling

Generally, failed DNS lookups result in an NXDOMAIN message, so if someone is fumbling with DNS (e.g., probing a domain for common names such as *mail.domain*, *smtp.domain*, *www.domain*, etc.) you can expect to see a spike in NXDOMAIN messages.

One potential false positive here is ISP-based DNS hijacking. When an ISP engages in DNS hijacking, it will not send an NXDOMAIN response, instead sending an IP address pointing to some internal service it controls. Check your upstream DNS services by sending bogus domains and verify that you actually get NXDOMAIN messages back.

---

4 Googlebot is a notable exception to this, and Google provides instructions on how to verify it (*http://bit.ly/verify-google*).

5 I once logged on to an account I had never used and was greeted by 3,000 spam messages.

Detecting and Analyzing Fumbling

> Until some brilliant researcher comes up with a better technique, scan detection will boil down to testing for X events of interest across a Y-sized time window.
>
> —Stephen Northcutt

Fumbling alarms can be used to detect scans, spam, and other phenomena where the attacker has next to no knowledge about the target network. In this section, we will discuss the creation of fumbling alerts, forensic analysis of fumbling, and re-engineering the network to more easily identify fumbling.

Building Fumbling Alarms

When tracking fumbles, the goal is to raise an alarm when there's suspicion that fumbling is not simply accidental. To do so, the alarm must first collect fumbling events using the rules discussed previously in this chapter. Mechanisms include:

1. Creating or consulting a map of targets to determine whether the attacker is reaching a real target.

2. Examining traffic for evidence of a failure to connect. Examples of failures to connect include:

   a. Asymmetric TCP sessions, or TCP sessions without ACK flags

   b. HTTP 404 records

   c. Email bounce logs

Innocuous fumbling (a false positive) is generally the result of some form of misconfiguration or miscommunication to the target. For example, if the DNS name for *destination.com* is moved from IP address A to IP address B, until the change thoroughly propagates through the DNS system, users will accidentally visit address A instead of B. These types of errors, when they occur, will come from multiple sources and will be consistent. Supposing that address C on the same network is dark (that is, it has no domain name), normal users may accidentally visit A for a while, but they will not visit C. Suspicious fumbling involves users who visit multiple nonexistent destinations; a user may visit A due to a configuration error, and she might possibly visit C due to chance, but if she visits A and C, then she's more likely scouting out a target.

Distinguishing malicious fumbling from innocuous failures is therefore, as Northcutt says, about deciding on a threshold—the number of events tolerated before you raise an alert. There are several techniques available for doing so, and simple thresholds on any of the constructs discussed in this chapter will support this approach; this process is covered in depth in Chapter 11.

An alternative approach is sequential hypothesis testing (SHT), a technique developed by Abraham Wald during World War II. The SHT approach is not in itself a statistical test, but a process for determining how many tests to conduct. For scan detection, the gold standard approach was developed by by Jaeyeon Jung et al. in their 2004 paper "Fast Portscan Detection Using Sequential Hypothesis Testing," presented at the IEEE Symposium on Security and Privacy.

Another approach, taken from network traffic development, is a *leaky bucket algorithm*. These algorithms imitate the titular "leaky bucket" by maintaining a counter that, left to its own devices, decrements to zero over time. The bucket is "filled" when events occur, and drains at a constant rate over time. When the bucket exceeds a predefined threshold, it raises an alert. Figure 13-5 shows an example of a leaky bucket in action.

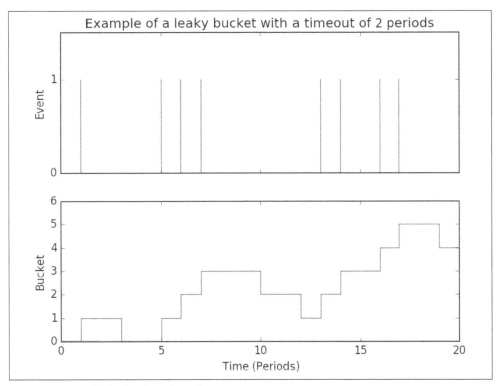

Figure 13-5. A leaky bucket algorithm in action

Both sequential hypothesis testing and leaky buckets facilitate the fast analysis of scanning phenomena. However, the thing about malicious fumbling is that the attackers, generally, have no particular reason to be subtle. If someone is scanning a site, he's going to hit everything quickly. Statistical methods are primarily useful to find the attacker *quickly*, and consequently have more use in active defense rather than in alarm generation.

Put another way, the challenge in fumbling detection is not in detecting the phenomena quickly; it's figuring out what's going on *outside* of the fantastically obvious scans that can easily consume all of your time and effort. Internet background radiation comprises an enormous number of transient phenomena, and those are lost in the noise of obvious attacks.

Forensic Analysis of Fumbling

Scanning *qua* scanning is basically of no interest. Every idiot on the planet scans the internet, and a number of them scan it multiple times daily. There is some worm-based scanning (such as with Code Red and SQL Slammer, if you want to get truly Jurassic) that has gone on for *years* without any noticeable effect. Scanning is like rain: it's going to happen, and the real problem is identifying the damage that it causes.

When receiving a scan alarm, there are several basic questions to ask:

1. Who responded to the scanner? As far as I'm concerned, scanners can visit as much of my dark space as they like. What I'm really concerned about is whether anyone in my network talked *back* to the scanner, and what they did afterward. More specific questions include:

   a. Did the scanner have a serious conversation with any host? Attack software usually rolls scanning and exploit into a two-step process. Consequently, my first question about any scan is whether it ended before the true exploit.

   b. Did any responding host have suspicious conversations afterward? Suspicious conversations include communications with external hosts (especially if it's an internal server), receipt of a file, and communications on odd ports.

2. Did the scanner find out something about my network I didn't know? Inventories are always at least *slightly* out of date, and attacks are taking place *all the time*. Given that, it makes sense to take advantage of the scanner's hard work for our own benefit. Questions to address this include:

   a. Did the scanner identify previously unknown hosts? If something that isn't already in your inventory responds to the fumbler, you need to identify, assess, and harden it.

   b. Did the scanner identify previously unknown services?

3. What else did the scanner do? Bots usually do multiple things at one time, and it's good to check whether the scanner scanned other ports, engaged in other types of probes, or tried multiple types of attacks.

There are several good questions to ask about fumblers in general. For example:

1. What else did the fumbler do? If the same address or source is sending mail to multiple targets, it's likely to be a spammer and, much like a scanner, is using a bot as a utility knife kind of tool.

2. Are there preferred targets? This particularly applies to fumbling with email addresses, because IP addresses are drawn from a much smaller pool. Are there common target addresses on your network? If so, they're good candidates for further instrumentation.

Engineering a Network to Take Advantage of Fumbling

Fumbling often takes advantage of common network configurations and assumptions. Most obviously, attackers scan common ports like 22 because they expect to encounter services there. You can take advantage of these assumptions to place more sensitive instrumentation, such as full packet capture, in certain places on the network.

Because malicious scans exploit the regularity of most target sites, you can make the lives of attackers a bit harder by configuring your site in a somewhat irregular way:

Rearrange addresses
Most scanning is linear: the attacker will hit address X, then X+1, and so on. Most administrators and DHCP implementations also assign addresses linearly. It's not uncommon to have a /24 or /27 where the upper half is entirely dark. Rearranging addresses so that they're scattered evenly across the network, or leaving large empty gaps elsewhere in the network, is a simple method that creates dark space.

Move targets
Port assignments are largely a social convention, and most modern applications should be able to handle a service located on an unorthodox port. Especially when dealing with internal services, which shouldn't be accessed by the outside world, port reassignment is a cheap mechanism to frustrate more basic scanners.

## CHAPTER 14

On Volume and Time

In this chapter, we look at phenomena that can be identified by comparing traffic volume against the passage of time. "Volume" may be a simple count of the number of bytes or packets, or it may be a construct such as the number of IP addresses transferring files. Based on the traffic observed, there are a number of different phenomena that can be pulled out, such as:

Beaconing
When a host on your network communicates with an unknown host at regular intervals, it is a possible sign of communications with command and control.

File extraction
Massive downloads are suggestive of someone stealing your internal data.

Denial of service (DoS)
DoS attacks can prevent your servers from providing service.

Traffic volume data is noisy. Most of the observables that you can directly count, such as the number of bytes over time, vary highly and with no real relationship between the volume of the event and its significance. In other words, there's rarely a significant relationship between the number of bytes and the importance of the events. This chapter will help you find unusual behaviors through scripts and visualizations, but a certain amount of human eyeballing and judgment are necessary to determine which behaviors to consider dangerous.

The Workday and Its Impact on Network Traffic Volume

The bulk of traffic on an enterprise network comes from people who are paid to work there, so their traffic is going to roughly follow the hours of the business day. Traffic will trough during the evening, rise around 0800, peak around 1300, and drop off around 1800.

To show how dominant the workday is, consider Figure 14-1, a plot showing the progression of the Sobig.F email worm across the SWITCH network (*http:// www.switch.ch*) in 2003. SWITCH is Switzerland and Lichtenstein's educational network, and makes up a significant fraction of the national traffic for Switzerland. The plot shows the total volume of SMTP traffic over time for a two-week period. Sobig.F propagates at the end of the plot, but what I want to highlight is the normal activity during the earlier part of the week, on the left. Note that each weekday is a notched peak, with the notch coming at lunchtime. Note also that there is considerably less activity over the weekend.

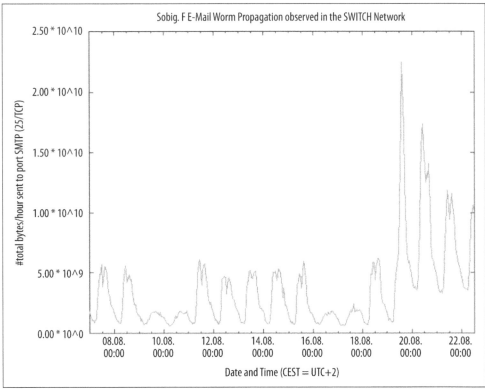

Figure 14-1. Mail traffic and propagation of a worm across Switzerland's SWITCH network (image courtesy of Dr. Arno Wagner)

This is a social phenomenon; knowing roughly where the address you're monitoring is (home, work, school) and the local time zone can help predict both events and volumes. For example, in the evening, streaming video companies account for a more significant fraction of traffic as people kick back and watch TV.

There are a number of useful rules of thumb for working with workday schedules to identify, map, and manage anomalies. These include tracking active and inactive periods, tracking the internal schedule of an organization, and keeping track of the time zone. The techniques covered in this section are a basic, empirical approach to time series analysis.

When working with site data, I usually find that it's best to break traffic into "on" (people are working) and "off" (people are at home) periods. The histogram in Figure 14-2 shows how this phenomenon can affect the distribution of traffic volume —in this case, the two distinct peaks correspond to the on-periods and off-periods. Modeling the two periods separately will provide a more accurate volume estimate without pulling out the heavier math used for time series analysis.

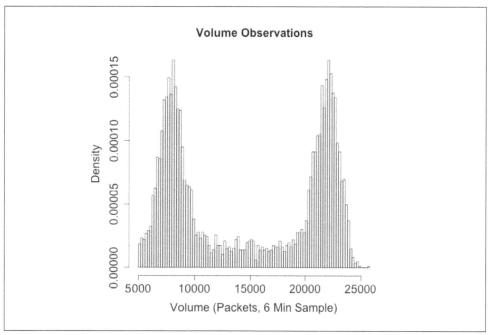

Figure 14-2. Distribution of traffic in a sample network, where the peak on the left is evening traffic, and the peak on the right is workday traffic

When determining on-periods and off-periods, consider the schedule of the organization itself. If your company has any special or unusual holidays, such as taking a founder's birthday off, keep track of those as potential off-days. Similarly, are there parts of the organization that are staffed constantly and other parts that are only 9 to 5? If something is constantly staffed, keep track of the shift changes, and you'll often see traffic repeat at the start of a shift as everyone logs on, checks email, and then starts working.

Business processes are a common source of false positives with volume analysis. For example, I've seen a corporate site where there was a sudden biweekly spike in traffic to a particular server. The server, which covered company payroll, was checked by every employee every other Friday and never visited otherwise. Phenomena that occur weekly, biweekly, or on multiples of 30 days are likely to be associated with the business's own processes and should be identified as such for future reference.

Beaconing

Beaconing is the process of systematically and regularly contacting a host. For instance, botnets will poll their command servers for new instructions periodically. This is particularly true of many modern botnets that use HTTP as a moderator. Such behavior will appear to you as information flows at regular intervals between infected systems on your site and an unknown address off-site.

However, there are many legitimate behaviors that also generate routine traffic flows. Examples include:

Keepalives
> Long-lived sessions, such as an interactive SSH session, will send empty packets at regular intervals in order to maintain a connection with the target.

Software updates
> Most modern applications include some form of automated update checkup. AV, in particular, regularly downloads signature updates to keep track of the latest malware.

News and weather

    Many news, weather, and other interactive sites regularly refresh the page as long as a client is open to read it.

Beacon detection is a two-stage process. The first stage involves identifying consistent signals. An example process for doing so is the *find_beacons.py* script shown in Example 14-1. *find_beacons.py* takes a sequence of flow records and dumps them into equally sized bins. Each input consists of two fields: the IP address where an event was found and the starting time of the flow, as returned by rwcut. rwsort is used to order the traffic by source IP and time.

The script then checks the median distance between the bins and scores each IP address on the fraction of bins that fall within some tolerance of that median. If a large number of flows are near the median, you have found a regularly recurring event.

Example 14-1. A simple beacon detector

```
#!/usr/bin/env python
#
#
# find_beacons.py
#
# input:
#        rwsort --field=1,9 | rwcut --no-title --epoch --field=1,9 | <stdin>
# command line:
# find_beacons.py precision tolerance [epoch]
#
# precision: integer expression for bin size (in seconds)
# tolerance: floating point representation for tolerance expressed as
# fraction from median, e.g. 0.05 means anything within (median -
# 0.5*median, median + 0.5*median) is acceptable
# epoch: starting time for bins; if not specified, set to midnight of the first
# time read.

# This is a very simple beacon detection script which works by breaking a traffic
# feed into [precision] length bins.  The distance between bins is calculated and
# the median value is used as representative of the distance.  If all the distances
# are within tolerance% of the median value, the traffic is treated as a beacon.

import sys

if len(sys.argv) >= 3:
    precision = int(sys.argv[1])
    tolerance = float(sys.argv[2])
else:
    sys.stderr.write("Specify the precision and tolerance\n")

starting_epoch = -1
```

```
if len(sys.argv) >= 4:
    starting_epoch = int(sys.argv[3])

current_ip = ''

def process_epoch_info(bins):
    a = bins.keys()
    a.sort()
    distances = []
    # We create a table of distances between the bins
    for i in range(0, len(a) -1):
        distances.append(a[i + 1] - a[i])

    distances.sort()
    median = distances(len(distances)/2)
    tolerance_range = (median - tolerance * median, median + tolerance *median)
    # Now we check bins
    count = 0
    for i in distances:
        if (i >= tolerance_range[0]) and (i <= tolerance_range[1]):
            count+=1
    return count, len(distances)

bins = {}     # Checklist of bins hit during construction; sorted and
              # compared later. Associative array because it's really
              # a set and I should start using those.
results = {} # Associative array containing the results of the binning
              # analysis, dumped during the final report.

# We start reading in data; for each line I'm building a table of
# beaconing events.  The beaconing events are simply indications that
# traffic 'occurred' at time X.  The size of the traffic, how often it occurred,
# how many flows is irrelevant.  Something happened, or it didn't.
for i in sys.stdin.readlines():
    ip, time = i.split('|')[0:2]
    if ip != current_ip:
        results[ip] = process_epoch_info(bins)
        bins = {}

    if starting_epoch == -1:
        starting_epoch = time - (time % 86400) # Sets it to midnight of that day
    bin = (time - starting_epoch) / precision
    bins[bin] = 1

a = bins.sort()
for i in a:
    print "%15s|%5d|%5d|%8.4f" % (ip, bins[a][0], bins[a][1],
                                 100.0 * (float(bins[a[0]])/float(bins[a[1]])))
```

The second stage of beacon detection is inventory management. An enormous number of legitimate applications, as we saw earlier, transmit data periodically. NTP, routing protocols, and AV tools all dial home on a regular basis for information updates.

SSH also tends to show periodic behavior, because administrators run periodic maintenance tasks via the protocol.

File Transfers/Raiding

Data theft is still the most basic form of attack on a database or website, *especially* if the website is internal or an otherwise protected resource. For lack of a better term, I'll use *raiding* to denote copying a website or database in order to later disseminate, dump, or sell the information. The difference between raiding and legitimate access is a matter of degree, as the point of any server is to serve data.

Obviously, raiding should result in a change in traffic volume. Raiding is usually conducted quickly (possibly while someone is packing up her cubicle) and often relies on automated tools such as wget. It's possible to subtly raid, but that would require the attacker to have both the time to slowly extract data and the patience to do so.

Volume is one of the easiest ways to identify a raid. The first step is building up a model of the normal volume originating from a host over time. The *calibrate_raid.py* script in Example 14-2 provides thresholds for volume over time, as well as a table of results to plot.

Example 14-2. A raid detection script

```
#!/usr/bin/env python
#
# calibrate_raid.py
#
# input:
#       Nothing
# output:
#       Writes a report containing a time series and volume estimates to stdout
# commandline:
# calibrate_raid.py start_date end_date ip_address server_port period_size
#
# start_date: The date to begin the query on
# end_date: The date to end the query on
# ip_address: The server address to query
# server_port: The port of the server to query
# period_size: The size of the periods to use for modeling the time
#
# Given a particular IP address, this generates a time series (via rwcount)
# and a breakdown on what the expected values at the 90-100% thresholds would
# be.  The count output can then be run through a visualizer in order to
# check for outliers or anomalies.
#
import sys,os,tempfile

start_date = sys.argv[1]
```

```
end_date = sys.argv[2]
ip_address = sys.argv[3]
server_port = int(sys.argv[4])
period_size = int(size.arg[5])

if __name__ == '__main__':
    fh, temp_countfn = tempfile.mkstemp()
    os.close(fh)
    # Note that the filter call uses the IP address as the source, and the
    # server port as the source.  We're pulling out flows that originated
    # FROM the server, which means that they should be the data from the
    # file transfer.  If we used daddress/dport, we'd be logging the
    # (much smaller) requests to the server from the clients.
    #
    os.system(('rwfilter --saddress=%s --sport=%d --start-date=%s ',
              '--end-date=%s --pass=stdout | rwcount --epoch-slots',
           ' --bin-size=%d --no-title > %s') % (
                   ip_address, server_port, start_date, end_date, period_size,
                   temp_countfn))

    # A note on the filtering I'm doing here.  You *could* rwfilter to
    # only include 4-packet or above sessions, therefore avoiding the
    # scan responses.  However, those *should* be minuscule, and
    # therefore I elect not to in this case.


    # Load the count file into memory and add some structure
    #
    a = open(temp_countfn, 'r')
    # We're basically just throwing everything into a histogram, so I need
    # to establish a min and max
    min = 99999999999L
    max = -1
    data = {}
    for i in a.readlines():
        time, records, bytes, packets = map(lambda x:float(x),
                                            i[:-1].split('|')[0:4])
        if bytes < min:
            min = bytes
        if bytes > max:
            max = bytes
        data[time] = (records, bytes, packets)
    a.close()
    os.unlink(temp_countfn)
    # Build a histogram with hist_size slots
    histogram = []
    hist_size = 100
    for i in range(0,hist_size):
        histogram.append(0)
    bin_size = (max - min) / hist_size
    total_entries = len(data.values)
    for records, bytes, packets in data.values():
```

```
        bin_index = (bytes - min)/bin_size
        histogram[bin_index] += 1

    # Now we calculate the thresholds from 90 to 100%
    thresholds = []
    for i in range(90, 100):
        thresholds.append(0.01 * i * total_entries)
    total = 0
    last_match = 0 # index in thresholds where we stopped
    # First, we dump the thresholds
    for i in range(0, hist_size):
        total += histogram[i]
        if total >= thresholds[last_match]:
            while thresholds[last_match] < total:
                print "%3d%% | %d" % (90 + last_match, (i * bin_size) + min)
    a = data.keys()
    a.sort()
    for i in a:
        print "%15d|%10d|%10d|%10d" % (i, data[i][0], data[i][1], data[i][2])
```

Visualization is critical when calibrating volume thresholds for detecting raiding or other raiding anomalies. We discussed the problem with standard deviations in Chapter 11, and a histogram is the easiest way to determine whether a distribution is even remotely Gaussian. In my experience, a surprising number of services regularly raid hosts—web spiders and the Internet Archive being among the more notable examples. If a site is strictly internal, backups and internal mirroring are common false positives.

Visualization can identify these outliers. The example in Figure 14-3 shows that the overwhelming majority of traffic occurs below about 1,000 MB/10 min, but those few outliers above 2,000 MB/10 min will cause problems for *calibrate_raid.py* and most training algorithms. Once you have identified the outliers, you can record them in a whitelist and remove them from the filter command using --not-dipset. You can then use rwcount to set up a simple alert mechanism.

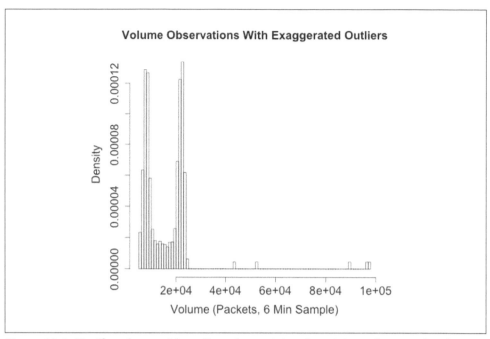

Figure 14-3. Traffic volume with outliers; determining the origin and cause of outliers will reduce alerts

Locality

Locality is the tendency of references (memory locations, URLs, IP addresses) to cluster together. For example, if you track the web pages visited by a user over time, you will find that the majority of pages are located in a small and predictable number of sites (spatial locality), and that users tend to visit the same sites over and over (temporal locality). Locality is a well-understood concept in computer science, and serves as the foundation of caching, CDNs, and reverse proxies.

Locality is particularly useful as a complement to volumetric analysis because users are generally predictable. Users typically visit a small number of sites and talk to a small number of people, and while there are occasional changes, we can model this behavior using a *working set*.

Figure 14-4 is a graphical example of a working set in operation. In this example, the working set is implemented as an LRU (Least Recently Used) queue of fixed size (in this case, four references in the queue). This working set is tracking web surfing, so it gets fed URLs from an HTTP server logfile and adds them to the stack. Working sets only keep one copy of every reference they see, so a four-reference set like the one shown in Figure 14-4 will only show four references.

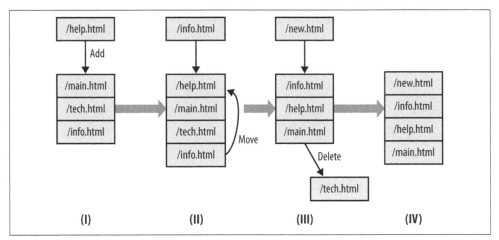

Figure 14-4. A working set in operation

When a working set receives a reference, it does one of three things:

1. If there are empty references left, the new reference is enqueued at the back of the queue (I to II).

2. If the queue is filled AND the reference is present, the reference is moved to the back of the queue.

3. If the queue is filled AND the reference is NOT present, then the reference is enqueued at the back of the queue, and the reference at the front of the queue is removed.

The code in Example 14-3 shows an LRU working set model in Python.

Example 14-3. Calculating working set characteristics

```
#!/usr/bin/env python
#
#
# Describe the locality of a host using working_set depth analysis.
# Inputs:
#       stdin - a sequence of tags
#
# Command-line args:
#       first: working_set depth

import sys

try:
    working_set_depth = int(sys.argv[1])
except:
```

```
        sys.stderr.write("Specify a working_set depth at the command line\n")
        sys.exit(-1)

working_set = []

i = sys.stdin.readline()
total_processed = 0
total_popped = 0
unique_symbols = {}
while i != '':
    value = i[:-1] #Ditch the obligatory \n
    unique_symbols[value] = 1 # Add in the symbol
    total_processed += 1
    try:
        vind = working_set.index(value)
    except:
        vind = -1

    if (vind == -1):
        # Value isn't present as an LRU cache; delete the
        # least recently used value and store this at the end
        working_set.append(value)
        if len(working_set) > working_set_depth:
            del working_set[0]
        working_set.append(value)
        total_popped +=1
    else:
        # Most recently used value; move it to the end of the working_set
        del working_set[vind]

# Calculate probability of replacement stat
p_replace = 100.0 * (float(total_popped)/float(total_processed))

print "%10d %10d %10d %8.4f" % (total_processed, unique_symbols,
                                working_set_depth, p_replace)
```

Figure 14-5 shows an example of what working sets will look like. This figure plots the probability of replacing a value in the working set as a function of the working set size. Two different sets are compared here: a completely random set where references are picked from a set of 10 million symbols, and a model of user activity using a Pareto distribution. The Pareto model is adequate for modeling normal user activity, if actually a bit *less* stable than user behavior under normal circumstances.

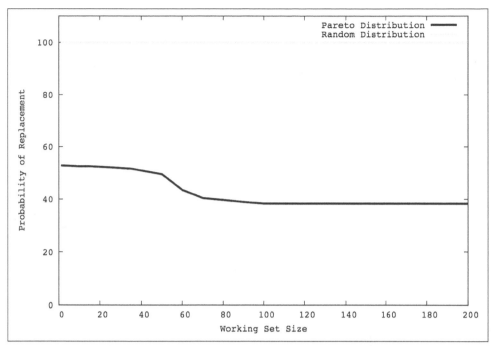

Figure 14-5. Working set analysis

Note the "knee" in the Pareto model, around the 60-element size, while the random model remains consistent at a 100% replacement rate. Working sets generally have an ideal size after which increasing the set's size is counterproductive. This knee is representative of this phenomenon—you can see that the probability of replacement drops slightly before the knee, but remains effectively stable afterward.

The value of working sets is that once they're calibrated, they reduce user habit down to two parameters: the size of the queue modeling the set and the probability that a reference will result in a queue replacement.

DDoS, Flash Crowds, and Resource Exhaustion

Denial of service is a goal, not a specific strategy. A DoS attack results in a host that cannot be reached from remote locations. Most DoS attacks are implemented as *distributed denial of service* (DDoS) attacks in which the attacker uses a network of captured hosts in order to implement the attack. There are several ways an attacker can implement a DoS, including but not limited to:

Service level exhaustion
> The targeted host runs a publicly accessible service. Using a botnet, the attacker starts a set of clients on the target, each conducting some trivial but service-specific interaction (such as fetching the home page of a website).

SYN flood

The SYN flood is the classic DDoS attack. Given a target with an open TCP port, the attacker sends clients against the attacker. The clients don't use the service on the port, but simply open connections using a SYN packet and leave the connections open.

Bandwidth exhaustion

Instead of targeting a host, the attacker sends a massive flood of garbage traffic toward the host, intending to overwhelm the connection between the router and the target.

Simple attacks

Be wary of physical insider attacks. An insider can DoS a system simply by unplugging it.

All these tactics produce the same result, but each tactic will appear differently in network traffic and may require different mitigation techniques. Exactly how many resources the attacker needs is a function of how the attacker implements DDoS. As a rule of thumb, the higher up an attack is on the OSI model, the more stress it places on the target and the fewer bots are required by the attacker. For example, bandwidth exhaustion hits the router and basically has to exhaust the router interface. SYN flooding, the classic DDoS attack, has to simply exhaust the target's TCP stack. At higher levels, tools like Slowloris (*http://bit.ly/slowloris-comp-sec*) effectively create a partial HTTP connection, exhausting the resources of the web server.

This has several advantages from an attacker's perspective. Fewer resources consumed means fewer bots involved, and a legitimate session is more likely to be allowed through by a firewall that might block a packet crafted to attack the IP or TCP layer.

DDoS and Routing Infrastructure

DDoS attacks aimed specifically at routing infrastructure will produce collateral damage. Consider a simple network like the one in Figure 14-6. The attacker hitting subnetwork C is exhausting not just the connection at C, but also the router's connection to the internet. Consequently, hosts on networks A and B will not be able to reach the internet and will see their incoming internet traffic effectively drop to zero.

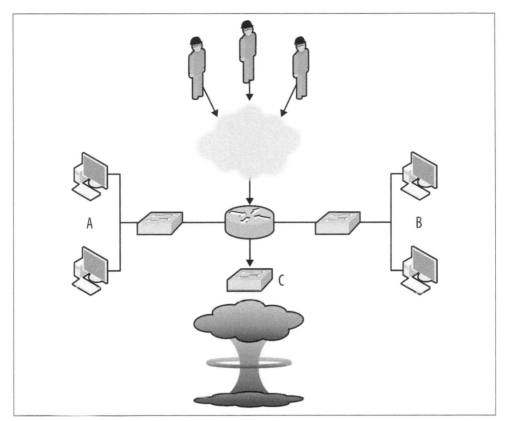

Figure 14-6. DDoS collateral damage

This type of problem is not uncommon on colocated services, and emphasizes that DDoS defense is rooted in network infrastructure. I am, in the long run, deeply curious to see how cloud computing and DDoS are going to marry. Cloud computing enables defenders to run highly distributed services across the internet's routing infrastructure. This, in turn, increases the resources the attacker needs to take out a single defender.

With DoS attacks, the most common false positives are *flash crowds* and cable cuts. A flash crowd is a sudden influx of legitimate traffic to a site in response to some kind of announcement or notification. Alternate names for flash crowds such as *SlashDot effect*, *farking*, or *Reddit effect* provide a good explanation of what's going on.

These different classes of attacks are usually easily distinguished by looking at a graph of incoming traffic. Some idealized images are shown in Figure 14-7, which explains the basic phenomena.

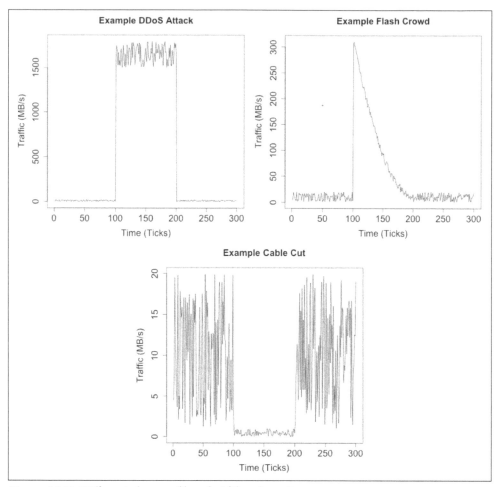

Figure 14-7. Different classes of bandwidth exhaustion

The images in Figure 14-7 describe three different classes of bandwidth exhaustion: a DDoS attack, a flash crowd, and a cable cut or other infrastructure failure. Each plot is of incoming traffic and equivalent to sitting right at the sensor. The differences between the plots reflect the phenomena causing the problems.

DDoS attacks are mechanical. The attack usually switches on and off instantly, as the attacker is issuing commands remotely to a network of bots. When a DDoS attack starts, it almost instantly consumes as much bandwidth as is available. In many DDoS plots, the upper limit on the plot is dictated by the networking infrastructure: if you have a 10 GB pipe, the plot maxes at 10 GB. DDoS attacks are also *consistent*. Once they start, they generally keep humming along at about the same volume. Most of the time, the attacker has grossly overprovisioned the attack. Bots are being removed while the attack goes on, but there are more than enough to consume all the available bandwidth even if a significant fraction are knocked offline.

DDoS mitigation is an endurance contest. The best defense is to provision out bandwidth before the attack starts. Once an attack actually occurs, the best you can do at any particular location is to try to identify patterns in the traffic and block the ones causing the most damage. Examples include:

- Identifying a core audience for the target and limiting traffic to the core audience. The audience may be identified by IP address, netblock, country code, or language, among other attributes. What is critical is that the audience has a limited overlap with the attacker set. The script in Example 14-4 provides a mechanism for ordering /24s by the difference between two sets: historical users you trust and new users whom you suspect of being part of a DDoS attack.

- Spoofed attacks are *occasionally* identifiable by some flaw in the spoofing. The random number generator for the spoof might set all addresses to x.x.x.1, as an example.

Example 14-4. An example script for ordering blocks

```
#!/usr/bin/env python
#
# ddos_intersection.py
#
# input:
#       Nothing
# output:
#       A report comparing the number of addresses in two sets, ordered by the
#       largest number of hosts in set A which are not present in set B.
#
#   command_line:
#   ddos_intersection.py historical_set ddos_set
#
#   historical_set: A set of historical data giving external addresses
#   which have historically spoken to a particular host or network
#   ddos_set: A set of data from a ddos attack on the host
#   This is going to work off of /24's for simplicity.
#
import sys,os,tempfile

historical_setfn = sys.argv[1]
ddos_setfn = sys.argv[2]
blocksize = int(sys.argv[3])

mask_fh, mask_fn = tempfile.mkstemp()
os.close(mask_fh)
os.unlink(mask_fn)
```

```
os.system(('rwsettool --mask=24 --output-path=stdout %s | ' +
                     ' rwsetcat | sed 's/$/\/24/' | rwsetbuild stdin %s') %
                     (historical_setfn, mask_fn))

bins = {}
# Read and store all the /24s in the historical data
a = os.popen(('rwsettool --difference %s %s --output-path=stdout | ',
             'rwsetcat --network-structure=C') % (mask_fn, historical_setfn),'r')
# First column is historical, second column is ddos
for i in a.readlines():
    address, count = i[:-1].split('|')[0:2]
    bins[address] = [int(count), 0]

a.close()
# Repeat the process with all the data in the ddos set
a = os.popen(('rwsettool --difference %s %s --output-path=stdout | ',
             'rwsetcat --network-structure=C') % (mask_fn, ddos_setfn),'r')
for i in a.readlines():
    address, count = i[:-1].split('|')[0:2]
    # I'm intersecting the maskfile again; since I originally intersected it against
    # the file I generated the maskfile from, any address that I find in the file
    # will already be in the bins associative array
    bins[address][1] = int(count)

#
# Now we order the contents of the bins.  This script is implicitly written to
# support a whitelist-based approach--addresses which appear in the historical
# data are candidates for whitelisting, and all other addresses will be blocked.
# We order the candidate blocks in terms of the number of historical addresses
# allowed in, decreasing for every attacker address allowed in.
address_list = bins.items()
address_list.sort(lambda x,y:(y[1][0]-x[1][0])-(y[1][1]-x[1][1]))
print "%20s|%10s|%10s" % ("Block", "Not-DDoS", "DDoS")
for address, result in address_list:
    print "%20s|%10d|%10d" % (address, bins[address][0], bins[address][1])
```

This type of filtering works more effectively if the attack is focused on striking a specific service, such as DDoSing a web server with HTTP requests. If the attacker is instead focused on traffic flooding a router interface, the best defenses will normally lie upstream from you.

As discussed in Chapter 13, people are impatient while machines are not, and this behavior is the easiest way to differentiate flash crowds from DDoS attacks. As the flash crowd plot in Figure 14-7 shows, when the event occurs, the initial burst of bandwidth is followed by a rapid falloff. The falloff is because people have discovered that they can't reach the targeted site and have moved on to more interesting pastures until some later time.

Flash crowds are public affairs—for some reason, *somebody* publicized the target. As a result, it's often possible to figure out the origin of the flash crowd. For example, HTTP referer logs will include a reference to the site. Flash crowd verification may be solved simply by Googling—look for news articles, recent mentions of the site, any public news that might mention the site and result in the traffic spike.

Cable cuts and mechanical failures will result in an actual drop in traffic. This is shown in the cable cut figure, where all of a sudden traffic goes to zero. When this happens, the first follow-up step is to try to generate some traffic *to* the target, and ensure that the problem is actually a failure in traffic and not a failure in the detector. After that, you need to bring an alternate system online and then research the cause of the failure.

DDoS and Force Multipliers

Functionally, DDoS attacks are wars of attrition: how much traffic can the attacker throw at the target, and how can the target compensate for that bandwidth? Attackers can improve the impact of their attacks through a couple of different strategies: they can acquire more resources, attack at different layers of the stack, and rely on internet infrastructure to inflict additional damage. Each of these techniques effectively serves as a force multiplier for attackers, increasing the havoc with the same number of bots under their control.

The process of resource acquisition is really up to the attacker. The modern internet underground provides a mature market for the rental and use of botnets. An alternative approach, used notably by some of Anonymous, involves volunteers. Early examples of this included a family of JavaScript and C# DDoS tools under the moniker LOIC (Low Orbit Ion Cannon) that were used to conduct DDoS attacks. The LOIC family of tools were, in comparison to hardcore malware, fairly primitive, but arguably, they weren't intended to be anything more than that given their hacktivist audience. LOIC was notoriously insecure, but variants persist.

These techniques rely on processing asymmetry: the attacker in some way juggles operations so that the processing demand on the server per connection is higher than the processing demand on the client. Development decisions will impact a system's vulnerability to a higher-level DDoS attack.[1]

Attackers can also rely on internet infrastructure to conduct attacks. This is generally done by taking a response service and sending the response to a forged target address. The classic example of this, the Smurf attack, consists of a ping where the host A, wanting to DDoS site B, sends a spoofed ping to a broadcast address. Every host

---

1 This is true historically as well. Fax machines are subject to *black fax* attacks, where the attacker sends an entirely black page and wastes toner.

receiving the ping (i.e., everything sharing the broadcast address) then drowns the target in responses.

The most common modern form of this attack uses *DNS reflection*: the attacker sends a spoofed request to a DNS resolver, which then sends an inordinately informative and helpfully large packet in response.

Applying Volume and Locality Analysis

The phenomena discussed in this chapter are detectable using a number of different approaches. In general, the problem is not so much detecting them as differentiating malicious activity from legitimate but similar-appearing activity. In this section, we discuss a number of different ways to build detectors and limit false positives.

Data Selection

Traffic data is noisy, and there's little correlation between the volume of traffic and the malice of a phenomenon. An attacker can control a network using ssh and generate much less traffic than a legitimate user sending an attachment over email. The basic noisiness of the data is further exacerbated by the presence of garbage traffic such as scanning and other background radiation (see Chapter 13 for more information on this).

The most obvious values to work with when examining volume are byte and packet counts over a period. They are also generally so fantastically noisy that you're best off using them to identify DDoS and raiding attacks and little else.

Because the values are so noisy and so easily disrupted, I prefer working with constructed values such as flows. NetFlow groups traffic into session approximations; I can then filter the flows on different behaviors, such as:

- Filtering traffic that talks only to legitimate hosts and not to dark space. This approach requires access to a current map of the network, as discussed in Chapter 19.

- Splitting short TCP sessions (four packets or less) from longer sessions, or looking for other indications that a session is legitimate, such as the presence of a PSH flag. See Chapter 13 for more discussion on this behavior.

- Further partitioning traffic into commands, fumbles, and file transfers. This approach, discussed in Chapter 18, extends the filtering process to different classes of traffic, some of which should be rare.

- Using simple volume thresholds. Instead of recording the byte count, for example, record the number of 100-, 1,000-, 10,000-, and 100,000+-byte flows received. This will reduce the noise you're dealing with.

Whenever you're doing this kind of filtering, it's important to not simply throw out the data, but actually partition it. For example, if you count thresholded volume, record the 1–100, 100+, 1,000+, 10,000+ and 100,000+ values as separate time series. The reason for partitioning the data is purely paranoia. Any time you introduce a hard rule for what data you're going to ignore, you've created an opening for an attacker to imitate the ignored data.

Less noisy alternatives to volume counts are values such as the number of IP addresses reaching a network or the number of unique URLs fetched. These values are more computationally expensive to calculate as they require distinguishing individual values; this can be done using a tool like `rwset` in the SiLK suite or with an associative array. Address counts are generally more stable than volume counts, but at least splitting off the hosts that are only scanning is (again) a good idea to reduce the noise.

Example 14-5 illustrates how to apply filtering and partitioning to flow data in order to produce time series data.

Example 14-5. A simple time series output application

```
# gen_timeseries.py
#
# Generates a time series output by reading flow records and partitioning
# the data, in this case into short (<=4 packet) TCP flows and long
# (>4 packet) TCP flows.
#
# Output:
# Time <bytes> <packets> <addresses> <long bytes> <long packets> <long addresses>
#
# Takes as input:
# rwcut --fields=sip,dip,bytes,packets,stime --epoch-time --no-title
#
# We assume that the records are chronologically ordered; that is, no record
# will produce an stime earlier than the records preceding it in the
# output.

import sys
current_time = sys.maxint
start_time = sys.maxint
bin_size = 300 # We'll use five-minute bins for convenience
ip_set_long = set()
ip_set_short = set()
byte_count_long = 0
byte_count_short = 0
```

```
packet_count_long = 0
packet_count_short = 0
for i in sys.stdin.readlines():
    sip, dip, bytes, packets, stime = i[:-1].split('|')[0:5]
    # Convert the non-integer values
    bytes, packets, stime = map(lambda x: int(float(x)), (bytes, packets, stime))
    # Now we check the time binning; if we're onto a new bin, dump and
    # reset the contents
    if (stime < current_time) or (stime > current_time + bin_size):
        ip_set_long = set()
        ip_set_short = set()
        byte_count_long = byte_count_short = 0
    packet_count_long = packet_count_short = 0
        if (current_time == sys.maxint):
            # Set the time to a 5-minute period at the start of the
            # currently observed epoch.  This is done in order to
            # ensure that the time values are always some multiple
            # of five minutes apart, as opposed to dumping something
            # at t, t+307, t+619, and so on.
            current_time = stime - (stime % bin_size)
        else:
            # Now we output results
            print "%10d %10d %10d %10d %10d %10d %10d" % (
                current_time, len(ip_set_short), byte_count_short,
                packet_count_short,len(ip_set_long), byte_count_long,
                packet_count_long)
            current_time = stime - (stime % bin_size)
    else:
        # Instead of printing, we're just adding up data
        # First, determine if the flow is long or short
        if (packets <= 4):
            # flow is short
            byte_count_short += bytes
            packet_count_short += packets
            ip_set_short.update([sip,dip])
        else:
            byte_count_long += bytes
            packet_count_long += packets
            ip_set_long.update([sip,dip])

if byte_count_long + byte_count_short != 0:
    # Final print line check
    print "%10d %10d %10d %10d %10d %10d %10d" % (
        current_time, len(ip_set_short), byte_count_short,
        packet_count_short,len(ip_set_long), byte_count_long,
        packet_count_long)
```

Keep track of what you're partitioning and analyzing. For example, if you decide to calculate thresholds for a volume-based alarm only for sessions from Bulgaria that have at least 100 bytes, then you need to make sure that the decision and the process are documented and that the same approach is used to calculate future thresholds.

Using Volume as an Alarm

The easiest way to construct a volume-based alarm is to calculate a histogram and then pick thresholds based on the probability that a sample will exceed the observed threshold. The *calibrate_raid.py* script in Example 14-2 is a good example of this kind of threshold calculation. When generating alarms, consider the time of day issues discussed in "The Workday and Its Impact on Network Traffic Volume" on page 273, and whether you want multiple models; a single model will normally cost you precision. Also, when considering thresholds, consider the impact of unusually *low* values and whether they merit investigation.

Given the noisiness of traffic volume data, expect a significant number of false positives. Most false positives for volume breaches come from hosts that have a legitimate reason for copying or archiving a target, such as a web crawler or archiving software. Several of the IDS mitigation techniques discussed in Chapter 3 are useful here; in particular, whitelisting anomalies after identifying that the source is innocuous and rolling up events.

Using Beaconing as an Alarm

Beaconing is used to detect a host that is regularly communicating with other hosts. To identify malicious activity, beaconing is primarily used to identify communications with a botnet command and control (C&C) server. To detect beacons, you identify hosts that communicate *consistently* over a time window, as is done with *find_beacons.py* (Example 14-1).

Beacon detection runs into an enormous number of false positives because software updates, AV updates, and even SSH cron jobs have consistent and predictable intervals. Beacon detection consequently depends heavily on inventory management. After receiving an alert, you will have to determine whether a beaconing host has a legitimate justification, which you can do if the beaconing is from a known protocol, is communicating with a legitimate host, or provides other evidence that the traffic is *not* botnet C&C traffic. Once identified as legitimate, the indicia of the beacon (the address and likely the port used for communication) should be recorded to prevent further false positives.

Also of import are hosts that are *supposed* to be beaconing, but don't. This is particularly critical when dealing with AV software, because attackers often disable AV when converting a newly owned host. Checking to see that all the hosts that are supposed to visit an update site do so is a useful alternative alarm.

Using Locality as an Alarm

Locality measures user habits. The advantage of the working set model is that it provides room for those habits to break. Although people are predictable, they do mail new contacts or visit new websites at irregular intervals. Locality-based alarms are consequently useful for measuring changes in user habits, such as differentiating a normal user of a website from someone who is raiding it, or identifying when a site's audience changes during a DDoS attack.

Locality is a useful complement to volume-based detection for identifying raiding. A host that is raiding the site or otherwise scanning it will demonstrate minimal locality, as it will want to visit all the pages on the site as quickly as possible. In order to determine whether a host is raiding, look at what the host is fetching and the speed at which the host is working.

The most common false positives in this case are search engines and bots such as Googlebot. A well-behaved bot can be identified by its `User-Agent` string; if the host is *not* identified as a bot by that string, you have a dangerous host.

A working set model can also be applied to a server rather than individual users. Such a working set is going to be considerably larger than a user profile, but it is possible to use that set to track the core audience of a website or an SSH server.

Engineering Solutions

Raid detection is a good example of a scenario in which you can apply analysis and are probably better off *not* building a detector. The histograms generated by *calibrate_raid.py* and analysis done by counting the volume a user pulls over a day are ultimately about determining how much data a user will realistically access from a server.

This same information can be used to impose rate limits on the servers. Instead of firing off an alert when a user exceeds this threshold, use a rate limiting module (such as Apache's Quota) to cut the user off. If you're worried about user revolt, set the threshold to 200% of the maximum you observe and identify outliers who need special permissions to exceed even that high threshold.

This approach is going to be most effective when you've got a server whose data radically exceeds the average usage of any one user. If people who access a server tend to use less than a megabyte of traffic a day, whereas the server has gigabytes of data, you've got an easily defensible target.

Further Reading

1. C. Dietzel, A. Feldmann, and T. King, "Blackholing at IXPs on the Effectiveness of DDoS Mitigation in the Wild," *Proceedings of the 2016 Passive and Active Measurement (PAM) Conference*, Heraklion, Greece, 2016.

2. S. Dietrich, D. Dittrich, and P. Reiher, *Internet Denial of Service: Attack and Defense Mechanisms* (London: Pearson Education, 2005).

3. J. Mirkovic, J. Martin, and P. Reiher, "A Taxonomy of DDoS Attacks and DDoS Defense Mechanisms," *ACM SIGCOMM Computer Communication Review* 34:2 (2004): 39–53.

4. J. McHugh and C. Gates, "Locality: A New Paradigm in Anomaly Detection," *Proceedings of the 2003 New Security Paradigms Workshop (NSPW)*, Ascona, Switzerland, 2003.

## CHAPTER 15

On Graphs

A *graph* is a mathematical construct composed of one or more *nodes* (or *vertices*) connected together by one or more *links* (or *edges*). Graphs are an effective way to describe communication without getting lost in the weeds. They can be used to model connectivity and provide a comprehensive view of that connectivity while abstracting away details such as packet sizes and session length. Additionally, graph attributes such as centrality can be used to identify critical nodes in a network. Finally, many important protocols (in particular, SMTP and routing) rely on algorithms that model their particular network as a graph.

This chapter is focused on the analytic properties of graphs. We begin by describing what a graph is and then developing examples for major attributes: shortest paths, centrality, clusters, and clustering coefficient.

Graph Attributes: What Is a Graph?

A graph is a mathematical representation of a collection of objects and their interrelationships. Originally developed in 1736 by Leonhard Euler to address the problem of crossing the bridges of Koenigsberg,[1] graphs have since been used to model everything from the core members of conspiracies to the frequency of sounds uttered in the English language. Graphs are an extremely powerful and flexible descriptive tool, and that power comes because they are extremely fungible. Researchers in mathematics, engineering, and sociology have developed an extensive set of constructed and observed graph attributes that can be used to model various behaviors. The first challenge in using graphs is deciding which attributes you need and how to derive them. The following attributes represent a subset of what can be done with graphs, and are

---

1 Modern-day Kaliningrad.

chosen for their direct relevance to the traffic models built later. Any good book on graph theory will include more attributes because at some point, someone has tried just about anything with a graph.

At the absolute minimum, a graph is composed of *nodes* and *links*, where a link is a connection between exactly two nodes. A link can be *directed* or *undirected*; if a link is directed, then it has an *origin* and a *destination*. Conventionally, a graph is either composed entirely of directed links, or entirely of undirected links. If a graph is undirected, then each node has a *degree*, which is the number of links connected to that node. Nodes in a directed graph have an *indegree*, which is the number of links with a destination that is that node, and an *outdegree*, which is the number of links whose origin is the node (Figure 15-1).

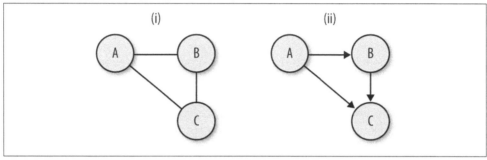

Figure 15-1. Directed and undirected graphs: in (i), the graph is undirected and each node has degree 2; in (ii), the graph is directed and node a has outdegree 2, indegree 0, node b has outdegree 1, indegree 1, and node c has outdegree 0, indegree 2

In network traffic logs, there are a number of candidates for conversion to graphs. In flow data, IP addresses can be used as nodes and flows between them can be used as links. In HTTP server logs, nodes can be individual pages linked together by `Referer` headers. In mail logs, email addresses can be nodes, and the links between them can be mail. Anything expressed as a communication from point A to point B is a suitable candidate.

A disclaimer about the code in this section of the book: it is intended primarily for educational purposes, so in the interests of clearly pointing out how various algorithms or numbers work, I've avoided optimization and a lot of the exception trapping I'd use in production code. This is particularly important when dealing with graph analysis, since graph algorithms are notoriously expensive. There are a number of good libraries available for doing graph analysis, and they will process complex graphs much more efficiently than anything I hack together here.

The script in Example 15-1 can create directed or undirected graphs from lists of pairs (for example, the output of `rwcut --field=1,2 --no-title --delim=' '`). There are a couple of methods under the hood for implementing graphs; in this case,

I'm using *adjacency lists*, which I feel are the most intuitively obvious. In an adjacency list implementation, each node maintains a table of all the links adjacent to it.

Example 15-1. Basic graphs

```python
#!/usr/bin/env python
#
# basic_graph.py
#
# Library
# Provides:
#       Graph object, which as a constructor takes a flow file
#
import os, sys

class UndirGraph:
    """ An undirected, unweighted graph class. This also serves as the base class
    for all other graph implementations in this chapter. """
    def add_node(self, node_id):
        self.nodes.add(node_id)

    def add_link(self, node_source, node_dest):
        self.add_node(node_source)
        self.add_node(node_dest)
        if not self.links.has_key(node_source):
            self.links[node_source] = {}
        self.links[node_source][node_dest] = 1
        if not self.links.has_key(node_dest):
            self.links[node_dest] = {}
        self.links[node_dest][node_source] = 1
        return

    def count_links(self):
        total = 0
        for i in self.links.keys():
            total += len(self.links[i].keys())
        return total/2 # Compensating for link doubling in undirected graph

    def neighbors(self, address):
        # Returns a list of all the nodes adjacent to the node address;
        # returns an empty list if there are no nodes (technically impossible with
        # these construction rules, but hey).
        if self.nodes.has_key(address):
            return self.links[address].keys()
        else:
            return None

    def __str__(self):
        return 'Undirected graph with %d nodes and %d links' % (len(self.nodes),
                                                    self.count_links())
```

```
    def adjacent(self, sip, dip):
        # Note that we've defined the graph as undirected during construction;
        # consequently links only has to return the source.
        if self.links.has_key(sip):
            if self.links[sip].has_key(dip):
                return True

    def __init__(self):
        #
        # This graph is implemented using adjacency lists; every node has
        # a key in the links hashtable, and the resulting value is another hashtable.
        #
        # The nodes table is redundant for undirected graphs, since the existence of
        # a link between X and Y implies a link between Y and X, but in the case of
        # directed graphs it'll provide a speedup if we're just looking for a
        # particular node.
        self.links = {}
        self.nodes = set()

class DirGraph(UndirGraph):
    def add_link(self, node_source, node_dest):
        # Note that in comparison to the undirected graph, we only
        # add links in one direction.
        self.add_node(node_source)
        self.add_node(node_dest)
        if not self.links.has_key(node_source):
            self.links[node_source] = {}
        self.links[node_source][node_dest] = 1
        return

    def count_links(self):
        # This had to be changed from the original count_links since we're now
        # using an undirected graph.
        total = 0
        for i in self.links.keys():
            total += len(self.links[i].keys())
        return total


if __name__ == '__main__':
    #
    # This is a stub executable that will create and then render an
    # undirected graph assuming that it receives some kind of
    # space-delimited set of (source, dest) pairs on input.
    #
    a = sys.stdin.readlines()
    tgt_graph = DirGraph()
    for i in a:
        source, dest = i.split()[0:2]
        tgt_graph.add_link(source, dest)
    print tgt_graph
```

```
print "Links:"
for i in tgt_graph.links.keys():
    dest_links = ' '.join(tgt_graph.links[i].keys())
    print '%s: %s' % (i, dest_links)
```

Graph Construction Versus Graph Attributes

It's really tempting when working with graphs to start creating complicated relations between network attributes and graph attributes, such as deciding direction points from client to server, or weighting links with the traffic between nodes.

I have found that such constructions are more trouble than they're worth, however. It's better to start with a simple graph and examine its attributes rather than trying to build up a complicated graph representation. With that in mind, here are two rules for converting raw data into graphs:

Define communication
> A link should represent a communication between two nodes; with flow data that may mean that a link only occurs when the flow has 10 or more packets and an ACK flag high in order to throw out scanning and failed login attempts.

Define node identity
> Should nodes be IP addresses, or IP addresses and ports in combination? I've found it useful to split the ports into services (everything under 1024 is unique; everything above that is *client*) and then use an IP:service combination.

Labeling, Weight, and Paths

On a graph, a *path* is a set of links connecting two nodes. In a directed graph, paths follow the direction of the link, while in an undirected graph they can move in either direction. Of particular importance in graph analysis are *shortest paths*, which as the name implies are the shortest set of links required to get from point A to point B (see Example 15-2).

Example 15-2. A shortest path algorithm

```
#!/usr/bin/env python
#
# apsp.py -- implements weighted paths and Dijkstra's algorithm

import sys,os,basic_graph

class WeightedGraph(basic_graph.UndirGraph):
    def add_link(self, node_source, node_dest, weight):
        # Weighted bidirectional link aid. Note that we keep the
        # associative array, but now instead of simply setting the value to
```

```
        # 1, we add the weight value.  This reverts to an unweighted
        # graph if we always use the same weight.
        self.add_node(node_source)
        self.add_node(node_dest)
        if not self.links.has_key(node_source):
            self.links[node_source] = {}
        if not self.links[node_source].has_key(node_dest):
            self.links[node_source][node_dest] = 0
        self.links[node_source][node_dest] += weight
        if not self.links.has_key(node_dest):
            self.links[node_dest] = {}
        if not self.links[node_dest].has_key(node_source):
            self.links[node_dest][node_source] = 0
        self.links[node_dest][node_source] += weight

    def dijkstra(self, node_source):
        # Given a source node, create a map of paths for each vertex
        D = {}  # Tentative distance table
        P = {}  # predecessor table

        # The predecessor table exploits a unique feature of shortest paths:
        # every subpath of a shortest path is itself a shortest path, so if
        # you find that (B,C,D) is the shortest path from A to E, then
        # (B,C) is the shortest path from A to D.  All you have to do is keep
        # track of the predecessor and walk backward.

        infy = 999999999999  # Shorthand for infinite
        for i in self.nodes:
            D[i] = infy
            P[i] = None

        D[node_source] = 0
        node_list = list(self.nodes)
        while node_list != []:
            current_distance = infy
            current_node = None
            # First find the node with the smallest distance; that'll
            # be node_source in the first call as it's the only one
            # where D=0.
            for i in node_list:
                if D[i] < current_distance:
                    current_distance = D[i]
                    current_node = i
            node_index = node_list.index(i)
            del node_list[node_index] # Remove it from the list
            if current_distance == infy:
                break # We've exhausted all paths from the node,
                    # everything else is in a different component
            for i in self.neighbors(current_node):
                new_distance = D[current_node] + self.links[current_node][i]
                if new_distance < D[i]:
                    D[i] = new_distance
```

```
            P[i] = current_node
            node_list.insert(0, i)
    for i in D.keys():
        if D[i] == infy:
            del D[i]
    for i in P.keys():
        if P[i] is None:
            del P[i]
    return D,P

def apsp(self):
    # Calls dijkstra repeatedly to create an all-pairs shortest paths table
    apsp_table = {}
    for i in self.nodes:
        apsp_table[i] = self.dijkstra(i)
    return apsp_table
```

An alternative formulation of shortest paths uses *weighting*. In a *weighted graph*, links are assigned a numeric weight. When weights are assigned, the shortest path is no longer simply the smallest number of connected links from point A to point B, but the set of links whose total weight is smallest. Figure 15-2 shows these attributes in more detail.

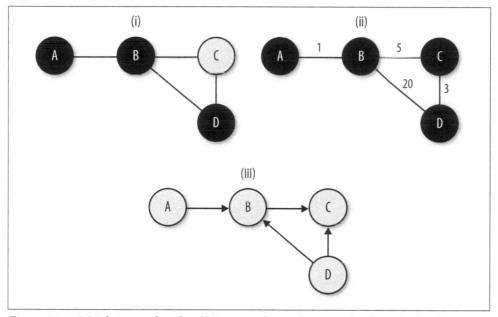

Figure 15-2. Weighting and paths: (i) in an undirected, unweighted graph, the shortest path from A to D involves the least nodes; (ii) in a weighted graph, the shortest path generally has the lowest total weight; (iii) in a directed graph, the shortest path might not be achievable

Shortest paths are a fundamental building block in graph analysis. In most routing services, such as Open Shortest Path First (OSPF), finding shortest paths is the goal. As a result, a good number of graph analyses begin by building a table of the shortest paths between all the nodes by using an All Pairs Shortest Paths (APSP) algorithm on the graph. The code in Example 15-2 provides an example of using *Dijkstra's algorithm* on a weighted, undirected graph to calculate shortest paths.

Dijkstra's algorithm is a good shortest path algorithm that can handle any graph whose link weights are positive. Shortest path algorithms are critical in a number of fields, and there are consequently a huge number of algorithms available depending on the structure of the graph, the construction of the nodes, and the amount of knowledge of the graph that the individual nodes have.

Shortest paths effectively define the distance between nodes on a graph, and serve as the building blocks for a number of other attributes. Of particular importance are *centrality* attributes (see Example 15-3). Centrality is a concept originating in social network analysis; social network analysis models the relationships between entities using graphs and mines the graphs for attributes showing the relationships between these entities in bulk. Centrality, for which there are several measures, is an indicator of how important a node is to the graph's structure.

Example 15-3. Centrality calculation

```
#/usr/bin/env python
#
#
# centrality.py
#
# Generates centrality statistics for a dataset.
#
# input:
# A table of pairs in the form source, destination with a space separating them.
# Weight is implicit; the weight of a link is the number of times a pair appears.
#
# command line:
# calc_centrality.py n
# n: integer value, the number of elements to return in the report
#
# output:
# 7-column report of the form rank | betweenness winner | betweenness
# score | degree winner | degree score | closeness winner | closeness
# score
import sys,string
import apsp

n = int(sys.argv[1])

closeness_results = []
```

```
degree_results = []
betweenness_results = []

target_graph = apsp.WeightedGraph()

# Load up the graph
for i in sys.stdin.readlines():
    source, dest = i[:-1].split()
    target_graph.add_link(source, dest, 1)

# Calculate degree centrality; the easiest of the bunch since it's just the
# degree
for i in target_graph.nodes:
    degree_results.append((i, len(target_graph.neighbors(i))))

apsp_results = target_graph.apsp()

# Now, calculate the closeness centrality scores
for i in target_graph.nodes:
    dt = apsp_results[i][0] # This is the distance table
    total_distance = reduce(lambda a,b:a+b, dt.values())
    closeness_results.append((i, total_distance))

# Then calculate betweenness centrality scores

bt_table = {}
for i in target_graph.nodes:
    bt_table[i] = 0

for current_node in target_graph.nodes:
    # Reconstruct the shortest paths from the predecessor table;
    # for each entry in the distance table, walk backward from that
    # entry to the corresponding origin to get the shortest path, then
    # count the nodes in that path on the master bt table
    pred_table = apsp_results[i][1] # We have the predecessor table
    sp_list = apsp_results[i][0]
    if current_node in sp_list.keys():
        path = []
        for working_node in sp_list.keys():
            if working_node != current_node:
                # We should be done with working-node at this point, count
                # the nodes there for bt score
                for i in path:
                    bt_table[i] += 1
            else:
                path.append(working_node)
                working_node = pred_table[working_node]

for i in bt_table.keys():
    betweenness_results.append((i,bt_table[i]))

# Order the tables; remember that betweenness and degree use higher score, closeness
```

```
# lower score
degree_results.sort(lambda a,b:b[1]-a[1])
betweenness_results.sort(lambda a,b:b[1]-a[1])
closeness_results.sort(lambda a,b:a[1]-b[1])

print "%5s|%15s|%10s|%15s|%10s|%15s|%10s" %
  ("Rank", "Between", "Score", "Degree", "Score","Close", "Score")
for i in range(0, n):
    print "%5d|%15s|%10d|%15s|%10d|%15s|%10d" % ( i + 1,
                                        str(betweenness_results[i][0]),
                                        betweenness_results[i][1],
                                        str(degree_results[i][0]),
                                        degree_results[i][1],
                                        str(closeness_results[i][0]),
                                        closeness_results[i][1])
```

We're going to consider three metrics for centrality in this book: *degree*, *closeness*, and *betweenness*. Degree is the simplest centrality measure; in an undirected graph, the degree centrality of a node is the node's degree.

Closeness and betweenness centrality are both associated with shortest paths. The closeness centrality represents the ease of transmitting information from a particular node to any other node in the graph. To calculate the closeness of a node, you calculate the sum total distance between that node and every other node in the graph. The node with the *lowest* total value has the highest closeness centrality.

Like closeness centrality, betweenness centrality is a function of the shortest paths. Betweenness centrality represents the likelihood that a node will be part of the shortest path between any two particular nodes. The betweenness centrality of a node is calculated by generating a table of all the shortest paths and then counting the number of paths using that node.

Centrality algorithms are all relative measures. Operationally, they're generally best used as ranking algorithms. For example, finding that a particular web page has a high betweenness centrality means that most users when browsing are going to visit that page, possibly because it's a gatekeeper or an important index. Observing user surfing patterns and finding that a particular node has a high closeness centrality can be useful for identifying important news or information sites.

Components and Connectivity

If two nodes in an undirected graph have a path between them, then they are *connected*. The set of all nodes that have paths to each other composes a *connected component*. In directed graphs, nodes can be *weakly connected* (if the paths exist when direction is ignored) or *strongly connected* (if the paths exist when direction is accounted for).

A graph can be broken into its components by using a *breadth-first search* (BFS), which is a search that progresses by picking a node, examining all the neighbors of that node, and then examining each of those nodes' neighbors in turn. This contrasts with a *depth-first search* (DFS), which examines a single neighbor, then a neighbor of that neighbor, and so on. The code in Example 15-4 shows how to use a breadth-first search to break a graph into components.

Example 15-4. Calculating components and clustering coefficient

```
#!/usr/bin/env python
#
#
import os,sys, basic_graph

def calculate_components(g):
    # Creates a table of components via a breadth-first search
    component_table = {}
    unfinished_nodes = {}
    for i in g.nodes.keys():
        unfinished_nodes[i] = 1
    node_list = [g.nodes.keys()[0]]
    component_index = 1
    while node_list != []:
        current_node = node_list[0]
        del node_list[0]
        del unfinished_nodes[current_node]
        for i in g.neighbors(current_node):
            component_table[i] = component_index
            node_list.insert(0, i)
        if node_list == [] and len(unfinished_nodes) > 0:
            node_list = [unfinished_nodes.keys()[0]]
    return component_table
```

Clustering Coefficient

Another mechanism for measuring the relationships between nodes on a graph is the *clustering coefficient*. The clustering coefficient is the probability that any two neighbors of a particular node on a graph are neighbors of each other. Example 15-5 shows a code snippet for calculating the clustering coefficient.

Example 15-5. Calculating clustering coefficient

```
def calculate_clustering_coefficients(g):
    # Clustering coefficient for a node is the
    # fraction of its neighbors who are also neighbors with each other
    node_ccs = {}
    for i in g.nodes.keys():
        mutual_neighbor_count = 0
```

```
neighbor_list = g.neighbors(i)
neighbor_set = {}
for j in neighbor_list:
    neighbor_set[j] = 1
for j in neighbor_list:
    # We grab the neighbors and find out how many of them are in the
    # set
    new_neighbor_list = g.neighbors[j]
    for k in new_neighbor_list:
        if k != i and neighbor_list.has_key(k):
            mutual_neighbor_count += 1
# We now calculate the coefficient by dividing by d*(d-1) to get the
# fraction
cc = float(mutual_neighbor_count)/((float(len(neighbor_list) *
                                        (len(neighbor_list) -1 ))))
    node_ccs[i] = cc
total_cc = reduce(lambda a,b:node_ccs[a] + node_ccs[b], node_ccs.keys())
total_cc = total_cc/len(g.nodes.keys())
return total_cc
```

The clustering coefficient is a useful measure of "peerishness." A graph of a pure client/server network will have a clustering coefficient of zero—a client talks only to servers, and servers talk only to clients. We've had some success using clustering as a measure of the impact of spam on large networks. As an example of this, Figure 15-3 shows the impact of the shutdown of McColo, a bulletproof hosting provider, on the SMTP network structure of a large network. Following McColo's shutdown, the clustering coefficient for SMTP rose by about 50%.

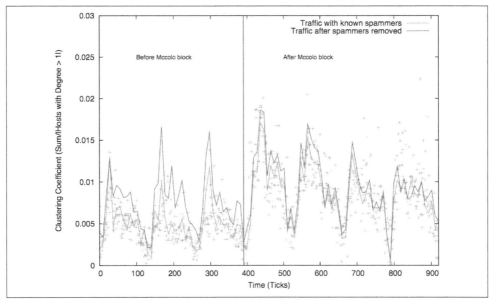

Figure 15-3. Clustering coefficient and large email networks

The relationship between peerishness and spam may be a bit obscure. SMTP, like DNS and other early internet services, is very sharing-oriented. An SMTP client in one interaction may operate as a server for another interaction, so we expect clients and servers to swap roles over time. Spammers, however, operate effectively as *super-clients*—they talk to servers, but never operate as a server for anyone else. This behavior manifests as a low clustering coefficient. Remove the spammers, and the SMTP network starts to look more like a peer-to-peer network and the clustering coefficient rises.

Analyzing Graphs

Graph analysis can be used for a number of purposes. Centrality metrics are a useful tool both for engineering and for forensic analysis, while components and graph attributes can be used to generate a number of alarms.

Using Component Analysis as an Alarm

In Chapter 13 we discussed detection mechanisms that relied on the attacker's ignorance of a particular network, such as blind scanning and the like. Connected components are useful for modeling a different type of attacker ignorance. An attacker might know *where* various servers and systems are located on a network, but not *how they relate to each other*. Organizational structure can be identified by looking at connected components, and a number of attacks—such as APT and hit-list attacks, which may know the target but not how its components relate to each other—can be identified by examining these components.

To understand how this phenomenon can be used as an alarm, consider the graphical example in Figure 15-4. In this example, the network is composed of two discrete components (say, engineering and marketing), and there is little interaction between them. When an attacker appears and tries to communicate with the hosts on the network, he combines these two components to produce one huge component that does not appear under normal circumstances.

To implement this type of alarm, you must first identify a service that can be divided into multiple components. Good candidates are services such as SSH that require some form of user login; permissions mean that certain users won't have access, which breaks the network into discrete components. SMTP and HTTP are generally bad candidates, though HTTP is feasible if you are looking exclusively at servers that require user login, and you limit your analysis to *just* those servers (e.g., by using an IPset).

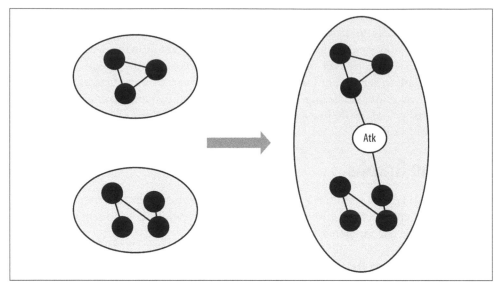

Figure 15-4. An attacker artificially links discrete components

After you've identified your set of servers, identify components to monitor. And after you identify a component, calculate its size—the number of nodes within the component as a function of the time taken to collect it (for example, 60 seconds of NetFlow). The distribution is likely to be sensitive not only to the time taken to collect the traffic, but also the time of day. Breaking traffic at least into on/off periods (as discussed in Chapter 14) is likely to help.

There are two ways to identify components: either by size order or by tracking hosts within the components. In the case of size order, you simply track the sizes of the largest component, the second-largest component, and so on. This approach is simple, robust, and relatively insensitive to subtle attacks. It's not uncommon for the largest component to make up more than one-third of the total nodes in the graph, so you need a fairly aggressive attack to disrupt the size of the component. The alternative approach involves identifying nodes by their component (e.g., component A is the component containing address 127.0.1.2).

Using Centrality Analysis for Forensics

Centrality is a useful tool for identifying important nodes in a network, and for identifying nodes that communicate at much lower volumes than traffic analysis can identify.

Consider an attack where the attacker infects one or more hosts on a network with malware. These infected hosts now communicate with a command and control server that was previously not present. Figure 15-5 shows this scenario in more depth.

Before hosts A, B, and C are infected, one node shows some degree of centrality. Following infection, a new node (*Mal*) is the most central node in the set.

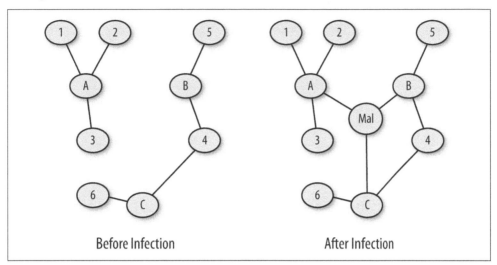

Figure 15-5. Centrality in forensics

This kind of analysis can be done by isolating traffic data into two sets, a *pre-event set* and a *post-event set*. For example, after finding out that the network received a malicious attachment at a particular time, I can pull traffic before that time to produce a pre-event set and traffic after that time to find a post-event set. Looking for newly central nodes gives me a reasonable chance of identifying the command and control server.

Using Breadth-First Searches Forensically

Once you've identified that a malicious host is communicating on your network, the next step is to find out who it's talking to, such as the host's C&C or other infected hosts on the network. Once you've found that out, you can repeat the process to find out who *they* talked to in order to identify other targets.

This iterative investigation is a breadth-first search. You start with a single node, look at all of its neighbors for suspicious behavior, and then repeat the process on *their* neighbors (see Example 15-6). This type of graph-based investigation can help identify other infected hosts, suspicious targets, and other systems on the network that need investigation or analysis.

Example 15-6. Examining a site's neighbors

```
#!/usr/bin/env python
#
```

```
# This is a somewhat ginned-up example of how to use breadth-first searches to
# crawl through a dataset and identify other hosts that are using BitTorrent.
# The crawling criteria are as follows:
#     A communicates to B on ports 6881-6889
#     A and B exchange a large file (> 1 MB)
#
# The point of the example is that you could use any criteria you want and put
# multiple criteria into constructing the graph.
#
#
# Command line:
# crawler.py seed_ip datafile
#
# seed_ip is the IP address of a known BitTorrent user
# datafile
import os, sys, basic_graph

def extract_neighbors(ip_address, datafile):
    # Given an ip_address, identify the nodes adjacent to that
    # address by finding flows that have that address as either a source or
    # destination.  The other address in the pair is considered a neighbor.
    a = os.popen("""rwfilter --any-address=%s --sport=1024-65535 --dport=1024-65535 \
    --bytes=1000000- --pass=stdout %s | rwfilter --input=stdin --aport=6881-6889 \
    --pass=stdout | rwuniq --fields=1,2 --no-title""" % (ip_address,datafile), 'r')
    # In the query, note the fairly rigorous port definitions I'm using -- everything
    # starts out as high.  This is because, depending on the stack implementation,
    # ports 6881-6889 (the BT ports) may be used as ephemeral ports.  By breaking
    # out client ports in the initial filtering call, I'm guaranteeing that I
    # don't accidently record, say, a web session to port 6881.
    # The 1 MB limit is also supposed to constrain us to actual BT file transfers.
    neighbor_set = set()
    for i in a.readlines():
        sip, dip = i.split('|')[0:2].strip()
    # I check to see if the IP address is the source or destination of the
    # flow; whichever one it is, I add the complementary address to the
    # neighbor set (e.g., if ip_address is sip, I add the dip).
        if sip == ip_address:
            neighbor_set.add(dip)
        else:
            neighbor_set.add(sip)
    a.close()
    return neighbor_set

if __name__ == '__main__':
    starting_ip = sys.argv[1]
    datafile = sys.argv[2]
    candidate_set = set([starting_ip])
    while len(candidate_set) > 0:
        target_ip = candidate_set.pop()
    target_set.add(target_ip)
        neighbor_set = extract_neighbors(target_ip, datafile)
        for i in neighbor_set:
```

```
        if not i in target_set:
            candidate_set.add(i)
    for i in target_set:
        print i
```

Using Centrality Analysis for Engineering

Given limited monitoring resources and analyst attention, effectively monitoring a network requires identifying mission-critical hosts and assigning resources to protecting and watching them. That said, in any network, there's a huge difference between the hosts that people *say* they need and the hosts they actually use. Using traffic analysis to identify critical hosts helps differentiate between what's important on paper and what users actually visit.

Centrality is one of a number of metrics that can be used to identify criticality. Alternatives include counting the number of hosts that visit a site (which is effectively degree centrality) and looking at traffic volume. Centrality is a good complement to volume.

Further Reading

1. M. Collins and M. Reiter, "Hit-List Worm Detection and Bot Identification in Large Networks Using Protocol Graphs," *Proceedings of the 2007 Symposium on Recent Advances in Intrusion Detection*, Queensland, Australia, 2007.

2. T. Cormen et al., *Introduction to Algorithims*, 3rd ed. (Boston, MA: MIT Press, 2009).

3. L. Li et al., "Towards a Theory of Scale-Free Graphs: Definition, Properties, and Implications (Extended Version)."

4. igraph (*http://bit.ly/igraph-pack*), an (R graph library).

5. Neo4j (*http://www.neo4j.org*), a scalable graph database.

6. NetworkX (*http://networkx.github.io/*), a Python graph library.

## CHAPTER 16

On Insider Threat

This chapter is about the problem of collecting and analyzing data when dealing with *insider threat*. Insider threat involves attacks coming from a member of an organization. When planning and executing attacks, insiders can take advantage of physical location, trust, and better knowledge of the organization. Where an outsider will blindly search within a network to find valuable targets, the insider will know (and possibly have created) the highest-value information. Where an outsider relies on rainbow tables and exploits, the insider can charm other users out of passwords or use common admin tools she needs as part of her job. Where the outsider's behavior is obviously aberrant, the insider can hide it, or, if caught, explain it away.

For a network security analyst, insider threat work should focus on collecting and synthesizing data, rather than detection. Insider threat investigations begin and end with people—cues from inside the organization that someone is at risk, and interviews with the insiders at the end. The network security team should expect to support other investigators by providing and analyzing data that forms a part of a larger picture.

Insider threat detection is hard; it involves a low-frequency, high-threat event that has a significant and damaging risk of blowback. Many of the biggest cues about insider threat involve indicia that someone is isolated or on his way out of the job—problems at work, antagonistic relationships with coworkers, and so on. However, at some point, everybody is going to have a bad day; therefore, distinguishing between daily grumbles and actual threats is critical to an effective program. Insider threat is best handled preventatively, by the organization addressing and eliminating the conditions that risk insider threats showing up in the first place. If the insider threat program consists exclusively of generating and following up on alerts, then the ops floor will be overburdened, and users will chafe under the constraints.

The analysis team should consequently be prepared to support investigations raised in response to common insider threat risks: specifically, the integration and synthesis of data from diverse (often legacy or embedded) sources such as physical access logs, video monitors, and traces of network traffic and assets.

Brian Kelley: The Risk of False Positives

Robert Hanssen is widely known as the FBI counterintelligence agent who spent 22 years selling secrets to the Soviet Union and the Russian Federation. Fewer people know about Brian Kelley, the CIA analyst who was a false positive in the Hanssen case. Kelley was identified as the mole in 1998, aggressively investigated by the FBI, and eventually had his clearance suspended (and not reinstated until after Hanssen was arrested several years later, in 2001).[1] Kelley himself believed that his suspension triggered Hanssen, who had been lying low for a few years, to start leaking again.

Kelley is, unfortunately, a good example of the damage that a false positive can cause. He was under constant investigation and his career was effectively scuttled for years. Insider threat investigations impact people's lives, so be cautious and thorough before pulling the trigger.

When insider threat analysis does involve detection, it will rarely find definitive evidence; rather, insider threat detection will uncover hints that something is amiss that combine with other evidence. Insider threat detection involves managing an enormous number of false positives, and making a judgment call about when to move from simple monitoring to more focused analysis to action.

This chapter is organized around two core concepts: differentiating insider attacks from external attacks, and a discussion of the types of attacks insiders conduct and how to observe them. The remainder of this chapter covers each topic in depth, followed up by pointers to supporting material. Several notable examples of insider threat cases are covered in sidebars; pointers are provided in each case to some material describing what happened and when.

Insider Threat Versus Other Classes of Attacks

Before diving into insider threat behavior in depth, let's emphasize that "insider threat" does *not* necessarily mean malice, and insider threat detection is not simply a matter of finding the villain. There are a good number of insider cases that involve

---

1 See P. Early, "Brian J. Kelley, My Friend the Spy Expert" (*http://www.peteeearley.com/2011/09/26/brian-j-kelley-my-friend-the-spy-expert/*) and M. McKay, "To Catch a Spy: Probe to Unmask Hanssen Almost Ruined Kelley" (*http://www.cbsnews.com/news/to-catch-a-spy-30-01-2003/*) (*60 Minutes* Transcript).

sysadmins "adopting" systems within a network and managing them long after they've left, inadvertently adding security holes and backdoors in the process. Insider threat is about risk, and while malice is part of that risk, so are fear, panic, and stupidity.

Terry Childs

Terry Childs is an example of a particular IT-centric form of insider threat. Childs was a CCIE who developed a key part of San Francisco's governmental IT infrastructure. After being reassigned, he refused to hand over control to anyone else, until he was eventually arrested and forced to turn over the passwords.[2]

Articles on Childs's motivation emphasize several common factors: he was the sole architect of the system, he took great pride in it, he didn't trust anyone else to manage it, and he was worried he was going to be fired.[3] This combination, in particular the sole ownership of the system, is an example of how bus factor (see "Applying Sector-Based Workflow to Insider Threat" on page 324) is common in IT, and can be an insider threat risk.

The simplest definition of an insider threat is that it's a threat to an organization posed by a member of that organization. Being a member of the organization gives the insider significant advantages: better knowledge of the organization, trust to exploit, physical presence, and the like.

Insiders differ from outsiders in that they have knowledge of their environment that the outsiders lack. Leveraging this knowledge means that defensive detection techniques that rely on the attacker making mistakes are less likely to apply to an insider. Consider, for example, how an insider and an outsider will approach the problem of finding and copying valuable information from a network.

We'll assume the outsider is smart: she uses a spear-phishing attack to drop an exploit kit into the network. With the exploit kit, the attacker probes inside the network and identifies a fileshare—she copies the contents of the entire fileshare, compresses the results, encrypts them, and then slowly transfers the results to an external server.

Now let's consider an insider. He opens up the fileshare on his desktop, copies the three most valuable files to a USB stick, and walks out the door.

---

2 See D. Kravets, "San Francisco Admin Charged with Hijacking City's Network" (*https://www.wired.com/ 2008/07/sf-city-charged/*).

3 See G. Newsom, "Why Government Should Outsource Technology" (*http://slate.me/2vdOTvO*), P. Venezia, "Why San Francisco's Network Admin Went Rogue" (*http://www.infoworld.com/article/2653004/misadven tures/why-san-francisco-s-network-admin-went-rogue.html*), and R. McMillan, "Terry Childs Juror Explains Why He Voted to Convict" (*http://www.pcworld.com/article/195198/article.html*).

Table 16-1 shows the differences in various areas. The outsider's behavior is moderated through the network, while the insider can rely on hard-to-detect behaviors like direct physical access. The outsider is ignorant of the network's structure, while the insider knows where things are. Finally, the outsider must forge or steal credentials, while the insider already has them. Each of these impacts the defender's ability to find hostile behaviors.

Table 16-1. Observables for technical events

Behavior	Insider	Outsider
Access	Can exploit physical access and resources	Network moderated
Resources/ targets	Aware of targets and value	Must probe to identify targets of value
Credentials	May already have credentials, can acquire out of band	Must acquire credentials, using password cracking, exploits, etc.
Tools	More likely to rely on existing sysadmin tools and privileges	More likely to rely on malware
Monitoring	More likely to be aware of monitoring, will intentionally evade	Evasion will not be tailored to specific network, relies on delay and encryption
Attacks	Data theft, specific sabotage	May be completely unaware of network's value

---

Tailored Damage: Roger Duronio

Roger Duronio was a system administrator for UBS Paine Webber. After a series of incidents, he quit his job over an unexpectedly small bonus. Before leaving the company, he installed a custom-written application to systematically destroy UBS's trading infrastructure before trading began on March 4, 2002.[4] Duronio's logic bomb went off, hitting UBS's infrastructure and causing millions of dollars in damage. As part of his vengeance plan, Duronio shorted UBS's stock, planning to make a profit after his bomb damaged the company's trading abilities.

This attack is an example of an insider tailoring their damage very specifically to the environment and their knowledge of it. Not only was the bomb tailored to cripple a specific system, but as an insider, Duronio was aware of how this particular attack would damage UBS.

For our purposes, the largest difference between insider and outsider attacks is that the outsider is *moderated via the network*. Control, exploit, transfer, communication,

---

4 See United States Department of Justice, US Attorney, District of New Jersey, "Former UBS Computer Systems Manager Gets 97 Months for Unleashing 'Logic Bomb' on Company Network" (*http://bit.ly/former-ubs-atty*) and M. Worman, "Information Ordnance: Logic Bombs, Forensics, and the Tragical History of Roger Duronio" (*http://bit.ly/information-ordnance*).

credential theft—*everything* must be done through the network. That communication may be delayed, it may be encrypted, or it may be hidden, but it must be done via some network channel. Insiders can exploit physical access and out-of-band communications. This means a much heavier reliance on host- and service-based monitoring, as well as potentially accessing physical logs and integrating them with network data.

The second most significant difference is that insiders will often exploit their knowledge of the system to ensure that they aren't detected, and to tailor damage specifically to their environment. Attacker behaviors that we generally expect to see from outsiders, particularly reconnaissance and fumbling (see Chapter 13), will be much rarer in the case of insider attacks.[5] Insiders stealing intellectual property or other assets are also likely to be less obvious than an outsider in the data they take.[6]

Third, insiders can exploit an organization's trust in ways that outsiders just can't. Insiders can rely on their own credentials, using administrative tools or social connections to gain the access they need. Insiders are also more likely to use their knowledge to tailor what they steal, whereas outsiders will try to steal whatever's available

Avoiding Toxicity

Insider threat investigations can backfire when they push too hard. Properly managing an insider threat program means recognizing not only that yes, a trusted employee can go bad, but also that trust is bidirectional. Insider threat recognition requires that users trust their security personnel; if the relationship between security and employees goes toxic—if the security team assumes all users are guilty—then insider threat programs risk becoming self-fulfilling prophecies.

Insider threat investigations are crises; investigators should expect to be in constant communication with the C-suite with regular briefs, updates, and status information moving up the chain of command. During the crisis, the team should update information daily. Once the crisis is done, it should be put away. I feel it's a good idea to rotate analysts out of insider threat investigations, keeping them from doing them consecutively because each investigation degrades the participants' trust in everything.

On that note, I'll reiterate: the best way to handle insider threats is to keep them from happening in the first place. If you are handling a disproportionate number of insider

---

5 As always, there are many exceptions. Insiders *may* probe inside the network if they're not sure where an asset is, but we'll focus on their distinctive behavior here.

6 Note that this is also a function of motivation; an insider looking to steal data for profit has less motivation to take everything than an insider looking to publish everything she can get her hands on on a leak site.

threat cases, that is a sign of deeper organizational problems. Big brother is not the solution here.

When an insider is apprehended, it's always a gut-punch for the organization. Insiders exploit institutional trust, and once you find an insider, you're shaking that trust. The situation is exacerbated with false positives, where you risk damaging institutional trust, losing a valuable employee, and making the insider aware you're looking for them.

Insider Motivations Versus Risk

In every insider threat case I've been involved in, there has been a head-slapping moment where we ask why the warning signs weren't heeded. This may be survivorship bias—the insider threat cases I've been involved in all started after the insider was caught—but I think it's also a case of how we want organizations to work. We want people to trust each other, and insiders break that. Afterwards, you ask, "Why?"

There are a number of classic motivations. A Cold War model for recruiting spies used the acronym *MICE*: Money, Ideology, Compromise, and Ego. While it's not perfect, as it's about creating insider threats rather than detecting them, it has some use—Duronio was motivated by money and ego, Hanssen by pure ego (he really didn't do anything with the money). That said, ideology and compromise have a very Cold War feel to them, and aren't necessarily as relevant now, with the potential exception of hacktivism.

In the case of IT personnel, misplaced ownership is a common problem—Childs is a reasonable example and isn't unique. It's not uncommon for IT personnel to acquire so much knowledge of core systems that they become indispensible, which is a problem if they're an insider threat or if they get run over by a bus.

Modes of Attack

I will now discuss the types of attacks an insider may *uniquely* conduct. These attacks rely on the insider's particular capabilities within the organization: knowledge of the internal structure and trust. In the following subsections, I will discuss several modes of attack, as well as observable data for identifying them.

Data Theft and Exfiltration

By far, the most common form of insider attack involves the exfiltration and theft of data for future use.

Monitoring file access requires that current versions of the files be in a monitorable location, such as a common Sharepoint, Google Drive, or the like. A well-defined checkin/checkout process for shared documents can ensure that the documents are in a location where they can be monitored for usual access.

Observables for data theft include excessive file access or copying, indicated either by an increase in data volume or users accessing files they have never accessed before (see Chapter 14 for information on volume thresholds and locality violations). If a user starts to fumble on the filesystem, that is also a potential indicator (see Chapter 13 for more information). Also pay attention to physical indicators, such as file access in off-hours, or use of physical tools such as USB drives.

Credential Theft

Credential theft occurs when the insider needs privileges that she doesn't have for the current attack. This kind of behavior is a precursor to other types of attacks, most notably sabotage and data exfiltration. Insider credential theft differs from external credential theft because it's more likely to be a form of social engineering (such as the ever popular "Hey Bob, I need your password to fix your computer!").

Since the act of credential theft will likely be conducted out of band, a defender is more likely to see indications that the credentials are being used anomalously after the fact.

Observables of credential theft include logins from unusual hosts (the user has never touched the host before, or the host is outside of the network or new) and logins from unusual physical locations. Multiple logins from diverse locations is suspicious, and may indicate two users working with the same account. Fumbling (see Chapter 13) is a good indicator that the user is unfamiliar with the host, and may be an indicator that she is looking for specific files or exploring the host.

Sabotage

Sabotage scenarios involve the insider damaging company assets, such as by installing malware on the network. The Duronio case is an example of a sabotage attack. Duronio not only took advantage of his administrative knowledge to plant his attack within the network and damage UBS activity, but engineered it specifically to hit at UBS's core functions.

Observables for sabotage include identifying changes to software or the subversion of systems—change control of critical applications or administrative software is helpful here (see Chapter 19 for more discussion). Understanding what core functions exist within your system is critical to managing sabotage; inventory and mapping (see Chapter 18) will help you to understand what systems require more monitoring and represent the highest risk.

Insider Threat Data: Logistics and Collection

Insiders are usually aware that they're being monitored. What they usually aren't aware of is the *extent* of monitoring. Anecdotally, insiders will be very cautious where they know they're being watched, and careless when they assume they aren't.

This means, for the defender, that the more *diverse* the data collected is, the better. Strategies include both collecting data from diverse sources, and collecting data redundantly—the same phenomenon observed at different locations. The problem, of course, with collecting all this data is that you then have an enormous pile of data to sift through. Triggered data collection—that is, accessing specific sources as needed rather than continuously feeding them to the SIEM—is important here.

Because analysts will often be using older, lower-priority, more obscure, and in many cases proprietary embedded data, there's a strong need for prior preparation and inventory. Insider threat investigations can stretch back to years' worth of data, and the team is well served to know ahead of time how hard it will be to acquire this data. In particular, data acquisition at these scales is often an ongoing process involving staging up data from multiple archives.

Applying Sector-Based Workflow to Insider Threat

Given the high false positive rate and enormous amount of data to process when dealing with insider threat, insider threat monitoring lends itself well to sector-based workflow (see Chapter 20 for more information on this). In this case, the sectors are groups of users based on the risk they represent.

In this approach, the ops team breaks users into different sectors based on risk. A simple staging model can break activity down by risk combined with trust, as follows:

Low-risk, high-trust (LR/HT)
> This should be the organization's default category, and represent the majority of users. These users are subject to *default monitoring*, which is to say nothing tailored to a specific user, not associated with a specific identity, and focusing primarily on external threats.

High-risk, high-trust (HR/HT)
> This category includes administrators, security analysts, and other personnel who are trusted, but who can cause exceptional damage. It may also include users who are outside world–facing, depending on your organization. These users will have more activities audited—for example, sysadmins may have all of their administrative tasks logged and achievable only from specified accounts. High-risk trusted users should be aware of the extent that they are being monitored; it is part of the responsibility.

Low-risk, low-trust (LR/LT)

This category includes new hires and employees who have recently resigned but did not have significant responsibilities. These users may have some additional monitoring in place, or they may be subject to additional controls.

High-risk, low-trust (HR/LT)

These are users who are subject to extensive and potentially tailored monitoring depending on the threat and the circumstances.

In this breakdown, analysts would spend the majority of their time checking the HR/HT and HR/LT groups. HR/HT users may be regularly audited, while HR/LT users have additional monitoring that they are not aware of. The expectation is that HR/HT should be a fairly static group, without much turnover, and the HR/LT group should be small, ideally zero.

Different events (organizational or technical) may cause different transitions. Examples of events that might move a user into a lower trust sector include:

Disciplinary action

If a user has been written up for disciplinary violations, threatened other employees, etc.

Financial pressure

Declarations of bankruptcy, gambling addiction, and other situations where the insider needs cash.

Quitting

If the employee quits, then elevated monitoring is likely to be part of the exit plan.

The risk factors listed here refer to a user's position within an organization, and are likely to remain relatively static over time. These cues are also of use for identifying targets for APT and spear phishing attacks:

Senior personnel

Senior members of an organization (managers, CEOs) have elevated access and authority.

Assistants to senior personnel

Senior executives live by their assistants, and the easiest way to subvert, access, or damage them is often to work through their assistants.

Public personnel

Users who are publicly noticeable represent an elevated risk.

Bus factor
> An indication of how critical a user is to your organization outside of the org chart. The term "bus factor" comes from software engineering circles and refers to the damage that would happen to projects if that particular user were run over by a bus.

Physical Data Sources

When dealing with insider threat locations, it is useful to be able to reconstruct where within a facility a particular event occurred. To this end, the analyst can look at physical data sources such as mobile device records and physical access control logs, and if necessary use network-based techniques.

Mobile devices (tablets, cellphones) usually have at least GPS tracking built into them, and mobile device management software (examples of which include MobileIron, Cisco, Meraki, and the like) will usually report this information.

Physical access records include video recordings and logs from physical access tools such as Datawatch Systems or Kastle Systems card logs (among other vendors). These are the logs showing badge access into a facility and can be helpful for associating physical access with network access. Note that access control log formats will be vendor-specific, and interpreting them may require using a specific vendor-provided tool. Be prepared to develop some interstitial software to export and process the data in your preferred console.

Basic network-based techniques will focus on tracking where within an organizational network (*if* the traffic is within the network) a host is located. This can be as simple as checking the IP address of a host, or it can require running a `traceroute` to the host to determine where it is within the organization's routing infrastructure.

Keeping Track of User Identity

In addition to access records, expect to need to use multiple redundant data sources to track insiders. If insiders are, for example, aware that they have to move through a web proxy to access the outside world, expect them to move their traffic outside of that proxy server and that you will likely have to fall back to NetFlow.

Be aware that insider threat investigations may involve setting up *new* log collection capabilities, as the analysis team may be called in several months before any final decision.

Since the analyst is usually in a supporting role for an insider investigation, he often will have a clear idea of what particular user he needs to monitor. The hard part is associating that user's identity with observable phenomena, in particular when using redundant sources.

Further Reading

1. D. Cappelli, A. Moore, and R. Trzeciak, *The CERT Guide to Insider Threats: How to Prevent, Detect, and Respond to Information Technology Crimes* (Boston, MA: Addison Wesley Professional, 2012).

2. CERT Insider Threat Group home page (*https://www.cert.org/insider-threat/*).

3. DARPA ADAMS project (*https://opencatalog.darpa.mil/ADAMS.html*).

## CHAPTER 17

On Threat Intelligence

In this chapter, I will discuss the consumption and processing of *threat intelligence*. Threat intelligence is a process of sharing data about attacks—victims of attacks or investigators share contextual information. Threat intelligence can comprise a variety of data sources, including geolocation data, reputation information (often gussied-up geolocation data), and information on attacker techniques, malware signatures, and vulnerabilities.

I have divided this chapter into two major sections. In the first section, I discuss threat intelligence source data: the type of information that comprises threat intelligence, and formats you can expect to receive this information in. In the second section, I discuss the process of setting up a threat intelligence program for an organization.

Defining Threat Intelligence

For our purposes, I am going to define threat intelligence data as *contextual* data collected from *multiple sources* to *improve response*. By contextual data, I mean that threat intelligence is data collected to enhance event-based data such as IDS alerts or flow data. Threat intelligence data is collected and synthesized from multiple sources; this includes actions more related to conventional intelligence gathering. Finally, threat intelligence data is used to improve incident response—it provides information for hardening networks, identifies indicators of higher-risk attacks, and provides a means for operations teams to identify common threads.

I must emphasize an important point here: threat intelligence data is supplementary and contextual. You cannot run a detection program on threat intelligence alone; there must be some set of event data to apply threat intelligence to. A threat intelligence feed without a primary data source (incidents, network traffic) is useless. A threat intelligence feed that isn't relevant to the types of data you're collecting is equally useless.

Raw threat intelligence data appears in network feeds, in the same way that conversations appear in the air—it doesn't become a product until someone analyzes it and packages it. In this sense, "threat intelligence" is a term now applied to formerly informal or largely corporate processes of information sharing. That's a cynical way of stating a good thing; in the last few years, there's been an increasing recognition that threat intelligence needs to be treated more systematically, and that information security isn't a purely technical effort. This includes the establishment of standards with some traction (e.g., STIX and TAXII), the increasing acceptance of threat intel platforms (e.g., MISP), and the development of open organizations for sharing threat intel (the Information Sharing and Analysis Centers, or ISACs in particular have taken charge on this).

Data Types

Threat intelligence is a wide, undefined topic, and it's an area where people are *very* eager to sell data. In this section, I am going to (loosely) classify threat intelligence data along several different qualities. Specifically, these qualities are the *type* of intelligence delivered, the *maturity* of the data, its *origin*, and its *format*.

Types of threat intelligence data

We will consider three major types of threat intelligence data: network reputation information (e.g., IP addresses, URLs), IOCs (e.g., malware hashes), and TTPs (tools, techniques, and procedures).

Network reputation information refers to data that scores URLs, IP addresses, or other indicators for hostility. A reputation threat feed will generally consist of timed and dated lists of keys, and an explanation for why a key is marked as a threat. As a rule, reputation data is something that you can directly plug into your access control lists (ACLs) or network filters, or automatically annotate your SIEM data with.

A free example of this type of information is the rules provided by the Emerging Threats database (*https://rules.emergingthreats.net*), a free repository of threat intelligence encoded as lists of IP addresses and IDS rulesets. This information is subdivided into different categories, such as botnet command and control, and various named groups.

Indicators of compromise (IOCs) really describe anything that can be used to indicate that a host has been compromised by malware. IOC data is forensic and largely host-based, including information such as malware hashes or credentials.

TTPs are usually reports describing the methods and techniques used by attackers, meant to be read and processed by people for situational awareness. These can be general, perhaps signaling awareness of a new form of attack, or quite specific, detailing behavioral signatures for particular malware groups.

Finally, there is an *implicit* category of threat intelligence data that I think of as *secondary*. Secondary data is threat intelligence that is delivered to platforms within your organization for their use. The classic example is antivirus signatures—when you subscribe to an AV service, you receive regularly updated intelligence delivered to your AV clients.

Maturity and format of threat intelligence data

A key workflow problem for any threat intelligence organization is the process of collecting, vetting, and reformatting the data. Threat intelligence data comes in a number of distinct formats, most of which are not directly accessible to the end users.

In addition, we must discuss the current efforts toward developing standards. In the last decade or so, there have been a number of efforts to develop threat intelligence formats. The first of these were the IODEF (Incident Object Description Exchange Format) and IDMEF (Intrusion Detection Message Exchange Format) standards developed by the IETF in the mid-2000s.

Several providers have also created their own formats. The most notable of these is MISP (*http://www.misp-project.org*), the malware intelligence sharing platform, originally built by CIRCL (Luxembourg's CERT). MISP is an open source project with a thriving community. Similar projects include OpenIOC (*http://www.openioc.org/*), an outgrowth of Mandiant's (now part of FireEye) forensics tools, and AlienVault's Open Threat Exchange (OTX) standard (*https://otx.alienvault.com*).

The other major project is a collection of OASIS-backed standards grouped under the moniker STIX (Structured Threat Information Expression) (*https://oasis-open.github.io/cti-documentation/*). The actual project includes several standards; STIX itself is the standard for representing IOCs, while TAXII (Trusted Automated Exchange of Intelligence Information) is the transport protocol.

So, with all these standards, what ones to use? Probably both MISP and STIX—with IOC data, the syntax of how the data is recorded is usually less important than the semantics. All IOC reporting standards are some form of key/value pairing, and the more important questions are what the keys are, not how they're stored, and whether there are interoperability tools.

With that in mind, here are some common types of IOC fields you can expect:

File hashes
    Hashes of specific files associated with a compromise. Given the rapid pace at which hashes are replaced and move (see Chapter 6), IOC formats usually specify multiple common hashes. These include MD5, SHA1, SHA256, and the longer

formats (like SHA384 and SHA512). IOCs will usually hash the malware files, but also may hash filenames.

Network addresses
Domain names, IP addresses. These are often categorized as botnet sites, command and control servers, drop sites, and the like.

Target information
Email addresses, financial information (ABA routing numbers, credit card numbers, etc.).

Windows data
Portable Executable (PE) hashes, Registry information, and other Windows-specific data.

A final note: the tools are, to be honest, less important than the communities. The intent of all of these standards is to provide a way to share information that is more structured than an email, but the standards are useless *without intelligence to populate them*. In the case of the MISP and STIX standards, you should really pay the most attention to their resources pages to find the organizations that are sharing data, and which ones are most relevant to your organization.

Provenance of threat intelligence data

The first and oldest sources of threat intelligence data are mailing lists and publicly shared resources curated by private organizations such as the Spamhaus Project and the various national CERTs. These organizations have a distinct producer/consumer separation, and may be government or privately funded.

Know Your CERTS

The acronym *CERT* refers to a Computer Emergency Response Team, and is often interchangeable with *CSIRT* (Computer Security Incident Response Team). In this book, CERT (not the acronym) specifically refers to the subdivision of the Software Engineering Institute at Carnegie Mellon University. This is a distinct organization from the national CERTs. Almost every country on the planet has its own national CERT, which serves as an information clearinghouse for computer security issues within that country. The biggest and best-funded is the United States US-CERT, which is itself a division of the US Department of Homeland Security. Most CERTs are identifiable by the country code embedded somewhere in their name (KrCERT, JPCERT, CERT.at, BR CERT, etc.).

Information sharing organizations are another common source of this data—but I have to emphasize the word *sharing*. These organizations have a clear concept of

---

ingroup and outgroup, and if you want information from them, you have to find some way to join the group. The most easily accessible and directly useful for many organizations are the various information sharing and analysis centers;[1] these groups share information about sector-specific threats.

There are also proprietary threat intelligence feeds: subscription services that deliver threat intelligence data. These services, when you join them, provide a curated collection of threat intelligence information that is updated and maintained on a regular basis. This information is usually the best formatted, but it is also a total black box. You do not know where the information comes from.

Finally, there's "hidden" threat intelligence data. When I say this data is "hidden," what I mean is that you're buying it through another source—for example, you are getting threat intelligence via your AV and antispam systems, and may be getting it via other appliances as well.

Creating a Threat Intelligence Program

An effective threat intelligence program will focus on techniques for effectively incorporating threat intelligence into the operational workflow with minimal pain and frustration for the ops team. The responsibilities of the analysis team include identifying the goals and domain for threat intelligence data, and determining what type of data to purchase and apply.

Identifying Goals

The easiest way to waste money on threat intelligence data is to let the vendors decide what threat intelligence you buy. The first step the threat intelligence team needs to focus on is determining what the data will be used for, what data is relevant, and what is redundant.

When discussing what the data will be used for, there are a couple of basic goals for the team to consider. These are:

Improving hardening
> In this context, this means developing stronger and more rigorous defenses. Hardening requires that the ops team have a history of effectively aggressively blocking material—they have the experience, they have the policy support, and they have user buy-in. Network reputation information and up-to-date rule feeds are useful examples of this category of defenses.

---

[1] A comprehensive list of ISACs is available at *https://www.nationalisacs.org/member-isacs*.

Annotating attack data

Reputation feeds and network IOCs are useful sources for annotating attack data, which helps analysts determine in turn whether an attack represents a significant threat to the organization. Reputation feeds are usually reasonably easy to convert into actionable data such as IDS signatures or firewall rules, since they are generally just lists of IP addresses or names anyway. IOCs require more contextual information, understanding what the indicated address means and how it appears.

Supporting forensic investigations

Malware IOCs support investigations by providing clues that the team can use to identify how a system is compromised and additional cues for finding compromised system. For example, if a specific malware hash is an IOC for an attack, and that same attack has a specific command and control, they can query traffic for the command and control address to identify other compromised hosts.

Keeping current

For mature organizations, threat intelligence services that keep you up-to-date on current attacker TTPs are a vital tool for identifying potential new threats.

As a rule of thumb, annotation is usually the easiest task to start with—annotating an IDS feed with high-quality threat information can help an analyst get through false alerts more quickly and focus on the higher-priority alerts. Forensic investigation support assumes you have a team that is conducting forensic investigations and malware analysis.

In addition to operational impact, determine what sector you're involved in and how that impacts your threat intelligence needs. In particular, consider:

- Your national affiliations.
- Your industrial sector.
- What category of attacks you expect to deal with. Are you expecting to be the target of spear-phishing campaigns? Do you have a large number of industrial systems? Do you build/prototype software?
- Your software/hardware inventory.
- Whether you're already purchasing hidden threat intelligence (e.g., through regularly updated antispam or antivirus tools).

Underpinning all of these issues is the question: what are you going to do with the data? If you don't run an active remediation program, then bleeding-edge IOCs aren't going to help much.

Starting with Free Sources

Start with the newspaper—the easiest way to start collecting threat intelligence data is to read publicly available feeds of threat data. This includes reports from organizations like Cisco's Talos, Mandiant, FireEye, and the like. In addition, use news sites such as Dark Reading (*http://www.darkreading.com/*) as a jumping-off point.

The next step is to look into the organizations that provide threat intelligence data for your goals and sectors. If you have an industrial or national CERT, start checking to see what intelligence it provides. If there's a relevant ISAC for your organization, see about joining it. Also check organizations such as FIRST. Mailing lists such as full-disclosure (for malware) and NANOG (for networking issues) are critical.

Determining Data Output

The next phase of your threat intelligence project's maturity involves staging up the data you're acquiring for use. Based on the four classes of data that I discussed previously, you can expect the output to be as follows:

- *Hardening* data will translate into access controls. This includes firewall and ACL rules, as well as specialized alerts such as SiLK scripts based on the type of data.

- *Annotation* data is going to be fed to the analyst, so you should expect this data to be as close to the analyst as possible: well-maintained databases plugged into your SIEM, or merging the information with event data as it comes online.

- *IOC* data will need to be searched; for that purpose, you need some kind of platform for managing and interchanging IOCs. Examples include MISP.

- *TPP* data needs to be distributed. Regular roundtable meetings discussing the current state of the practice and reviewing the latest intelligence are a reasonable approach. Note that TPPs may be most effective as user briefings—for example, presentations to your ops team to provide them with up-to-date threats, or presentations to your C-suite to explain what problems the ops team is facing. An effective threat intelligence program will require multiple outputs for multiple audiences, delivered at varying levels of detail.

Purchasing Sources

As security companies mature, they tend to offer threat intelligence services. There's a simple reason for this: threat intelligence is gathered by observing attacks in action, and if your company is spending all of its time dissecting attacks, examining malware, and collecting information on how the internet operates, threat intelligence is a perfectly logical product. A good number of network security devices are hardware platforms for delivering threat intelligence—what you pay for, basically, is expertise.

With that in mind, the savvy consumer is going to quickly recognize that a lot of companies are selling threat intelligence data and aren't going to ask you questions about whether the data is relevant. Your responsibility as the consumer is to figure out what sources are germane to you and seek them out.

Questions to ask when evaluating the data:

- Does the data overlap other types I've already acquired? It's a fair step to begin by collecting threat intel feeds within orthogonal domains (for example, TTPs for situational awareness, then IP reputation data, then a malware feed, then IOCs).

- Does the data overlap data I'm getting elsewhere? For example, if I purchase an IOC feed, am I getting better results than I do from a mailing list or other public source? Using the free data as a reference point is useful here.[2]

- Are the feeds relevant and timely? Keep track of how much the ops team uses threat intelligence results—if an IOC feed isn't helping your ops team, consider whether it's worth paying for.

Managing Names: A Problem in Construct Validity

If you do purchase threat intelligence data, expect to spend a fair amount of time just coordinating names. For example, MITRE's ATTACK repository lists a GROUP0007, which Mandiant calls APT 28 and CrowdStrike calls Fancy Bear. While there's a certain amount of marketing behind this, it's not *entirely* marketing. Determining exactly what is a threat group is a function of construct validity.

Each threat intelligence company creates different constructs for defining attack groups. These techniques will grow out of the organization's history and practice. For example, a simple question like "Are these two computers on the same botnet?" is a construct argument—a network guy will likely look at command and control, a malware guy at the malware samples. The only person who knows is the person who owns the botnet, and he's not talking.

As discussed in Chapter 1, construct validity requires a certain amount of transparency that you may not find in this case. As such, you will want to examine the IOCs provided by each provider and cross-reference them to see when they overlap.

---

2 One thing to note in passing: even if all the threat intelligence feed does is repackage public sources, you may want to ask whether you want to spend your time repackaging the public sources.

Brief Remarks on Creating Threat Intelligence

This chapter is primarily focused on threat intelligence from a consumer perspective. I view creating data as a complementary task after you have a working program running. To create threat intelligence data, you have to have threats to learn from, which means both that you're observing threats and that they're ones you don't have prior knowledge of. So, the prerequisites for creating threat intelligence include:

- A threat intelligence program mature enough to determine whether what you're dealing with is novel.

- Manpower to investigate threats. This likely involves at least a working forensics and remediation program (more than just patch and restore).

- Channels for sharing the data. If your threat intelligence is mature enough to determine novelty, you should be in contact with ISACs and other organizations to share your data with.

- Enough incidents to generate intelligence.

On the last point, while you can generate intelligence from being hit repeatedly, if you run a large enough network, you can also instrument your network to *proactively* collect and share threat intelligence. In particular, you can collect dark space data, run honeypots to collect intelligence, scan your web logs for IOCs, and share that information. The end state of many information security companies is threat intelligence, because they're capitalizing on the most basic resource needed to start creating threat intelligence: a plethora of different attacks to examine.

Further Reading

1. The ACM Workshops on Information Sharing and Collaborative Security (WISCS) are an excellent source of research and technology on threat intelligence.

2. H. A. Slatman, "A Curated List of Awesome Threat Intelligence Resources," available at *https://github.com/hslatman/awesome-threat-intelligence*. This is a giant curated list of threat intelligence feeds and tools, well worth perusing.

3. J. Dietle, *Effective Threat Intelligence: Building and Running an Intel Team for Your Organization* (CreateSpace Independent Publishing, 2016).

Application Identification

It used to be so easy to identify applications in network traffic: you looked at the port number, or if that failed, you looked at a couple of header packets for identification information. But these identifiers have become muddier over the past decade, in particular as users seek to hide certain classes of traffic (BitTorrent!) and as privacy advocates push for increased encryption.

There are still methods for identifying traffic that do not rely on payload. Most protocols have a well-defined sequence and certain predictable behaviors that mark them so you don't have to look at the payload. By looking at the hosts to which a session talks and at packet sizes, a surprising amount of information is available.

This chapter is broken into two major sections. The first section focuses on techniques for identifying a protocol, starting with the most obvious methods and moving toward more complex techniques such as behavioral analysis. The second section discusses the contents of application banners and some methods for finding behavioral and payload information for analysis.

This chapter is very much a companion to Chapters 6 and 7; however, those chapters are more focused on the data that you can collect. This chapter is focused on application identification specifically, and is intended as a prelude to Chapter 19.

Mechanisms for Application Identification

In a perfectly safe and secure computing environment, you could just examine the configuration file on each server and it would tell you all the traffic that the server allows. Unfortunately, there are many hidden ways of starting traffic that undermine this simple strategy. You may have hosts on your system you don't know about that were started by users with innocent or not-so-innocent goals of their own. Services can be started by administrators or ordinary users outside of your startup configuration. And legitimate servers can be taken over by intruders and used for things you never intended. Although many of the techniques in this section are commonly applied by snoopers who don't have access to your servers' configuration files, you should be using the techniques as well so you know what is really happening.

Port Number

Port numbers are the first way to check what a service is, and while there's no technical requirement that a particular service runs on a particular port, there are social conventions that tend to make it so. IANA maintains a public registry (*http://bit.ly/ port-list*) of port numbers and their associated services. Although port number assignment is effectively arbitrary, and users have an active interest in evading detection by using previously untouched port numbers (or, slightly more deviously, by using common port numbers), the well-known ports still carry enough official and innocent traffic to make them the first-pass mechanism for identifying protocols. Techniques we'll discuss later in this section often use port numbers as an assertion on the user's part. For example, a user talking on port 80 is effectively asserting that she's talking to a web server.

Port number assignment is chaotic because all anyone really has to do is pick a number and hope nobody else is using it. The official registry maintained by IANA (*http:// bit.ly/iana-port*) focuses on protocols designed as part of the RFC process. Other registries and lists include a Wikipedia page (*http://bit.ly/tcp-udp-ports*), SpeedGuide.net (*http://bit.ly/sg-ports*), and the SANS Internet Storm Center (*http://bit.ly/sans-isc*), which provides a mini-messageboard per port with useful insights.

So, a huge number of ports are reserved for certain applications, and another huge number are used conventionally for other applications—but there are a small set of applications that actually matter. Table 18-1 lists the ports that I worry about the most, with a short description explaining why in each case.

Table 18-1. Ports to care about

Port	Name	Meaning
The Holy Trinity		
80/tcp	HTTP	Not only is HTTP the basic protocol for nearly everything on the internet now, it's also the most commonly imitated protocol. Users will drop traffic on port 80 to evade firewall rules.
25/tcp	SMTP	Email is the most critical service after HTTP, and also one of the most attacked.
53/udp	DNS	Another critical foundational protocol; DNS attacks will seriously damage networks.
Infrastructure and Management		
179/tcp	BGP	Border Gateway Protocol; a core protocol for internetwork routing.

Port	Name	Meaning
161-162/udp	SNMP	System Network Management Protocol; used to manage routers and other devices.
22/tcp	SSH	The administrative workhorse.
23/tcp	Telnet	If I see Telnet, I kill the connection. It is obsolete and should be replaced by other protocols, notably SSH.
123/udp	NTP	Network Time Protocol; used to coordinate clocks on networks.
389/tcp	LDAP	Lightweight Directory Access Protocol; manages directory services.
File Transfer		
20/tcp	FTP-data	Along with 21, makes up FTP.
21/tcp	FTP	The FTP control port. Another service I kill if I see it. Use SFTP.
69/tcp	TFTP	Trivial file transfer; largely used by system administrators and hopefully never seen crossing a border router.
137–139/tcp & udp	NETBIOS	NetBios is the infrastructure used for Service Message Block (SMB) and in particular provides sharing features for Windows and (via Samba) Unix systems. Pounded by attacks over its history.
Email		
143/tcp	IMAP	Internet Message Access Protocol; one of the two standard email client protocols.
110/tcp	POP3	Post Office Protocol; the other standard email client protocol.
Databases		
1521/tcp	Oracle	The primary Oracle server port.
1433/tcp & udp	SQL Server	Microsoft SQL Server's port.
3306/tcp	MySQL Server	MySQL's default port.
5432/tcp	Postgresql Server	Postgres's default port.
File Sharing		
6881–6889/tcp	BitTorrent	The default BitTorrent client ports.
6346–6348/tcp & udp	Gnutella	BearShare and LimeWire's default Gnutella ports.
4662/tcp & udp	eDonkey	Default port for eDonkey clients.

On Unix and Windows systems, port assignment is supposed to be controlled by the */etc/services* file (*WINDOWS\\SYSTEM32\\DRIVERS\\ETC\\SERVICES* on Windows hosts). A dump of the file, shown in Example 18-1, shows that it's a simple database listing a service name and the corresponding host.

Example 18-1. The contents of /etc/services

```
# Catting /etc/services without header info
$ cat /etc/services | egrep -v '^#' | head -10
rtmp            1/ddp       # Routing Table Maintenance Protocol
tcpmux          1/udp       # TCP Port Service Multiplexer
tcpmux          1/tcp       # TCP Port Service Multiplexer
nbp             2/ddp       # Name Binding Protocol
compressnet     2/udp       # Management Utility
compressnet     2/tcp       # Management Utility
compressnet     3/udp       # Compression Process
compressnet     3/tcp       # Compression Process
echo            4/ddp       # AppleTalk Echo Protocol
rje             5/udp       # Remote Job Entry
```

The names in the *services* file are used by `getportbyname` and any other port lookup functions to identify protocols. This does *not*, of course, mean that the users are really invoking those services, just that *services* say the ports are supposed to be used by the services. To get a list of all the services I have listening on a host, I use `netstat -a`, as discussed in Chapter 6. An example output is shown in Example 18-2.

Example 18-2. netstat and /etc/services/

```
# I'm running a Django web server on port 8000, and I run netstat
$ netstat -a | grep LISTEN
tcp4    0    0  localhost.irdmi    *.*            LISTEN
tcp46   0    0  *.8508             *.*            LISTEN
tcp46   0    0  *.8507             *.*            LISTEN
$ cat /etc/services | grep irdmi
irdmi2          7999/udp    # iRDMI2
irdmi2          7999/tcp    # iRDMI2
irdmi           8000/udp    # iRDMI
irdmi           8000/tcp    # iRDMI
```

`netstat` consults */etc/services* to determine what the port number is named, and you can always find the real port number in */etc/services*. However, there is no guarantee that the service is actually what the named service is.

It's appropriate at this point to make a digression into the raving paranoia characteristic of a network traffic analyst. `netstat` is obviously a great tool for identifying which ports are open on your host, but if you want more certainty, scan the machine vertically and compare the results.

Port Assignment

Any symmetric TCP or UDP transaction uses two port numbers: the *server port* is used by the client to send traffic to the server, and the *client port* is used by the server to respond. Client ports are short-lived and recycled from a pool of *ephemeral ports*; the size and allocation of the pool is a function of the TCP stack in question and user configuration.

There are several conventions regarding port assignment. The most important is the distinction between port numbers 1024 and below: nearly every operating system that has a socket on one of these requires root or administrative access. When used legitimately, this means only the administrator can start a service such as a web or email server. But this property also makes services on those ports attractive to attackers, because subverting those processes grants root privileges.

Generally, ports below 1024 are used only to run server sockets. This isn't to say that you couldn't use them for clients, only that it would be contrary to standard practice and mildly insane because you're using a client port with root access. Technically, an ephemeral port can be any port above 1024, but there are a number of conventions in their assignment.

IANA has assigned a standard range (49152 to 65535) for ephemeral ports (*http://bit.ly/iana-port*). However, this range is still in the process of being adopted, and different operating systems will have different default ranges. Table 18-2 lists common port assignments.

Table 18-2. Port assignment rules for various operating systems

Operating system	Default range	Controllable
Windows, through XP	1025–5000	Partly, through `MaxUserPort` in *Tcpip \Parameters*
Windows, Vista onward	49152–65535	Yes, via `netsh`
macOS	49152–65535	Yes, through `net.inet.ip.portrange` family in `sysctl`
Linux	32768–65535	Yes, through */proc/sys/net/ipv4/ip_local_port_range*
FreeBSD	49152–65535	Yes, through `net.inet.ip.portrange` family in `sysctl`

Application Identification by Banner Grabbing

Banner grabbing and its companion function, OS fingerprinting, are scanning techniques used to determine server and operating system information. They rely on the convention that the first thing most applications do when woken up is identify themselves. Most server applications respond to an open socket by passing their protocol, their current version, or other configuration information. If they don't do it automatically, they will often do so with a little prodding.

Banner grabbing can easily be done manually using any "keyboard to the socket" tool, such as netcat (see Chapter 7 for more information). Example 18-3 shows active banner grabbing using netcat to collect some data. Note that I am able to pull information from several servers without actually using the protocol in question.

Example 18-3. Examples of active banner grabbing with netcat

```
# Open a connection to an SSH server.
# Note that I receive information without the need for actual
# interaction with the server.
$ netcat 192.168.2.1 22
SSH-2.0-OpenSSH_6.1
^C
# Open an IMAP connection.
# Again, note that I have to do nothing with mail itself.
$ netcat 192.168.2.1 143
* OK [CAPABILITY IMAP4rev1 LITERAL+ SASL-IR LOGIN-REFERRALS
  ID ENABLE STARTTLS AUTH=PLAIN AUTH=LOGIN] Dovecot ready.
```

An alternative to active banner grabbing is passive banner grabbing, which can be done using tcpdump. Since a banner is really just text that appears at the beginning of a session, grabbing the payload of the first five or six packets will provide banner data as well.

bannergrab.py is a very simple banner grabbing script using Scapy. It's not trying to parse banner contents—it's just grabbing the first load of information it sees. This can be quite informative. Example 18-4 shows the contents from the SSH dump.

Example 18-4. Grabbing client and server banners using Scapy

```
#!/usr/bin/env python
#
#
# bannergrab.py
# This is a Scapy application that loads up a banner file and drops
# out the client and server banners.  To do so, it
# reads the contents of the client and server files from the session,
# extracts ASCII text, and dumps it to screen.
#
```

```
from scapy.all import *
import sys
sessions = {}

packet_data = rdpcap(sys.argv[1])
for i in packet_data:
    if not sessions.has_key(i[IP].src):
        sessions[i[IP].src] = ''
    try:
        sessions[i[IP].src] += i[TCP].payload.load
    except:
        pass

for j in sessions.keys():
    print j, sessions[j][0:200]


$ bannergrab.py ssh.dmp
WARNING: No route found for IPv6 destination :: (no default route?)
192.168.1.12
216.92.179.155 SSH-2.0-OpenSSH_6.1
```

Example 18-5 shows a pull from *www.cnn.com*.

Example 18-5. A pull from cnn.com

```
57.166.224.246 HTTP/1.1 200 OK
Server: nginx
Date: Sun, 14 Apr 2013 04:34:36 GMT
Content-Type: application/javascript
Transfer-Encoding: chunked
Connection: keep-alive
Vary: Accept-Encoding
Last-Modified: Sun
157.166.255.216
157.166.241.11 HTTP/1.1 200 OK
Server: nginx
Date: Sun, 14 Apr 2013 04:34:27 GMT
Content-Type: text/html
Transfer-Encoding: chunked
Connection: keep-alive
Set-Cookie: CG=US:DC:Washington; path=/
Last-Modified

66.235.155.19 HTTP/1.1 302 Found
Date: Sun, 14 Apr 2013 04:34:35 GMT
Server: Omniture DC/2.0.0
Access-Control-Allow-Origin: *
Set-Cookie: s_vi=[CS]v1|28B31B23851D063C-60000139000324E4[CE];
        Expires=Tue, 14 Apr 2
23.6.20.211 HTTP/1.1 200 OK
```

```
x-amz-id-2: 287KOoW3vWNpotJGpn0RaXExCzKkFJQ/hkpAXjWUQTb6hSBzDQioFUoWYZMRCq7V
x-amz-request-id: 8B6B2E3CDBC2E300
Content-Encoding: gzip
ETag: "e5f0fa3fbe0175c47fea0164922230d4"
Acc

192.168.1.12 GET / HTTP/1.1
Host: www.cnn.com
Connection: keep-alive
Accept: text/html,application/xhtml+xml,application/xml;q=0.9,*/*;q=0.8
User-Agent: Mozilla/5.0 (Macintosh; Intel Mac OS X 10_8_3) AppleWebK
23.15.9.160 HTTP/1.1 200 OK
Server: Apache
Last-Modified: Wed, 10 Apr 2013 13:44:28 GMT
ETag: "233bf1-3e803-4da01de67a700"
Accept-Ranges: bytes
Content-Type: text/css
Vary: Accept-Encoding
Content-Encoding

63.85.36.42 HTTP/1.1 200 OK
Content-Length: 43
Content-Type: image/gif
Date: Sun, 14 Apr 2013 04:34:36 GMT
Connection: keep-alive
Pragma: no-cache
Expires: Mon, 01 Jan 1990 00:00:00 GMT
Cache-Control: priv

138.108.6.20 HTTP/1.1 200 OK
Server: nginx
Date: Sun, 14 Apr 2013 04:34:35 GMT
Content-Type: image/gif
Transfer-Encoding: chunked
Connection: keep-alive
Keep-Alive: timeout=20
```

In Example 18-5, the client is midway through the dump (at 192.168.1.12). Note the sheer number of web servers; this is a common feature with modern websites, and you can expect to see dozens of servers involved in constructing a single page. Also note the information provided: the server sends content information, the server name, and a bunch of configuration data. The client string includes a variety of acceptable formats and the User-Agent string, which we'll discuss in more depth later.

Banner grabbing is fairly simple. The challenge lies in identifying what the banners *mean*. Different applications have radically different banners, which are often complete languages in themselves.

Application Identification by Behavior

In the absence of payload, it's often difficult to tell what an application *is*, but an enormous amount of information is still available about what an application *does*. Behavioral analysis focuses on finding cues for the application's behavior by examining features such as the packet sizes and connection failures.

Packet sizes in any IP protocol are bound by the *maximum transmission unit* (MTU), the maximum frame size defined by the layer 2 protocol. When IP attempts to send a packet larger than the MTU, the original packet is split into the number of MTU-sized packets that are required to transmit it. In tcpdump and NetFlow data, this means that the maximum packet size you will ever see is controlled by the shortest MTU of the route taken by that packet so far. Because the internet is dominated by Ethernet, this imposes an effective limit of 1,500 bytes on packet sizes.

We can use this limit to split network traffic into four major categories:

Fumbling
Covered in Chapter 13, this consists of failed attempts to open connections to targets.

Control traffic
Small, fixed-size packets sent by clients and servers at the beginning of a session.

Chatter
Packets less than the MTU in size, of varying size and sent back and forth between clients and servers. Chatter messages are characteristic of chat protocols like ICQ and AIM, as well as the command messages for many protocols such as SMTP and BitTorrent.

File transfer
Asymmetric traffic where one side sends packets almost entirely of MTU size and the other side sends ACKs in response. Characteristic of SMTP, HTTP, and FTP.

Control packets are, when available, the most interesting information you can find on a service because their sizes are often specified by the service itself. Control messages are often implemented as templates of some form, with specific areas to fill in the blanks. As a result, even with the payload obscured, the sizes can often be used to identify them.

Histograms, presented in "Histograms" on page 210, are useful for comparing protocols via the lengths of their control messages. As an example, consider Figure 18-1. This is a plot of histograms for short flows (less than 1,000 bytes in total) from clients to BitTorrent and web servers.

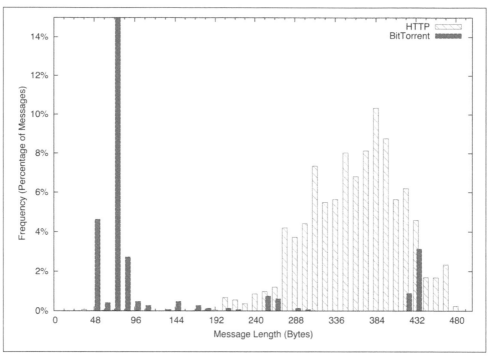

Figure 18-1. Histogram comparing BitTorrent and HTTP short flow sizes

For a web client, this consists primarily of issuing the HTTP GET request and then receiving a file. The GET requests, as you can see in Figure 18-1, are spread over a somewhat normalized distribution between about 200 and 400 bytes. Conversely, the BitTorrent packets have a huge peak between 48 and 96 bytes, a function of the 68-byte BitTorrent handshake message.

Histograms can be checked visually, as in Figure 18-1, or numerically by calculating the L1 (or Manhattan) distance (*http://bit.ly/l1-norm*). In a histogram, you calculate the L1 distance as the sum of the differences between each bin. Normalized to percentages, this provides a value between 0 and 2, with 0 indicating that the two histograms are identical and 2 indicating that the two histograms are complete opposites. Example 18-6 shows how to calculate the L1 distance in Python.

Example 18-6. Calculating L1 distance in Python

```
#!/usr/bin/env python
#
#
# calc_l1.py
#
# Given two datafiles consisting purely of sizes and a histogram
# specification (bin size, max bin size), calculate the L1 distance
```

```
# between two histograms.
#
# command line:
#         calc_l1 size min max file_a file_b
#
# size: the size of a histogram bin
# min: the minimum size to bin
# max: the maximum size to bin
#
#
import sys

bin_size = int(sys.argv[1])
bin_min = int(sys.argv[2])
bin_max = int(sys.argv[3])
file_1 = sys.argv[4]
file_2 = sys.argv[5]

bin_count = 1 + ((bin_max - bin_min)/bin_size)
histograms = [[],[]]
totals = [0,0]

for i in range(0, bin_count):
    for j in range(0,2):
        histograms[j].append(0)

# Generate histograms
for h_index, file_name in ((0, file_1), (1,file_2)):
    fh = open(file_name, 'r')
    results = map(lambda x:int(x), fh.readlines())
    fh.close()
    for i in results:
        if i <= bin_max:
            index = (i - bin_min)/bin_size
            histograms[h_index][index] += 1
            totals[h_index] += 1

# Compare and calculate L1 distance
l1_d = 0.0
for i in range(0, bin_count):
    h0_pct = float(histograms[0][i])/float(totals[0])
    h1_pct = float(histograms[1][i])/float(totals[1])
    l1_d += abs(h0_pct - h1_pct)

print l1_d
```

Chatting and file transfers can be examined by identifying the individual packet sizes or, in the case of flow files, comparing the mean packet sizes for the flow (flow bytes divided by flow packets). If one side is close to the MTU, odds are that it's a file transfer, and if both sides are roughly asymmetric and greater than 40 bytes per packet, some form of chatter may be going on. To illustrate this graphically, consider the plots in Figures 18-2 and Figure 18-3. These show the packet sizes for a file transfer (HTTP) and chat (AIM) session, respectively.

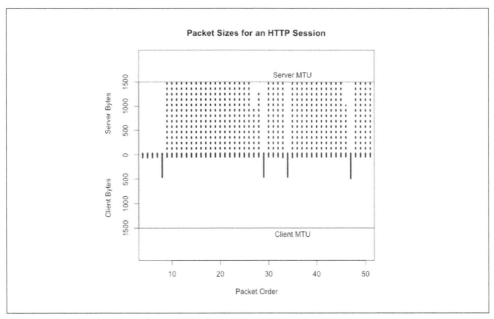

Figure 18-2. Packet sizes for an HTTP session

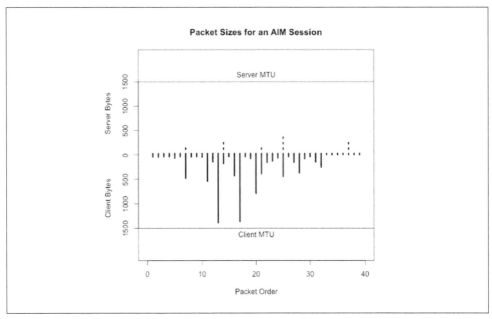

Figure 18-3. Packet sizes for an AIM session

Application Identification by Subsidiary Site

Network-aware applications rarely exist in a vacuum. Software updates, registration servers, database updates, advertising, and user tracking are all examples of network-based functionality that an application can conduct without a user being aware of them. At the same time, users may visit support forums, talk on message boards, or require access to information just to run the application.

As example of this behavior, consider two applications: antivirus and BitTorrent. Any antivirus application needs to contact its home servers on a regular basis in order to update the knowledge base. This activity is so predictable that it's not uncommon for malware to explicitly disable the update addresses on the local host. Any host running AV should be contacting these addresses on a regular basis, and anyone who does is likely to be running AV.

Now consider BitTorrent. A considerable amount of work has been done in recent years to decentralize the protocol. In the late 2000s, it was possible to identify trackers and then identify users by finding out who was communicating with the trackers. Although tracker identification is less effective now, BitTorrent users still need to find their files, and the relevant magnet links are concentrated on sites such as the Pirate Bay, KickassTorrents, and other specialized torrent sites. Find a user who visits the Pirate Bay, then find someone engaging in huge file downloads on weird ports, and you have probably found a BitTorrent user. Once you've identified a server or host running a particular service, look at who else is talking to it.

Application Banners: Identifying and Classifying

Application banners can provide a lot of information about applications, servers, operating systems, and versions of all these things. Unfortunately, the format of these banners changes radically with each service, almost like a different language. The good news is that, with the exception of web browsers, most application banners are relatively simple. The bad news is that web browsers will make most of the banners you see.

Non-Web Banners

This section discusses server banners for servers not using the web. Banners can provide information on the operating system and the protocol, or can be obfuscated to prevent scanners from acquiring intelligence.

SMTP banners are defined in RFC 5321. On client login, an SMTP server should respond with a 220 status code (the greeting), along with some domain information. Given that SMTP servers are one of the services most commonly targeted by scanners, it's not unusual to find SMTP banners reduced to a bare minimum by system administrators.

Microsoft defines the default banner for MS Exchange as:

```
220 <Servername> Microsoft ESMTP MAIL service ready at
    <RegionalDay-Date-24HourTimeFormat> <RegionalTimeZoneOffset>
```

with optional customization. An example banner for Exchange is:

```
220 mailserver.bogodomain.com Microsoft ESMTP MAIL service ready at
    Sat, 16 Feb 2013 08:34:14 +0100
```

SSH is defined in RFC 4253. On client login, an SSH server sends a brief message providing an identification string. According to the protocol definition, the identification string will be of the form:

```
SSH-protoversion-softwareversion SP comments CR LF
```

where SP is a space, CR is a carriage return, and LF is a line feed. All modern implementations of SSH should use 2.0 for the protocol version, but a server that supports previous versions of SSH should identify its version as 1.99. Comments are optional.

The following banner is an example of SSH before version 2.0, which should be rare:

```
SSH-1.99-OpenSSH_3.5p1
```

Everything else should be 2.0 or above:

```
SSH-2.0-OpenSSH_4.3
```

As these examples show, the first step to identifying a banner is usually to find the relevant technical documentation. This may be an RFC for an IETF-engineered protocol such as IMAP, POP3, SSH, or SMTP. For protocols that do not involve the IETF, some searching may be required to identify the developer of the protocol and any support sites. For example, BitTorrent's protocol is currently specified at the *theory.org* wiki (*http://bit.ly/bt-spec*).

Web Client Banners: The User-Agent String

Web clients send browsers a complicated configuration string defining their capabilities and preferences: the platform the browser runs on, the operating system, and a variety of configuration details. This string, the User-Agent, is defined in RFC 2616, but can become phenomenally complicated (as well as informative) fairly quickly.

Some User-Agent strings are shown sorted by browser in Example 18-7.

Example 18-7. Example User-Agent strings by browser

```
Firefox:
Mozilla/5.0 (X11; U; Linux x86_64; en-US; rv:1.8.1.12) Gecko/20080214
         Firefox/2.0.0.12
Mozilla/5.0 (Windows; U; Windows NT 5.1; cs; rv:1.9.0.8) Gecko/2009032609
         Firefox/3.0.8
```

```
Mozilla/5.0 (X11; U; Linux i686; en-US; rv:1.8) Gecko/20051111 Firefox/1.5

Internet Explorer:
Mozilla/5.0 (compatible; MSIE 9.0; Windows NT 6.1; WOW64; Trident/5.0; SLCC2;
          Media Center PC 6.0; InfoPath.3; MS-RTC LM 8; Zune 4.7)
Mozilla/5.0 (compatible; MSIE 10.0; Windows NT 6.1; Trident/6.0)
Mozilla/5.0 (compatible; MSIE 9.0; Windows NT 6.1; Trident/5.0; Xbox)

Safari:
Mozilla/5.0 (Macintosh; Intel Mac OS X 10_6_8) AppleWebKit/534.57.1
          (KHTML, like Gecko) Version/5.1.7 Safari/534.57.1
Mozilla/5.0 (iPad; CPU OS 6_0 like Mac OS X) AppleWebKit/536.26
          (KHTML, like Gecko) Version/6.0 Mobile/10A403 Safari/8536.25

Opera:
Opera/9.80 (Windows NT 6.0) Presto/2.12.388 Version/12.11
Opera/9.80 (Macintosh; Intel Mac OS X 10.8.2) Presto/2.12.388 Version/12.11
Opera/9.80 (X11; Linux i686; U; ru) Presto/2.8.131 Version/11.11
Mozilla/5.0 (Windows NT 6.1; rv:2.0) Gecko/20100101 Firefox/4.0 Opera 12.11

Chrome:
Mozilla/5.0 (Windows NT 6.2; WOW64) AppleWebKit/535.24
          (KHTML, like Gecko) Chrome/19.0.1055.1 Safari/535.24
Mozilla/5.0 (Macintosh; Intel Mac OS X 10_7_3) AppleWebKit/535.19
          (KHTML, like Gecko) Chrome/18.0.1025.151 Safari/535.19
Mozilla/5.0 (Linux; Android 4.0.4; Galaxy Nexus Build/IMM76B)
          AppleWebKit/535.19 (KHTML, like Gecko) Chrome/18.0.1025.133
          Mobile Safari/535.19
Mozilla/5.0 (iPhone; U; CPU iPhone OS 5_1_1 like Mac OS X; en)
          AppleWebKit/534.46.0 (KHTML, like Gecko) CriOS/19.0.1084.60
          Mobile/9B206 Safari/7534.48.3

Googlebot:
Mozilla/5.0 (compatible; Googlebot/2.1; +http://www.google.com/bot.html)

Bingbot:
Mozilla/5.0 (compatible; bingbot/2.0; +http://www.bing.com/bingbot.htm)

Baiduspider:
Mozilla/5.0 (compatible; Baiduspider/2.0; +http://www.baidu.com/search/
spider.html)
```

The User-Agent strings in Example 18-7 follow a basic structure that is derived from the original RFC 2616 specification along with various detritus from the browser wars. These attributes are broken down as follows:

1. An initial tag, usually Mozilla/4.0 or higher. The use of Mozilla as the default string is a relic of the browser wars. Suffice it to say that almost every browser automatically masquerades as Mozilla.

2. A set of values in parentheses that will tell you what the browser *really* is. These values vary based on the browser make and configuration, but usually contain the actual browser name, the OS, and a number of optional parameters.

3. Following the parentheses (usually) is a tag naming the layout engine for the software; the layout engine is the browser's toolkit for rendering HTML, and the same engine can be used by multiple browsers. Common engines include Gecko (used by Firefox, Mozilla, and SeaMonkey), WebKit (used by Safari and Chrome), Presto (Opera), and Trident (IE).

As Example 18-7 shows, the actual composition of the string is very much a function of the browser, the OS, and the idiosyncratic whims of the implementer.

Further Reading

1. M. Collins and M. Reiter, "Finding Peer-to-Peer File Sharing Using Coarse Network Behaviors," *Proceedings of the 2007 ESORICS Conference*, Hamburg, Germany, 2007.

2. H. Inoue et al., "NetADHICT: A Tool for Understanding Network Traffic," *Proceedings of the 2007 Large Installation System Administration Conference (LISA)*, Dallas, TX, 2007.

3. The NetADHICT home page (*http://bit.ly/netADHICT*).

4. Michael Zalewski's p0f (*http://bit.ly/p0fv3*).

5. *http://www.useragentstring.com*.

## CHAPTER 19

On Network Mapping

In this chapter, we discuss mechanisms for managing the rate of false positives produced by detection systems by reducing make-work. Consider this scenario: I create a signature today to identify the IIS exploit of the week, and sometime tomorrow afternoon it starts firing off like crazy. Yay, somebody's using an exploit! I check the logs, and I find out that I am not in fact being attacked by this exploit because my network *actually doesn't run IIS*. Not only have I wasted analysts' time dealing with the alert, but I've wasted *my* time writing the original alert for something to which the network isn't vulnerable.

The process of inventory is the foundation of situational awareness. It enables you to move from simply reacting to signatures to continuous audit and protection. It provides you with baselines and an efficient anomaly detection strategy, it identifies critical assets, and it provides you with contextual information to speed up the process of filtering alerts.

Creating an Initial Network Inventory and Map

Network mapping is an iterative process that combines technical analysis and interviews with site administrators. The theory behind this process is that any inventory generated by design is inaccurate to some degree, but accurate enough to begin the process of instrumentation and analysis. Acquiring this inventory begins with identifying the personnel responsible for managing the network.

The mapping process described in this book consists of four distinct phases, which combine iterative traffic analysis and asking a series of questions of network administrators and personnel. These questions inform the traffic analyses, and the analyses lead to more queries. Figure 19-1 shows how the process progresses: in phase I you identify the space of IP addresses you are monitoring, and in each progressive phase you partition the space into different categories.

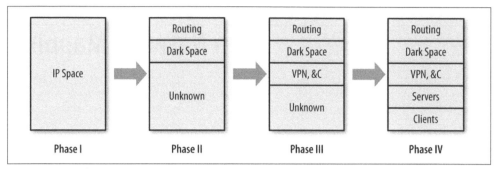

Figure 19-1. The mapping process

Creating an Inventory: Data, Coverage, and Files

In a perfect world, a network map should enable you to determine, based on addresses and ports, the traffic you are seeing on any host on the network. But the likelihood of producing such a perfect map of an enterprise network is pretty low because by the time you finish the initial inventory, *something* on the network will have changed. Maps are dynamic and consequently have to be updated on a regular basis. This updating process provides you with a facility for continuously auditing the network.

A security inventory should keep track of every addressable resource on the network (that is, anything attackers could conceivably reach if they had network access, even if that means access inside the network). It should keep track of which services are running on the resource, and it should keep track of how that system is monitored. An example inventory is shown in Table 19-1.

Table 19-1. An example worksheet

Address	Name	Protocol	Port	Role	Last seen	Sensors	Comments
128.2.1.4	www.server.com	TCP	80	HTTP server	2013/05/17	Flow 1, Log	Primary web server
128.2.1.4	www.server.com	TCP	22	SSH server	2013/05/17	Flow 1, Log	Administrators only
128.2.1.5–128.2.1.15	N/A	N/A	N/A	Client	2013/05/17	Flow 2	Workstations
128.2.1.16–128.2.1.31	N/A	N/A	N/A	Empty	2013/05/17	Flow 2	Dark space

Table 19-1 has an entry for each unique observed port and protocol combination on the network, along with a role, an indicator of when the host was last seen in the sensor data, and the available sensor information. These fields are the *minimum* set that you should consider when generating an inventory. Additional potential items to consider include the following:

- The Role field should be enumerable, rather than an actual text field. Enumerating the roles will make searching much less painful. A suggested set of categories is:
  - — *Service* Server, where *Service* is HTTP, SSH, etc.
  - — Workstation, to indicate a dedicated client
  - — NAT, to indicate a network address translator
  - — Service Proxy for any proxies
  - — Firewall for firewalls
  - — Sensor for any sensors
  - — Routing for any routing equipment
  - — VPN for VPN concentrators and other equipment
  - — DHCP for any dynamically addressed space
  - — Dark for any address that is allocated in the network but has no host on it
- Identifying VPNs, NATs, DHCP, and proxies, as we'll discuss in a moment, is particularly important—they mess up the address allocation and increase the complexity of analysis.
- Keeping centrality or volume metrics is also useful. A five-number summary of volume over a month is a good starting point for anomaly detection.
- Per-host whitelists are a useful tool for anomaly management (see Chapter 3 for a more extensive discussion). The inventory is a good place to track per-host whitelist and rule files.
- Ownership and point of contact information is critical. One of the most time-consuming steps after identifying an attack is usually finding out who owns the victim.
- Keeping track of the specific services on hosts, and the versions of those services, helps track the risk that a particular system has to current exploits. This can be identified by banner grabbing, but it's more effective to just scan the network using the inventory as a guideline.

Table 19-1 could be kept on paper or in a spreadsheet, but it really should be kept in an RDBMS or other storage system. Once you've created the inventory, it will serve as a simple anomaly detection system, and should be updated regularly by automated processes.

Phase I: The First Three Questions

The first step of any inventory process involves figuring out what is already known and what is already available for monitoring. For this reason, instrumentation begins at a meeting with the network administrators.[1] The purpose of this initial meeting is to determine what is monitored:

- What addresses make up the network?
- What sensors do I have?
- How are the sensors related to traffic?

Start with addresses, because they serve as the foundation of the inventory. More specific questions to ask include:

Is the network IPv4 or IPv6?
> If the network is IPv6, there's going to be a lot more address space to play with, which reduces the need for DHCP and NATing. The network is more likely to be IPv4, however, and that means that if it is of any significant size, there's likely to be a fair degree of aliasing, NATing, and other address conservation tricks.

How many addresses are accessible or hidden behind NATs?
> Ideally, you should be able to get a map showing the routing on the network, whether there are DMZs, and what information is hidden behind NATs. These individual subnets are future candidates for instrumentation.

How many hosts are on the network?
> Determine how many PCs, clients, servers, computers, and embedded systems are on the network. These systems are the things you're defending. Pay particular attention to embedded systems such as printers and teleconferencing tools because they often have network servers, are hard to patch and update, and are frequently overlooked in inventories.

This discussion should end with a list of all your potential IP addresses. This list will probably include multiple instances of the same ephemeral spaces. For example, if there are six subnets behind NAT firewalls, expect to see 192.168.0.0/16 repeated six times. You should also get an estimate of how many hosts are in each subnet and in the network as a whole.

The next set of questions to ask involves current instrumentation. Host-based instrumentation (e.g., server logs and the like, as discussed in Chapter 5) are not the primary target at this point. Instead, the goal is to identify *whether* network-level

---

1 Preferably at a brewpub.

collection is available. If it is available, determine what is collected, and if not, determine whether it can be turned on. More specific questions to ask include:

What is currently being collected?
> A source doesn't have to be collected "for security purposes" to be useful. NetFlow, for example, is primarily used as a billing system, but can be useful in monitoring as well.

Are there NetFlow-capable sensors?
> For example, if Cisco routers with built-in NetFlow instrumentation are available, use them as your initial sensors.

Is any IDS present?
> An IDS such as Snort can be configured to just dump packet headers. Depending on the location of the IDS (such as if it's on the border of a network), it may be possible to put up a flow collector there as well.

At the conclusion of this discussion, you should come up with a plan for initially instrumenting the network. The goal of this initial instrumentation should be to capitalize on any existing monitoring systems and to acquire a systematic monitoring capability for cross-border traffic. As a rule of thumb, on most enterprise networks it's easiest to turn on deactivated capabilities such as NetFlow, and it's progressively more difficult, respectively, to add new software and hardware.

The default network

Throughout this chapter, I use asides to discuss more concrete methods to answer the high-level questions in the text. These asides and examples involve a hefty number of SiLK queries and at least a little understanding of how SiLK breaks down data.

The default network is shown in Figure 19-2. As described by SiLK, this network has two sensors: router 1 and router 2. There are three types of data: `in` (coming from the cloud into the network), `out` (going from the network to the cloud), and `internal` (traffic that doesn't cross the border into the cloud).

In addition, there exist a number of IP sets. `initial.set` is a list of hosts on the network provided by administrators during the initial interview. This set is composed of `servers.set` and `clients.set`, comprising the clients and servers. `servers.set` contains `webservers.set`, `dnsservers.set`, and `sshservers.set` as subsets. These sets are accurate at the time of the interview, but will be updated as time passes.

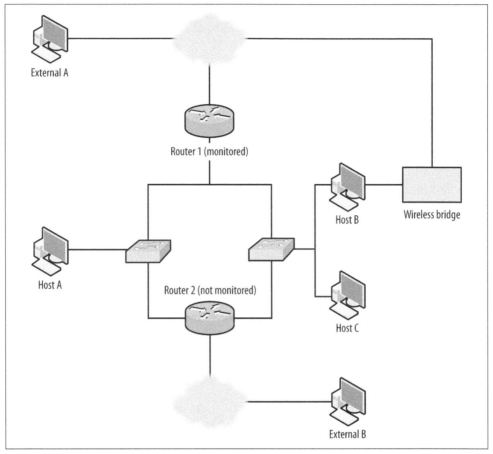

Figure 19-2. Unmonitored routes in action

Phase II: Examining the IP Space

You'll need to consider the following questions:

- Are there unmonitored routes?
- What IP space is dark?
- Which IP addresses are network appliances?

Following phase I, you should have an approximate inventory of the network and a live feed of, at the minimum, cross-border traffic data. With this information, you can begin to validate the inventory by comparing the traffic you are receiving against the list of IP addresses that the administrators provided you. Note the use of the word *validate*—you are comparing the addresses that you observe in traffic against the addresses you were told would be there.

Your first goal is to determine whether instrumentation is complete or incomplete, and in particular whether you have any unmonitored routes to deal with—that is, legitimate routes where traffic is not being recorded. Figure 19-2 shows some common examples of dark routes. In this figure, a line indicates a route between two entities:

- The first unmonitored route occurs when traffic moves through router 2, which is not monitored. For example, if host A communicates with external address B using router 2, you will not see A's traffic to B or B's traffic to A.

- A more common problem in modern networks is the presence of wireless bridges. Most modern hosts have access to multiple wireless networks, especially in shared facilities. Host B in the example can communicate with the internet while bypassing router 1 entirely.

The key to identifying unmonitored routes is to look at *asymmetric* traffic flow. Routing protocols forward traffic with minimal interest in the point of origin, so if you have *n* access points coming into your network, the chance of any particular session going in and out of the same point is about *1/n*. You can expect *some* instrumentation failures to result on any network, so there are always going to be broken sessions, but if you find *consistent* evidence of asymmetric sessions between pairs of addresses, that's good evidence that the current monitoring configuration is missing something.

The best tool for finding asymmetric sessions is TCP traffic, because TCP is the most common protocol in the IP suite that guarantees a response. To identify legitimate TCP sessions, take the opposite approach from Chapter 13: look for sessions where the SYN, ACK, and FIN flags are high, with multiple packets or with payload.

Identifying asymmetric traffic

To identify asymmetric traffic, look for TCP sessions that carry a payload and don't have a corresponding outgoing session. This can be done using `rwuniq` and `rwfilter`:

```
$ rwfilter --start-date=2013/05/10:00 --end-date=2013/05/10:00 --proto=6 \
  --type=out --packets=4- --flags-all=SAF/SAF --pass=stdout | \
  rwuniq --field=1,2 --no-title --sort | cut -d '|' -f 1,2 > outgoing.txt
# Note that I use 1,2 for the rwuniq above, and 2,1 for the rwuniq below.
# This ensures that the fields are present in the same order when
# I compare output.
$ rwfilter --start-date=2013/05/10:00 --end-date=2013/05/10:00 --proto=6 \
  --type=in --packets=4- --flags-all=SAF/SAF --pass=stdout | rwuniq \
  --field=2,1 --no-title --sort | cut -d '|' -f 2,1 > incoming.txt
```

Once these commands finish, I will have two files of internal IP and external IP pairs. I can compare these pairs directly using `-cmp` or a handwritten routine. Example 19-1 shows a Python example that generates a report of unidirectional flows.

Example 19-1. Generating a report of unidirectional flows

```python
#!/usr/bin/env python
#
#
# compare_reports.py
#
# Command line: compare_reports.py file1 file2
#
# Reads the contents of two files and checks to see if the same
# IP pairs appear.
#
import sys, os
def read_file(fn):
    ip_table = set()
    a = open(fn,'r')
    for i in a.readlines():
        sip, dip = map(lambda x:x.strip(), i.split('|')[0:2])
        key = "%15s:%15s" % (sip, dip)
        ip_table.add(key)
    a.close()
    return ip_table

if __name__ == '__main__':
    incoming = read_file(sys.argv[1])
    outgoing = read_file(sys.argv[2])
    missing_pairs = set()
    total_pairs = set()
    # Being a bit sloppy here, run on both incoming and outgoing to ensure
    # that if there's an element in one not in the other, it gets caught
    for i in incoming:
        total_pairs.add(i)
        if not i in outgoing:
            missing_pairs.add(i)
    for i in outgoing:
        total_pairs.add(i)
        if not i in incoming:
            missing_pairs.add(i)
    print missing_pairs, total_pairs
    # Now do some address breakdowns
    addrcount = {}
    for i in missing_pairs:
        in_value, out_value = i.split(':')[0:2]
        if not addrcount.has_key(in_value):
            addrcount[in_value] = 0
        if not addrcount.has_key(out_value):
            addrcount[out_value] = 0
        addrcount[in_value] += 1
        addrcount[out_value] += 1
    # Simple report, number of missing pairs, list of most commonly occurring
    # addresses
    print "%d missing pairs out of %d total" % (len(missing_pairs),
```

```
                                    len(total_pairs))
s = addrcount.items()
s.sort(lambda a,b:b[1] - a[1]) # lambda just guarantees order
print "Most common addresses:"
for i in s[0:10]:
    print "%15s %5d" % (i[0],addrcount[i[0]])
```

This approach is best done using passive collection because it ensures that you are observing traffic from a number of locations outside the network. Scanning is also for identifying dark spaces and backdoors. When you scan and control the instrumentation, not only can you see the results of your scan on your desktop, but you can compare the traffic from the scan against the data provided by your collection system.

Although you can scan the network and check whether all your scanning sessions match your expectations (i.e., you see responses from hosts and nothing from empty space), you are scanning from only a single location, when you really need to look at traffic from multiple points of origin.

If you find evidence of unmonitored routes, you need to determine whether they can be instrumented and why they aren't being instrumented right now. Unmonitored routes are a security risk: they can be used to probe, exfiltrate, and communicate without being monitored.

Unmonitored routes and dark spaces have similar traffic profiles to each other; in both cases, a TCP packet sent to them will not elicit a reply. The difference is that in an unmonitored route, this happens due to incomplete instrumentation, while a dark space has nothing to generate a response. Once you have identified your unmonitored routes, any monitored addresses that behave in the same way should be dark.

Identifying dark space

Dark spaces can be found either passively or actively. Passive identification requires collecting traffic to the network and progressively eliminating all address that respond or are unmonitored—at that point, the remainder should be dark. The alternative approach is to actively probe the addresses in a network and record the ones that don't respond; those addresses should be dark.

Passive collection requires gathering data over a long period. At the minimum, collect traffic for at least a week to ensure that dynamic addressing and business processes are handled. For example:

```
$ rwfilter --type=out --start-date=2013/05/01:00 --end-date=2013/05/08:23 \
    --proto=0-255 --pass=stdout | rwset --sip-file=light.set
# Now remove the lit addresses from our total inventory
$ rwsettool --difference --output=dark.set initial.set light.set
```

An alternative approach is to ping every host on the network to determine whether it is present:

```
$ for i in `rwsetcat initial.set`
  do
  # Do a ping with a 5-second timeout and 1 attempt to each target
    ping -q -c 1 -t 5 ${i} | tail -2 >> pinglog.txt
  done
```

pinglog.txt will contain the summary information from the ping command, which will look like this:

```
--- 128.2.11.0 ping statistics ---
1 packets transmitted, 0 packets received, 100.0% packet loss
```

The contents can be parsed to produce a dark map.

Of these two options, scanning will be faster than passive mapping, but you have to make sure the network will return echo reply messages (ICMP type 0) to your pings.

Another way to identify dynamic spaces through passive monitoring is to take hourly pulls and compare the configuration of dark and lit addresses in each hour.

Finding network appliances

Identifying network appliances involves either using traceroute, or looking for specific protocols used by them. "Network appliances" in this context really means router interfaces. Router interfaces are identifiable by looking for routing protocols or checking for "ICMP host not found" messages (also known as "network unreachable" messages), which are generated only by routers.

Every host mentioned by traceroute except the endpoint is a router. If you check for protocols, candidates include:

BGP

BGP is commonly spoken by routers that route traffic across the internet, and won't be common inside corporate networks unless you have a very big network. BGP runs on TCP port 179:

```
# This will identify communications from the outside world with BGP speakers
# inside
$ rwfilter --type=in --proto=6 --dport=179 --flags-all=SAF/SAF \
  --start-date=2013/05/01:00 --end-date=2013/05/01:00 --pass=bgp_speakers.rwf
```

OSPF and EIGRP

These are common protocols for managing routing on small networks. EIGRP is protocol number 88, OSPF protocol number 89:

```
# This will identify communications with OSPF and EIGRP speakers.
# Note the use of internal; we don't expect this traffic to be cross-border.
$ rwfilter --type=internal --proto=88,89 --start-date=2013/05/01:00 \
  --end-date=2013/05/01:00 --pass=stdout | rwfilter --proto=88 \
    --input-pipe=stdin --pass=eigrp.rwf --fail=ospf.rwf
```

RIP

Another internal routing protocol, RIP is implemented on top of UDP using port 520:

```
# This will identify communications with RIP speakers
$ rwfilter --type=internal --proto=17 --aport=520 \
  --start-date=2013/05/01:00 --end-date=2013/05/01:00 --pass=rip_speakers.rwf
```

ICMP

Host unreachable messages (ICMP type 3, code 7) and time exceeded messages (ICMP type 11) both originate from routers:

```
# Filter out ICMP messages. The longer period is because ICMP is much rarer
# than TCP and UDP.
$ rwfilter --type=out --proto=1 --icmp-type=3,11 --pass=stdout \
  --start-date=2013/05/01:00 \
  --end-date=2013/05/01:23 | rwfilter --icmp-type=11 --input-pipe=stdin \
  --pass=ttl_exceeded.rwf --fail=stdout | rwfilter --input-pipe=stdin \
  --icmp-code=7 --pass=not_found.rwf
$ rwset --sip-routers_ttl.set ttl_exceeded.rwf
$ rwset --sip=routers_nf.set not_found.rwf
$ rwsettool --union --output-path=routers.set routers_nf.set routers_ttl.set
```

The results of this step will provide you with a list of router interface addresses. Each router on the network will control one or more of these interfaces. At this point, it's a good idea to go back to the network administrators in order to associate these interfaces with actual hardware.

Phase III: Identifying Blind and Confusing Traffic

You'll need to consider the following questions:

- Are there NATs?
- Are there proxies, reverse proxies, or caches?
- Is there VPN traffic?
- Are there dynamic addresses?

After completing phase II, you will have identified which addresses within your network are active. The next step is to identify which addresses are going to be problematic. Life would be easier for you if every host were assigned a static IP address, that address were used by exactly one host, and the traffic were easily identifiable by port and protocol.

Obviously, these constraints don't hold. Specific problems include:

NATs

These are a headache because they alias multiple IP addresses behind a much smaller set of addresses.

Proxies, reverse proxies, and caches

Like a NAT, a proxy hides multiple IP addresses behind a single proxy host address. Proxies generally operate at higher levels in the OSI stack and often handle specific protocols. Reverse proxies, as the name implies, provide aliases for multiple server addresses and are used for load balancing and caching. Caches store repeatedly referenced results (such as web pages) to improve performance.

VPNs

Virtual private network (VPN) traffic obscures the contents of protocols, hiding what's being done and how many hosts are involved. VPN traffic includes IPv6-over-IPv4 protocols such as 6to4 and Teredo, and encrypted protocols such as SSH and TOR. All of these protocols encapsulate traffic, meaning that the addresses seen at the IP layer are relays, routers, or concentrators rather than the actual hosts doing something.

Dynamic addresses

Dynamic addressing, such as that assigned through DHCP, causes a single host to migrate through a set of addresses over time. Dynamic addressing complicates analysis by introducing a lifetime for each address. You can never be sure whether the host you're tracking through its IP address did something after its DHCP lease expired.

These particular elements should be well documented by network administrators, but there are a number of different approaches for identifying them. Proxies and NATs can both be identified by looking for evidence that a single IP address is serving as a frontend for multiple addresses. This can be done via packet payload or flow analysis, although packet payload is more certain.

Identifying NATs

NATs are an enormous pain to identify unless you have access to payload data, in which case they simply become a significant pain. The best approach for identifying NATs is to quiz the network administrators. Failing that, you have to identify NATs through evidence that there are multiple addresses hidden behind the same address. A couple of different indicia can be used for this:

Variant `User-Agent` strings

The best approach I've seen to identify NATs is to pull the `User-Agent` strings from web sessions. Using a script such as *bannergrab.py* from Chapter 18, you can pull and dump all instances of the `User-Agent` string issuing from the NAT. If you see different instances of the same browser, or multiple browsers, you are likely looking at a NAT.

There is a *potential* false positive here. A number of applications (including email clients) include some form of HTTP interaction these days. Consequently, it's best to restrict yourself to explicit browser banners, such as those output by Firefox, IE, Chrome, and Opera.

Multiple logons to common servers

Identify major internal and external services used by your network. Examples include the company email server, Google, and major newspapers. If a site is a NAT, you should expect to see redundant logins from the same address. Email server logs and internal HTTP server logs are the best tools for this kind of research.

TTL behavior

Recall that time-to-live (TTL) values are assigned by the IP stack and that initial values are OS-specific. Check the TTLs coming from a suspicious address and see if they vary. Variety suggests multiple hosts behind the address. If the values are the same *but below the initial TTL for an OS*, you're seeing evidence of multiple hops to reach that address.

Identifying proxies

Proxy identification requires you to have both sides of the proxy instrumented. Figure 19-3 shows the network traffic between clients, proxies, and servers. As this figure shows, proxies take in requests from multiple clients and send those requests off to multiple servers. In this way, a proxy behaves as *both* a server (to the clients it's proxying for) and a client (to the servers it's proxying to). If your instrumentation lets you see both the client-to-proxy and proxy-to-server communication, you can identify the proxy by viewing this traffic pattern. If it doesn't, you can use the techniques discussed for NAT identification. The same principles apply because, after all, a proxy is a frontend to multiple clients, like a NAT firewall.

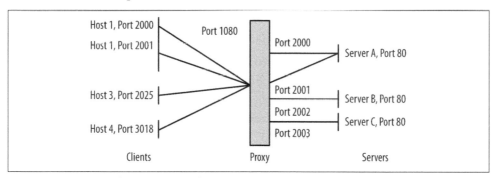

Figure 19-3. Network connections for a proxy

To identify a proxy using its connectivity, first look for hosts that are acting like clients. You can tell a client because it uses multiple ephemeral ports. For example, using rwuniq, you can identify clients on your network as follows:

```
$ rwfilter --type=out --start-date=2013/05/10:00 --end-date=2013/05/10:01 \
  --proto=6,17 --sport=1024-65535 --pass=stdout | rwuniq --field=1,3 \
  --no-title | cut -d '|' -f 1 | sort | uniq -c | egrep -v '^[ ]+1' |\
  cut -d ' ' -f 3 | rwsetbuild stdin clients.set
```

That command identifies all combinations of source IP address (`sip`) and source port number (`sport`) in the sample data and eliminates any situation where a host only used one port. The remaining hosts are using multiple ports. It's possible that hosts that are using only seven or eight ports at a time are running multiple servers, but as the distinct port count rises, the likelihood of them running multiple servers drops.

Once you've identified clients, the next step is to identify which of the clients are *also* behaving as servers (see "Identifying servers" on page 369).

VPN traffic can be identified by looking for the characteristic ports and protocols used by VPNs. VPNs obscure traffic analysis by wrapping all of the traffic they transport in another protocol, such as GRE. Once you've identified a VPN's endpoints, instrument there. Once the wrapper has been removed from VPN traffic, you should be able to distinguish flows and session data.

Identifying VPN traffic

The major protocols and ports used by VPN traffic are:

IPsec

IPsec refers to a suite of protocols for encrypted communications over VPNs. The two key protocols are AH (Authentication Header, protocol 51) and ESP (Encapsulating Security Payload, protocol 50):

```
$ rwfilter --start-date=2013/05/13:00 --end-date=2013/05/13:01 --proto=50,51 \
  --pass=vpn.rwf
```

GRE

GRE (Generic Routing Encapsulation) is the workhorse protocol for a number of VPN implementations. It can be identified as protocol 47:

```
$ rwfilter --start-date=2013/05/13:00 --end-date=2013/05/13:01 --proto=47 \
  --pass=gre.rwf
```

A number of common tunneling protocols are also identifiable using port and protocol numbers, although unlike standard VPNs, they are generally software-defined and don't require special assets specifically for routing. Examples include SSH, Teredo, 6to4, and TOR.

Phase IV: Identifying Clients and Servers

After identifying the basic structure of the network, the next step is to identify what the network does, which requires profiling and identifying clients and servers on the network. Questions include:

- What are the major internal servers?
- Are there servers running on unusual ports?
- Are there FTP, HTTP, SMTP, or SSH servers that are not known to system administrators?
- Are servers running as clients?
- Where are the major clients?

Identifying servers

Servers can be identified by looking for ports that receive sessions and by looking at the spread of communications to ports.

To identify ports that are receiving sessions, you either need access to pcap data or flow instrumentation that distinguishes the initial flags of a packet from the rest of the body (which you can get through YAF, as described in "YAF" on page 166). In a flow, the research then becomes a matter of identifying hosts that respond with a SYN and ACK:

```
$ rwfilter --proto=6 --flags-init=SA|SA --pass=server_traffic.rwf \
  --start-date=2013/05/13:00 --end-date=2013/05/13:00 --type=in
```

This approach won't work with UDP, because a host can send UDP traffic to any port it pleases without any response. An alternate approach, which works with both UDP and TCP, is to look at the *spread* of a port/protocol combination. I briefly touched on this in "Identifying proxies" on page 367, and we'll discuss it in more depth now.

A server is a public resource. This means that the address has to be sent to the clients, and that, over time, you can expect multiple clients to connect to the server's address. Therefore, over time, you will see multiple flows with distinct source IP/source port combinations all communicating with the same destination IP/destination port combination. This differs from the behavior of a client, which will issue multiple sessions from different source ports to a number of distinct hosts. Figure 19-4 shows this phenomenon graphically.

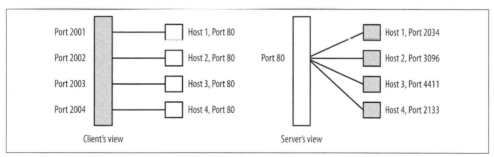

Figure 19-4. A graphical illustration of spread

Spread can easily be calculated with flow data by using the `rwuniq` command. Given a candidate file of traffic originating from one IP address, use the following:

```
$ rwuniq --field=1,2 --dip-distinct candidate_file | sort -t '|' -k3 -nr |\
  head -15
```

The more distinct IP addresses talk to the same host/port combination, the more likely is it that the port represents a server. In this script, servers will appear near the top of the list.

By using spread and direct packet analysis, you should have a list of most of the IP:port combinations that are running servers. This is always a good time to scan those IP:port combinations to verify what's actually running: in particular, search for servers that are *not* running on common ports. Servers are a public resource (for some limited definition of "public"), and when they appear on an unusual port, it may be an indication that a user didn't have permissions to run the server normally (suspicious behavior) or was trying to hide it (also suspicious behavior, especially if you've read Chapter 13).

Once you've identified the servers on a network, determine which ones are most important. There are a number of different metrics for doing so, including:

Total volume over time
> This is the easiest and most common approach.

Internal and external volume
> This differentiates servers accessed only by your own users from those accessed by the outside world.

Graph centrality
> Path and degree centrality often identify hosts that are important and that would be missed using pure degree statistics (number of contacts). See Chapter 15 for more information.

The goal of this exercise is to produce a list of servers ordered by priority, from the ones you should watch the most to the ones that are relatively low profile or, potentially, even removable.

Once you have identified all the servers on a network, it's a good time to go back to talk to the network administrators.[2] This is because you will almost invariably find servers that nobody knew were running on the network, examples of which include:

- Systems being run by power users
- Embedded web servers

---

2 Preferably at a place that serves vodka.

- Occupied hosts

Identifying Sensing and Blocking Infrastructure

Questions to consider:

- Are there any IDSs or IPSs in place? Can I modify their configuration?
- What systems do I have log access to?
- Are there any firewalls?
- Are there any router ACLs?
- Is there an antispam system at the border, or is antispam handled at the mail server, or both?
- Is AV present?

The final step of any new instrumentation project is to figure out what security software and capabilities are currently present. In many cases, these systems will be identifiable more from an *absence* than a presence. For example, if no hosts on a particular network show evidence of BitTorrent traffic (ports 6881–6889), it's likely that a router ACL is blocking BitTorrent.

Updating the Inventory: Toward Continuous Audit

Once you've built an initial inventory, queue up all the analysis scripts you've written to run on a regular basis. The goal is to keep track of what's changed on your network over time.

This inventory provides a handy anomaly-detection tool. The first and most obvious approach is to keep track of changes in the inventory. Sample questions to ask include:

- Are there new clients or servers on the network?
- Have previously existing addresses gone dark?
- Has a new service appeared on a client?

Changes in the inventory can be used as triggers for other analyses. For example, when a new client or server appears on the network, you can start analyzing its flow data to see who it communicates with, scan it, or otherwise experiment on it in order to fill the inventory with information on the new arrival.

In the long term, keeping track of what addresses are known and monitored is a first approximation for how well you're protecting the network. It's impossible to say "X is more secure than Y"; we just don't have the ability to quantitatively measure the X factor that is attacker interest. But by working with the map, you can track coverage either as a strict number (out of X addresses on the network, Y are monitored) or as a percentage.

Further Reading

1. U. Shankar and V. Paxson, "Active Mapping: Resisting NIDS Evasion Without Altering Traffic," *Proceedings of the 2003 IEEE Symposium on Security and Privacy*, Oakland, CA, 2003.

2. A. Whisnant and S. Faber, "Network Profiling Using Flow," Report CMU/SEI-2012-TR-006, Carnegie Mellon University Software Engineering Institute, Pittsburgh, PA, 2012, available at *http://resources.sei.cmu.edu/library/asset-view.cfm?assetID=28115*.

3. C. Hosmer, *Passive Python Network Mapping* (Rockland, MA: Syngress Publishing, 2015).

4. C. McNab, *Network Security Assessment*, 3rd ed. (Sebastopol, CA: O'Reilly Media, 2016).

## CHAPTER 20

On Working with Ops

In this chapter, I will discuss how an analysis team can effectively interact with and support an ops team. The concept of an independent "analysis team" is still new in information security, and there are no experts at this yet. There are, however, a good number of traps we can avoid.

This chapter is divided into two major sections. The first section is a brief discussion of the roles and stresses of operations environments. The second section attempts to classify major operational workflows—how operations environments are likely to execute decisions—and provides some guidelines for ensuring that ops and analytics can effectively support each other.

Ops Environments: An Overview

A *Security Operations Center* (SOC) is an organization focused on active security incident response.[1] The SOC's role is to process information about the state of an organization's security and respond to that information; they are effectively first responders to security alerts. Everything that goes wrong in information security ends up on the SOC floor.

SOC work is stressful; the stress comes from the constant flow of alerts the SOC must process. The penalty for conducting an attack is very low, and because of this, any open network is subject to a constant stream of attacks. New attacks do not replace old attacks; they supplement them. Any analyst with more than a month's experience may be conversant with attacks that have been going on for more than five years. Attacks are constant, increasing, and fire off alerts all the time.

---

1 SOCs have a number of different names. I personally prefer the chewier but more descriptive *Computer Security Incident Response Team* (CSIRT).

SOC work is tedious. Because the penalty for attacking is so low, attackers run non-threatening attacks all the time. Analysts must differentiate between the constant stream of nonthreatening attacks and the constant stream of potentially threatening attacks. Operational SOC work is a constant process of picking up alerts, validating that they aren't threats, and moving on to the next alerts.

SOC work is frustrating. Due to internal siloing, user pushback, and omnipresent vulnerabilities, the things that an analyst can actually *do* to defend a network are limited. They can tweak defenses, pull machines off the network for remediation, and write reports. Aggressive defenses require fights, and the security organization has to be careful about which fights it picks.

Because of these factors, analysts are always choked for time. I want to emphasize this point: *the most valuable resource in any SOC is analyst time*. Well-run SOCs have service level agreements (SLAs) and IDS configurations that produce just enough alerts for the SOC to handle, but this is a fraction of the potential problems they could be addressing but don't have the resources to address.

The most important thing for any analytics group to understand is that analysts are stressed, working at capacity, and don't have a lot of spare cycles. Good SOC managers often limit access to analysts for precisely this reason—they don't have a lot of time to spend on the ivory tower.

For analysis teams, this means that building and maintaining trust is critical. The material in this chapter is unsexy but critically important; I really consider it more important than anything involving machine learning, pattern recognition, or classification. The reason it's important is because there are *so many areas* where a well-equipped and aware analysis team can improve ops *without* looking to build a better IDS. There's a lot of important work to be done on inventory, task allocation, data parsing, workflow management, visualization, and deduplication. Spend your time here, and you're more likely to make a concrete difference.

Operational Workflows

In this section, we will discuss five operational workflows. These workflows are:

Escalation
> The basic workflow on most operational floors. Escalation workflow progressively filters alerts from frontline analysts to backend experts.

Sector
> Sector workflow is an alternate to escalation workflow where alerts are allocated to specialized teams of analysts based on the alert, its targets, and its impact.

Hunting

Hunting is a specialized form of data analysis done by experienced analysts. It tends to be self-directed and driven by analyst intuition; the output may be alerts or security action, but it also produces TTPs for junior analysts to operate.

Hardening

Hardening is a situational reaction to audits or alerts about new threats, and consists of taking an inventory and then triaging vulnerable assets in that inventory.

Forensic

Forensic workflow is a situational reaction to an alert about a host within the network being compromised.

Escalation Workflow

The most common form of operational workflow is the escalation workflow, a helpdesk-like process of promotion. This workflow is characterized by multiple *tiers* of analysts who progressively filter information to experts. If you peruse standards such NIST 800-61 or best practices guides, you will see some variant of this workflow discussed. It's not uncommon to find tools for managing these workflows that come directly from helpdesk management. For example, Remedy is a bread-and-butter tool for managing escalation workflows in helpdesks or ops floors.

In an escalation workflow, the inputs are alerts, and the outputs are security decisions. These decisions are primarily reports, but can also include incident responses such as forensic analysis, or changes to the instrumentation. Figure 20-1 shows an example of this workflow with the key characteristics of the process. An escalation workflow is initiated by alerts, generally dropped into a SIEM console by one or more sensors. Tier 1 analysts grab the alerts and process them. When a tier 1 analyst can't process an alert, he escalates it to a tier 2 analyst, and so on until the last tier is reached (which is generally tier 3).

How Many Alerts?

As a rule of thumb, tier 1 analysts can process approximately 100 alerts in a shift, or about 12 alerts an hour. Of these dozen, 10 of them will be immediately dismissed as obvious false positives or non-threats. The remaining two will require the analyst to conduct some investigation or file a report.

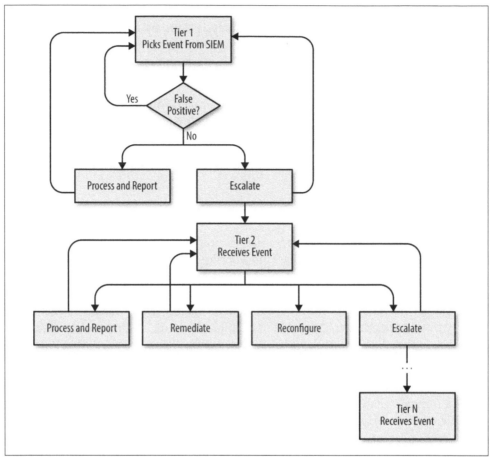

Figure 20-1. Escalation workflow

Tiers are based on seniority, skill, and responsibilities. Tier 1 analysts are primarily alert processors—this is a junior and generalist position where the analyst learns the ropes of an organization. Ideally, tier 1 work is heavily workflow-based; analysts should have very well-defined processes to help them move through the enormous volume of false positives they process.

Higher-tier analysts are increasingly autonomous and specialized. Precisely how many tiers an organization offers is up in the air. I generally prefer to refer to "junior," "senior," and "expert" analysts to clearly delineate responsibilities. Senior (tier 2) analysts begin to specialize and are more autonomous than junior analysts, but are still focused primarily on SIEM. Expert (tier 3) analysts have a deep understanding of the organization's network traffic and are usually experts on critical fields within the system.

As a reactive process, the escalation workflow is a necessary component for incident response. However, the approach is well known for burnout—a rule of thumb is that tier 1 analysts will last between six months and a year before leaving or being promoted to tier 2. This hefty turnover, especially in the lower tiers, results in concomitant training costs and a constant problem of knowledge management.

Analysis teams working with an escalation workflow should look into processes to help analysts handle more alerts and processes that provide awareness of false negatives. Given the turnover in analysis teams, the most effective place to start working is on improving the reproducibility and throughput of junior analyst work. Inventory and organizational information are particularly useful here—much of what a junior analyst does is based on determining what the target of the alert is, and whether that target is vulnerable to the problem raised by the alert.

Also of use are tools that speed up looking up and representing anomalous behavior and building up the inventory and other situational information. Much of a tier 1 analyst's work is threat assessment: based on an indicator such as an IP address, has this host talked to us recently? If a scan is seen, who responded to the scan? Automating these types of queries so the analyst simply has to process rather than fetch the data can result in a faster turnaround time and reduce errors.

At a more strategic level, the analysis team can evaluate the coverage provided by the detection systems. Coverage metrics (see Chapter 19) can help to estimate how many problems are slipping past the detectors.

Sector Workflow

The sector workflow is an alternative to the escalation workflow that divides alerts into discrete areas of expertise. In information security, sector workflows are rare—in my experience, the overwhelming majority of ops floors use an escalation workflow, and the majority of tools are written to support it. That said, sector workflows are common outside of information security, in air traffic control, combat information centers, and the like.

Figure 20-2 shows the basic process. A sector workflow is a "foundational" workflow in the same way that an escalation workflow is: it begins with alerts delivered to the SIEM console and ends with analysts deciding on defensive actions. However, whereas an escalation workflow assumes analysts are generalists and assigns alerts to tier 1 analysts without preference, a sector workflow assigns alerts to analysts based on different sectors of expertise.

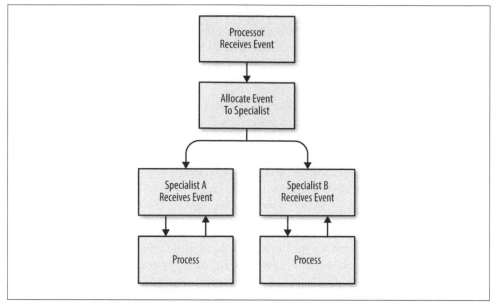

Figure 20-2. Sector workflow

Exactly *how* tasks are divided into sectors is the major challenge in building a sector workflow. Done well, it enables analysts to develop deep expertise on a particular network or class of problems. Done poorly, analysts end up in feast or famine situations —a disproportionate number of alerts end up in the hands of a small group of analysts, while the remainder are stuck occupying space.

An analysis team can support sector workflows by reviewing and evaluating sector allocation. A number of different partitioning techniques exist, including:

Network-based

Divide the network into subnets and allocate subnetworks to analysts as their domains. Analysts working in subnet sectors should be divided by workload, rather than total number of IP addresses.

Service-based

Service-based sectors assign analysts to particular services, such as web servers, email, and the like. Service-based allocation requires a good understanding of what services are available, which ones are critical, and which ones are as yet undiscovered.

Publish/Subscribe

In a publish/subscribe system, analysts *choose* which assets on the network to monitor. This requires that the analysts have a good understanding of what assets are important.

Attack-based
> In an attack-based system, analysts are divided by classes of attacks. For example, an attack-based division might have teams handling spam, DDoS attacks, scanning, etc.

Hunting Workflow

Hunting is a specialized form of exploratory data analysis focused on filling in gaps on network attributes. In contrast to the other workflows discussed in this chapter, a hunting workflow is open-ended and analyst-driven; it is a senior analyst activity.

Hunting requires both skilled analysis and an environment that facilitates open queries. Figure 20-3 shows a hunting workflow; this workflow is similar to the workflows for exploratory data analysis in Chapter 11 and is really a refinement of those workflows to deal with the realities of how hunting starts and proceeds. Hunting is characterized, in comparison to the generic EDA process, by the following:

- It is predicated on deep expertise on the observed environment. An analyst begins the hunting process by finding unexpected or unknown behavior on a network, which requires the analyst to have a pretty good intuition for how the network normally behaves.

- It works with the data in place. When an analyst is hunting, she is generally focused on an aberration in the network as currently observed. The tools or capabilities that are in place are what the analyst can use.

- It generally produces a very concrete product: either an answer to a security question, or TTPs (tools, techniques, and procedures) for junior analysts.

- It depends heavily on raw data sources such as logfiles, packet dumps, and flow records.

Hunting Maturity

Hunting is a technique used by senior analysts with a comprehensive understanding of the target network and access to extensive data sources. This workflow requires an advanced analysis team with a good understanding of what they already know and a desire to understand what on their network they *don't* know.

This is a roundabout way of saying that you can't stand up a hunting program with a single analyst, and you can't stand up a hunting program if your data collection consists of a Snort feed. You have bigger fish to fry.

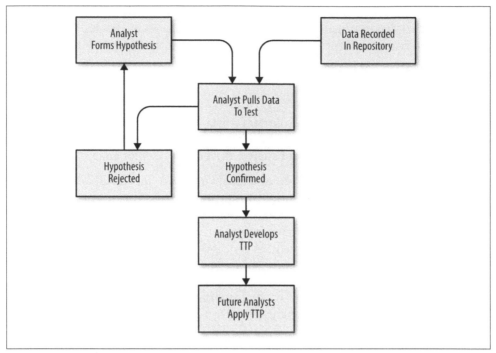

Figure 20-3. Hunting workflow

Hardening Workflow

Hardening is the process of assessing a network for potential vulnerabilities and then reconfiguring the network to reduce the potential for damaging attacks. In comparison to the escalation and sector workflows, hardening is situational—it is generally triggered as part of an audit or in response to an announced vulnerability, as opposed to being a continuous process.

Figure 20-4 shows the key components of a hardening workflow. As this figure shows, the workflow begins with the ops team receiving information on a potential vulnerability. This information is generally acquired in one of two ways: either the team is continuously auditing the network for vulnerable systems and receives an alert about such a system, or the team has received information on a new common mode vulnerability. In either case, the hardening workflow is inventory-driven—after receiving a notification, the ops team must create an inventory of vulnerable assets.

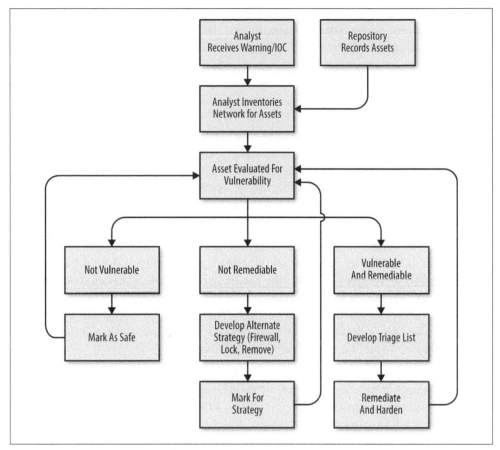

Figure 20-4. Hardening workflow

After identifying vulnerable assets, the ops team must decide on courses of action. This phase is triage-oriented—in general, there are more assets than the team can effectively address, and in some cases the assets *cannot* be patched or rectified (a particular problem with embedded systems). As a result, the ops team will usually end up with a prioritized list of courses of action: some hosts will be patched before others, and some hosts will not be patched but taken offline or heavily blocked.

When executed on a regular basis (as part of a process of continuous audit and identification), hardening is a proactive defensive strategy and can reduce the workload on other parts of the ops team. That said, hardening depends heavily on quality inventory—identifying vulnerable assets is the core of a hardening workflow, and it is easy to skip assets.

There are several ways that an analysis team can improve hardening work. The first is by working to improve the quality of inventory by mapping and assessing the assets in a network continuously, rather than simply as part of the hardening process (see Chapter 7 for more information on assessment). In addition, analytics work on population and locality (see Chapter 14 for more information) can help inform operations by giving them an understanding of how heavily used an asset is and the potential impact of its loss.

A hardening scenario

Consider a situation where vulnerability researchers publicize a widespread vulnerability in a common HTTP library (let's call it Heartbleed). This kind of vulnerability is likely announced through some vulnerability clearinghouse such as US-CERT, although it may also appear on mailing lists or occasionally as a front-page newspaper item. On receipt of the announcement, the SOC team must create a mechanism to determine which hosts within the network are vulnerable to an exploit.

The SOC team collates information from multiple sources and determines that the vulnerability is limited to a specific set of versions of Nginx, Apache, and a family of embedded web servers. At this time, the hardening workflow forks into two different courses of action: one for software, one for embedded. The Nginx and Apache servers can (theoretically) be identified and patched. The embedded web servers are barely identifiable, as the vulnerable installation has passed through three different manufacturers and now runs a dozen different host strings.

Based on this information, the SOC team scans the network on ports 80 and 443 for web servers and creates an inventory of those servers. Of the 100 web servers they find, 60 are not vulnerable, and 40 are. Of the 40 vulnerable web servers, 4 of them are mission critical—they cannot be shut down and patched without affecting the company's core business processes. After interviewing the team running those servers, the SOC team determines that the servers do not have to communicate across the network's border. They prepare to aggressively lock down those servers, allowing access from a limited set of networks within the company. The remaining 36 servers are patched.

Forensic Workflow

A forensic workflow refers to an investigation into breaches or damage. This is, like hardening, a situational workflow, but one driven by a confirmed alert. A forensic workflow is about assessing damage: determining what assets within a network have been infected, what damage the attacker did, and how to prevent the attack from recurring.

Figure 20-5 is a high-level description of a forensic workflow. As the figure shows, the workflow begins with a confirmed incident—evidence of an attack, or an alert from a user. From this information, the ops team identifies hosts that have been compromised. This is done by isolating indicators of compromise (IOCs) from infected hosts and using this information to identify the extent of damage throughout the network.

Like the hardening workflow, a forensic workflow is largely asset-based; the metric for success is based on examining a list of assets. However, in a forensic workflow that list of assets grows dynamically during the investigation process—identifying a new IOC necessitates examining hosts on the network for evidence of that IOC. A forensic workflow consequently resembles a graph walk where each node is an asset, and the links are paths of communication.

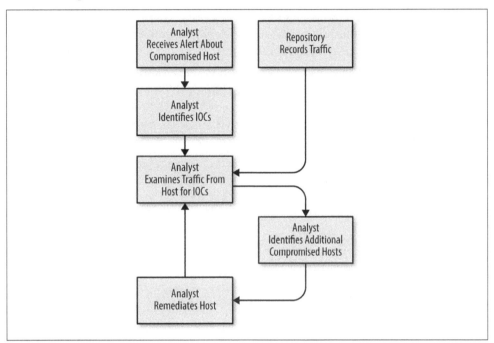

Figure 20-5. Forensic workflow

Switching Workflows

The workflows described here aren't set in stone, and it's not uncommon to see an ops floor use some combination of them. In particular, an analysis shop might use an escalation workflow for its tier 1 analysts, while tier 2 analysts use a sector workflow and tier 3 analysts are working in a hunting flow. Workflows may also be situational and temporary; this is particularly true for forensic, hardening, and hunting workflows, which happen due to specific events and should have clearly defined end states.

Further Readings

1. J. Bollinger, B. Enrigh, and M. Valites, *Crafting the InfoSec Playbook: Security Monitoring and Incident Response Master Plan* (Sebastopol, CA: O'Reilly Media, 2015).

2. P. Cichonski et al., "Computer Security Incident Handling Guide," NIST Special Publication 800-61r2, available at *http://nvlpubs.nist.gov/nistpubs/SpecialPublica tions/NIST.SP.800-61r2.pdf*.

3. C. Zimmerman, "Ten Strategies of a World-Class Cybersecurity Operations Center," MITRE, available at *https://www.mitre.org/publications/all/ten-strategies-of-a-world-class-cybersecurity-operations-center*.

4. The Argus group website, particularly *http://www.arguslab.org/anthrosec.html*. Among its many projects, the lab run by Simon Ou at the University of South Florida runs the only anthropological study of CSIRTs that I know of. I can't stress how important their work on analyst stress (in particular their model for burnout) is.

5. The ThreatHunting Project: Hunting for Adversaries in Your IT Environment (*http://www.threathunting.net*).

## CHAPTER 21

Conclusions

In this book, I have discussed techniques for collecting, processing, and applying data to deal with information security problems, and specifically ways to use that data to inform security decisions. This discussion is only half the story, though; every network is different, and every insecure network is insecure in its own way.

I encourage you, more than anything else, to *look at the data*. Constructs are good, statistics are good, but the fundamental tool for data analysis is *data*. Whatever you start with will be terrible: the first result of any data collection effort is finding out how bad the data collection was. However, until you collect that data, until you poke at your network, and until you understand what weirdness is going on—the ancient developer who insists that USENET is part of his essential workflow, the guy who thought putting the timeserver on .123, the web server on .80, and the HTTPS server on .187—life is going to be confusing. Well, more confusing—the internet is really weird.

Index

port numbers, 340-343
Applied Security, 180
APSP (All Pairs Shortest Paths), 306
archive data, 127
ArcSight, 89, 124
ARP (Address Resolution Protocol), 175
ASCII, 238
ASPack, 241
assessment, active domain data
    defined, 108
    with nmap, 115-118
asymmetric traffic flow, 361-363
asynchronous transfer mode (ATM), 41
attack models, 199
attacker
    behavior overview, 199-202
    challenges to validity of detection/defense
        system, 16
    text encoding as tool, 239-242
attacks, threats vs., 1
AV (antivirus) systems, 104, 351

B

backscatter, 262-263
bag tools, 162
bag, defined, 162
bandwidth exhaustion, 286
banner
    identifying/classifying, 351-354
    non-web, 351
    web client banners: User-Agent string, 352
banner grabbing, 344-346
bar plots, 212
base-rate fallacy, 48
base64 encoding, 239
basic access authentication, 266
beaconing
    as alarm, 295
    characteristics of, 276-279
bell curve, 231
Berkeley Packet Filter (BPF), 36-41
    address filtering in, 39
betweenness (centrality metric), 308
BFS (breadth-first searches), 309, 313
BGP protocol, 364
binary classifiers, 45
    failure modes, 47
    ROC curves and, 220
bins, 210

BitTorrent
    blocking of traffic, 371
    histogram, 211, 347
    identification by subsidiary site, 351
bivariate data, 215-217
black-box systems
    email rules/filtering, 83
    ruleset problems, 51
blacklist services, 84
botnets, 291
bots, as general-purpose software systems, 1
boxplot (box-and-whiskers plot), 213-215
BPF (Berkeley Packet Filter), 36-41
    address filtering in, 39
breadth-first searches (BFS), 309, 313
Bro, 46
broadcast address, 177
buffer, rolling, 36

C

cable cuts, 287, 291
cables, monitoring, 26
CAN (controller area network), 41
canonical name (CNAME) records, 188
Carnegie Mellon University, 44, 137, 332
categorical variables, 209
ccTLDs (country code TLDs), 182
CDN (content distribution network), 185, 192
CEF (Common Event Format), 89
Censys, 198, 264
centrality (graph attribute)
    about, 306-308
    engineering use of, 315
    forensic use of, 312
CERT
    Carnegie Mellon vs. national organizations,
        332
    SiLK, 137
CERT Network Situational Awareness (NetSA)
    Group, 44, 137
Childs, Terry, 319
Christmas tree packet, 262
CIDR (Classless Inter-Domain Routing), 28
CIDR (Classless Internet Domain Routing)
    block, 176
Cisco Systems
    NetFlow, 41
    Sourcefire, 46
    SpamCop, 197

anomaly-based IDSs, 56
beacon detection, 295
binary classifiers, 47
DoS attacks and, 287
in real-time detection, 130
insider attacks and, 318
NXDOMAIN message, 267
volume breaches, 295
fat-fingering, 249, 265
Fibre Channel, 41
file transfers/raiding, 279-281
filesystem monitoring, 101-103
filtering
BPF addresses, 39
packet data, 37-41
rwfilter tool, 144-152
fitting/estimation of data, 228-233
goodness of fit tests, 231-233
K-S, 232
normal distribution questions, 228
QQ plots, 230-231
S-W tests, 232
visualization to test against a distribution, 228-231
five-number summary, 212-215
flags, fumbling detection and, 261
flash crowds, 287, 291
flow
fumbling detection, 261-263
in NetFlow, 42
rwptoflow tool, 168
flow filtering, unidirectional, 261-263
forensic analysis
EDA and, 205
fumbling and, 270
forensic workflow, 375, 382
frequency (histogram element), 210
fumbling behaviors, 253-271
alarms for, 268
automated systems, 254
defined, 253
detecting and analyzing, 268-271
DNS fumbling, 267
forensic analysis of, 270
HTTP fumbling, 265
ICMP messages and, 264
identifying, 255-264
IP fumbling, 257-258
lookup failures, 254

network engineering to defeat, 271
scanning, 255, 260
service-level, 265-267
SMTP fumbling, 267
TCP fumbling, 259-264
web crawlers and robots.txt, 266

G

gaps, in scatterplot, 216
gateway address, 177
Gaussian distribution, 231
Generic Routing Encapsulation (GRE), 368
generic TLDs (gTLDs), 182
GeoIP, 180
geolocation, 128, 180-181
goodness of fit tests, 231-233
K-S, 232
S-W tests, 232
Google, 36, 197
graph analysis, 311-315
breadth-first searches, 313
centrality analysis for engineering, 315
centrality analysis for forensics, 312
component analysis as alarm, 311-312
shortest paths, 303-306
graphs, 299-315
about, 299-303
analyzing, 311-315
centrality, 306-308
clustering coefficient, 309-311
components and connectivity, 308
construction vs. attributes, 303
defined, 299
path, 303-308
rules for converting raw data into, 303
weighting, 305
GRE (Generic Routing Encapsulation), 368
gTLDs (generic TLDs), 182

H

Hamming distance, 248
Hanssen, Robert, 318
hardening workflow
about, 380-382
defined, 375
scenario, 382
hardware, MAC addresses for, 175
hash functions
defined, 102

security of, 102
heartbeat signals, 119
HIDS (host-based IDSs), 45
HIPS (host intrusion prevention system), 104
histograms
    and univariate data, 210
    generating, 210
    protocol comparison with, 347
history, problems of, 13
hit list, 255
Homeland Security, U.S. Department of, 14, 46, 332
homoglyphs, 251
horizontal scan, 112, 255
host domain, 91-105
    AV systems, 104
    command history, 103
    data, 92
    defined, 6
    filesystem, 101-103
    HIPS, 104
    historical data, 103
    network and, 92
    network interfaces, 93-96
    process information, 98-101
    sensors in, 91-105
    user login history, 103
    UUIDs, 96-98
host intrusion prevention system (HIPS), 104
host-based IDSs (HIDS), 45
HTTP fumbling, 265
HTTP log data, 78-81
    CLF, 79
    critical headers, 79
    ELF, 80
hunting workflow, 375, 379

I

IANA (see Internet Assigned Numbers Authority)
ICANN (Internet Corporation for Assigned Names and Numbers), 178, 182
ICMP (Internet Control Message Protocol)
    data from, 41
    frame and packet formats, 37
    router interfaces and, 365
    type 3 messages and fumbling, 264
IDMEF (Intrusion Detection Message Exchange Format), 331

IDNs (internationalized domain names), 252
IDSs (see intrusion detection systems)
IETF (Internet Engineering Task Force), 331
ifconfig tool, 93
IMPACT, 14
Incident Object Description Exchange Format (IODEF), 331
indegree (of node), 300
indicators of compromise (IOCs), 330, 383
information security operations center (see security operations center (SOC))
inline tools, 124
insider threats, 201, 317-326
    avoiding toxicity when investigating, 321
    Terry Childs case, 319
    compared to other classes of attacks, 318-321
    credential theft, 323
    data logistics/collection, 324-326
    data theft/exfiltration, 322
    Roger Duronio case, 320
    Robert Hanssen case, 318
    Brian Kelley case, 318
    modes of attack, 322
    motivations vs. risk, 322
    off-days and, 276
    physical data sources, 326
    sabotage, 323
    sector-based workflow analysis, 324
    user identity tracking, 326
instrumentation
    and internal validity, 13
    inventory and, 361
intelligence (see threat intelligence)
interested attacker, 201
internal validity
    about, 13
    defined, 12
internationalized domain names (IDNs), 252
Internet Archive, 197
Internet Assigned Numbers Authority (IANA)
    IP address allocation, 178
    IP suite protocols, 36
    IPv4 Address Register, 28
    port number assignment, 340, 343
    TLD definitions, 182
Internet Control Message Protocol (see ICMP)
Internet Corporation for Assigned Names and Numbers (ICANN), 178, 182

operational workflows, 374-383
    escalation workflow, 375-377
    forensic workflow, 382
    hardening workflow, 380-382
    hunting workflow, 379
    sector workflow, 377-379
    switching workflows, 383
ops (operations) team, 373-383
    operational workflows, 374-383
    ops environment overview, 373
    tier classifications in, 376
ordinal variable, 209
organizationally unique identifier (OUI), 27,
    174
OS fingerprinting, 344
OSI (Open Systems Interconnection) model
    layers of, 20
    lookup process and, 173
OSPF (Open Shortest Path First), 306
OSPF protocol, 364
OUI (organizationally unique identifier), 27,
    174
outdegree (of node), 300
outliers, 215

P

packet
    Christmas tree packet, 262
    fumble detection, 263
packet capture, 5
packet data, 36-44
    filtering, 37-41
    limiting data captured from each packet, 37
    NetFlow traffic summarization, 41-44
    non-Ethernet, 41
    rolling buffers, 36
    rwptoflow tool, 168
pairs plots, 218
parallelization, 134
parent process ID (PPID), 100
passive banner grabbing, 344
passive discovery, 119
password management, 118
PAT (Port Address Translation), 31
paths, on graphs, 303-308
pcap data, 44
PCRE (Perl Compatible Regular Expression),
    246
peer-to-peer worm propagation, 200

peerishness, 310
people, as last line of defense, 206
Perl Compatible Regular Expression (PCRE),
    246
PF_RING, 46
phishing attacks, 200
physical taps, 26
PID (process ID), 99
pie charts, 212
ping, 108-110
ping sweep, 109
PMAPs (prefix maps), 163-165
pointer (PTR) record, 191
population validity, 12
Port Address Translation (PAT), 31
port mirroring, 23
port numbers
    application identification, 340-343
    assignment, 340, 343
PPID (parent process ID), 100
predictable phenomena, 56
prefetching data, 58
prefix maps (PMAPs), 163-165
print-stat/print-volume-stat commands, 151
process ID (PID), 99
process information, host
    command and path, 100
    CPU, 100
    memory, 100
    PID and PPID, 99
    start time, 100
    UID, 100
process sampling, 101
Project Sonar, 264
proxies, 33
    identification for network inventory, 367
    logs, 60
ps (process sampling tool), 101
pstree, 101
PTR (pointer) record, 191
Python, xvi, xix
    GeoIP library, 180
    histogram creation, 210
    regular expressions, 244, 246
    report of unidirectional flows, 361
    split method, 243

Q

qualitative variables, 209

About the Author

Michael Collins is the chief scientist for RedJack, LLC, a network security and data analysis company located in the Washington, DC, area. Prior to his work at RedJack, Dr. Collins was a member of the technical staff at the CERT Network Situational Awareness Group at Carnegie Mellon University. His primary focus is on network instrumentation and traffic analysis, in particular on the analysis of large traffic datasets. Dr. Collins graduated with a PhD in electrical engineering from Carnegie Mellon University in 2008. He holds master's and bachelor's degrees from the same institution.

Colophon

The animal on the cover of *Network Security Through Data Analysis* is a European merlin (*Falco columbarius*). There is some debate as to whether the North American and the European/Asian varieties of merlin are actually different species. Carl Linnaeus was the first to classify the bird in 1758 using a specimen from America, then in 1771 the ornithologist Marmaduke Tunstall assigned a separate taxon to the Eurasian merlin, calling it *Falco aesalon* in his book *Ornithologica Britannica*.

Recently, it has been found that there are significant genetic variations between North American and European types of merlin, supporting the idea that they should be officially classified as distinct species. It is believed that the separation between the two kinds happened more than a million years ago, and since then the birds have existed completely independently of each other.

The merlin is more heavily built than most other small falcons and can weigh almost a pound, depending on the time of year. Females are generally larger than males, which is common among raptors. This allows the male and female to hunt different types of prey animals and means that less territory is required to support a mating pair. Merlins normally inhabit open country, such as scrubland, forests, parks, grasslands, and moorland. They prefer areas with low and medium-height vegetation because it allows them to hunt easily and find abandoned nests that they take on as their own. During the winter, European merlins are known to roost communally with hen harriers, another bird of prey.

Breeding occurs in May and June, and pairs are monogamous for the season. The merlins will often use the empty nests of crows or magpies, but it is also common (especially in the UK) to find merlins nesting in crevices in cliffs or buildings. Females lay three to six eggs, which hatch after an incubation period of 28 to 32 days. The chicks will be dependent on their parents for up to four weeks before starting out on their own.

In medieval times, chicks were taken from the nest and hand-reared to be used for hunting. *The Book of St. Albans*, a handbook of gentleman's pursuits, included merlins in the "Hawking" section, calling the species, "the falcon for a lady." Today, they are still trained by falconers for hunting smaller birds, but this practice is declining because of conservation efforts. The most serious threat to merlins is habitat destruction, especially in their breeding areas. However, since the birds are highly adaptable and have been successful at living in settled areas, their population remains stable around the world.

Many of the animals on O'Reilly covers are endangered; all of them are important to the world. To learn more about how you can help, go to *animals.oreilly.com*.

The cover image is from Wood's *Animate Creation*. The cover fonts are URW Typewriter and Guardian Sans. The text font is Adobe Minion Pro; the heading font is Adobe Myriad Condensed; and the code font is Dalton Maag's Ubuntu Mono.

Learn from experts.
Find the answers you need.

Sign up for a **10-day free trial** to get **unlimited access** to all of the content on Safari, including Learning Paths, interactive tutorials, and curated playlists that draw from thousands of ebooks and training videos on a wide range of topics, including data, design, DevOps, management, business—and much more.

Start your free trial at:

oreilly.com/safari

(No credit card required.)

Milton Keynes UK
Ingram Content Group UK Ltd.
UKHW012035270824
447508UK00009B/175